Advance praise for
The Transfer Experience

"This book is a timely and much-needed call to action to more effectively meet the transfer needs of our postsecondary students. The research contained within these chapters presents a playbook for both campus and state higher education officials to create and execute a strategy that will better serve students, campuses, and states alike."—*Robert E. Anderson, President, State Higher Education Executive Officers Association (SHEEO)*

"Helping students achieve their educational goals is a win for everyone and brings the 'American Dream' closer to reality. A key, underused strategy in reaching this goal is an effective, holistic transfer system that begins when a student enters an institution of higher education and continues through completion. *The Transfer Experience* is authored by 'transfer warriors' who understand and are passionate about transfer. This book is a comprehensive educational masterpiece that challenges and inspires higher education leaders and policymakers to skillfully and purposefully foster transfer student success, thereby enhancing the quality of life for students."—*Paula K. Compton, Associate Vice Chancellor, Articulation and Transfer, Ohio Department of Higher Education*

"The achievement and graduation of transfer students in higher education is one of the most important issues confronting colleges and universities. Given that nearly half the undergraduate enrollees are in community colleges, we have to work together across the community college and 4-year sector to find structures, programs, and policies to strengthen their success. The editors and contributors provide nuanced perspectives on how transfer student success must be addressed."—*Scott E. Evenbeck; Founding President, Stella and Charles Guttman Community College; and University Professor, Baruch College, City University of New York*

"Transfer is a vital mechanism for closing the racial and income equity gaps in higher education as well as an unnecessarily complex issue that too often leaves students stranded on their academic journeys. I share the editors and contributors' holistic philosophy of the transfer student experience and particularly appreciate their emphasis on the student's pre-transfer academic preparation. This handbook is an essential tool for ensuring these students are propelled to degree completion."—*Janet L. Marling, Executive Director, The National Institute for the Study of Transfer Students, University of North Georgia*

"As a former vice president of student affairs and enrollment management at one of America's leading community colleges, and as a three-time university chancellor, I have attended more conferences and read more books about student success than I can recall. *The Transfer Experience*, edited by Gardner, Rosenberg, and Koch, is clearly one of the best I have ever read. Filled with proven nuggets of successful initiatives, this is required reading for faculty and administrators who are committed to creating a more equitable and successful system of postsecondary education. College access, student success, and equity are core principles of democracy and each is achievable."—*Charlie Nelms; Chancellor Emeritus, North Carolina Central University; and Vice President Emeritus, Indiana University*

"*The Transfer Experience* is a gift to educators who view transfer as a social justice imperative. Transfer matters now, perhaps more than ever, and this text offers the most comprehensive, evidence-based analysis of the transfer experience. The editors and contributors offer a transformational view of the transfer journey that goes beyond a mechanistic, processual experience. Shattering outmoded transfer assumptions, the editors and contributors take care to present a more thoughtful, holistic view of transfer keeping in mind that underserved, first-generation, adult learners should be assisted in every way to fulfill their hopes and dreams of earning a bachelor's degree. This text offers fertile ground for significant equity and justice dialogue, transformational changes, and policy considerations."—*Laura I. Rendón, author of* Sentipensante Pedagogy: Educating for Wholeness, Social Justice and Liberation

THE TRANSFER EXPERIENCE

THE TRANSFER EXPERIENCE

A Handbook for Creating a More Equitable and Successful Postsecondary System

Edited by John N. Gardner,
Michael J. Rosenberg, and Andrew K. Koch

Foreword by John Hitt and Sanford Shugart

Copublished with

Gardner Institute

Brevard, North Carolina

1996-2021 25™ ANNIVERSARY

PUBLISHING, LLC.

STERLING, VIRGINIA

COPYRIGHT © 2021 BY STYLUS PUBLISHING, LLC.

Published by Stylus Publishing, LLC.
22883 Quicksilver Drive
Sterling, Virginia 20166-2019

Library of Congress Cataloging-in-Publication Data
Names: Gardner, John N., editor. | Rosenberg, Michael J. (College administrator), editor. | Koch, Andrew K. (Andrew Karl), editor. | Hitt, John C., writer of foreword. | Shugart, Sanford, writer of foreword.
Title: The transfer experience : a handbook for creating a more equitable and successful postsecondary system / edited by John N. Gardner, Michael J. Rosenberg, and Andrew K. Koch ; foreword by John Hitt and Sanford Shugart.
Description: First edition. | Sterling, Virginia : Stylus Publishing, LLC, 2021. | "Copublished with Gardner Institute." | Includes bibliographical references and index. |
Identifiers: LCCN 2021005568 (print) | LCCN 2021005569 (ebook) | ISBN 9781620369470 (paperback) | ISBN 9781620369463 (hardback) | ISBN 9781620369487 (library networkable e-edition) | ISBN 9781620369494 (consumer e-edition)
Subjects: LCSH: Students, Transfer of--United States. | Transfer students--Services for. | Transfer students--United States. | Community college students--Services for--United States. | Academic achievement--United States.
Classification: LCC LB2360 .T734 2021 (print) | LCC LB2360 (ebook) | DDC 378.1/6--dc23
LC record available at https://lccn.loc.gov/2021005568
LC ebook record available at https://lccn.loc.gov/2021005569

13-digit ISBN: 978-1-62036-946-3 (cloth)
13-digit ISBN: 978-1-62036-947-0 (paperback)
13-digit ISBN: 978-1-62036-948-7 (library networkable e-edition)
13-digit ISBN: 978-1-62036-949-4 (consumer e-edition)

Printed in the United States of America

All first editions printed on acid-free paper
that meets the American National Standards Institute
Z39-48 Standard.

Bulk Purchases

Quantity discounts are available for use in workshops and for staff development.

Call 1-800-232-0223

First Edition, 2021

Dedicated to the transfer students—past, present, and future—and to our fellow educators who strive to support their success.

CONTENTS

ONLINE COMPENDIUM

Case Studies and Other Resources

Although more than a century old, the innovation of vertical transfer—the movement of students from community colleges to universities—remains one of the most interesting, promising, and underperforming inventions in American higher education. This book is dedicated to addressing this underperformance our country can no longer afford and should no longer tolerate. Community college students represent the largest sector in higher education, comprising more than 40% of undergraduates. They are more diverse, more likely to be first generation, more likely to come from the lower two quintiles of income, more likely to come from recent immigrant families assimilating into the American economy and cultures, and much less likely to have access to enrollment in a selective and/or costly college/university experience. For all these reasons, improving the performance of the college transfer systems, and creating them where they scarcely exist, ought to be a significant priority for both community colleges and universities.

As present and former community college and university presidents, respectively, we have seen up close the power of an effective transfer system, unleashing enormous potential by granting access for large numbers of proven community college students to an advanced education in a highly selective university. While we served our rapidly growing institutions in the greater Orlando, Florida, region as presidents of a large community college and a large public university, we engaged the opportunity—the necessity, really—of redesigning the entire transfer ecosystem around making successful transfer and graduation from both institutions the norm rather than the exception. The resulting model, branded as "DirectConnect to UCF" and overviewed in a case study later in this book, has produced more than 50,000 bachelor's degree graduates (nearly all with a completed associate degree, as well) through transfer since its implementation in 2005. These successful transfer students add substantial diversity to the graduating classes of the university on all the dimensions previously mentioned, giving new vigor to the promise of opportunity through higher education.

In Florida, there has been a long-standing and widespread recognition that the state is producing fewer baccalaureate degrees than are needed to support a modern economy. Successive legislatures and governors have established and supported two institutional systems of higher education. One is a collection of 28 colleges that fulfill the role of the traditional community college, awarding a wide range of associate degrees and a limited number of baccalaureates. The other is a system of 12 baccalaureate-granting institutions, some of which offer extensive graduate and professional programs, including medicine and law. The two systems include institutions with the largest and smallest enrollments of their type, both in Florida and, in some cases, nationally.

Informal discussions among presidents of the primary university and the approximately half-dozen colleges serving the east-central region of Florida (roughly the Orlando Standard Metropolitan Statistical Area) led to the conclusion that, as leaders of the public higher education institutions serving a population of more than 2 million, we were obligated to develop a regional plan that offered increased access to high-quality degrees in fields leading to immediate employment or further study tied to attainment of advanced degrees.

Given the ongoing growth of the population of central Florida and the absence of increased funding for increased enrollments from state coffers, we clearly needed an inventory of resources required to support the growth necessary to support the required enrollments. We soon saw that Florida owed debts of gratitude to policymakers from previous times who crafted and implemented both the "two-plus-two" model of undergraduate education and the "common course numbering system." The two-plus-two concept eased the transfer of credit from Florida's community colleges to its universities, while the creation of a common course numbering system made transfer much more student- and institution-friendly by ensuring that all courses in public institutions with the same name and number ideally included the same content.

Undertaking this ongoing project requires a willingness to rethink what transfer students experience, not only in the transactions around the term of transfer but also end-to-end across both institutions. This partnership requires redesign of curriculum; support services; admission into both institutions; shared institutional goals for transfer; shared performance metrics; and, most importantly, a value proposition made to students that will sustain their commitment to a rational decision and pathway to success.

This work will not typically emerge from "the middle" of a college or university. Faculty and staff at all levels involved in the transactions around transfer will be inclined to view them "transactionally." What will be needed is strategic leadership, specifically and especially from chief executive officers and chief academic officers who have already seen the value of viewing higher education as an ecosystem in need of tuning to the needs and interests of students and communities, rather than narrow interests of institutional ambition. They will be the leaders, using insights like those in the pages that follow, who choose to measure their institutions by their impact more than their image.

The contributors to this volume have taken a unique and comprehensive look at the total experience of transfer students. Their perspectives are steeped in the best research on patterns of success and failure among students, with an eye toward institutional practices that can lead to quantum improvements in transfer student outcomes. They place the responsibility for the redesign of systems squarely on the institutional partners, while situating the discussion in historic, public policy, and social justice frameworks. The result is a powerful primer for any institutional leaders who believe their students can perform at dramatically higher levels—preparing for transfer, achieving transfer efficiently, and progressing to the bachelor's degree—if we get the systems right. And "getting the systems right" is the charge we offer you, readers!

This book straddles the world of the best scholarship, heavily citing the primary research literature, and the world of practice, offering useful questions and practical strategies for institutional teams to consider, detailed case studies, and pragmatic suggestions for improved performance. This text also provides a robust rationale for the work ahead, rooted in not only the arguments for the development of future talent but also solid moral and ethical logic for the social justice and equity agendas that animate much of what higher education has tasked itself to do. Recent news of scandals in elite college admissions only underscores the need to reengage every tool available to us to make the promise of equality and opportunity real for all the people we serve. Significant improvements in the success of college transfer programs and students may contribute more to this agenda than any other effort we can conceive. Again, you, our readers, will determine this.

As we look back on the period of our overlapping presidencies in a shared geographic region, we offer this reflection for your consideration. One of the most important steps we both took in our presidencies was building our joint-institutional and presidential professional and personal partnership to increase the attainment of social justice outcomes for our region by vastly increasing our number of successful transfer students—both at the sending and receiving institutional levels. The editors of this book chose us to provide this foreword to offer you, in whatever your capacity, the opportunity to emulate this kind of partnership fundamentally based on collaboration rather than competition. America needs and deserves this in as many of our communities as possible, hundreds of which have both community college and baccalaureate-level institutions serving the same citizenry. We have been inspired and continually rededicated to this effort, and we believe you can and should be as well.

John Hitt
President Emeritus
University of Central Florida

Sanford Shugart
President
Valencia College

Timing Is Everything: Who We Are and Why This Book Is Needed Now

We come to this volume as three postsecondary educators with more than a century of collective experience advocating for transfer students and guiding undergraduate improvement. While our biographies are included at the end of this book, we would like to share a bit about our interest in and experience with transfer.

The principal architect of what is called "the first-year experience" as well as many other education reform efforts, John N. Gardner, was an undergraduate in the early 1960s at an independent liberal arts college in Ohio. Although he never knowingly met a transfer student during his undergraduate years, nearly 2 decades later as a chief academic officer in a public university system for five small "regional" campuses, he personally witnessed and attempted to mitigate many issues students faced transferring between campuses in the same university system. Working with many institutions throughout his career, he encountered firsthand the invidious prejudice directed toward 2-year colleges, their students, and their faculty. As a result, he became the co-designer of a transfer student success improvement strategy facilitated by the nonprofit Gardner Institute for Excellence in Undergraduate Education known as "Foundations of Excellence Transfer Focus." That process helps community colleges study and redefine their transfer-sending mission and 4-year institutions study and redesign their transfer-receiving efforts and has informed various other forms of transfer work Gardner and his colleagues have conducted. Approximately 75 2- and 4-year institutions have participated in this process at the time of this book's publication.

Much of Michael J. Rosenberg's career in higher education has been in academic advising and student success, with a heavy emphasis on the success of transfer students. As the director of student affairs and academic advising at the University of Cincinnati's College of Allied Health Sciences, Rosenberg was the liaison for transfer students—both those transferring between colleges within the university and those transferring to the university from other institutions. Later, at Gateway Community & Technical College in northern Kentucky, Rosenberg was the first director of transfer, spearheading efforts to build partnerships with local universities to increase the opportunity for transfer students, including the first public-private co-enrollment program in the state. He became acquainted with the other editors while acting as co-leader of the institution's Foundations of Excellence Transfer Focus process. Through that work, he worked to address the challenges faced by Gateway students, about two thirds of whom were attending college part time to pursue a bachelor's degree.

His doctoral research culminated in a large-scale statewide survey of all transfer-bound students in the Kentucky Community & Technical College System. In his current role as director of planning at Penn State University, he is involved with strategic planning efforts on and among all 24 of Penn State's campuses.

Andrew K. Koch directly felt the implications of transfer through the postsecondary educational experiences of three of his children. Each of those experiences has been different: one son transferred between community colleges, a second transferred from a community college to a regional comprehensive university, and a third son transferred from a regional comprehensive public university to a flagship public research university. Koch's experiences with transfer student support at colleges and universities have also been shaped by his professional work, which spans nearly 2 decades. During the late 1990s and first decade of the 21st century, Koch helped lead the Student Access, Transition, and Success Programs department at Purdue University. As department head, he helped lead an effort to transform the way Purdue brought transfer students into the university—adding a spring orientation program for midyear transfers, redesigning summer/fall orientation for transfers, and so on. Since joining the Gardner Institute in 2010, Koch has participated in efforts to refine the Foundations of Excellence Transfer Focus process, support a transfer redesign process undertaken by the Kentucky Community & Technical College System, and put forth comparable effort with seven Tulsa-area institutions funded by the Charles and Lynn Schusterman Family Foundation.

Through these experiences, all three of us have come to believe fervently that transfer students are often neglected and, in some cases, exploited. While we believe much of this discrimination is unintentional, unintentional discrimination is still discrimination, and our desire to stand as advocates for transfer students inspired us to compile the book you are now reading.

A grant awarded to the Gardner Institute in 2016 from the Bill & Melinda Gates Foundation offered the three of us the opportunity to ask, "What can and should we be doing on a national scale to improve the lives of transfer students?" After scanning the national environment regarding transfer, convening and interviewing focus groups, participating in workshops with experts who had built successful programs, and gleaning insights from faculty, staff, and students across the country and beyond—we discovered a broad collection of important thinkers, researchers, and practitioners leading this important transfer reform work. Some of these works include *The Transfer Playbook* (Wyner et al., 2016); *Building Transfer Student Pathways for College and Career Success* (Poisel & Joseph, 2018), edited by Mark Allen Poisel and Sonya Joseph; *The Transfer Handbook: Promoting Student Success* (American Association of Collegiate Registrars and Admissions Officers, 2015); and the multitude of resources available through the National Institute for the Study of Transfer Students (NISTS). Many of the individuals involved in this Gates Foundation–funded project contributed chapters to this book. (Note: The findings and conclusions contained within this volume are those of the authors and do not necessarily reflect positions or policies of the Foundation.)

ACKNOWLEDGMENTS

We openly and readily acknowledge that we did not produce this book alone. We are grateful for the contributions of those we mention here and their willing provision of time, energy, and/or content to make our efforts both intellectually stimulating and deeply meaningful. We are indebted for their commitment to our cause.

First and foremost, we must thank our chapter contributors. This publication reflects the great wisdom about the transfer experience our chapter contributors brought to their writing. Their content made this book the useful tool it is. We could never have produced a volume of this quality on our own.

We also express profound gratitude to our senior editor at Stylus Publishing, David Brightman. His sound guidance, seemingly infinite patience, and ongoing encouragement throughout the writing and compilation process sustained our efforts. Thank you, David, for giving life to our idea and helping us deliver it.

We offer thanks to our colleagues at the Bill & Melinda Gates Foundation. The work that inspired us to assemble this book stemmed from a planning grant from the Gates Foundation centered on an exploration of transfer and digital learning on a national scale. Specifically, we gratefully acknowledge the Gates Foundation's Nazeema Alli, Kelly DeForrest, Mandee Eckersley, Rupal Nayar, Bree Olofson, and Rahim Rajan for their guidance and support during the planning grant. We thank them and all the other staff from the Gates Foundation who helped expand our transfer student success knowledge and network.

The volume's quality is greatly enhanced because of the great care and commitment that our dear colleague Betsy O. Barefoot, the cofounder and senior scholar of the John N. Gardner Institute for Excellence in Undergraduate Education, brought to these written words. She thoughtfully reviewed each chapter—catching issues we no longer saw and further tightening each chapter's message. Her keen intelligence and comprehensive style knowledge makes this book much more readable.

We are especially grateful to the members of our three respective families who helped us find the time to write this book. Without them, few things in life would be possible. Even less would be meaningful.

We must also thank the Gardner Institute colleagues who contributed time and support—adjusting schedules, helping with conference calls and virtual meetings, and even providing meals as we conducted our work.

Last, but absolutely not least, we salute the nation's millions of transfer students. They are the inspiration for this book. Their talents, potential, and dreams for their future fuel our efforts. Our sincerest hope is that they will benefit as your institutions apply the recommendations found here—and that both your and their experiences lead to learnings at least as deep as those we realized from our writing. This book is a product of our past and present. The transfer students of the United States and you, our readers, are our nation's future.

We know no writing project is ever perfect, and we acknowledge and own the limitations of this publication—limitations made even more real through the uncertainties arising from the realities of COVID-19. Even so, we hope this volume is the genesis of new ideas that result in the continued improvement of the transfer experience. We further hope that those improvements lead to more just and promising outcomes across the higher education landscape today.

John N. Gardner
Michael J. Rosenberg
Andrew K. Koch
September 2020

References

American Association of Collegiate Registrars and Admissions Officers. (2015). *The transfer handbook: Promoting student success*. Author.

Poisel, M. A., & Joseph, S. (Eds.). (2018). *Building transfer student pathways for college and career success*. University of South Carolina: National Institute for the Study of Transfer Students, National Resource Center for the First-Year Experience and Students in Transition.

Wyner, J., Deane, K. C., Jenkins, D, & Fink, J. (2016). *The transfer playbook: Essential practices for two- and four-year colleges*. Aspen Institute.

INTRODUCTION

John N. Gardner, Michael J. Rosenberg, and Andrew K. Koch

We don't treat transfer students very well. This poor treatment is not because American educators and policymakers don't care about them. There's not an intentional animus against this population of students or an overarching disregard for them. No, we do not treat transfer students very well because, to put it simply, most of our colleges and universities are simply not designed for them.

At most institutions, transfers lack advocates. This handbook seeks to hasten the creation of a brighter future for transfer students—one in which institutions are much more actively aware of the challenges facing these students, are strongly promoting the success of transfers as learners, and are taking action to assist them in moving seamlessly through the various way-stations of the academic process that culminate in the "walk across the stage" moment. To achieve these aspirations, a rethinking and redesign of the entire transfer experience is necessary.

This handbook is intended as a comprehensive resource for higher educators and policymakers who wish to improve the success of transfer students. We believe this work is needed for the following reasons:

- Transfer is a primary route to a bachelor's degree in U.S. higher education.
- Degree attainment rates for transfer students are far too low.
- Transfer is still a relatively low priority for campus leaders, faculty, staff, and policymakers.
- Transfer student experiences and outcomes reveal a pervasive, institutionalized pattern of prejudice and discrimination, resulting in long-term inequities in U.S. higher education outcomes, especially obstacles to upward mobility and social justice.
- Major goals like Lumina Foundation's Goal 2025—to increase the proportion of Americans with high-quality degrees, certificates, and other credentials to 60% by that year will be impossible to attain until we increase transfer degree attainment rates.
- Transfer needs a call to action, and we intend this volume to serve as such.

As we were in the final process of completing the work for the volume you're now reading, we found ourselves at the onset of one of the great social disruptions in our shared history. Everyday academic rhythms ended in March 2020 as the realities of COVID-19 began sending waves of challenge and change across the educational spectrum.

1

The virus and its effects will obviously have significant implications for transfer and transfer students. However, at this point in our shared history, we cannot begin to understand the pandemic's effects on both the process of transfer and the new ways transfer students will experience college without simply being speculative. For this reason, we elect to acknowledge that the impact of COVID-19 on transfer merits a much deeper analysis—perhaps an entire book of its own. But this is not that book. The work you are reading now examines transfer in all its pre-COVID-19 complexities. The issues and opportunities we explore in the pages that follow existed before the pandemic and will inevitably continue long after it passes.

Why a Focus on Transfer? Why Now?

As mentioned previously, the mobility of students and their academic work has become commonplace. Most baccalaureate earners in the United States now carry credit from more than one institution. There are multiple reasons for this new reality—high school dual credit programs, the increasing financial burden of student loan debt, displaced workers finding their way back to college for recredentialing, increasing numbers of underrepresented students entering the higher educational space—the list grows and changes year to year.

We owe these students a hard look at our institutional practices. Whether 2-year or 4-year, public or private, open-access or highly selective, most institutions design their policies around "home-grown" students—those who accept an admission offer as first-year students and stay until they complete an associate or baccalaureate credential. While understandable, this design has led to massive inequities in the treatment of transfers.

We hope to bring the lived realities of the many different types of transfer students into the spotlight so we might better understand their challenges and also how we, as the institutional leaders, faculty, administrators, and staff tasked with giving these students the best educational experience feasible, can help them reach their goals. In short, this book is about exposing and undoing an unjust design that limits possibilities for a large number of postsecondary students in the United States.

Toward a New Definition of Transfer

As context, we want to be explicit both how we are and are not defining *transfer*. Fundamentally, we argue that "the transfer experience" is the sum of everything the student goes through at both the sending *and* receiving institutions. We reject the notion that transfer is primarily an "event," a "phase," or even a "transition" within the total undergraduate experience.

How did we come to take this intentionally comprehensive and holistic view of student transfer? We believe that an operational focus on transfer students is much too narrow. Transfer is typically seen as an administrative function—a mechanical process whereby students move and "articulate" from one autonomous institution to another. This function is usually under the purview of the functional areas of admissions or enrollment management. Therefore, transfer is not approached as a fundamental "academic" matter or process.

A natural assumption exists that transfer is a 2-year to 4-year institutional phenomenon, dealt with largely through one-size-fits-all policies. While this "traditional transfer" path may still be the norm, there are many other types of transfer: 2-year to 2-year, 4-year to 4-year, 4-year to 2-year, "swirling," concurrent enrollment, for-profit to not-for-profit, and on and on. Transfer exists within the same geographic area, as well as across regional boundaries, state lines, and international borders. A singular approach to the transfer process from every conceivable angle is an impossibility. As a result, we believe it is imperative that we view the transfer experience as unique to *each* student and institution.

That said, we acknowledge that this book is primarily focused on vertical transfer from 2- to 4-year institutions in the pursuit of a bachelor's degree. We made this choice primarily because of the evidence of overwhelming societal and economic benefits associated with earning a baccalaureate degree.

Another typical assumption underpinning how institutions approach "transfer" operationally is to define *transfer* as a sequence of consecutive events, steps, and activities. These are typically the following:

1. The student decides to transfer from one institution to another—with whatever input from the sending institution might have influenced or facilitated this decision.
2. The student applies for admission to a receiving institution.
3. The student also applies for financial aid.
4. The receiving institution reviews applicable credits and awards "transfer credit."
5. The receiving institution offers overall onboarding to include academic advising/orientation.
6. The student registers and enrolls at the receiving institution.

Transfer, thus, is examined as a "stage" or period of student development during the overall collegiate experience. This period—starting with the decision to transfer and concluding with starting classes at a new institution—is often viewed through the lens of "transition" and "adjustment." We argue that while the actual decision to transfer is significant, it ignores what has been happening to the student academically before implementing a transfer decision and what happens to a student academically after matriculating at a receiving institution.

While considering the steps and stages of transfer is necessary, we would argue this is insufficient for the ultimate purpose of increasing transfer students' academic success and baccalaureate attainment. Only by viewing transfer holistically across a student's entire educational experience can we truly improve outcomes.

At the most elementary level of understanding, a student must accumulate credits before transferring. Thus, the starting place for enhancement of transfer student success would be to examine the actions both the student and the sending institution take to make a student academically successful in learning and receiving academic credits early in the sending college experience. Unfortunately, when most institutions seek enhancements to enhance transfer, that focus often falls at the point where the student begins to implement their decision to transfer. We lose far too many students by this point in the pipeline.

In like manner, conventional views of transfer usually do not focus on what happens to transfer students *after* registration and onboarding at the receiving institution. As an upshot, institutions may lose focus on the extended period of a transfer student's undergraduate experience involving everything the student does from accumulating as few as 15 semester credit hours (or the equivalent) at a sending institution, transferring, and then working on accumulating 105 more. Thus, we argue consideration of the transfer experience must continue until the eventual awarding of the student's desired credential.

We must break our preoccupation with a focus for transfer rate improvement based solely on the mechanics of articulation, awarding of transfer credits, and simply enrolling students. If we don't focus more broadly, we will have limited success improving transfer student outcomes.

Advocating for a Point of View and Specific Corrective Actions in the Name of Social Justice

Despite the massive number of students legitimately classified as transfers, supporting transfer students remains a relatively low priority on many campuses—especially among faculty and administrative leadership. We believe this is due partly to a correctable lack of awareness about the lived experience of many students pre- and post-transfer at both sending and receiving institutions. Additionally, both implicit and explicit biases often exist against students who have transferred for a number of reasons: negative assumptions about academic skills; prejudices regarding student backgrounds; preference for focusing on first-time, first-year students; or perhaps even a case of "We don't know what to do with them, so we'll just do nothing."

The national data are telling (Fink & Jenkins, chapter 2, this volume). Multiple studies demonstrate that when transfer students make a successful transition to a baccalaureate-granting institution—by which we mean finding a new institution, moving themselves and their credits, and embarking on the remainder of a baccalaureate course of study—their academic performance typically meets or exceeds the performance of their peers who began their college experience at that institution. Nevertheless, while an enormous majority of these students, when asked, state that they desire a bachelor's degree in the future, only a sliver of the pie chart of "completers" represents transfers.

Close to half of underrepresented, first-generation, and adult students begin their education at a community college or equivalent (see Del Real Viramontes & Jain, chapter 4, this volume). These three groups are the backbone of the transfer student population. Since our system, as currently constructed, does not seem to further many of these students' academic efforts, there then arises an unmistakable *social justice* imperative for improving this system (see Rosenberg & Koch, chapter 3, this volume).

That call for social justice underpins our motivations. We want this book to raise awareness, provoke reflection, and provide a guide for institutional self-examination and change. Thus, we must express our strong belief that our higher education system has not done nearly enough for this population. We believe these students are as deserving and demonstrably as able as any other students. We believe they have been neglected. We know that as a country we cannot provide more equitable trajectory to attaining the "American dream" unless we improve our performance with this cohort.

How to Use This Book

To maximize the potential of this book in leading toward concrete improvements for your institution, we strongly recommend the following:

1. Consider our recommendations and discussion questions, offered at the end of each chapter, for potential applicability at your institution.
2. Consider how you can tell your own institution's "transfer story."
3. Create an institution-wide reading group to digest and discuss what you find here. Perhaps divide up the book so that individuals can review and report on individual chapters.
4. Better yet, create a more formal task force to conduct a self-study of your institution's current approaches, outcomes, and priorities with respect to transfer students and produce a set of recommended action items. Then, implement those recommendations.
5. Use this book as a basis for preparation for a retreat/summit to consider the current status of transfer at your institution.
6. Engage a wide cross-section of your campus educators in the substance of this book: faculty, academic administrators, student affairs professionals, student success professionals, cabinet-level leaders, governing board members, student government leaders and—most importantly—the transfer students themselves.

An Introduction to the Chapters

We strove to include strong voices from across the spectrum of higher education to provide insight into student transfer and how to improve transfer outcomes.

We thank our colleagues John Hitt and Sanford Shugart for providing the foreword. Their extraordinarily successful professional, personal, and institutional partnership is a gold standard that we hope all will emulate.

The first section of the book (chapters 1–4) illustrates the context of transfer in American history and contemporary society: how we came to have "transfer" in the first place, who these students are, where they come from, and why institutions must reframe transfer as a social justice imperative.

Most American college and university educators assume that we have always had transfer students. Not at all. Transfer students are a unique American phenomenon. We invited the thinker we regard as *the* historian of transfer, Stephen J. Handel of the College Board, to retrace for us the origins of our transfer student landscape. You will be surprised and perhaps troubled by what he relates.

Current transfer policies and practices are extremely complex and difficult for the most informed educators to adequately comprehend. An impressive array of institutional barriers, largely unintentionally created by public policymakers and educators alike, make it extremely difficult to better our transfer success rates. Two excellent researchers, John Fink and Davis Jenkins of Columbia University's Community College Research Center, expose a number of myths about transfer students and institutional performance to challenge and motivate our thinking.

Two of this book's coeditors, Michael J. Rosenberg and Andrew K. Koch, make the case that addressing inequities in transfer should be considered a social justice imperative by all institutions of higher education. They suggest the current systems for transfer students and the uneven outcomes among many underrepresented populations perpetuate racial, ethnic, and family wealth inequities.

We turn to José Del Real Viramontes of the University of Illinois and Dimpal Jain of California State University–Northridge for an exploration of theoretical frameworks that center the student of color in the transfer process. Using special emphasis on a case study about Latinx students, the chapter explores transfer-receptive culture and community cultural wealth models to offer insight into providing more effective interventions for any number of student subpopulations.

In the second section (chapters 5–11), we take a deeper dive into several of the functional areas of the institution that directly impact the transfer student experience from start to finish. Our collection of contributors provides solid, functional advice on how to improve service to transfers.

Our second contribution from Stephen J. Handel is framed as a personal discussion aimed directly at admissions professionals—a realm Handel knows intimately from his time as the chief undergraduate and transfer admissions officer for the University of California system. This discussion has larger implications and application value to a broad range of other professionals who are advocates for transfer student success. He sheds a great deal of light on how the whole process of transfer admissions could be significantly improved.

Paying for college is a top concern among all college students, not just transfers. The federal aid system, as currently designed, can present any number of roadblocks for transfers, especially those who attend multiple institutions or enroll part time.

Additionally, community college transfer-bound students are likely to be less well-off financially than their non-transferring compatriots, so all our approaches for meeting these students' needs for financial support should be explored. We have turned to Jason Taylor of the University of Utah for a comprehensive overview of how transfer students are and are not supported by our country's complex panoply of financial aid practices.

When students transfer, they may have difficulty earning credit for their previous academic work or their accumulation of knowledge outside the formal classroom-equals-credit higher educational structure. Kathy Silberman and Rose Rojas of the Curriculum and Transfer Articulation office at Maricopa Community College call for a "revolution" in the way institutions manage their prior learning assessment (PLA) processes, which, if offered properly, can provide an enormous boost to the odds of student success.

Building on the concepts of the previous chapter, Michelle Alvarez, Tess Diver, and Jamie Holcomb examine a relatively new movement to provide more recognition and support of transfer students through what is known as competency-based education (CBE)—providing credit for learning experiences outside the "traditional" higher education model. The three discuss how this fast-growing educational model provides opportunities for baccalaureate attainment for students whose life circumstances can stand in the way of traditional college attendance. They discuss methods of orienting, advising, and mentorship for students in this emerging learning paradigm.

One of the many inequities that transfer students experience is inadequate recognition of their previous academic work. Transfer students would be in an even stronger position in the employment market if they were, on their ultimate path to a bachelor's degree, recognized for completing the requirements for their associate degree. As well, their sending institutions—typically community colleges—are also not recognized for awarding these degrees, which can be problematic in this time of performance-based funding and budgeting. One way to rectify this state of affairs is through retroactive degree certification, more commonly known as reverse-credit transfer to provide "credit when it's due." The country's leading researcher on reverse transfer, Debra D. Bragg of the University of Washington, and her colleague, Heather N. McCambly from Northwestern University, will explicate for us this growing practice.

Most state public university systems, both 2- and 4-year, have state-level governance structures, which are in the position to offer a huge boon to student success efforts. Our book would not have been complete without a powerful illustration of how the resources of an entire state system can be brought to bear on improving transfer students' chances of greater success and mobility. For this important insight, we turn to Angela Bell, vice chancellor of Research and Policy Analysis for the University of Georgia System, who will help us understand what can be done cooperatively at the campus and state system levels to leverage the odds for improvement in the transfer realm.

One population of transfer students facing especially strenuous challenges, for which they are charged a significant differential in tuition and fees, is international students. Without their presence on both 2- and 4-year U.S. campuses, our higher education enterprise would be very different. In their chapter, Jason Chambers, Karen Ramos, and Sarah Mackey of the University of Cincinnati identify the special challenges faced by this population and offer reflection and suggestions about what can be done to help students from beyond our domestic borders.

The third section (chapters 12–15) focuses on the most important work of the academy: teaching and learning. Given our comprehensive definition of *transfer* as being all inclusive of the entire sending and receiving academic experience, we must focus on how to make transfer students more academically successful.

The chief academic officer or provost of any institution guides the faculty's overall academic direction. The individual in this leadership position holds the power to create a transformative academic environment for transfer students. Mark Canada, executive vice chancellor for academic affairs at transfer-friendly Indiana University Kokomo, offers counsel and guidance to academic leaders in any sector in promoting a fertile learning ground for transfers and for engaging faculty in the transfer process and rewarding them for their service in this area.

Andrew K. Koch, one of the editors of this volume, and his research partner and big-data decision support expert, Brent M. Drake of the University of Nevada Las Vegas, examine inequities in student performance in foundational, high-risk, and high-enrollment *gateway courses*. They draw upon unique new research to offer a quantitative view of how outcomes differ in these courses along racial and socioeconomic lines. They also provide suggestions for how institutional research offices can serve as windows for faculty into how their students perform as well as revealing systemic inequities. Knowledge of these inequities coupled with action creates lasting change.

Along those lines, we move to the faculty who educate the students in these gateway courses. Stephanie M. Foote of the Gardner Institute offers suggestions for intentional, liberating pedagogy and curricular redesign in these courses which often serve as barriers to transfer student progress.

As the world of higher education integrates itself more and more into the online environment, institutions must be attentive and intentional about their pedagogies in the digital realm. Susannah McGowan of Georgetown University puts her curriculum design experience to work in providing a unique definition of *digital learning* and illustrates how technology can facilitate a smooth student integration into the online learning space—specifically looking at how this integration can benefit transfer students.

In the fourth and final section (chapters 16–17), we conclude by focusing on important "best practices" presented in the form of two detailed institutional case histories of how to put these collective improvements into practice in a sustainable and continually improvable manner. We will consider the nation's two largest transfer-receiving institutions: Arizona State University and the University of Central Florida—which have much to offer that is replicable, even for smaller institutions. These exemplars are designed to inspire our readers by what is truly possible.

Finally, the conclusion offers recommendations that we are convinced can be pursued, either in part or in their collective whole, by any postsecondary institution that has responsibility for transfer students. We believe our conclusions will allow you to transition the information presented in this book to practical application for increased transfer student success.

An Online Compendium and Companion Publication of Important Resource Information

We also wished to highlight some inspirational case studies from institutions who have made a commitment to bolster the successes of transfer students. Because of length considerations, we provide these brief cases in an online compendium, which can be accessed at https://styluspub.presswarehouse.com/browse/book/9781620369470/The-Transfer-Experience. These case studies are an integral part of the "case" we strive to make.

In this digital compendium, you will find:

1. A second case study from Guttman Community College. As the previously mentioned case study focuses on how the college works with its own transfer students, this case study focuses on how Guttman College is working as part of a broader consortium of its transfer partner institutions.
2. A case study from one of America's newest community colleges, the City University of New York's (CUNY) Stella and Charles Guttman Community College. Approximately 5 years old, this remarkable college has become a community college gold standard for achieving many outcomes, including retention and graduation rates and intentionally preparing students for transfer to CUNY "senior" colleges. This case study focuses on Guttman Community College's overall campus strategy in engaging and preparing transfer students.
3. A case study about consolidation and partnership—how the consolidation of Georgia State University and Perimeter College provides increased opportunities and challenges in the area in and around Atlanta for thousands of transfer students.
4. A case study of a truly unique urban research university that is a partnership of two Association of American Universities research universities: IUPUI, which serves many transfers in the Hoosier state.
5. A case study of Kean University of New Jersey, which illustrates a special partnership with a community college campus, Ocean County College, and how it is drawing from that partnership to design a new regional transfer effort called Kean Skylands. The case study shows how a regional university is addressing common issues associated with transfer by not having students physically "transfer" at all.

6. A case study of how a state consortium of 36 private colleges and universities have provided greater access and opportunity for community college transfers: the North Carolina Independent Colleges and Universities, in partnership with the North Carolina Community College System.

7. A case study of the University Center of the Mountains, based at Hazard Community and Technical College in a geographically isolated and economically challenged region of the country, eastern Kentucky. This multi-institutional partnership of a dozen colleges and universities brings a variety of baccalaureate and master's degree options to this area.

8. A case study about the Transfer Pride initiative at one of the most selective, public universities in the United States—the University of California, Los Angeles. Rather than trying to get transfer students to assimilate, UCLA celebrates students' transfer identity while integrating them into the campus fabric.

9. A case study about the Interstate Passport, an effort to support transfer students who wish and need to cross state lines by means of a consortium based in the Western Interstate Commission for Higher Education (WICHE). Schools participating in the Passport program guarantee seamless transfer of lower-division general education requirements among its members, allowing students to move more quickly through their academic programs post-transfer.

10. A case study of the American Public University System (APUS), one of the nation's largest 100% online universities, focused on transfer students who are currently active duty military, former active duty military, retired active duty military, and their spouses/partners. A for-profit, regionally accredited university, APUS demonstrates a high degree of intentionality about addressing the needs of a unique population of transfer students.

11. And finally, a description of how seven higher education institutions (one community college, two research universities, one public historically Black university, one private university, and two regional public universities) came together to first create the Tulsa (OK) Transfer Collaborative, and proceeded to create what we hope will become a permanent higher education consortial structure. This work, initiated by the Schusterman Family Foundation, is an inspiration in its emergence in the time of and in spite of COVID-19.

The Online Compendium: Case Studies and Other Resources also includes information about Phi Theta Kappa, the honor society at 2-year institutions in the United States, and Tau Sigma, an honor society at 4-year institutions for incoming transfer students. These organizations highlight student success, provide networking and leadership training, and offer scholarships to this population. We also include information about the National Institute for the Study of Transfer Students, the premier professional organization for transfer advocacy, and its wealth of information and resources.

To conclude, we hope this volume will serve as a pathway to understanding and a spur to action. Progress is possible. In the 1980s, another cohort of students was neglected, considered low priority, and discriminated against: first-year students. We once believed broadly that students failed because of their own shortcomings. Such a view would be laughable today as a result of the first-year experience reform movement.

Our hope is that we, the higher education community, can marshal our resources and muster the will to affect a similar attitudinal sea change in the world of transfer students. We are calling for as much attention to be paid to improving the transfer experience as there now is for the first-year experience. We hope you will join us in this endeavor!

PART ONE

TRANSFER IN CONTEXT

LOOKING BACK TO SEE THE FUTURE

The Transfer Pathway as Historical Mirage

Stephen J. Handel

Democracy, if it continue, must include the masses and maintain their sympathy and interest.

—William Rainey Harper (1905, p. 12)

The conflict between open-door admission and performance of high quality often means a wide discrepancy between the hopes of entering students and the means of their realization. . . . As a result, while some students of low promise are successful, for large numbers failure is inevitable and structured.

—Burton R. Clark (1960, p. 571)

The transfer pathway between community colleges and 4-year universities was an extraordinary educational leap of faith when it was first seriously contemplated at the start of the last century. Although legislation that precipitated the Morrill Acts of 1862 and 1890 (Lucas, 1994) had opened opportunities for more individuals to attend higher education, authentic access to a college degree remained limited to individuals with the means or the standing to take full advantage of this opportunity. The transfer pathway was built on an emerging consensus, however, that the nation would need a better educated citizenry; that the economic and cultural future of America was at least partially dependent on providing opportunities for individuals to earn additional skills offered only in higher education. Students interested in a college degree who were otherwise unable to attend a 4-year institution directly from high school could, if they successfully completed a program of study at a community college, transfer to one of America's storied public or private 4-year institutions.

Today, over 100 years later, the idea of transfer remains a remarkably progressive ideal, a fashioning of democratic opportunity and egalitarian aspiration, as in tune with the nation's consciousness in the current day as it was in the last century. During the past 100 years, authentic access to higher education via a community college has become a reality beyond what its original framers had in mind—visionary leaders such as Harry Tappan, William Rainey Harper, Alexis Lange, and David Gordon Starr (Winter, 1964). Today, a community college is within driving distance of most Americans (American Association of Community Colleges, 2018). Moreover, the fact that these institutions are open access—an admissions policy unaddressed by the originators of these colleges—means, in theory at least, that anyone in the United States can go to college and transfer to the nation's best 4-year colleges and universities. In a country where admission to the most selective institutions has become increasingly fraught at the first-year level, the access offered by the transfer pathway, by comparison, remains astonishingly progressive.

Simply put, the transfer pathway is one of the most extraordinary educational innovations in the history of U.S. higher education. But transfer—as an innovation or as a practice—is largely a mirage in traditional histories of American collegiate life.

Despite the uniqueness of the transfer pathway and its potential for authentic change in the way we serve students in postsecondary education, it is rarely treated separately from the broader fortunes of community colleges. This is surely an important perspective, but it is not the entire story. Moreover, the transfer idea must, by definition, include a robust partnership with 4-year institutions. This partnership, such as it is, is rarely addressed in histories of 4-year institutions. When policymakers and others cite failures in the transfer pathway—and they have—the fault is usually laid at the door of the community college. Although 4-year institutions are criticized occasionally regarding the acceptance of community college credit, for example, their role as full partners in the transfer process, is rarely noted (Handel, 2010).

This short treatment will not balance the scales for an updated and comprehensive historical analysis of transfer as an educational innovation of its own. If you are interested in more information along those lines, there are several general, but excellent histories of community colleges. Besides Brint and Karabel (1989) and Dougherty (1994) described earlier, see treatments by Beach (2012), Cohen and Brawer (2008), and Witt et al. (1994).

My modest purpose here is to demonstrate that the transfer pathway remains critical in this century as surely as it was in the last one. We appreciate that both the foundational narrative of the transfer pathway and its legacy are debated (Handel, 2013a). However, for those of us who see transfer as a pivotal educational pathway for students who might not otherwise have access to higher education, we insist that students' attempts to transfer from a 2- to 4-year institution is something more than a prosaic transactional reality; that is, it represents—whether the originators of the junior college intended this or not—a radical investment in the intellectual potential of everyday Americans. We would also insist that the necessity of transfer, and its optimism in the transformative potential of higher education, is more important today than ever.

The Public Promise and the Private Calculation: Transfer's Creation Story

Before there could be transfer, there had to be a place for students to transfer *from*, namely the junior college. Henry P. Tappan, president of the University of Minnesota in the 1870s, is credited with first proposing a collegiate-like institution separate from high schools and universities (or, in another version, extending high school by 2 additional years) that would ultimately be called a community college (Witt et al., 1994). However, William Rainey Harper at the University of Chicago turned this idea into reality. In a short paper published in 1901, Harper proposed that high school graduates be admitted to a "lower division" or a general education curriculum, which would be separate from an "upper-division" curriculum offered at a university (Harper, 1901). Under his plan, students who successfully completed the course of study in the lower division would be qualified to transfer to the university to earn the baccalaureate degree. Students uninterested in continuing their studies or who did not perform well enough to be admitted as transfer students, would earn a 2-year "associate degree" and enter the workforce.

In this early incarnation, Harper's (1901) notion about a transfer pathway is not much more than a necessary transaction for students to advance from a small, 2-year institution, he calls ("for the lack of a better term" p. 34) a junior college, to the larger and better resourced university. Harper's rationale for creating the junior college is premised almost entirely on his strategy to establish a new higher education system that would privilege emerging U.S. research universities, while supporting the expansion of the free comprehensive public high school system. To accomplish this, Harper stressed the need to thin the number of small, mostly denominational, colleges dotting the U.S. landscape at that time. His position was that these institutions, while having numerous virtues, lacked the resources to provide the advanced education that would be needed to train a growing intellectual and professional class in the United States. In his writings on this topic (see Harper 1901, 1905), Harper takes considerable pains to demonstrate that small colleges were in no position financially to grow the necessary libraries, laboratories, and faculty that would allow them to adequately train students at the highest levels of scholarship, and any attempt to do so would necessarily detract from the education these institutions should provide to students in the lower division. Harper emphasized that many of these small colleges could ensure their survival by becoming either 2-year institutions or aligning themselves to public high schools by offering 2 additional years of schooling.

Harper (1901) devoted little attention to the practical matter of how and why students might transfer from a junior college to a 4-year institution, yet he was not oblivious that his proposal required a fundamental reordering of American higher education in the first years of the 20th century:

> The change of certain colleges into junior colleges . . . and the close association of such colleges with the universities—all this contributes toward a system of higher education (something which does not now exist in America), the lack of which is sadly felt in every sphere of educational activity. (pp. 44–45)

As other historians have noted, Harper's beliefs were aligned with a broader progressive movement in the United States that sought new avenues for individuals to achieve greater levels of economic opportunity (Brint & Karabel, 1989; Dougherty, 1994). As noted earlier, some states had begun to capitalize on the opportunities inherent in the Morrill Land-Grant Acts, which sowed the seeds for the establishment of America's greatest public research universities, including those in Michigan, Wisconsin, and California. The free public high school was also educating greater numbers of students throughout the United States, fueling a belief that the industrial might of the nation would be bolstered when citizens had additional opportunities to climb "ladders of ascent" based on individual drive and initiative as opposed to limited opportunities offered through wealth, status, and position alone (Brint & Karabel, 1989).

Harper's prescience in seeing the value of a new higher education structure was not unique. Progressive leaders at several of the nation's most prestigious institutions were enthusiastic supporters of this higher education reordering. In addition, local political leaders were interested in realizing the advantages that a publicly funded college might provide to the local community (Dougherty, 1994). As Brint and Karabel (1989) note, the community college movement was aided by

> the support and encouragement of the nation's great universities—among them, Chicago, Stanford, Michigan, and Berkeley—which, far from opposing the rise of the junior college as a potential competitor for students and resources, enthusiastically supported its growth. (p. 23)

The Limits of Aspiration

Although there was a genuine enthusiasm for the creation of junior colleges—or some variant in high schools that might provide students with increased educational options—there was also an implicit limit on the extent to which a student could take advantage of these new opportunities. While transfer from a junior college to a 4-year university was understood to be one of the major advantages of attending these colleges in the first place, access was constrained by the economic necessities and expectations of the age.

Identifying the reasons for these aspirational limits is not complicated, even if they are not immediately apparent. For university leaders, the growth of junior colleges would be beneficial for two reasons. First, it would unburden them of having to teach lower-division, general education courses, a responsibility that Harper (1901) indicated, for example, was akin to the aims of the high school, preparatory school, or academy rather than the university:

> The work of the freshman and sophomore years is only a continuation of the academy or high school work. It is a continuation, not only of the subject-matter studied, but of the methods employed. It is not until the end of the sophomore year that university methods of instruction may be employed to advantage. (p. 34)

Second, diverting most college-bound students to junior colleges rather than to universities would provide 4-year institutions with the ability to select students for further postsecondary education. University leaders very much coveted the opportunity to admit only the very best of students since that was viewed as necessary to strengthen the standards of scholarship and prestige for their institutions. Although junior colleges offered an opportunity for individuals to participate in higher education, the universities would nonetheless retain the authority for who might receive advanced training.

For local political leaders, the transfer pathway was also seen as one of the characteristics that would enhance the reputation of these new junior colleges. Those students who successfully transferred to the university would be justly celebrated. But the junior college would also offer something of value to students who did not transfer: terminal degrees that would serve as vocational training for local workforce needs (Dougherty, 1994; Eells, 1941). A better educated citizenry, especially in communities located far away from state or research universities, was one of the bets placed by local boosters interested in establishing a community college in their hometown. Dougherty (1994) concludes that

> local business strongly supported the community college in part because it shared the general interest in educational opportunity. But three other interests were as or more important: securing publicly subsidized employee training, fostering local economic development, and burnishing local pride. (p. 134)

The creation of a transfer pathway that, in effect, was limited to students who qualified to attend a 4-year institution was neither a secret nor a cynical ploy to subvert the intentions of students who wished to earn a 4-year degree. Surely institutional self-interest was at play: universities wishing to unload the teaching of lower-division courses elsewhere and maintain their prerogative to select only the best students, and community colleges wishing to establish a unique mission that was not dependent on the willingness of universities to admit their students via transfer. But one need not vilify either higher education segment for its institutional provincialism; it was merely an outgrowth of the times. The proportion of the U.S. population attending college in the early decades of the 20th century was a fraction of what it is today (Cohen & Brawer, 2008). More importantly, there was no college-going culture of national prominence at the beginning of the junior college movement. Earning a high school diploma was sufficient for most individuals who, after graduation, were able to secure stable jobs. To say that universal transfer for all community college students was unsupported is to presume that such an ideal was even contemplated in the first place. This position is hardly countenanced even today.

Nevertheless, what Harper and other political and educational leaders could not have foreseen was the extraordinarily attractive claim the transfer pathway had on the minds of prospective students (Brint & Karabel, 1989; Dougherty, 1994). It was a narrative perfectly embodied in an often-recited American cultural narrative: the idea that individuals with ambition and opportunity could create the life they wished to live by simply working diligently to achieve it. As postsecondary education became increasingly important for full economic and cultural participation in American life, the transfer pathway was to become the avenue of presumed access to the baccalaureate degree and all that it promised for working class students who had few comparable avenues for advancement. That the transfer pathway did not—and does not to this day—live up to this expectation is not the fault of community college students writ large; it is, rather, a failure of the imagination in all of us who are advocates for this transformative educational pathway.

Transfer and Student Aspirations

The original boosters of the community college and transfer pathway, especially William Rainey Harper, could not have foreseen the extraordinary growth of American higher education in the 20th century. Today, community colleges enroll about 43% of all undergraduates, making it the largest segment in U.S. higher education with nearly 1,200 campuses spread across the country (American Association of Community Colleges, 2018). For their part, 4-year institutions, public and private, are lauded for their scholarship and productivity and regularly rated as among the best institutions in the world (Cole, 2009). Two- and 4-year institutions have made it possible for more Americans to earn postsecondary certificates and degrees than any other industrialized country. Although 4-year institutions are better resourced, more generally praised for their academic accomplishments, and typically viewed as places for students to experience stereotypical college life, the presence of the community college—and its open-door access enrollment policy—embodies higher education's greatest aim to make postsecondary life possible for any person in the United States.

Students who attend college for the first time at a 2-year institution typically enter with a goal to transfer and earn the baccalaureate degree. This goal has not wavered in the entire history of the community college movement. Surveys of student intentions conducted in the 1920s to today verify the constancy of this goal is to transfer to a 4-year institution and earn the baccalaureate degree (Brint & Karabel, 1989, Dougherty, 1994; Handel, 2010, 2013b; Handel & Williams, 2012). More recently, in a 2009 survey by the U.S. Department of Education, 80% of all new, first-time community-college students aspired to earn bachelor's degrees. The desire was especially strong among students from groups traditionally underrepresented in higher education, such as Latinx Americans, African Americans, and those in the lowest income quartile (see Handel, 2013b). Between 1966 and 1999, when the University of California Los Angeles Cooperative Institutional Research Program surveyed the educational aspirations of community college students separately from those entering 4-year institutions, the proportion of 2-year-college students whose educational goal was a bachelor's degree (or higher) never dropped below 70% (Handel 2013b).

Still, one could reasonably argue that such intentions are, as one colleague expressed to me, "merely aspirational," implying that most students have inflated goals and unrealistic expectations. I do not think this premise unfair; I would only argue that it is irrelevant. It is certainly true that students in 2- and 4-year institutions often find themselves facing an unconsidered reality as they pursue their educational goals at 17 or 18 years of age. Yet we never question the goals of students who enter the 4-year institution; we rarely question that a desire to "complete" a degree is disingenuous or "merely aspirational." Indeed, as colleges and universities scramble to increase the degree completion rates at their institutions in response to government and public pressure, one might argue that students with substantive aspirations for a 4-year degree are precisely the kinds of students one would encourage to finish a degree.

Despite the extraordinary esteem that first-time community college students have held for the transfer function, the number of students who transfer has always been relatively low. National figures place the proportion at around 12% (Century Foundation, 2013; Putnam, 2015). But this is an imperfect estimate, which includes only those students who attend community colleges on a full-time basis (most attend part time). Still, it is almost impossible to derive a precise national transfer number since data are not compiled centrally. More generously, the actual transfer rate is probably somewhere between 25% and 35% of first-time community college students (Handel, 2013c).

Contemporary researchers and practitioners have a variety of theories as to why more community college students fail to transfer to 4-year institutions. They often point to factors such as decreasing state support for higher education, insufficient financial aid, doubts about the value of higher education degrees in relation to cost, and the increased need for remedial education in collegiate settings. Yet a brief look at the historical record is instructive, even if not definitive.

At the start of the community college movement, as noted previously, leaders wished to establish their institutional identities separate from that of universities. Exemplifying this perspective, Eells (1941) quotes an unidentified junior college leader:

> I wonder if the junior colleges are going to take over this program of fitting people to live, or are just preparatory institutions to the 4-year colleges and universities; whether we are going to assert our right to a "place in the sun" to serve men and women, fitting them for life at that level, or whether we are just going to be a tail for the universities to wag. (p. 17)

Moreover, local boosters saw early the value of workforce training as a way of enhancing the regional economy. Upon entry to the community college, a student was faced almost immediately with competing programmatic choices, most of which did not support moving along a transfer pathway. In addition, 4-year institutions, which were separate and in no small way competitors for the same students, rarely devoted the resources to articulate courses and programs for transfer students. This situation prevented students who were intent on transfer from gaining a clear idea about how the courses they completed at a community college might transfer to the receiving institution.

Institutional provincialism can only be a partial description of why the transfer function has not operated historically as well as perhaps students believe it should. Despite the egalitarian foundation inherent in the community college mission, embodied perfectly by its own open access admissions policy, most higher education leaders (both 2 year and 4 year), along with their local, state, and national political leaders, believed in the transfer creation story as an educational abstraction; a utopian ideal unmoored from regular reality. Even today, any higher education leader can describe with uncanny familiarity how the transfer pathway provides access to any student who, regardless of personal background, may gain access to the baccalaureate degree through hard work and ambition. But believing that *any* student could achieve this goal is something quite different than believing *all* students should achieve it.

Early advocates of community colleges and transfer argue that the nation does not need so many well-educated individuals, that there were insufficient jobs for these students. What the economy needed, at best, was more workers with *some* college. Implicit in this concern was an appreciation that the driving force of a college education is to prepare students for the world of work. While earning a degree in philosophy or history might be fine for those of means and standing, others simply cannot afford to indulge in such intellectual luxuries.

Another familiar argument is that most students attending community colleges simply do not have the qualifications to earn a higher-level degree. This idea gained greater currency throughout the century as the community college's open-access policy become more widely applied. Open access created a curious contradiction for many higher education leaders. To presume that all students attending a community college could transfer to 4-year college or university was, on its face, not defendable since these students did nothing to *earn* their way into higher education. Ironically, such a position turns on its head the transformative rationale for transfer and why it was so greatly esteemed by students who might not otherwise have access to the baccalaureate degree.

Despite the failure of transfer thus far to accommodate the aspirations of students who might benefit from this opportunity, their plans have not changed. There is something quite remarkable about the strong and unwavering collegiate aspirations of students who, in another time or in another country, would not have had an opportunity to go to college. Although Harper may have viewed transfer as an aspirational goal befitting only a relatively few students, most community college students—then as now—*took him at his word.*

Cooling Out and Moving On

If Harper's 1901 essay represents the first, full embodiment of what we call the transfer pathway, Burton Clark's 1960 essay describing the "cooling out" function of the community college is an equally influential scholarly event contributing to transfer's creation story. Appearing as it does at almost the exact middle point of transfer's history is only convenient; yet Clark's essay remains essential reading for not only students in various fields but also career-long transfer advocates. Whether one agrees with Clark's conclusions or not, there can be no denying that his ideas frame the dialectic that has fueled the debate over the effectiveness of the transfer pathway for the past 6 decades.

Clark's (1960) essay advances a single question, but it is big and, by the standards of scholarship, shocking: Do community colleges fail students or do the students fail themselves? Simply put, he concludes that student failure in U.S. community colleges—and by failure he means a failure to transfer—is "structured" and largely inevitable. He presumes from the start that no nation so committed to universal collegiate access can fully absorb all students who wish to earn a 4-year degree. Nor can every student who wishes to earn such a degree have the intellectual wherewithal to do so. As a result, community colleges are complicit in a delicate process of "cooling out" students' intentions, redirecting them to programs of study or workforce training that might be better aligned either to explicit workforce needs or the intellectual abilities of the individual student.

Clark's position forced an historic shift in the way we view student performance in community colleges; in fact, it opened up for debate the serious possibility that there *was* such a thing as failure in a 2-year college. Halfway through the community college movement no one really questioned what happened to students who chose to enter higher education by enrolling in their local 2-year institution. Founding fathers such as Harper would argue that a failure to transfer is not failure at all. It merely represents an outcome of a system that is, by design, elitist. Even today, Derek Bok (2017), former president of Harvard University, articulates a similar vision of 4-year institutions more generally:

> Until late in the century, dropout rates were seldom even considered a responsibility of the college. If students failed to stay the course, their departure was largely attributed to their lack of ability or perseverance, not to any failing on the part of the institution. (p. 7)

Even if they failed to gain admission to the University of Chicago, they would leave with a terminal associate degree and get on with their lives. For other community college enthusiasts, completion of terminal degrees (absent transfer) was viewed as a success since a student's successful transfer was only an occasional celebration (perhaps in the same way we celebrate the very few student-athletes who achieve their ambition to "go pro") (Eells, 1941). Although Clark's perspective does not vary from Harper and other community college boosters, he names what was heretofore unexpressed: The authentic function of the community college was not to ensure transfer to a 4-year institution but to manage and redirect over-earnest student expectations toward goals that were seen as more attainable, such as applied workforce credentials and degrees that would lead to gainful employment. There was little point in arguing about low transfer rates since the very structure of the community college was to "cool" aspirations rather them "warm" them.

Clark's perspective, often inappropriately viewed as *only* an assault on the mission of community college (it was also an assault on higher education broadly), has galvanized the work of dozens of researchers, spurred the publication of scores of research studies, and focused the way in which policymakers have analyzed transfer. To this day, Clark delineates the rules of engagement for judging—usually negatively—community colleges and transfer at almost the complete exclusion of 4-year institutions. (If you believe this conclusion overbroad, consider how rarely 4-year institutions are blamed for low transfer rates, even though they are the institutions responsible for the number of transfer students who are admitted.)

Like Harper, I doubt Clark suspected that his sociological meta-analysis could have generated so much thinking and research on this topic. Clark's pronouncement did not alone galvanize opposition to the cooling out function, but it set the course alight. As the 1960s gained momentum, education leaders, as well as students largely *unrepresented* in the nation's most elite institutions, began to question the increasing vocationalization of the community college as a strategy to "track" the powerless away from traditional higher education. Citing Clark's cooling-out schema, these constituencies understood what failure looked like in a country that offered mass access to higher education but did less to ensure the success of students who took advantage of this opportunity. This criticism plagued community colleges for most of the decades following the 1960s. Community college professionals viewed this criticism as especially harsh and unfair given their passion—then and now—to provide unparalleled access to the advantages of higher education degrees, certifications, and training (Dougherty, 1994; Handel, 2013a).

So, what *is* failure at a community college? That we lack an answer even today undermines the potential of the transfer pathway.

Transfer Nation: A Personal Perspective

Despite the extraordinary growth of community colleges in the United States, the transfer pathway steadily languished through the later decades of the 20th century, despite students' stated preference to earn a 4-year degree (Cohen & Brawer, 2008). As noted earlier, this was due to competition for students' academic attention in other areas of the community college curriculum. It was also due to 4-year institutions' lackluster enthusiasm for transfer students. And it was part of sustained belief that too much education was probably a bad thing.

The start of the new century, however, presented some startling reminders of the need for an educated citizenry regardless of how and where individuals accessed higher education. As worldwide communications technologies grew more sophisticated, a far more interconnected global economy emerged. The unprecedented growth in new knowledge—and the skills needed to manage this "information age"—became increasingly clear. This global village promised economic advantages, but only to those who could enter its city limits. It also posed new dangers, as the unprecedented financial meltdown that came to be known as the Great Recession demonstrated. Our internet-connected lives keep us tethered to an astonishing amount of news and information, but we have little time to evaluate its importance or its potential influence on our lives. If there was ever a time in which the skills of a liberal arts education—critical thinking, quantitative reasoning, historical context, ethnical discernment—would be more important, it would be now.

It is my belief—sheer speculation that historians only later will be able to verify—that this confluence of events will boost the popularity of the transfer pathway for several reasons. First, the bachelor's degree has become the most important credential for economic life in America. Whether you believe it represents an excessive labor market credential or a well-documented constellation of invaluable intellectual skills, the baccalaureate is the ticket that must be punched to participate in American economic and cultural life (Baker, 2014).

Of course, as documented earlier, community college students' pursuit of the 4-year degree has been sustained throughout the last century, despite economic upheavals and international crises. They also understand that the new economy will require them to retool and reeducate regularly. Since most graduate and professional programs require the bachelor's degree as the price of admission, smart men and women will keep their options open, as they should, by earning a 4-year degree.

Second, if the Great Recession taught Americans anything, it was to be more skeptical of higher education's value proposition. As the cost of higher education has increased, U.S. families are asking harder questions about its "payoff." As tuition has moved upward faster than the cost of almost anything else in America, families are leveraging their limited higher education budgets by using community colleges more judiciously than ever before (Spencer, 2018).

Third, shifting demographics and a widening gap between the haves and have-nots will boost enrollment in community colleges. Demographer Nathan Grawe (2017) rather ominously predicts that in less than a decade, higher education will see 280,000 fewer high school graduates, the inexorably result of a "birth dearth" spurred by the economic instability of the Great Recession. With prospective college students participating in a higher education buyer's market, Grawe and others argue that community colleges will likely lose in the competition for students to 4-year institutions. Perhaps this is true, but not if 4-year institutions continue to boost the price of admission via tuition and, more critically, if America's current economic divide should grow wider. Moreover, those students who *are* graduating from high school in the next decade will be from groups that have been traditionally underrepresented in higher education and who have found community college to be far more welcoming than more traditional institutions.

Fourth, this "transfer nation" is a place where there will be far fewer traditionally aged high-school graduates to fill the nation's college classrooms and a rapidly increasing proportion of prospective college students from groups traditionally underrepresented in 4-year institutions, as well as a widening breach between the rich and poor. Thus, 4-year institutions will, for the first time in the history of the community college movement, need 2-year institutions more than the reverse. This transition may finally make it possible for the leaders of these institutions to see that they are owners too of the transfer pathway and are responsible for its effectiveness as surely as community college are. From this realization will come easier credit transfer, better transfer orientation programs, speedier credit evaluations, competitive tuition discounting, and all the other things that smooth the pathway to a baccalaureate degree.

Optimism has always been the heart of the transfer pathway. It will continue to propel our work to fulfill the transformative possibilities of U.S. higher education as perfectly embodied in the transfer pathway.

Recommendations

1. Review your institution's history regarding transfer. This historiography might include internal memoranda, catalog copy, or minutes from board of trustee meetings. What kind of historical record can be written about your institution's focus on or concern with transfer students? Keep in mind that a lack of recorded history also tells an important story.
2. Using the expertise of your institutional research department or faculty members skilled in survey design, develop a simple method of assessing the educational aspirations of transfer students on your campus. Compare those results with whatever extant data you possess about the aspirations of previous cohorts of transfer students. Have these aspirations changed over time?
3. Assess the extent to which Clark's "cooling out function" exists at your institution. Does your college or university see differential rates of success among some sets of students over others? What might be the structural barriers at your institution that impede the academic progress of some students?

Discussion Questions

1. The success of the transfer process is often assessed by counting the number of students who successfully transfer from a community college to a 4-year institution without reference to some external standard. Since community colleges also serve students with educational intentions other than transfer, what is a reasonable standard that educators can use to judge whether the transfer pathway is working well for students at a particular institution?
2. What is an institution's obligation to students who wish to transfer but do not? Do all students with transfer intentions deserve the chance to earn a bachelor's degree at a 4-year institution?
3. Community colleges are often criticized for low student transfer rates, but what is the responsibility of 4-year institutions that set the requirements for admission? Is the responsibility for transfer students different for 2-year colleges versus the 4-year colleges or universities?

4. Given the historic difficulty of increasing the number of students who transfer from 2- to 4-year institutions, should community colleges revise their institutional missions to serve only students with associate degrees or certificate intentions?

References

American Association of Community Colleges (2018). *Fast facts*. Author.

Baker, D. (2014). *The schooled society: The educational transformation of global culture*. Stanford University Press.

Beach, J. M. (2012). *Gateway to opportunity? A history of the community college in the United States*. Stylus Publishing.

Bok, D. (2017). *The struggle to reform our colleges*. Princeton University Press.

Brint, S., & Karabel, J. (1989). *The diverted dream: Community colleges and the promise of educational opportunity in American, 1900–1985*. Oxford University Press.

Century Foundation. (2013). *Bridging the higher education divide: Strengthening community colleges and restoring the American dream*. Author.

Clark, B. R. (1960, May). The "cooling out" function in higher education. *American Journal of Sociology, 65*(6), 569–576. https://doi.org/10.1086/222787

Cohen, A. M., & Brawer, F. B. (2008). *The American community college* (5th ed.). Jossey-Bass.

Cole, J. R. (2009). *The great American university: Its rise to preeminence; its indispensable national role; why it must be protected*. PublicAffairs.

Dougherty, K. J. (1994). *The contradictory college: The conflicting origins, impacts, and futures of the community college*. State University of New York.

Eells, W. C. (1941). *Present status of junior college terminal education*. American Association of Community Colleges.

Grawe, N. D. (2018). *Demographics and the demand for higher education*. Baltimore: The John's Hopkins Press.

Handel, S. J. (2010, September 19). Silent partners in transfer admissions. *The Chronicle of Higher Education*. https://www.chronicle.com/article/Silent-Partners-in-Transfer/124514

Handel, S. J. (2013a). *Recurring trends and persistent themes: A brief history of transfer*. The College Board.

Handel S. J. (2013b, September 23). Two-year students have long had four-year dreams. *The Chronicle of Higher Education*. https://www.chronicle.com/article/2-Year-Students-Have-Long-Had/141787

Handel, S. J. (2013c, Winter). Community college students earning the baccalaureate: The good news could be better. *College and University, 89*(2), 22–26, 28–30.

Handel, S. J., & Williams, R. A. (2012). *The promise of the transfer pathway*. The College Board.

Harper, W. R. (1901). *The prospects of the small college*. University of Chicago Press. https://play.google.com/store/books/details?id=2RwBAAAAYAAJ&rdid=book-2RwBAAAAYAAJ&rdot=1

Harper, W. R. (1905). *The trend in higher education.* The University of Chicago Press.

Lucas, C. J. (1994). *American higher education: A history.* St. Martin's Griffins.

Putnam, R. D. (2015). *Our kids: The American dream in crisis.* Simon and Schuster.

Spencer, K. (2018, April 5). Middle-class families increasing look to community colleges. *The New York Times.* https://www.nytimes.com/2018/04/05/education/learning/community-colleges-middle-class-families.html

Winter, C. G. (1964, December). *History of the community college movement in California.* (ERIC Document 346 902). California State Department of Education. https://files.eric.ed.gov/fulltext/ED346902.pdf

Witt, A. A., Wattenbarger, J. L., Gollattscheck, J. F., & Suppinger, J. E. (1994). *America's community colleges: The first century.* The American Association of Community Colleges.

2

INSTITUTIONAL BARRIERS TO BACCALAUREATE TRANSFER FOR COMMUNITY COLLEGE STUDENTS

John Fink and Davis Jenkins

Community colleges are the entry point to college for over 40% of undergraduates. Most students who enter higher education through a community college aspire to earn a bachelor's degree or higher (Horn & Skomjsvold, 2011). Yet, only about a third of students end up transferring to a 4-year institution, and less than 15% earn a bachelor's degree within 6 years of starting college (Jenkins & Fink, 2016, Shapiro et al., 2017). Scholars have studied numerous aspects of the transfer student experience, including barriers to completion of a bachelor's degree such as integration into the university (Bahr et al., 2013), transfer shock (Flaga, 2006; Hills, 1965), encountering less transfer-affirming university cultures (Herrera & Jain, 2013; Jain et al., 2011), lack of credit transferability (GAO, 2017; Simone, 2014), the resulting effects on transfer student completion (Monaghan & Attewell, 2015), time to degree, excess credits, and unnecessary costs for students and taxpayers (Belfield et al., 2017; Cullinane, 2014; Xu et al., 2016). Too often students are blamed for the difficulties they experience transferring—or they blame themselves (Kadlec & Gupta, 2014). In reality, many substantial barriers to successful transfer are created by colleges and universities themselves. The good news is that these barriers can also be undone in ways that benefit not only students but also institutions themselves (Jenkins et al., 2014).

In the following pages, we synthesize research we and others have done to shed light on institutional barriers to transfer success and how colleges and universities can work together to remove them. We give particular focus to barriers that affect students early on in their educational journey for two reasons. First, related work on early academic momentum suggests that students benefit from a strong start in college (Adelman, 2005, 2006; Attewell & Monaghan, 2016; Jenkins & Bailey, 2017). Second, many (if not most, as we will review in this chapter) bachelor's degree–seeking community college students do not even transfer to a 4-year institution, let alone complete the bachelor's degree. Yet, we find that the barriers bachelor's degree–seeking community college students encounter early—before transferring—are relatively understudied in the transfer literature. For these reasons we examine the following set of institutional barriers, with the purpose of shedding light on these key issues to inform institutional redesign to improve transfer student success.

Institutional Barriers to Baccalaureate Transfer for Community College Students

1. The paths to successful transfer and degree completion are unclear.
2. Colleges and universities fail to provide adequate advising and progress monitoring to help prospective transfer students explore, enter, and progress along transfer pathways.
3. Colleges fail to help students gain "aspirational" momentum in a field of interest.
4. Dual enrollment offerings are not designed to help students actively explore interests and develop goals for college and career.

Barrier #1: The Paths to Successful Transfer and Degree Completion Are Unclear

Most entering community college students intend to earn a bachelor's degree or higher, yet the vast majority are not successful in reaching this goal and instead encounter a complicated process with little accurate guidance.

How Would You Fare as a Transfer Student?

Go to your (or your local) community college's or university's websites and put yourself in the shoes of a student. You are just starting at the community college and want to transfer and get a bachelor's degree in marketing. Take a few minutes and try to figure out the following (try it on your phone, which is likely how most students are looking at the website):

- What are the local university transfer destinations that offer marketing? What are the local career opportunities for marketing graduates, and what is the typical starting wage?
- For a particular university in which you are interested, what are the requirements and timeline for transfer admissions? What courses do you need to take at the community college that you know will apply to the marketing degree at the university? What courses should you take this first semester at community college?
- Whom can you contact for more information or assistance at the community college, and is that information available? What about at the university?

After completing this exercise, consider the following: How easy or difficult was it to find this information? How many clicks did it take? How accurate or updated was the information?

Jaggars and Fletcher (2014) asked community college students to do just this in a set of activity-based focus groups and found that few students could figure out the paths. Some colleges have tried this same exercise with their own faculty and find that they too are often unable to map the path to transfer (Bailey et al., 2015a). Schudde et al. (2018) examined the websites of 20 community colleges in Texas, evaluating the accessibility and usefulness of these colleges' online transfer information. About half of the colleges evaluated presented transfer information in a very accessible way online (e.g., easy to find on the homepage, small number of clicks to access), and about half of the colleges' information was rated highly in the usefulness domain (e.g., simple and succinct language, links to further resources led to their intended location). However, there was wide variability in the quality of the colleges' online transfer information when taking both accessibility and usefulness into account. Schudde et al. (2018) found that for most colleges there was room for improvement on either accessibility or usefulness of information, and that for some colleges transfer information was both difficult to access and not useful. Students encountering these websites might be referred to a list of transfer partners with links that either led to tangentially related information (e.g., the university's general website or admission pages) or links that were broken altogether. In follow-up interviews with community college advising staff, interviewees similarly expressed frustration in trying to access transfer information from university websites.

The lack of clear information about transfer requirements may in part explain why so few bachelor's-intending students who make substantial progress at community college do not even enroll (let alone complete) at a 4-year institution. Xu et al. (2016) tracked a cohort of Virginia community college entrants who indicated that they intended to earn a bachelor's degree and found that after 8 years only 23% ever transferred to a 4-year institution (authors used National Student Clearinghouse data to also track both transfers in- and out-of-state).

Taking a broader view on the barriers encountered by students in the California Community College system, the Campaign for College Opportunity's *Transfer Maze* report described the transfer system in California as chaotic, and as a result costly to community college students seeking bachelor's degrees (Bustillos, 2017). In an example of the challenges encountered by entering community college students, the *Transfer Maze* report profiled Ben Newsum, a student who completed high school early and, at age 17, started at a community college in 2012 seeking a bachelor's degree. Over 5 years later, Newsum was finally admitted to his major at University of California Davis, after attending five different community colleges and accumulating 95 credits (though only 70 were required for transfer) (Bustillos, 2017). As the report further described, the lack of clear pathways for transfer and resulting complexity for community college students seeking to transfer into 4-year institutions in California have been drivers of low transfer rates, which disproportionately affect Latino and Black community college students. Six years after starting at a California community college, only 38% of students ever transferred to a 4-year institution (34% Black students and only 29% of Latino students; see Bustillos, 2017).

Even for students who successfully transfer and complete a bachelor's degree, there is no "well-trodden" transfer pathway.

Many community colleges and universities have put a great deal of energy into developing articulation agreements intended to clarify the path for community college students seeking to transfer. Many states have also developed such agreements for their public higher education systems. Most of them are based on a "2+2" model in which students take 2 years of lower-division, general education coursework, followed by 2 years of courses in their major at a university.

In reality, very few students actually follow this ideal 2+2 model. In a blog post reporting further on results from Jenkins and Fink's (2016) *Tracking Transfer* report, Fink (2017) explored transfer enrollment patterns among successful bachelor's degree completers who started at community college. Fink derived an enrollment sequence for each successful community college transfer student using term-by-term National Student Clearinghouse (NSC) enrollment data on whether students were enrolled at a community college, a 4-year institution, or not enrolled, and collapsing term-by-term data into year-by-year results using students' highest institution attended for each year. As shown in Figure 2.1, Fink found that only 8% of bachelor's degree graduates who started in a community college followed the 2+2 pattern. The 2+3, 3+3, and 2+4 patterns were slightly more common than the 2+2, although there wasn't anywhere near a majority pattern. Interestingly, about one in five students "stopped-out" for a year or more, re-enrolled and subsequently completed, all within our relatively short tracking period of 6 years from first entering community college.

Figure 2.1. Enrollment patterns among bachelor's degree graduates who started at a community college.

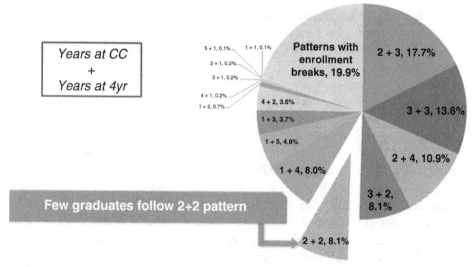

Source. Fink, 2017.

Few successful transfer students follow the 2+2 enrollment sequence, and, as the study by Xu et al. (2016) shows, few students are able to cleanly take all of their lower-division requirements in their first 2 years at a community college and then seamlessly transfer into upper-division coursework at the university. Over 40% of baccalaureate-seeking community college students in their sample transferred to a university with fewer than 60 college credits (the number typically required for an associate degree). While little more than a quarter (27%) of such students transferred to a 4-year institution in the third year following their start at a community college, some students transferred sooner (16%), and most (57%) transferred 3 years or more after starting at the community college.

Barrier #2: Colleges and Universities Fail to Provide Adequate Advising and Progress Monitoring to Help Prospective Transfer Students Explore, Enter, and Progress Along Transfer Pathways

Transfer-intending community college students may not successfully make the leap to a 4-year institution because they are unable to navigate the complex transfer maze. Colleges offer advising and other assistance to help students prepare for successful transfer by exploring careers and developing a plan, but generally it is up to students to seek it out (Karp, 2013). The focus of intake advising for new students is typically to determine if they need to go through remedial instruction and to schedule their first term classes, rather than help students look at options. Most community colleges offer college success courses for new students, but often these courses are not required, and the content varies. Some such courses provide opportunities for career and transfer exploration and planning, but many do not. The typical community college career and transfer centers and related services are under-resourced and use is not required for all students (Karp et al., 2017). There is evidence that students who need these sorts of supports for exploration and planning are the least likely to make use of them (Bailey et al., 2015b; Jaggars & Fletcher, 2014). Furthermore, having a sense of purpose or direction can be extremely motivating for students. Research on college students more generally indicates that student who choose a major that is a good fit for their interests are more likely to complete (Allen & Robbins, 2010; Tracey & Robbins, 2006).

And most community colleges do not help students develop an academic plan or monitor their progress on their plan (Jaggars & Karp, 2016). One symptom of this is that colleges do not help students gain momentum for transfer. Currently, community college entrants—even those who enter intending to transfer and earn a bachelor's degree—earn college-level credits at a slower pace compared to students who enter college through a 4-year institution. Part of this is due to the fact that community college students are more likely to enroll part time or to take remedial credits, which do not count toward a degree. In their study of 2- and 4-year college students in Virginia, Xu et al. (2016; see also Xu, Jaggars, et al., 2018) tried to account for these differences by comparing groups of 2- and 4-year entrants who were matched on numerous student characteristics, including whether or not they started college as a full-time student, and if they had ever taken a remedial course. Even when using this matched sample, as is shown in Figure 2.2 (top panel), 4-year entrants on average took a higher course load each semester than do similar community college students. This, combined with the fact that community college students take more remedial courses that do not count toward a degree, means that community college students fall further and further behind their 4-year peers in earning credits over time (see Figure 2.2, bottom panel).

Figure 2.2. Lack of early momentum of community college entrants compared to 4-year entrants.

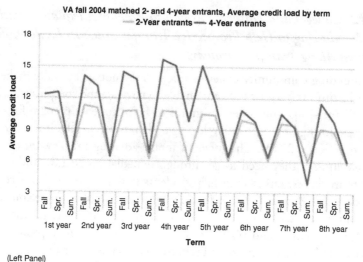

(Left Panel)

(Right Panel)

Source. Xu et al., 2016.

Another symptom of the failure of community colleges to help students develop a transfer plan, gain momentum, and monitor student progress is that many students intend to transfer and make good progress, but do not matriculate at a 4-year institution. In their study of transfer-aspiring community college students in Virginia, Xu et al. (2016) found that even among students who earned substantial numbers of college-level credits at the community college, the majority still did not make the leap to a 4-year institution. For example, the transfer rate for the bachelor's-seeking community college entrants who earned 40 to 59 college-level credits at the community college was only 36%. Almost half of students (43%) who earned 60 or more college-level credits did not transfer to a 4-year institution within 8 years of first starting at the community college (see Figure 2.3). As Xu et al.'s findings suggest, prospective transfer students are making substantial progress but not transferring. Even though they have proved themselves to be capable students, they are not transferring and thus falling short of their educational (and economic) potential. Racking up credits without a clear sense that they are making progress toward their end goals, many students become frustrated and do not end up transferring.

Two recent reports detailing barriers to transfer in California echo findings from Xu et al.'s (2016) study of Virginia students and further describe the barrier of unclear transfer pathways. Researchers at the RP Group are working to understand how

Figure 2.3. Transfer rates among bachelor's degree–seeking community college entrants in Virginia, by pre-transfer credit and degree completion.

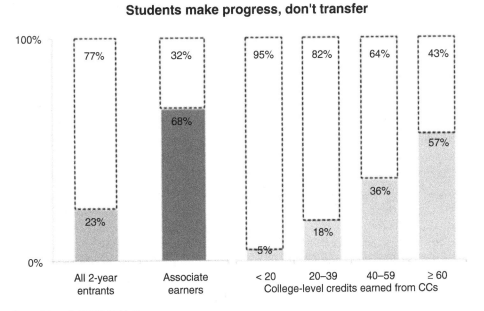

Source. Xu et al. (2016), Table 9.

to increase transfer rates out of the California Community College (CCC) system. In a 2017 technical report, the RP Group tracked cohorts of transfer-intending students in the CCC system and found large proportions of students that were eligible for transfer (having earned 60 or more transfer-level units including transfer-level math and English) but had not enrolled at a university (Cooper et al., 2017). Also, researchers found that there was a large number of students who had earned 60 or more transfer units but still had not completed a transfer-level math course. While the authors found that not passing transfer-level math was a major barrier to successful transfer, they also noted that there were a substantial number of students who *had* completed transfer-level math, as well as transfer-level English and many transfer-level units, but still did not transfer.

Keeping options open or adding further complexity? Considering different programs of study at multiple potential transfer destinations complicates transfer advising exponentially.

In addition to transfer advising and related support services being under-resourced and not mandatory at many community colleges, advising and support for transfer-intending students is particularly challenging in "thick" transfer markets, where lots of potential transfer destinations exist. Think about your local community college. How many different 4-year colleges do you think its students transfer to? Research we did with the Aspen Institute and National Student Clearinghouse to identify high-performing transfer partnerships profiled in the *Transfer Playbook* revealed some even more astonishing figures: In an entering community college cohort nationally, students transferred from one of 803 community colleges to one of 1,803 4-year institutions, resulting in 44,135 unique 2/4 transfer partnerships (Wyner et al., 2016; Xu et al., 2017; Xu, Ran, et al., 2018). The typical community college sent transfer students to 31 different 4-year institutions, and this likely underestimates the true number of institutions students transfer to as it counts only students who transferred once to a 4-year institution (i.e., does not account for "swirling" transfer enrollments). The number of 4-year transfer destinations a community college sends students to likely depends on the number of local 4-year institutions. For example, among urban community colleges the median number of different 4-year institutions students transferred to was 38, but even among rural community colleges the median number of 4-year transfer destinations was 23. With many transfer partners, particularly in "thick" transfer markets, community colleges must accomplish the daunting task of helping new transfer-intending students not only explore and clarify a program of interest but also plan out efficient transfer to a range of potential 4-year destinations. If students are considering multiple majors and multiple transfer destinations, sorting out the idiosyncratic transfer requirements can be extremely time consuming. See Xu et al. (2017) and Xu, Ran, et al. (2018) for full data definitions and further descriptive detail on transfer partnerships. Results on the median number of receiving institutions for transfers from community colleges are based on further analysis by authors on an updated cohort (fall 2010) of community college entrants who transferred to 4-year institutions using the same definitions and Analysis of National Student Clearinghouse data. See also Fink and Jenkins (2017b) for additional examples of measures of performance for transfer partnerships.

In the context of complex transfer networks, how can colleges create seamless transfer pathways and help students explore, enter, and progress through these pathways? To illustrate the tangled web of institutions sending and receiving transfer students, we visualize in Figure 2.4 the network of transfer from public 2-year to public 4-year institutions in Texas. Drawing from publicly available institution-level transfer reports provided by the Texas Higher Education Coordinating Board (THECB, n.d.), this network shows transfer student movement from community colleges to public universities in Texas. The transfer network shows the variation in the number of students transferring within each partnership (represented by the weight of lines in between nodes in Figure 2.4), as well as the variation in bachelor's degree completion among transfer students in each partnership (represented by the shades of grey in between nodes in Figure 2.4). Importantly, note that Figure 2.4 presents a relatively simplified illustration of student transfer, as it does not show transfer within sectors (e.g., between community colleges) or student transfer out of universities. Even without the phenomenon of "transfer swirl," transfer networks are complex. Given the myriad combinations of institutions sending and receiving transfer students, it may be that institutions, which have finite resources to create and sustain highly effective transfer partnerships, should prioritize their major transfer partners to maximize their impact with students.

As demonstrated in the lower panel of Figure 2.4, colleges can find value in examining transfer volume and outcomes for each of their top partners. In a 2017 Community College Research Center Analytics publication, we outlined a set of performance metrics for colleges to derive for each of their top transfer destinations to help in identifying partnerships to prioritize (Fink & Jenkins, 2017a). These metrics include, specific to transfer students in a given partnership, the rate at which students transfer with a community college award, bachelor's degree completion rate, total time to degree, the percentage of the institution's transfers who transferred to this partner, and the percentage of the institution's transfer bachelor's degree completers who completed at this partner (see Fink & Jenkins, 2017a).

This figure shows the movement of fall 2012 transfer students from community colleges to public universities in Texas (THECB, n.d.). Darker gray nodes represent community colleges and the lighter gray nodes represent universities. The size of the nodes show the total number of transfer students sent or received from all other institutions, and the size of the lines in between nodes depict the number of students transferring between institutions. An example breakdown of transfer number and completion rates by top destinations is provided for the Lone Star College System in the lower panel.

For transfer students, how good is the advice to "get your gen eds out of the way"?
To deal with the complexity of navigating major and transfer destination choice simultaneously, students are often instructed to "get your gen eds out of the way" to buy more time to explore major program options. The assumption is that this advice will provide students more flexibility, as all of the general coursework students will take while they are figuring out their plan will count toward whatever path they eventually select (Bailey et al., 2015b).

Figure 2.4. Texas transfer network.

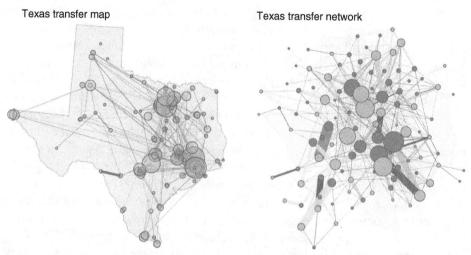

Lone Star College System		
Top Destination Institutions	Number of Transfers	BA Completion Rate
University of Houston	954	54%
Sam Houston State University	659	64%
U. of Houston-downtown	614	56%
Texas State University	173	60%
Texas A&M University	106	76%
Texas Southern University	77	38%
U. of Texas at Austin	71	75%
Prairie view A&M University	65	66%
U. of Texas at Arlington	63	59%
Texas Tech University	52	44%

One indication that students are not taking the "right" courses pre-transfer is the large number of excess credits among transfer students that successfully graduated with a bachelor's degree. Fink et al. (2017) used data mining techniques to examine the transcript of bachelor's graduates who started at a community college, comparing the course-taking patterns among graduates with many excess credits compared to graduates with very few excess credits. Both before and after they transferred to the 4-year institution, graduates with more excess credits also took larger proportions of their coursework in 100- and 200-level courses and smaller proportions in 300-level courses. Additionally, transfer students who took 100-level courses, and especially 100-level math courses, in the first two terms after they transferred-in to a 4-year institution also graduated with more excess credit. Fink et al. (2017) proffer that the reason is that specific bachelor's majors often carry specific major-specific general education requirements, in addition to major prerequisite courses. This explanation is backed up by some university transfer staff, who, when asked what they would like community colleges to do to improve transfer success for their students, say that it would lead to better outcomes if community colleges would help students choose a major early on (Wyner et al., 2016). So rather than keeping their options open, encouraging students to take any gen ed courses to satisfy distribution requirements turns out to be bad advice for students. Fink et al.'s (2017) findings suggest that early exploration and development of a plan for transfer into a specific bachelor's degree program will help to reduce the number of credits students take that do not apply toward their major.

Barrier #3: Colleges Fail to Help Students Gain "Aspirational" Momentum in a Field of Interest

New research from Xueli Wang (2017) at the University of Wisconsin–Madison suggests that early classroom experiences can play a pivotal role in developing students transfer momentum. Xueli Wang's research has focused on transfer momentum for students in STEM, but we believe that her work is more broadly applicable to other subjects as well.

Uninspiring gateway courses inhibit transfer momentum.
There is a substantial body of evidence that early momentum—earning a substantial number of college-level credits in students' field of interest during their first year—is a strong leading indicator that a student will likely complete a degree over a longer period. Wang (2017) reviews this evidence in a chapter that appeared in the *Higher Education: Handbook of Theory and Research* and then lays out a theoretical model grounded in research to explain the mechanisms by which momentum would lead to higher rates of degree completion for community college students.

Much of Wang's recent work is based on a study of over 1,600 students who started in comprehensive community colleges in a Midwest state and who indicated an intent to major in STEM or were taking STEM courses in their first term (other than remedial math). Wang (2017) examined the transcripts of these students to see what course-taking patterns were associated with momentum toward transfer in a STEM major. She also surveyed these students in fall 2014 during their first term and then again 18 months later in their second year. The survey instrument Wang developed for this purpose asks students questions about their high school course-taking in math and science, perceived self-efficacy in these subjects, extent to which they sought out transfer information and advising, engagement in active learning in STEM classes, and support from friends and family. This information on students' experiences gleaned from these surveys, together with data on students' demographic characteristics and transcript records, enables Wang and her colleagues to gain insights into the factors that propel students along program paths in a way that research that relies on analysis of student transcripts and demographic characteristics alone cannot.

Findings from this research suggest two sets of practices that colleges can adopt to increase community college student transfer momentum: First, they should ensure that students take a college-level course in a field of interest in their first term, and second, they should ensure that students have ample opportunities to engage in active learning, particularly in critical required introductory courses in the student's field of interest.

Ensure that students take a college-level course in a field of interest in their first term.
In a study published in 2016, Wang examined how course-taking patterns are related to whether or not community college students pursue pathways in STEM (Wang, 2016). She analyzed survey and transcript data from a nationally representative sample of baccalaureate-seeking community college students who took at least one college-level STEM course in their first term and used data mining techniques to examine the connection of student characteristics and course-taking patterns to whether the student transferred to a bachelor's degree program in STEM or another field, or didn't transfer at all.

A key finding from this research is that the early course-taking pattern most common among students who transferred to a bachelor's program in STEM was taking a transferable STEM course in the first term, followed by math courses in subsequent terms. This finding is noteworthy since community college students are often encouraged to take math courses (sometimes at the developmental level) as prerequisites to courses in STEM and other subject areas. This finding is also consistent with the idea, emphasized in the guided pathways model, that students need to begin the process of exploring career and college interests from the start (Jenkins et al., 2018). One way to do this is to require that students take a college-level course in a field of interest in their first term. This way, they can see early on if they are excited about a particular field and, if not, can continue to explore other areas.

Research on student decision-making about majors in 2- and 4-year institutions indicates that early major switching does not hurt students' longer-term chances of completion and may even help them find a field they are interested in (Kopko, 2017). However, changing one's mind about majors later in the students' tenure means that they will likely be unable to apply at least some credits they have already taken toward their new major, which increases the time and cost of earning a degree and may decrease the chances that they do so.

For early course-taking to serve a way to help students explore potential majors, of course, there needs to be a mechanism for helping new students identify career and academic fields in which they have an interest. Redesigning the new student experience to enable students to explore career and college options (and develop a full-program plan by the end of the first term) is a central strategy of guided pathways reforms. Prerequisite remedial requirements can also prevent students from taking a college-level course of interest in term one. In light of the growing evidence for "corequisite" approaches that contextualize academic support into college-level coursework (Rodriguez et al., 2018; Scott-Clayton, 2018), colleges should explore how they can provide integrated supports in key college-level program gateway courses in not only math and English but also other subjects.

Ensure that students have ample opportunities to engage in active learning, particularly in critical required introductory courses in the student's field of interest.

In another analysis, Wang, Sun, et al. (2017) looked at how active learning in required math and other STEM classes contributed to students' intention to transfer in STEM. Wang, Sun, et al. surveyed the students who entered 2-year colleges intending to major in STEM or took college-level STEM courses in their first term. The survey gauged the extent to which students were engaged in various active learning experiences including critical thinking, problem-solving, questioning, or analyzing information in STEM courses required for their programs. Using a path analysis of the survey data, the researchers found that experience of active learning in initial required STEM courses had a direct and positive effect on students' intent to transfer in STEM. Additionally, the researchers found that the effect of active learning on the intent to transfer was mediated by the students' sense of transfer efficacy. This means that the experience of active learning was associated with a stronger sense among that they were capable of transferring, which in turn strengthened their intention to transfer. As Wang, Sun, et al. state, "For those who were interested in majoring in STEM, active learning experiences pulled them toward these fields instead of pushing them away" (p. 610).

For colleges seeking to strengthen pathways to success for students, these findings indicate that active learning not only is associated with better academic outcomes in students' courses, as previous research has shown (e.g., Freeman et al., 2014) but also can increase students' motivation to progress in their program. As such, colleges should make every effort to ensure that introductory courses are well taught, including providing ample opportunities for students to explore questions, solve problems, and analyze information. The sense of confidence as learners that students gain from engaging in active learning and doing well academically helps them gain momentum in their field.

Barrier #4: Dual Enrollment Offerings Are Not Designed to Help Students Actively Explore Interests and Develop Goals for College and Career

In the past 2 decades, the number of high school students participating in some type of "dual enrollment" program has expanded tremendously. This growth has been particularly pronounced in the community college sector. From 1995 to 2015, fall enrollments of students age 17 or younger at public 4-year institutions grew from 72,000 to 220,000, while at community colleges they grew from 163,000 to 745,000 (Institute of Education Sciences, n.d.). The potential of dual enrollment as a mechanism for college acceleration could be better realized if college leaders and policymakers approached it more strategically—with the "end in mind." For most dual enrollment students (and most community college entrants generally), the educational end goal is a bachelor's degree or higher. Whether or not community college dual enrollment students return to a community college or matriculate at a 4-year institution after high school, they are all community college transfer students in that they seek to earn a bachelor's degree by starting their coursework at a community college. In other words, community college dual enrollment students are often future community college transfer students. Given the increasing prominence of dual enrollment as a strategy to accelerate college completion and reduce costs, community colleges and universities partnering to tackle transfer at scale must not overlook students for which dual enrollment serves as their on-ramp into college.

Several rigorous studies have found evidence that students who take college courses in high school are more likely to go to college and complete college credentials than are students who do not take such courses. A recent review by the U.S. Department of Education's What Works Clearinghouse (WWC) indicates that many of these studies meet the WWC's rigorous standards of evidence (U.S. Department of Education, 2017). Several studies have found particular benefits of dual enrollment for students from underrepresented groups, including low-income students and students of color, although the size of the effects vary depending on the study (An, 2013; Karp et al., 2007; Taylor, 2015).

Tracking a national cohort of dual enrollment students using National Student Clearinghouse data, Fink et al. (2017) found substantial variation, both within and across states, in whether or not students first attended a community college or university after high school and their eventual degree outcomes. The study also found troublesome gaps in college completion between former dual enrollment students from lower-income families and higher-income families—with several states having gaps of more than 10, or in some cases even 20, percentage points depending whether students first entered a community college or university after high school. Despite the potential benefits, Fink et al.'s study raised important questions about why dual enrollment students in some states do substantially better in college than in others and why there are large achievement gaps between different income groups in some states. For example, not all dual enrollment courses are delivered in the same manner. Some are taught by credentialed teachers in high schools, some are taught on college campuses, and some are offered online. A growing number of colleges have established early college high schools, which provide a more comprehensive curriculum, not just discrete courses.

Despite the rapid spread of dual enrollment nationally, many schools, colleges and states have not carefully tracked what courses dual enrollment students are taking, where former dual enrollment students enroll in college after high school, how their dual enrollment credits are transferred and applied toward their degree programs, and the extent to which these credits reduce their time to degree. There is some evidence that dual enrollment students are unable to apply many of the credits they earn to bachelor's degrees in their major field of interest (Greater Texas Foundation, 2015). If colleges are to improve rates of college-going and completion by dual enrollment students generally, and those from disadvantaged backgrounds in particular, they will need to monitor their dual enrollment students more closely, both while they are still in high school and after they graduate.

Based on our work with community colleges thinking about implementing their dual enrollment programs more strategically, to reduce institutional barriers and provide these students clearer pathways for transfer and bachelor's degree completion, we suggest college leaders consider the following questions on their campus:

- What courses are our dual enrollment students taking and how are they selecting them?
- Are our dual enrollment students gaining momentum in a program of study in high school?
- Where do our dual enrollment students go to college after high school, how many return to our college, and what's happening with dual enrollment students who don't go to college?
- How many end up earning college credentials, from which institutions, and in what majors?
- What are the course-taking patterns and outcomes among dual enrollment students who continued at our college after high school?
- Are dual enrollment students passing college-level math and critical program courses either in high school or in their first year in college (after high school)?
- Are dual enrollment credits being applied to students' degree programs?
- How do results vary by high school and program of study?
- How do results vary for students by race, income, gender, and geography?

Community college dual enrollment students are future community college transfer students. As colleges and universities work to strengthen transfer pathways, they should think strategically about how these pathways can be pushed down into high schools. Community colleges in particular can serve a key role as connector between local industry, university, and K–12 leaders. As a part of the Community College Research Center's work in states implementing guided pathways reforms, we encourage colleges to think about improving student success (including transfer and dual enrollment outcomes) through the guided pathways framework: Clarifying paths to student end goals, helping students choose and enter a path, keeping students on the path, and ensuring that students are learning (see Jenkins et al., 2018). A central component to guided pathways is that each student should have an individualized plan clearly laying out an educational pathway to their end goal. For students to create a plan, colleges need to help students explore, understand, and clarify their career and educational goals, including transfer destinations, bachelor's degree programs, and what kind of lifestyle and careers for which these pathways are designed to prepare students.

Recommendations: To Address Institutional Barriers, Reforms Must Be Made at Scale

Moving the needle on transfer student success will require these barriers to be tackled at scale. Reflecting on years of student success efforts through the "completion agenda," Bailey et al. (2015b) argued that many reforms do not result in substantial gains to student outcomes because they either affect a part of colleges' student population or they are directed at only one aspect of the student experience. The guided pathways reform model Bailey et al. describe addresses these shortcomings by providing a comprehensive framework for student success—targeting each component of the student experience (e.g., from connection, to intake, progression, and completion) at scale for all students at the college. To improve transfer outcomes at scale, college leaders should take a similar, comprehensive approach.

The sort of significant changes in practice that community colleges and universities need to make to strengthen transfer outcomes are highlighted in our research with the Aspen Institute to develop the *Transfer Playbook* (Wyner et al., 2016). The *Transfer Playbook* described the essential practices of highly effective 2- and 4-year institution partnerships, which we identified nationally as having better-than-expected transfer outcomes using National Student Clearinghouse data (controlling for institutional and student characteristics, see Xu et al., 2017). We visited six sets of highly effective transfer partnerships and found that these colleges were collaborating to remove barriers from student transfer pathways. Based on these visits, we identified three sets of practices that are characteristic of effective community college-university partnerships:

1. Make transfer student success a priority.
2. Create clear programmatic pathways with aligned high-quality instruction.
3. Provide tailored transfer student advising.

Readers are encouraged to access the *Transfer Playbook* and accompanying resources (including institutional self-assessment and planning tools), and as colleges and universities redesign themselves at scale transfer, we emphasize that equity implications of these practices need to be scrutinized. For example, Wang, Lee, et al. (2017) studied how a college's transfer services and students' perceived support for transfer may affect students' aspiration to transfer over time. They found that STEM majors and early STEM course takers who used transfer services increased their "aspirational momentum toward STEM transfer" (p. 311)—that is, their intent to transfer to a bachelor's program in STEM. However, the effects of transfer service usage were not evenly distributed across student groups. Men who more frequently used transfer services were more likely to sustain a commitment to transfer in STEM than were women who did the same. Moreover, with more perceived support for transfer, White students were more likely to maintain transfer aspirations, while Black and Hispanic students were less likely to do so. These findings exemplify the importance for college leaders to scrutinize the effects of particular practices on different student groups and consider how they may need to be adjusted or targeted to benefit particular groups.

To help community college students achieve their goals of transferring and earning bachelor's degrees or higher, institutional barriers must be removed to clear the pathway for transfer students. Through this chapter we aimed at providing insight on the major barriers transfer-intending students encounter early in their educational journey. These barriers describe not only institutional challenges but also opportune areas for institutional redesign that fosters improved and more equitable outcomes for students.

Questions for Further Discussion and Reflection

In closing, we offer some questions to start discussions around how to tackle the barriers outlined in this chapter:

1. How can 2- and 4-year institutions work together to more clearly map out transfer pathways for students?
2. What can leaders and faculty at 4-year institutions learn from auditing transfer student transcripts to see how courses are applying (or not) to their degree programs?
3. What would it look like for our community college to help all students explore career and academic interests, choose a direction, and develop a full-program plan early in their educational journey (within the first one to two terms)? How can universities help community colleges strengthen early career and transfer advising for their students?
4. How can our college ensure that all students have ample opportunities for active learning in introductory courses in their field of interest, in order to help them achieve "aspirational" momentum to transfer?
5. What would it look like for our community college to monitor students' progress along their transfer plans and, with assistance from our top partner universities, encourage and advise them to transfer in their major field of interest?

References

Adelman, C. (2005). *Moving into town—and moving on. The community college in the lives of traditional-age students.* U.S. Department of Education.

Adelman, C. (2006). *The toolbox revisited: Paths to degree completion from high school through college.* U.S. Department of Education.

Allen, J., & Robbins, S. (2010). Effects of interest–major congruence, motivation, and academic performance on timely degree attainment. *Journal of Counseling Psychology, 57*(1), 23–35. https://doi.org/10.1037/a0017267

An, B. P. (2013). The impact of dual enrollment on college degree attainment: Do low-SES students benefit? *Educational Evaluation and Policy Analysis, 35*(1), 57–75. https://doi.org/10.3102/0162373712461933

Attewell, P., & Monaghan, D. (2016). How many credits should an undergraduate take? *Research in Higher Education, 57*(6), 682–713. https://doi.org/10.1007/s11162-015-9401-z

Bahr, P. R., Toth, C., Thirolf, K., & Massé, J. C. (2013). A review and critique of the literature on community college students' transition processes and outcomes in four-year institutions. In M. B. Paulsen (Ed.), *Higher education: Handbook of theory and research* (pp. 459–511). Springer.

Bailey, T. R., Jaggars, S. S., & Jenkins, D. (2015a). *Implementing guided pathways at Miami Dade College: A case study.* Columbia University, Teachers College, Community College Research Center.

Bailey, T. R., Jaggars, S. S., & Jenkins, D. (2015b). *Redesigning America's community colleges: A clearer path to student success.* Harvard University Press.

Belfield, C., Fink, J., & Jenkins, D. (2017). *Is it really cheaper to start at a community college? The consequences of inefficient transfer for community college students seeking bachelor's degrees* (CCRC Working Paper No. 94). Columbia University, Teachers College, Community College Research Center.

Bustillos, L. T. (2017, September). *The transfer maze: The high cost to students and the state of California.* The Campaign for College Opportunity. http://collegecampaign.org/wp-content/uploads/2017/09/CCO-2017-TransferMazeReport-27.pdf

Chan, H-Y., & Wang, X. (2017). Momentum through course-completion patterns among 2-year college students beginning in STEM: Variations and contributing factors. *Research in Higher Education, 59,* 704–743. https://doi.org/10.1007/s11162-017-9485-8

Cooper, D. M., Fong, K., Karandjeff, K., Kretz, A., Nguyen, A., Purnell-Mack, R. D., & Schiorring, E. (2017). *Through the gate: Mapping the transfer landscape for California Community College students.* The RP Group.

Cullinane, J. P. (2014). *The path to timely completion: Supply- and demand-side analyses of time to bachelor's degree completion* (Doctoral dissertation). University of Texas, Austin, TX. https://repositories.lib.utexas.edu/handle/2152/24932

Fink, J. (2017). *Visualizing the many routes community college students take to complete a bachelor's degree.* https://ccrc.tc.columbia.edu/easyblog/visualizing-many-routes-bachelors-degree.html

Fink, J., & Jenkins, D. (2017a). *How to measure community college effectiveness in serving transfer students* (CCRC Analytics). Community College Research Center, Teachers College, Columbia University.

Fink, J., & Jenkins, D. (2017b). Takes two to tango: Essential practices of highly effective transfer partnerships. *Community College Review, 45*(4), 294–310. https://doi.org/10.1177/0091552117724512

Fink, J., Jenkins, D., Kopko, E., & Ran, F. X. (2018, February). *Using data mining to explore why community college transfer students earn bachelor's degrees with excess credits.* CCRC Working Paper No. 100. https://ccrc.tc.columbia.edu/publications/using-data-mining-explore-why-community-college-transfer-students-earn-bachelors-degrees-excess-credits.html

Fink, J., Jenkins, D., & Yanagiura, T. (2017). *What happens to students who take community college "dual enrollment" courses in high school?* Community College Research Center, Teachers College, Columbia University.

Flaga, C. (2006). The process of transition for community college transfer students. *Community College Journal of Research and Practice, 30*(1), 3–19. https://doi.org/10.1080/10668920500248845

Freeman, S., Eddy, S. L., McDonough, M., Smith, M. K., Okoroafor, N., Jordt, H., & Wenderoth, M. P. (2014). Active learning increases student performance in science, engineering, and mathematics. *Proceedings of the National Academy of Sciences of the United States of America, 111*(23), 8410–8415. https://doi.org/10.1073/pnas.1319030111

GAO. (2017). *Students need more information to help reduce challenges transferring credits.* (GAO-17-574). Government Accountability Office.

Greater Texas Foundation (2015). *GTF scholars: A scholarship program for Texas early college high school graduates.* http://media.cmgdigital.com/shared/news/documents/2016/04/19/GTFScholarsOverview_2.pdf

Herrera, A., & Jain, D. (2013). Building a transfer-receptive culture at four-year institutions. *New Directions for Higher Education, 2013*(162), 51–59. doi:10.1002/he.20056

Hills, J. R. (1965). Transfer shock: The academic performance of the junior college transfer. *The Journal of Experimental Education, 33,* 201–215. https://doi.org/10.1080/00220973.1965.11010875

Horn, L., & Skomsvold, P. (2011). *Community college student outcomes: 1994–2009* (NCES 2012-253). U.S. Department of Education, Institute of Education Sciences, National Center for Education Statistics.

Institute of Education Sciences, National Center for Education Statistics. (n.d.). *IPEDS (1995-2015).* U.S. Department of Education. http://nces.ed.gov/ipeds/datacenter/DataFiles.aspx

Jaggars, S. S., & Fletcher, J. (2014). *Redesigning the student intake and information provision processes at a large comprehensive community college* (CCRC Working Paper No. 72). Community College Research Center.

Jaggars, S. S., & Karp, M. M. (2016). Transforming the community college student experience through comprehensive, technology-mediated advising. *New Directions for Community Colleges, 2016:* 53–62. https://doi.org/10.1002/cc.20222

Jain, D., Bernal, S., Lucero, I., Herrera, A., & Solórzano, D. (2016). Toward a critical race perspective of transfer: An exploration of a transfer receptive culture. *Community College Journal of Research and Practice, 40*(12), 1013–1024. https://doi.org/10.1080/10668926.2016.1213674

Jain, D., Herrera, A., Bernal, S., & Solorzano, D. (2011). Critical race theory and the transfer function: Introducing a transfer receptive culture. *Community College Journal of Research and Practice, 35*(3), 252–266. https://doi.org/10.1080/10668926.2011.526525

Jenkins, D., & Bailey, T. (2017). *Early momentum metrics: Why they matter for college improvement* (CCRC Research Brief No. 65). Columbia University, Teachers College, Community College Research Center.

Jenkins, D., & Fink, J. (2016). *Tracking transfer: New measures of state and institutional effectiveness in helping community college students attain bachelor's degrees.* Community College Research Center, Aspen Institute, and the National Student Clearinghouse Research Center.

Jenkins, D., Kadlec, A., & Votruba, J. (2014). *Maximizing resources for student success: The business case for regional public universities to strengthen communtiy college transfer pathways.* http://hcmstrategists.com/maximizingresources/images/Transfer_Pathways_Paper.pdf

Jenkins, D., Lahr, H., Fink, J., & Ganga, E. (2018). *What we are learning about guided pathways.* Community College Research Center, Teachers College, Columbia University.

Kadlec, A., & Gupta, J. (2014). *Indiana regional transfer study: The student experience of 760 transfer pathways between Ivy Tech Community College and Indiana University.* Public Agenda.

Karp, M. M. (2013). *Entering a program: Helping students make academic and career decisions* (CCRC Working Paper No. 59). Columbia University, Teachers College, Community College Research Center.

Karp, M. M., Calcagno, J. C., Hughes, K. L., Jeong, D. W., & Bailey, T. R. (2007). *The postsecondary achievement of participants in dual enrollment: An analysis of student outcomes in two states*. University of Minnesota, National Research Center for Career and Technical Education.

Karp, M. M., Raufman, J., Efthimiou, C., & Ritze, N. (2017). Revising a college 101 course for sustained impact: Early outcomes. *Community College Journal of Research and Practice*, *41*(1), 42–55. https://doi.org/10.1080/10668926.2016.1152929

Kopko, E. M. (2017). Essays on the economics of education: Community college pathways and student success. (Doctoral dissertation). Columbia University, New York, NY. https://academiccommons.columbia.edu/catalog/ac:jwstqjq2dd

Monaghan, D. B., & Attewell, P. (2015). The community college route to the bachelor's degree. *Educational Evaluation and Policy Analysis, 37*(1), 70–91. https://doi.org/10.3102/0162373714521865

Rodriguez, O., Cuellar Mejia, M., & Johnson, H. (2018). *Remedial education reforms at California's community colleges early evidence on placement and curricular reforms*. Public Policy Institute of California.

Schudde, L., Bradley, D., & Absher, C. (2018, April). *Ease of access and usefulness of transfer information on community college websites in Texas* (CCRC Working Paper No. 102). https://ccrc.tc.columbia.edu/publications/ease-access-usefulness-transfer-information-community-college-websites-texas.html

Scott-Clayton, J. (2018, March 29). *Evidence-based reforms in college remediation are gaining steam—and so far living up to the hype Brookings*. https://www.brookings.edu/research/evidence-based-reforms-in-college-remediation-are-gaining-steam-and-so-far-living-up-to-the-hype/

Shapiro, D., Dundar, A., Huie, F., Wakhungu, P. K., Yuan, X., Nathan, A. & Hwang, Y. (2017). *Tracking transfer: Measures of effectiveness in helping community college students to complete bachelor's degrees* (Signature Report No. 13). National Student Clearinghouse Research Center.

Simone, S. A. (2014). *Transferability of postsecondary credit following student transfer or coenrollment* (NCES 2014-163). U.S. Department of Education, Institute of Education Sciences, National Center for Education Statistics.

Taylor, J. L. (2015). Accelerating pathways to college: The (in)equitable effects of community college dual credit. *Community College Review, 43*(4), 355–379. https://doi.org/10.1177/0091552115594880

Texas Higher Education Coordinating Board. (n.d.). *Texas higher education data: Academic performance of 2-year college transfer students at Texas public universities*. http://www.txhighereddata.org/reports/performance/ctctransfer/

Tracey, T. J. G., & Robbins, S. B. (2006). The interest–major congruence and college success relation: A longitudinal study. *Journal of Vocational Behavior, 69*, 64–89. https://doi.org/10.1016/j.jvb.2005.11.003

U.S. Department of Education, Institute of Education Sciences, What Works Clearinghouse. (2017). *Transition to college intervention report: Dual enrollment programs*. https://whatworks.ed.gov

Wang, X. (2016). Course-taking patterns of community college students beginning in STEM: Using data mining techniques to reveal viable STEM transfer pathways. *Research in Higher Education, 57*, 544–556. https://doi.org/10.1007/s11162-015-9397-4

Wang, X. (2017). Toward a holistic theoretical model of momentum for community college student success. In M. B. Paulsen (Ed.), *Higher education: Handbook of theory and research* (pp. 259–308). Springer.

Wang, X., Lee, S. Y., & Prevost, A. (2017). The role of aspirational experiences and behaviors in cultivating momentum for transfer access in STEM: Variations across gender and race. *Community College Review*, *45*(4), 311–330. https://doi.org/10.1177/0091552117724511

Wang, X., Sun, N., Lee S.Y., & Wagner B. (2017). Does active learning contribute to transfer intent among 2-year college students beginning in STEM? *The Journal of Higher Education*, *88*(4), 593–618. https://doi.org/10.1080/00221546.2016.1272090

Wyner, J., Deane, K. C., Jenkins, D., & Fink, J. (2016). *The transfer playbook: Essential practices for two- and four-year institutions.* The Aspen Institute College Excellence Program.

Xu, D., Jaggars, S. S., & Fletcher, J. (2016, April). *How and why does two-year college entry influence baccalaureate aspirants' academic and labor market outcomes?* (CAPSEE Working Paper). Center for Analysis of Postsecondary Education and Employment.

Xu, D., Jaggars, S. S., Fletcher, J., & Fink, J. E. (2018). Are community college transfer students "a good bet" for 4-year admissions? Comparing academic and labor-market outcomes between transfer and native 4-year college students. *Journal of Higher Education*, *89*, 478–502. https://doi.org/10.1080/00221546.2018.1434280

Xu, D., Ran, X., Fink, J., Jenkins, D., & Dundar, A. (2017). *Strengthening transfer paths to a Bachelor's degree: Identifying effective two-year to four-year college partnerships* (CCRC Working Paper No. 93). Community College Research Center, Teachers College, Columbia University.

Xu, D., Ran, F. X., Fink, J., Jenkins, D., & Dundar, A. (2018). Collaboratively clearing the path to a baccalaureate degree: Identifying effective 2- to 4-year college transfer partnerships. *Community College Review*, *46*(3), 231–256. https://doi.org/10.1177/0091552118772649

3

REFRAMING TRANSFER AS A SOCIAL JUSTICE IMPERATIVE

Michael J. Rosenberg and Andrew K. Koch

Our higher education system broadly discriminates against transfer students. While on first read this assertion may seem harsh and perhaps even hyperbolic, the statement's accuracy quickly comes to light when one objectively examines the evidence provided both in this chapter and the broader book of which it is a part. Coming to grips with this reality is the first step toward building a better future for this oft-mistreated population. Embracing our responsibility as a higher education community is crucial—because the success of transfer students is vital to the institutions they attend, the communities where they will live, the places where they will work, and the larger society to which they will contribute.

As this and many other chapters in this book illustrate, current transfer processes are not based on a full understanding of today's students and their needs. Often, most faculty and staff at an institution will not know that transfer students, considered collectively, potentially make up a majority of the undergraduate enrollment at their 4-year college or university. The first-time/full-time students enrolling in the fall get the headlines, but transfer students contribute as much if not more to the bottom line.

The lack of focus on and awareness about transfer students stands in direct opposition to institutional efforts to foster an inclusive, diverse academic environment. Failing to recognize the contributions transfer makes to a diverse and pluralistic learning environment borders on neglect at best and malfeasance at the worst.

Postsecondary educators and institutions across the United States must recognize and repair the largely flawed and unjust design of the transfer experience currently existing at many colleges and universities across the nation. That design is particularly rife with negative implications for the types of students that higher education in the United States has not served well historically—students from first-generation, low-income, and diverse racial and ethnic backgrounds who are disproportionately overrepresented in the transfer-bound populations at community colleges today. Viewed in this light, repairing the transfer model shifts from an institutional responsibility to a moral and societal obligation. In short, transfer must be *reframed* from an enrollment management mechanism to a social justice imperative.

This chapter sets out to make the case why the transfer process, as currently organized and experienced, is unjust. In Part One of this chapter, we provide a four-component framework for social justice in and through transfer—a structure to help reframe the discussion and action associated with transfer in ways that more directly acknowledge and address its social justice implications.

In Part Two, the first two components of the framework are applied to show how institutions can become aware of transfer inequities resulting from outdated or ill-crafted policies and practices. This content is contextualized with demographic information about today's transfer students as well as historical, theoretical, and organizational content to help readers understand how and why transfer operates as it does today, and what is at stake those operational structures remain unaltered.

In Part Three, application of the third and fourth components of the framework should create more just transfer outcomes through evidence-based interventions and continuous quality improvement efforts. Guidance on how individual educators can help move their institutions to take actions yielding more just outcomes for their transfer students is offered, as well as recommendations for institutional level action to reframe transfer as a social justice imperative.

Part One: A Framework for Social Justice in and Through Transfer

Institutions can benefit from a new, social justice–tinted lens for examining and acting on transfer as a social justice imperative. This framework, in turn, should inform more just action and change for what institutions do with and for their transfer students.

In other words, this framework should help postsecondary educators see if and how social justice is being inhibited in what their institutions are currently doing with transfer students. The framework should also move postsecondary educators beyond a new awareness—to support and guide more just outcomes *through* what they will change and redesign in their efforts.

Social justice can be defined as equal access to social mobility, opportunity, and privilege within a society. When this term appears in many institutional and departmental mission statements, the phrase often refers to efforts in the realm of diversity and inclusion. While such efforts are certainly admirable and undeniably necessary, this terminology constrains "social justice" to a single or few campus departments whose efforts are frequently focused on race, ethnicity, and, in certain academic disciplines, gender and identity. Regardless of a student's classification, all transfer students are in the process of transitioning from a previous postsecondary educational context or contexts into a new one. These equity-focused units are rarely primary providers of support for transfer students.

In this regard, transfers are what anthropologists have come to call "culturally liminal"—meaning that they are in an intermediate or "in-between" state. They are neither "of" the transfer-receiving institution or "apart" from it. During this liminal state, social hierarchies may be annulled or temporarily suspended; what was once deemed tradition may now become uncertain, and future outcomes once believed to be guaranteed may now be cast into doubt. This liminal state may be more than temporary in many ways—it can be sporadic or even permanent (Horvath et al., 2015).

Recognizing the liminal nature of many transfer students is important. Transfers may bring much-needed racial/ethnic, gender, identity, age, family income, and other forms of diversity to a campus. They are a uniquely diverse population in their own right. However, their needs go well beyond those that most diversity resource offices can or even should address. As such, they merit nuanced focus and support, requiring broad, cross-unit efforts. Failure to do so can lead to inequitable outcomes.

Colleges and universities often state proudly that their form of education is a driver of social mobility, opportunity, and career access. Concerning transfer students, however, simply stating that students are permitted to transfer in, have credit accepted, and enter programs is typically considered sufficient. Often, little further consideration is given to what actually happens to transfer students once they enroll and have moved beyond the mechanics of "transferring in."

In response to this dynamic, we offer a four-component framework for social justice in and through transfer. To wit:

1. *Equity in access and outcomes is a positive institutional goal.* Transfer students should be an identified population that is examined when assessing institutional performance in pursuit of this equity.
2. *Systemic conditions such as policies, practices, and processes may inherently advantage some students over others.* Institutions should examine if/how their transfer students are impacted by these policies, practices, and processes.
3. *Well-designed interventions can and often do improve outcomes for historically marginalized groups while maintaining and often raising expectations and standards.* Institutions should examine if/how their interventions serve or neglect transfer students.
4. *Ongoing advocacy and continuous, evidence-based improvements are necessary for lasting change.*

At its core, our approach to anchoring and operationalizing transfer in a social justice framework is done to level a particular playing field and allow all postsecondary participants a fair shot at successful completion of a baccalaureate degree. Doing so requires institutions to undertake efforts to identify and remove institutionally generated and/or perpetuated barriers that subtly but effectively inhibit fair and equitable treatment that enable transfer student success and collegiate completion. In the rest of this chapter, we use this framework to help both educators and/or institutions begin and/or continue to do just that.

Part Two: Building Awareness of and Understanding the Context for Inequitable Design in Transfer

The first component of the framework deals with building awareness of inequity in higher education access for transfer students, and the second focuses on systemic reasons—policies, practices, and procedures—that may discriminate against an institution's transfer students. This section begins with some demographic, historical, and theoretical background on why transfer is structured as it is at many 4-year colleges and universities across the United States today. Keep these factors in mind as you consider some of the common inequities faced by the transfer population.

What Is at Stake—The Demographic Context

Recent surveys indicate that the vast majority of students who begin their quest for a higher education credential at a community college state that they eventually hope to earn a bachelor's degree. Sadly, fewer than 16% eventually walk across the stage to collect a diploma (Jenkins & Fink, 2016). The associated issues only get worse when considering both the sheer number of students who attend community colleges as well as the demographic composition of that group.

Roughly 40% of U.S. first-time first-year students begin higher education in a community college (Doyle, 2009; Kena et al., 2015; Shapiro et al., 2015, 2017). This means that first-year student enrollment in community colleges is proportionately higher than in any other postsecondary sector in the United States—since community colleges constitute just slightly above one quarter (25.1%) of all U.S. postsecondary institutions, but enroll approximately two fifths of all first-year students (*The Chronicle of Higher Education*, 2018).

Students who enroll in community colleges are *diverse* in nearly all senses of the term. Over two fifths of Hispanic (42.6%), nearly one third of African Americans (31.3%), nearly two fifths of American Indians (39.3%), and nearly three tenths (29.4%) of students who identify as belonging to two or more race/ethnicity groups are enrolled in community colleges (*The Chronicle of Higher Education*, 2018). And over two fifths (42%) of all low-income students who go to college in the United States, do so in the community college (National Center for Public Policy & Higher Education, 2011). Students of color and students from low-income families are overrepresented in a sector that, as previously mentioned, constitutes just about a quarter of all U.S. postsecondary institutions.

These data really matter when it comes to transfer. Community colleges disproportionately function as the primary entry point for students from historically underrepresented race and ethnic groups as well as low-income families. Shapiro et al. (2017) and their National Student Clearinghouse Research Center colleagues report that lower-income students at community colleges were essentially as likely as students from higher-income families to earn an associate degree or certificate before they transferred to 4-year institutions. But low-income students were much less likely to earn a bachelor's degree after transferring than their counterparts from higher-income families. Specifically, nearly half of community college students from higher-income families (49%) earned a baccalaureate degree within 6 years of starting at the community college compared to slightly more than a third (35%) of students from low-income families. Given these outcomes, there is a disservice being done to these students, unintentionally or not. As the next section shows, that disservice is rooted in and contextualized by theory.

What Is at Stake—The Historical and Theoretical Contexts

The discussion of education through a social justice and access lens is nothing new, but a significant focus of that discussion has primarily been on K–12 systems and on potential support for students in systems considered "failing" by one metric or another. These discussions are, in contemporary contexts, largely seen as a state-level issue, since the majority of funding for primary and secondary schools comes from state and/or local sources.

Equity in postsecondary educational opportunity in the United States has "trickled up" from the Civil Rights era in the 1950s and 1960s, where the focus was largely on *de jure* racial discrimination. While many colleges and universities also draw extensive monies from individual states, the overarching dependence on federal financial aid (among other statutes) and student mobility across state lines make higher education a national issue—an issue with a level of importance often tied to the party controlling the congressional purse.

Transfer, however, has largely been excluded from the social justice conversation and the related examination of contemporary higher education policy. Politicians and the media often extol the accessibility of community colleges, while also stressing the importance of postsecondary education to the economic opportunities of low-income, minority, and first-generation college students. Spotlights are placed on remarkable success stories like that of Kansas Congresswoman Sharice Davids, a graduate of Kansas City's Johnson County Community College who eventually earned a juris doctor (JD) degree from Cornell Law School (Palmer, 2018).

As deeply inspiring as these accounts may be, they often mask the difficult realities of transfer students and the labyrinthine nature of the transfer experience. In other words, while we often focus on stories of the survivors of the wreck of the *S.S. Transfer*, we need to determine why so few made it to the lifeboats.

The structural difficulties that these baccalaureate-desiring students face, some argue, are a hard-coded feature rather than a bug. Burton Clark (1960) posited his well-discussed "cooling out" function of the community/junior college nearly 6 decades ago. Clark's idea was that students not starting at a 4-year college are discouraged, both explicitly and implicitly, from pursuing more advanced programs and degrees through their experiences at community colleges. Consequently, they are ultimately denied degrees, and by extension, the economic opportunity and stature that comes with such. The effect further privileges those who do earn those degrees. Clark's theory about the existence of a winnowing ethos at community colleges certainly might be contested. The evidence strongly suggests that transfer student discrimination is alive and well nearly 60 years after Clark first wrote his article (Jenkins & Fink, 2016).

The existing realities are that (a) transfer students largely do not reach their desired educational goals; (b) the institutions, largely the 4-year receiving institutions that are the gatekeepers to the baccalaureate, are not sufficiently responsive to the needs of this population; and (c) low-income students and students of color who disproportionately start their education in the community college bear the brunt of this flawed transfer design. Understanding how and why transfer students fare as poorly as they do—in essence, figuring out what makes the system so flawed for transfers—requires some knowledge of theory associated with "transfer student capital" and "social reproduction."

A professor in one of the contributors' graduate programs opined that the most important thing a student learns in college, regardless of their major, is how to successfully navigate a bureaucracy. That sort of knowledge, gained through lived experience, is key to a student's success. That functional knowledge mirrors what Laanan et al. (2011) term *transfer student capital*.

The concept of transfer student capital hinges on the notion of human capital put forth by Becker (1993) and Sweetland (1996) drawing on Bourdieu et al. (1990) and their discussions of social and cultural capital. Transfer student capital includes a student's synthesis of services and information accessible to them. A student accumulates transfer student capital through activities such as academic skill building, academic advising and counseling, perceptions of the transfer process, cognitive development through learning, and interactions with faculty and staff. One might even make an argument that the overall process of accumulating academic credit itself could be a source of transfer student capital.

Laanan et al. (2011) makes the case that the more transfer student capital students acquire, the more likely they are to resist "transfer shock"—the phenomenon (and phrase) coined by Hills (1965) referring to the GPA drop that typically follows when a student changes institutions. If an institution provides (and students take advantage of) appropriate levels of challenge and support through both curricular and cocurricular efforts, students should increase their overall level of transfer student capital, thus improving the odds of success as they move through the transfer process. Rosenberg (2016), drawing on Laanan's concept, found a strong correlation, controlling for age, gender, race, and SES, between a student's self-reported intent to transfer and their participation in transfer student capital-building activities such as those mentioned previously.

The concept of transfer student capital is closely aligned with a construct called *social reproduction theory*. Social reproduction theory acknowledges the Marxist notion that, in modern economies, workers produce commodities, and then further asks what educational systems produce the workers and why those systems do so (Bhattacharya, 2017). The chapter contributors acknowledge that this is a simplification, but delving fully into all aspects of social reproduction theory would be well beyond the scope of the chapter.

In his social reproduction thesis, Bourdieu et al. (1990) focused extensively on the relationship among education, family, and social class. In this scholarship, Bourdieu makes the point that "education plays an important role in aiding and abetting the reproduction of social inequality and social exclusion" (Tzanakis, 2011, p. 76). As Tzanakis notes, the "reproduction of these inequalities is argued by Bourdieu to be facilitated in schools where teachers' pedagogic actions promote the cultural capital of the dominant class by rewarding students who possess such capital and by penalizing others who do not," thereby denoting that "the school becomes a central agent of social exclusion and reproduction" (pp. 76–77).

While Bourdieu emphasizes that pedagogic actions used by schools to reproduce—often unknowingly—social values, norms, and structures, social reproduction does not simply occur through actions in the classroom. The pervasive nature of dominant norms in all aspects of academic life make social reproduction possible. In the transfer process, the view that transfers serve as a means to meet or boost enrollment numbers is one manner in which social norms are reproduced. We believe that this enrollment-related view of transfer dominates institutional perspectives about and activities for the transfer experience and transfer students. This view also explains why the most common reporting "home" for transfer student responsibility is the enrollment management division. As a result, the possibilities associated with transfer are deleteriously limited, as we illustrate in the next section.

How Transfer Is Frequently Viewed and Organized Today

In a large, statewide survey of transfer-bound students, transfer students listed their top concerns (which were reported at statistically significantly higher rates than other concerns) with transferring as (a) ability to pay for college, (b) time management, and (c) academic preparedness (Rosenberg, 2016). Taken together, these represent a concern with being able to balance the academic requirements of a baccalaureate program with the realities of everyday life and finances.

An examination of transfer through a more organizational and functional perspective exposes that addressing these sorts of concerns among transfers is not a high institutional priority at many colleges and universities. A chief executive officer's cabinet reflects the functional areas seen as most instrumental to the success of the institution. The frequent absence of explicitly delineated advocates for transfer at the highest level means, naturally, that any transfer advocate will have to cut through numerous levels of bureaucracy before getting the ear of decision-makers with sufficient influence to effect and maintain structural change. Lacking upper-level advocacy, the "invisible nature" of transfer students at many institutions means their concerns go unheeded, as their potential champions (to the extent any even exist) are often diffused across units.

The lack of attention to these students from an institutional, structural perspective is bad enough considering a sense of justice and equity. Making matters worse is that this information is *absolutely nothing new.* The lack of seamless academic integration of transfer students is reported again and again, both anecdotally and through academic study (Belfield et al., 2017; Laanan, 1998; Lang, 2009; Rhine et al., 2000). Yet the problem persists, even among campuses known to rely on transfer students to bolster their enrollment.

This obstinacy has real-life implications for the students who find themselves ill-served by these structures. Ever-increasing tuition, driven by cuts to public education by state governments; increases in costs; unfunded mandates; and so on, leave these students with mountains of unpaid student loan debt, often without a credential to show for their work. This failure is directly related, and primarily caused by, how institutions view and organize themselves for transfer.

This belief is supported by the findings from a survey of transfer practitioners undertaken by the Gardner Institute in 2017 as part of a planning grant funded by the Bill & Melinda Gates Foundation. The results showed that while the majority of colleges had an individual whom they considered a primary transfer advocate, that person was most often located within some part of the enrollment management division. Enrollment management proved to be far and away the most common location for transfer student advocacy and support. Fewer than 2% of respondents indicated that the primary transfer advocate was at the presidential/CEO or cabinet level (Rosenberg & Griffin, 2017).

There are distinct merits of an enrollment management connection with the transfer function, and we think very highly about the good intentions and merits of enrollment management leaders and personnel. An issue arises, however, when enrollment management serves as the sole—or at least the overwhelming primary—area with responsibility for transfer. This arrangement causes most institutions to view and treat transfer as largely an organizational sustainment exercise.

The limits of the "organizationally sustaining" raison d'être for transfer may be further understood by considering the earlier information about social reproduction theory. If viewed as a sole or even primary enrollment management responsibility, transfer students become largely a means for keeping enrollment numbers and revenue projections at levels needed to keep the organization running—to perpetuate or "reproduce" the college or university as an entity. The reproduction feeds budget models as it spits out transfer students.

This point is further supported by the findings of the aforementioned Rosenberg and Griffin (2017) survey. Those survey results showed that institutions generally do not consider transfer a social justice imperative—but rather, as mentioned before, largely an operations issue. That is, transfer is seen as the process of transporting *credits* out of one registrar's system and into another's, which depersonalizes a very human phenomenon. Almost 68% of respondents indicated that either the division of enrollment management (48.3%) or academic affairs (19.3%) was the primary "owner" of transfer advocacy, and nearly 46% stated that there were no campus advocates for transfer *at all* outside of enrollment management.

With a singular or overemphasized enrollment management focus, the goal of helping low-income and historically underrepresented transfer students earn baccalaureate degrees and achieve social mobility ceases to be the primary driver of transfer policy. If these goals were primary, the problems related to low-income students' baccalaureate completion rates likely would not be as acute as they are, nor would they have been tolerated over decades.

Examples of Inequity Toward Transfers

Based on our experiences and research, we believe that even a cursory examination using the first two components of the framework would reveal issues surrounding the transfer student experience at many institutions in the United States. While certainly not exhaustive, some examples of biased design in access and practice follow.

Inequity in admission practices at "elite" institutions. As a recent report by the Jack Kent Cooke Foundation illustrates, the more competitive an admissions process is at a 4-year institution, the less likely that institution is to accept transfer students from community colleges—favoring instead other 4-year students (Glynn, 2019). This approach effectively eliminates access for large swaths of the otherwise-qualified low-income, underrepresented, and first-generation college student population. These institutions are also then insulated from the talents these students bring—talents which help them graduate, by all indications, at rates comparable to first-time freshmen (Xu et al., 2018). The approach privileges one form of educational experience over another—thereby undermining the meritocratic promise associated with community colleges in particular and higher education in the United States in general.

To illustrate, Princeton University did away with transfer admissions altogether in 1990. While the University's administration undoubtedly discussed the implications, this decision conveyed a clear "if you didn't start here, you don't belong here" message. The same institution, 26 years later, made headlines by reversing its decision by admitting *13* transfer students out of over 1,400 transfer applicants (Jaschik, 2019).

Inequity toward "post-traditional" students. Even at moderately selective institutions such as typical regional 4-year public institutions, an implicit or explicit bias against the lived reality of transfer students often exists. Something as customary as new student orientation may be set up as long blocks of in-person presentations and activities. While appropriate for an 18-year-old student living in a residence hall, such an arrangement is potentially unworkable for an adult student with potential childcare and/or work responsibilities who likely would be unable to attend a 4-day series of welcome events.

Further, after evaluation of previously earned credits, students may learn that they are further from graduation than they had anticipated (Silberman & Rojas, chapter 7, this volume). Responsibilities for initiating an appeal to regain those credits often lie entirely with the students, who frequently must navigate a complex process at an entirely new institution with little accessible guidance.

Inequity in the design and availability of student information. The backbone of academic advising services for transfers is often some sort of transfer pathway indicating recommended course sequences for particular majors. These pathways may be difficult for a student to locate through a basic institutional website search prior to admission, and many individuals with whom a student may come into contact—faculty, resident advisors, financial aid professionals, and so on—may not even be aware of the existence of these sorts of articulations. These same individuals would likely have little problem pointing a first-year student to the campus library or recreation center.

Inequitable faculty bias toward transfer. Faculty may also have implicit or explicit biases toward transfer students—often centering on a perceived lack of individual academic acumen or concerns about curricular rigor at the institutions where the transfer students were previously enrolled. Frequently, these concerns exist in the complete absence of discussion with faculty counterparts at primary sending institutions or an evidence-based examination about who does or does not succeed in particular courses and curricula. The following anecdote should not sound uncommon in this age of expansive use of adjunct faculty.

After years of expressed frustration on the part of a department head, a 4-year institution held a meeting with its instructors and their counterparts from a local community college to discuss perceived rigor differences and instructional inadequacies in a particular course offered at both institutions—a course deemed pivotal to curricular sequences in a number of popular majors. Most of the sections taught at the 4-year university were taught by continuing term lecturers—instructors who had multiyear appointments to teach one or more sections of the course at the university.

Upon greeting the meeting attendees, the department head suddenly realized that over half of his continuing term lecturers were also teaching the same course at the nearby community college. The course content was practically identical—as evidenced by the syllabi shared in the meeting—and the majority of the instructors teaching the course were literally the same people. In addition, the courses at both institutions were approved by the same regional accreditor using the same evaluative standards. Yet, until that meeting, there was a pervasive belief at the university that the course and its community college instructors were somehow inferior.

This is not to say that all "equivalent" courses and experiences are, in fact, equal. However, egregiously misinformed biases such as this can lead to deleterious policies such as blanket rejection of transfer credit from certain institutions and institutional types with no option for a student to earn credit for prior learning. Also, some colleges flatly reject credit from courses taken virtually, even if the course is from a regionally accredited institution and uses the same syllabus as the "in-person" version of the course (Dohanos et al., 2019). While not necessarily unique to transfer students, the combination of rejected online credits, rejection of credits from certain institutions, and limited opportunity for prior learning assessment leaves many transfers with diminished credit for previous coursework.

In and of themselves, these sorts of issues represent known systemic inequality between transfer and non-transfer students. The lack of action from those in positions to effect change, despite firsthand knowledge of these issues, moves the issue into one of de facto discrimination. As a result, a fair shot at success is denied many transfer students, which include a large proportion of historically minoritized, first-generation, and adult students who begin their educational journeys toward a bachelor's degree at a community college.

Part Three—Evidence-Based Interventions and Continuous Quality Improvement Actions for More Just Transfer Outcomes

So far, this chapter has introduced both a need for reframing transfer as a social justice imperative and a four-component framework for social justice in and through transfer that institutions could use to guide a reframing effort and then offered considerations for the first two components in our four-part framework—illustrating the need for change in this unjust system.

To help institutions make that change, this section focuses on the remaining two components of the four-component framework. As explained earlier, these latter two components deal with how individual educators and the institutions of which they are a part can go about reframing transfer as a more just experience through both evidence-based interventions and continuous quality improvement efforts.

Interventions and actions which yield just outcomes for transfer students must reflect the context in which they are being applied. To address issues surrounding transfer on a more holistic level through a social justice lens, one must reconsider the nature of transfer itself. Rather than thinking about the archetypal transfer model— one where a student starts at a 2-year college, accumulates credits, and makes a transition either with or without an associate degree to a 4-year institution where they are left to sink or swim on the basis of academic merit—one must take a broader view.

As well, beyond the students themselves at a typical institution, little accurate data are available about who transfer students are and how they perform—both as a cohort and compared to their non-transferring peers. As well, the aspects of transfer student progression—such as performance in gateway coursework at both transfer-sending and transfer-receiving institutions—is not well scrutinized. In a performance-based budgeting world, any support program designed to assist a transfer student will have difficulty assessing impact and efficacy since equitable transfer student outcomes are generally not considered in state-performance funding models.

Further, transfer must also be seen as a process that has broader, and arguably higher-order, societal benefits. Transfer initiatives should openly recognize and consistently deliver on their social mobility promise.

The structure of the system itself must be thoroughly examined to determine where the "pain points" lie in the process. Taken alone, each of these points may be relatively innocuous, overcome by students whose perseverance has been demonstrated again and again. But the collective effect of these various bureaucratic issues may lead to an "academic death by a thousand paper cuts." To protect students from this potential fate, consider the continuum of the student experience from initial enrollment at a sending institution to the eventual earning of a bachelor's degree— while understanding the reality, as previously discussed in this chapter, that the students most in need have the least transfer student capital with which to navigate this process.

The awareness-building components of our framework shared previously provide the structure and examples of methods for how educators can become more conscious about erroneous assumptions, inequitable treatment, and gaps in support for transfer students. Following are some ways in which informed educators can help their institutions act continuously to improve the entire transfer experience—from the pre-transfer stage to the point where the transfer student obtains a baccalaureate degree.

The Transfer Student Experience as a Just Continuum—Thoughts and Questions to Guide Action

John N. Gardner provided a definition that can be used as a basis for this reframing:

> Transfer is the totality of the educationally purposeful experiences which we intentionally provide our students to enable them to pursue their educational and personal aspirations for academic movement from any of our colleges to some other learning environment that enables our students to pursue a form of educational credentialing not provided by their initial institution. (Ehasz et al., 2017)

Effectively, a student's transfer experience begins at initial enrollment, ends at degree completion and graduation, and includes every aspect of the academic experience in between.

Educators interested in creating just outcomes in the transfer experience might consider the transfer student experience as a five-part continuum. Each part deserves in-depth examination and redesign bolstered by evidence. In support of these efforts, both the five-part continuum and some guiding questions for each part follow.

Part 1: Pre-Enrollment—These are the "pieces and parts" a student navigates before beginning coursework. Consider first the application process—both online and in-person. What does the initial advising process look like? How does your institution perform credit evaluation—whether from International Baccalaureate (IB) or Advanced Placement (AP) exams, work experience, credit from other institutions, and so on? How is information about financial aid communicated, how are awards packaged, and appeals performed? Does the institution offer institutional aid to transfer students or reserve most of it for first-time, full-time, first-year students? How do students experience orientation and initial registration? How does your institution design and deliver placement testing? What about priority for registration? What about parity for access to on-campus residential accommodations? Is guidance available for exploratory students?

Part 2: First Institution (Transfer-Sending Institution) Experience—Once a student is enrolled, what safeguards does your institution put in place for a student to maintain an accurate academic path? When are they given information about transfer requirements at various destination institutions? Are transfer "pathways" clearly spelled out and accessible? Will their noncredit remediation needs throw them off an academic pathway? Do they have a guide for appropriate general education or pre-major courses in their eventual baccalaureate major? If those pre-major courses (e.g., advanced calculus for students desiring engineering) are not available, what options do students have to earn those credits? What ongoing advising and tutoring resources are available? Does the institution have a transfer center? What services exist to help them with "nonacademic challenges"? Are outcomes studied both in aggregate and disaggregated by (and in partnership with) primary transfer-receiving institutions to determine if/how transfer is actually facilitating progress for all students?

Part 3: The Transfer Move—This stage is where most institutions focus their efforts—the "bridge between campuses." For 2-year colleges: What sort of guidance is provided to students to ensure a proper institutional fit at their new destination? What is the transcript fee policy if a student has demonstrated financial need—or emergency financial needs? For 4-year colleges: What sort of recruitment messages are sent? How is the hand-off of financial aid handled? When does credit evaluation happen—and are previous credit evaluations from other institutions allowed to stand, especially among "horizontal" transfers from other 4-year schools? Does transfer orientation exist? Is there a transfer version of the first-year experience course available and, if so, is it required? Do registration policies send transfer students to the "back of the line" for course registration? Are housing options available for transfer students? Do the faculty from the primary-sending and primary receiving institutions discuss teaching, learning, and success in gateway courses that are foundational to successful completion in primary transfer-receiving programs of study?

Part 4: Receiving Institution Experience—How is admission of transfer students into desired majors, especially competitive majors, handled? If students have coursework gaps, such as missing general education courses, what is the remedy? How is advising performed in a student's receiving department? Is there a transfer center at the receiving institution? Do faculty examine transfer student performance in gateway courses and larger transfer-receiving programs of study? Do academic progression policies align with the transfer student experiences? Are transfer student outcomes studied in aggregate and disaggregated with the primary transfer-sending institutions to determine if/how transfer is actually facilitating social mobility?

Part 5: The Baccalaureate Emergence—Do institutional residency policies mirror the lived experiences of transfer students, or do they unnecessarily delay completion of a baccalaureate? Are clear graduation application instructions sent to transfer students? Are transfer students eligible for academic honors? Does the alumni office celebrate the successes of transfer students?

Any institution trying to address the inequality with which transfer students grapple could start by asking questions like these in a systematic manner. Whether performed in a formal planning process or by an ad hoc committee, great utility exists in gaining a deeper understanding of the realities of the transfer experience. Armed with that information, however, advocates for transfer must build a broad-based coalition which recognizes the need for action to address these inequities, as no one can create change alone.

Making the Case Within Your Institution

While at least a bare majority of institutions have designated advocates for transfer, these champions for transfer students often do not hold positions of significant organizational and/or academic leadership influence outside of the enrollment management realm and generally have little if any contact with top academic and/or administrative leadership.

While enrollment management is essential to any institution's success, an individual or an office dedicated to recruitment or retention typically does not have the sole power or authority to set policy, change or augment curricula, or even broadly debunk campus mythology surrounding its transfer students. Enrollment management involvement in transfer is imperative, but as currently structured at many institutions, this role is insufficient in striving to create equitable transfer learning and social justice goals.

Barring a broad-based institutional effort directed at improving transfer outcomes that engages all elements of campus, transfer advocates often have the somewhat thankless task of convincing major campus stakeholders to support their efforts. Campus leadership is under a constant barrage of requests for support, especially financially related support, from any number of offices, departments, and interest groups. Rising above that chorus is a challenge. Transfer advocates who singlehandedly push for change on an individual level, or even those who try to simply go "up the line," following the hierarchy on an institutional organizational chart, often become frustrated at the lack of progress or support. As well, single-office efforts to improve transfer outcomes are vulnerable to changes in institutional leadership, organizational structure, or unexpected changes in departmental priority.

Lasting change requires advocacy, responsibility, and intentionality. Advocacy requires intentionally organizing and, more importantly, constant, evidence-based, action to build support for efforts in the transfer arena. This sort of outreach generally isn't part of the job description for many transfer practitioners and instead begs for advocacy from a senior level position or person. Building networks of allies outside of the typical enrollment management/academic advising/registrar triumvirate is critical to changing the conversation about transfer on any campus. What follows is a potential guide for potential outreach and momentum-building efforts. This guide is adapted from *A Pocket Guide to Building Partnerships* by the World Health Organization (2003), but any number of networking and partnership strategies could also work here.

Know the institutional mission. A mentor of one of this chapter's contributors once quipped, "When you run into resistance, bring everything back to mission." While having data that demonstrates improved retention, persistence, and graduation rates can help people understand that a focus on transfer is *important*, illustrating a connection between transfer and the core values of an institution demonstrates that focus is an *imperative*. The connection to mission can be further enhanced by making the connection between transfer and equity apparent to all involved stakeholders, particularly faculty.

Every institution has a mission statement. Many of those statements implicitly or explicitly discuss the institutional role in the creation of a just and educated society, broadening economic opportunity for all who walk through the doors, the value of diversity, and ending injustice. If you have not done so already, consider how helping your institution improves the lives of transfer students aligns with its stated mission. That alignment is the start of the pitch.

Identify the stakeholders. Who else on your campus engages in work that could support the social justice mission of transfer? Perhaps consider the chair of the faculty senate, who could make a social justice–based case to the collective professoriate. In collective bargaining environments, involving union leaders in discussions about transfer students is vital for change to occur. Offices of diversity and inclusion or multicultural affairs champion the causes of campus subpopulations—within which transfer students are often richly represented. The campus fundraising, development, and alumni affairs offices are also fair game. Fundraising involves highlighting stories of student success, and few students have better stories than transfer students. Regardless of where you begin, once you identify a person or persons within the targeted office, be able to articulate the direct benefit to this department and its constituency of an increased focus on transfer—as well as how this focus will benefit the institution as a whole.

Establish points of contact and communication. Begin networking. Once a person or persons within the targeted offices is identified, invite them to lunch, coffee, or even a 15-minute meeting to break the ice. Come in with a bulleted list of talking points. In addition to transfer data, outline your best illustrations of why facilitating the transition of transfer students is a moral and ethical imperative that needs to involve multiple campus players. Once there's mutual interest, ask for a longer meeting to hammer out details. In that longer meeting, ask them who else they think should be a part of the conversation. See if they are willing to offer an invite.

Create strategy and assessment goals. The proverbial rubber meets the hypothetical road at this point, as you consider how championing transfer is a win–win case to advance to the institution's body politic. Consider what would be considered a "success" to your new partner. Identify how you would measure that success and outline an action plan, including communications. Get the wheels turning on the plan.

Report successes and institutionalize projects. Communicate your successes, to both internal and external audiences. If a program is working particularly well, work your channels to get those support systems backed by a budget. Make certain that everyone knows that it's a collaborative effort.

Other Recommendations for Action

1. Understand that many students in these transfer populations come to the institution with a baked-in assumption that the processes of successfully navigating a collegiate experience will be arduous and difficult. "Mystery shop" your own institution's student-facing processes with an eye toward a student's real experience. As you're following the process a typical student would follow, ask yourself whether a student with limited time, means, or experience would be successful in this effort. Personal experience goes a long way toward building knowledge for advocacy.
2. Perform regular audits of transfer pathways, articulation agreements, and credit acceptance policies to assure they're working in the best interests of students. If your institution does not have processes in place to perform those three audits, create them with an eye toward spotting inequitable trends.
3. When creating and/or reviewing transfer policy, outline policy intent, process, and expected outcome to a group of students. See if they understand what the institution is trying to accomplish. If it can't be easily explained, send it back to the drawing board with their feedback.
4. Work with institutional partners, both those with which you have a sending–receiving relationship and peer institutions with a similar transfer demographic. Avoid reinventing the proverbial wheel, and build problem-solving connections by involving the opinions and observations of other institutions and a diverse array of educators.
5. Find the area or areas where your state is prioritizing funds—sectors of workforce, various initiatives, and so on. Align your transfer message accordingly to justify additional pecuniary support.
6. Create a long-term campus plan for transfer. This can be done through a facilitated formal planning process like the Gardner Institute's Foundations of Excellence Transfer Focus or created in-house. This plan should be dynamic, involving a broad assortment of stakeholders and created to withstand changes in institutional leadership. Focus on including strong faculty representation, as they are often left out of policy conversations.
7. In all forms of evaluation, discussion, and planning for the transfer experience, focus on outcomes for both transfer students in aggregate and transfer students from various demographic groups. Recognizing that systemic racism and classism are often hidden—thereby making them difficult to spot, let alone rectify—make sure data about transfer students can be disaggregated by race/ethnicity, family income, and gender. Use these data continuously as a

focus of the conversations and work and to revise policy and practice in ways that eliminate inequitable gaps in achievement (Koch & Drake, chapter 13, this volume).

Concluding Thoughts on Transfer as a Social Justice Imperative

This chapter has provided a four-component framework for social justice in and through transfer, furnished historical and theoretical foundations for understanding how and why transfer must be reframed as a social justice imperative, and provided practical steps readers can take to move toward realizing a more just design for their institution's transfer experience.

Making transfer a social justice imperative is an evolutionary process, even if it may come across to some readers as a revolutionary idea. While this call to action may be rooted in theory of Marxist origins, we are by no means calling for the transfer students of the world to unite and overthrow the owners of the means of educational production. Rather, we are calling for concerned educators to begin examining evidence in a new way—evidence that may display current transfer practices are reinforcing inequity instead of mitigating it.

We encourage postsecondary educators and leaders, especially those who have yet to be involved in the transfer agenda at their institutions, to examine if and how their institutional approaches to transfer are or are not contributing to a just and equitable learning experience, and, ultimately social mobility. We also encourage them to see and understand how their role—either through action or inaction—might be perpetuating class- and race-based injustice.

Change will not come overnight. Nor will it come simply by moving responsibility for transfer from one area to another. This change will require caring and concerned educators throughout the transfer pipeline taking steps to mitigate these issues. We hope this chapter informs such action.

References

Becker, G. S. (1993). *Human capital: A theoretical and empirical analysis, with special reference to education.* University of Chicago Press.

Belfield, C. R., Fink, J., & Jenkins, D. (2017). *Is it really cheaper to start at a community college? The consequences of inefficient transfer for community college students seeking bachelor's degrees* (CCRC Working Paper 94). Columbia University, Teacher's College, Community College Research Center. https://academiccommons.columbia.edu/doi/10.7916/D8HX1NC5/download

Bhattacharya, T. (Ed.). (2017). How not to skip class: Social reproduction of labor and the global working class. In *Remapping class, recentering oppression* (pp. 68–93). Pluto Press.

Bourdieu, P., Passeron, J.-C., & Nice, R. (1990). *Reproduction in education, society and culture* (2nd ed.). Sage.

Chronicle of Higher Education. (2018, August 19). *The almanac of higher education 2018-19.* (2018). Author. (Access to this site requires a paid subscription.) https://www.chronicle.com/package/the-almanac-of-higher-education-2018-19/

Clark, B. R. (1960). The "cooling-out" function in higher education. *American Journal of Sociology, 65*(6), 569–576. https://doi.org/10.1086/222787

Dohanos, A., Swafford, M., & Morgan, A. (2019, February 20). *From community college to selective research institution: A humanities transfer pathway focused on student success.* Paper presented at the Ohio Undergraduate Education: Inspiring Practices for Student Success conference, Columbus, OH.

Doyle, W. R. (2009). Impact of increased academic intensity on transfer rates: An application of matching estimators to student-unit record data. *Research in Higher Education, 50*(1), 52–72. https://www.jstor.org/stable/29782905

Ehasz, M., Gardner, J. N., & Rosenberg, M. J. (2017, February 20). *A transfer reform agenda: An exemplar and more coming—How does your institution fit in?* Presentation at the Southern Association of Colleges and Schools Commission on Colleges, Dallas, TX.

Glynn, J. (2019). *Persistence: The success of students who transfer from community colleges to selective four-year institutions.* Jack Kent Cooke Foundation. https://www.jkcf.org/research/persistence/

Hills, J. R. (1965). Transfer shock: The academic performance of the junior college transfer. *The Journal of Experimental Education, 33*(3), 201–215. https://doi.org/10.1007/s11162-008-9107-6

Horvath, A., Thomassen, B., & Wydra, H. (2015). *Breaking boundaries: Varieties of liminality.* Berghahn.

Jaschik, S. (2019, January 22). The (missed) potential of transfer students at elite colleges. *Inside Higher Ed.* https://www.insidehighered.com/admissions/article/2019/01/22/study-finds-elite-institutions-admit-few-transfer-students-community?mc_cid=0584ea1166&mc_eid=1b711a3551

Jenkins, D., & Fink, J. (2016). *Tracking transfer: New measures of state and institutional effectiveness in helping community college students attain bachelor's degrees.* Community College Research Center, Aspen Institute, and the National Student Clearinghouse Research Center.

Kena, G., Musu-Gillette, L., Robinson, J., Wang, X., Rathbun, A., Zhang, J., Wilkinson-Flicker, S., Barmer, A., Velez, E. D., Nachazel, T. & Dziuba, A. (2015). *The condition of education 2015.* (NCES 2015-144). National Center for Education Statistics.

Laanan, F. S. (1998). *Beyond transfer shock: A study of students' college experiences and adjustment processes at UCLA* (Doctoral dissertation). https://www.library.ucla.edu/sel/grey-literature/dissertations/

Laanan, F. S., Starobin, S. S., & Eggleston, L. E. (2011). Adjustment of community college students at a four-year university: Role and relevance of transfer student capital for student retention. *Journal of College Student Retention: Research, Theory & Practice, 12*(2), 175–209. https://doi.org/10.2190/CS.12.2.d

Lang, D. W. (2009). Articulation, transfer, and student choice in a binary post-secondary system. *Higher Education, 57*(3), 355–371. https://doi.org/10.1007/s10734-008-9151-3

National Center for Public Policy & Higher Education. (2011, June). Affordability and transfer: Critical to increasing baccalaureate degree completion. *Policy Alert,* June, 1–8.

Palmer, T., Dial, S., & Plake, S. (2018, November 6). Newcomer Sharice Davids triumphs against Kevin Yoder in Johnson County. *KSHB 41–Kansas City.* https://www.kshb.com/news/political/newcomer-sharice-davids-triumphs-against-kevin-yoder-in-johnson-county

Rhine, T. J., Milligan, D. M., & Nelson, L. R. (2000). Alleviating transfer shock: Creating an environment for more successful transfer students. *Community College Journal of Research and Practice, 24*(6), 443–453. https://doi.org/10.1080/10668920050137228

Rosenberg, M. J. (2016). Understanding the adult transfer student—Support, concerns, and transfer student capital. *Community College Journal of Research and Practice, 40*(12), 1058–1073. https://doi.org/10.1080/10668926.2016.1216907

Rosenberg, M. J., & Griffin, B. (2017). *JNGI survey of transfer practitioners*. John N. Gardner Institute for Excellence in Undergraduate Education. http://www.jngi.org/surveytransfer-practitioners

Shapiro, D., Dundar, A., Huie, F., Wakhungu, P. K., Bhimdiwali, A., Nathan, A., & Young-sik, H. (2015). *Transfer and mobility: A national view of student movement in postsecondary institutions, fall 2008 cohort.* (Signature Report No. 9). National Student Clearinghouse.

Shapiro, D., Dundar, A., Huie, F., Wakhungu, P. K., Yuan, X., Nathan, A., & Hwang, Y. (2017). *Tracking transfer: Measures of effectiveness in helping community college students to complete bachelor's degrees.* (Signature Report No. 13). National Student Clearinghouse.

Sweetland, S. R. (1996). Human capital theory: Foundations of a field of inquiry. *Review of Educational Research, 66*(3), 341–359. https://doi.org/10.3102/00346543066003341

Tzanakis, M. (2011). Bourdieu's social reproduction thesis and the role of cultural capital in educational attainment: A critical review of key empirical studies. *Educate, 11*(1), 76–90. https://www.readyunlimited.com/wp-content/uploads/2013/02/Cultural-Capital-report1.pdf

World Health Organization & Stop TB Partnership. (2003). *A pocket guide to building partnerships.* World Health Organization. http://www.stoptb.org/assets/documents/countries/partnerships/building_partnerships_guide.pdf.

Xu, D., Jaggars, S. S., Fletcher, J., & Fink, J. E. (2018). Are community college transfer students "a good bet" for 4-year admissions? Comparing academic and labor-market outcomes between transfer and native 4-year college students. *The Journal of Higher Education, 89*(4), 478–502. https://doi.org/10.1080/00221546.2018.1434280

4

UTILIZING TRANSFORMATIVE THEORETICAL FRAMEWORKS FOR TRANSFER STUDENTS OF COLOR

José Del Real Viramontes and Dimpal Jain

Today, community colleges are one of the largest postsecondary segments in the United States, enrolling almost half of the undergraduate student population (American Association of Community Colleges, 2019). In particular, community colleges serve as a critical pathway for historically underserved groups in higher education, enrolling 43% of first-time full-time Latinx and 36% of African American undergraduate students in the United States (Ma & Baum, 2016). However, despite Latinx and African American students enrolling in community college in large numbers, there is a considerable gap in their educational attainment and transfer rates when compared to other racial/ethnic groups (Bailey et al., 2005; Gándara et al., 2012). For example, among first-time college students in the 2011 cohort, only 39.5% of Hispanic and 33.2% of Black students, compared with 49.8% of Asian and 50.4% of White students, successfully transferred from a 2-year institution to a 4-year institution (Shapiro et al., 2018).

Related to this disconnect between race and transfer, the goal of this chapter is to introduce higher education practitioners and leaders to theoretical frameworks that center the student of color experience in the transfer process. Our hope is that these frameworks can encourage 4-year institutions to develop more equitable transfer practices and policies and increase the number of community college students who transfer and graduate with their bachelor's degree and beyond.

This chapter is organized into four sections. The first section encourages institutions to create better transfer policies by using these transformative theoretical frameworks:

- critical race theory in education
- transfer receptive culture
- community cultural wealth

The second section highlights the transfer receptive culture for Latinx students at a predominantly White institution located in the Southwest to understand the challenges Latinx students experience during the post-transfer experience. The third section describes the various forms of community cultural wealth used by these Latinx students during the post-transfer process. The fourth section provides recommendations to develop a transfer receptive culture that acknowledges a student's community cultural wealth.

Transformative Theoretical Frameworks

According to the acclaimed sociologist Bonilla-Silva, theory is like medicine—it tastes bad, but it's good for you (Bonilla-Silva, 2014). In addition, feminist scholar bell hooks (2000) states, "[E]verything we do in life is rooted in theory. Whether we consciously explore the reasons we have a particular perspective or take a particular action there is also an underlying system shaping thought and practice" (p. 19). As advocates for students in higher education, we should not be intimidated by or avoid theory in everyday practice. We use theory more often than we think, such as when we begin to question data results, how and why programs are not fulfilling projected goals, and to investigate the reasons behind disparities in educational outcomes.

According to Harper (2012), higher education research in general, and community college research in particular, has historically been resistant to theorizing issues related to race and racism. In his review of top higher education journal articles that were race-related studies he found that scholars were reluctant to identify racism as an issue and instead relied on semantic moves or erasure to avoid discussing racism in a critical manner. Structural and institutional racism are real forces that have shaped higher education for hundreds of years, resulting in inequity in terms of access, retention, and academic success for students of color across multiple sectors of education (Smith et al., 2002).

When examining the racial inequities in the transfer function, which we know have persisted for decades (Crisp & Nuñez, 2014), critical race theory in education is an appropriate framework as it accounts for the role of race and racism in educational theory, policy, and practice (Solórzano, 1998). That is, critical race theory does not ignore how historical and contemporary racism has shaped the experiences of students of color as they go through transitions in the higher education pipeline, including transfer. There have been few studies in recent years that have employed a critical race theory framework while analyzing community college and transfer student issues (Acevedo-Gil et al., 2015; Giraldo et al., 2017; Jain, 2010; Ornelas & Solórzano, 2004). To expand on this previous work, we begin with a brief history of the development of critical race theory in education and describe how the theory has influenced both transfer receptive culture and community cultural wealth models—and can assist practitioners as they strive for a more equitable transfer practice.

Critical Race Theory in Education

Critical race theory emerged from critical legal studies and ethnic studies in a post–Civil Rights era (Ledesma & Calderón, 2015). Solórzano (1998), in addition to Ladson-Billings (1998) and Ladson-Billings and Tate (1995), provide the premise to develop critical race theory in education. Solórzano (1998) argues that critical race theory in education analyzes race and racism within an historical and contemporary context. Further, he points to how critical race theory in education challenges educational scholarship by drawing on theories and methodologies from other fields of study, such as sociology and gender studies, providing an interdisciplinary perspective.

Critical race theory in education highlights how educational practices and discourse can marginalize racial and ethnic groups (Solórzano, 1998). Solórzano (1998) provide five tenets that form the basic perspectives, research methods, and pedagogy of critical race theory in education:

1. The centrality and intersectionality of race and racism
2. The challenge to dominant ideology
3. The commitment to social justice
4. The centrality of experiential knowledge
5. The interdisciplinary perspective

Overall, critical race theory in education identifies and challenges racism as part of a larger goal of identifying and challenging all forms of subordination (Delgado & Stefancic, 2017).

Transfer Receptive Culture

The framework of a transfer receptive culture draws on critical race theory in education to examine the relationships between community colleges and baccalaureate-granting colleges and universities. Seeing the disproportionate numbers of students of color who attend community college versus those who leave without transferring or completing their degree, a transfer receptive culture focuses on the role of the receiving institution in accepting transfer students (Jain et al., 2011). A *transfer receptive culture* can be defined as a commitment by an institution to support community college students to transfer successfully—that is, to navigate the community college, take the appropriate coursework, apply, enroll, and successfully earn a baccalaureate degree in a timely manner. A transfer receptive culture is grounded in critical race theory in education and centers the experiences of race and racism in the transfer process.

A transfer receptive culture's foundation in critical race theory is important for two reasons. First, there continues to be a discrepancy between aspirations to transfer and actual transfer for students of color (Pérez et al., 2015; Rivas et al., 2007). Even when accounting for academic preparation and socioeconomic status, community colleges that enroll a high population of Latinx or African American students have lower transfer rates (Wassmer et al., 2004). Second, the completion of a bachelor's degree remains a key toward upward socioeconomic mobility within communities of color (Bahr et al., 2013). There is a real and urgent need to address institutional responses to the lack of students of color transferring to achieve degrees beyond an associate degree or a certificate.

Jain et al. (2011) and Jain et al. (2020) outline five elements that are necessary for colleges and universities to establish transfer from the community college as a normalized process. The five elements of a transfer receptive culture are divided between pre- and post-transfer efforts and include the following:

Pre-transfer

1. Establish the transfer of students, especially nontraditional, first-generation, low-income, and underserved students of color, as a high institutional priority that ensures stable accessibility, retention, and graduation.
2. Provide outreach and resources that focus on the specific needs of transfer students while complimenting the community college mission of transfer.

Post-transfer

3. Offer financial and academic support through distinct opportunities for non-traditional/reentry transfer students in which they are stimulated to achieve at high academic levels.
4. Acknowledge the lived experiences that students bring and the intersectionality between community and family.
5. Create an appropriate framework from which to assess, evaluate, and enhance transfer receptive programs and initiatives that can lead to further scholarship on transfer students.

To date, a transfer receptive culture has assisted numerous practitioners in rethinking their institutions' commitment to transfer and how to best strategize the implementation of the previous elements in their daily practice (Bernal et al., 2019). Cal Poly Pomona is one example of an institution that implemented a transfer receptive culture due to a steady increase in its transfer student population. Gomez and Santiago-González (2016) reviewed the institution's PolyTransfer Initiative which emphasized "recruitment, enrollment, engagement, retention, and increasing timely graduation of transfer students, especially among underrepresented minority and first-generation students" (Gomez & Santiago-González, 2016, p. 90). Team members focused on student integration, student involvement, and environmental pull factors; academic, social, and cultural capital; and transfer receptivity. They then implemented high-impact practices such as a pre-matriculation summer bridge program, peer mentoring, and ongoing graduate school preparation for transfer students. In addition to a transfer receptive culture, they also encouraged those involved in the transfer process for and with students of color and other marginalized student populations to consider the framework of community cultural wealth.

Community Cultural Wealth

The community cultural wealth model describes the array of knowledge, skills, abilities, and contacts possessed and used by communities of color to survive and resist macro- and micro-forms of oppression (Yosso, 2005). Yosso's community cultural wealth model also challenges Pierre Bourdieu's traditional forms of cultural capital, which have been used to explain why students of color do not succeed at the same rate as White students. *Cultural capital* can be defined as a person's set of knowledge and skills that affords them a higher social ranking. For Bourdieu, cultural capital, social capital, and economic capital can be acquired only through one's family and/or formal schooling (Bourdieu & Passeron, 1977). Yosso (2005) asserts that, by these standards, the dominant groups within society are able to maintain power because access to acquiring and learning strategies to use these forms of capital are limited. She asserts that Bourdieu's interpretation of capital makes White middle-class culture the standard, so that all other forms and expressions of "culture" are judged in comparison to this norm.

The community cultural wealth model draws from critical race theory to highlight the forms of cultural capital within marginalized groups that traditional cultural capital theory ignores and devalues. Community cultural wealth centers the wealth contributed by communities of color beyond narrow definitions of *capital* that relate to financial prominence and social status. Yosso's (2005) community cultural wealth model is made up of six forms of capital or assets students develop through the variety of cultural knowledge, skills, abilities, and contacts they possess. They are (a) aspirational, (b) linguistic, (c) familial, (d) social, (e) navigational, and (f) resistant capitals. They are defined in the list that follows:

1. *Aspirational capital* describes individual motivation developed and maintained to overcome challenges and barriers and to achieve personal and or community goals and dreams.
2. *Linguistic capital* describes the sets of skills and knowledges gained from being part of a bilingual family and/or building relationships across cultural, ethnic, and racial groups.
3. *Familial capital* includes cultural knowledges developed around family histories and promotes the well-being of family members and community.
4. *Social capital* includes networks of people who are part of an individual's immediate and extended social groups and who have the ability to provide information and access to resources.
5. *Navigational capital* describes the skills to navigate and negotiate different physical and social spaces/environments.
6. *Resistant capital* describes the skills and knowledge developed through challenging sociocultural and sociopolitical inequalities by engaging in oppositional or questioning behavior.

Together, a transfer receptive culture and community cultural wealth, both informed by critical race theory in education, allow for a critical look at institutional factors that hinder or support community college transfer students, and how receiving institutions can honor a student's community cultural wealth to better support them. One example of utilizing community cultural wealth as it applies to Latinx transfer students can be seen in the study employed by Martín (2014). Martín explored how students viewed their social and cultural capital before, after, and during a summer bridge program prior to enrollment at a community college. She found that participants entered the program with a deficit notion of their academic preparation and exchangeable capital, yet upon completion of the program they developed an understanding of their community cultural wealth and how they could leverage their forms of capital as they navigated the transfer pathway (Martín, 2014).

A transfer receptive culture views the transfer function as a racialized phenomenon and squarely places the responsibility of ensuring that community college students become transfer eligible, apply, enroll, and graduate on the baccalaureate-granting institution rather than on the student. In other words, the blame for not transferring is often placed on students, who are seen as lacking some type of personal quality or as deficient in some way. This becomes even more complex when the student is a student of color, and practitioners can unknowingly fall back on racist notions of a student of color's intelligence or ability to academically succeed (Valencia, 1997). For example, academic solutions are often based on "fixing" students of color so that they can become "college ready" versus looking at how an institution can be "student ready" (McNair et al., 2016) and ensure that the college/university is addressing institutional issues related to student equity and diversity.

By utilizing a community cultural wealth framework, we know that students of color come from culturally rich communities and possess valuable assets and it is often institutional barriers, rather than personal intrinsic barriers, that prevent them from transferring. By using community cultural wealth and transfer receptive culture as a lens to transfer work, one may see transfer students of color not as a problem for an institution to solve, but rather as an opportunity to invite and receive the resiliency and brilliance that students of color provide to their campus.

Transfer Receptive Culture for Latinx Students: An Illustration

We used a study (Del Real Viramontes, 2018) that took place at Southwest State University (SSU, a pseudonym), a predominantly White institution located in the southwestern United States, to illustrate how critical it is for academic and student affairs/student success practitioners to consider approaching their work with transformative theoretical frameworks. This study focused on Latinx students, who use the community college as a pathway into higher education. This study used community cultural wealth and transfer student capital to help better understand these transfer student's challenges and to explore how they believed the institution did or did not address them.

Experiences of Latinx Students at the Community College

Community colleges' open admissions policy, coupled with low tuition and geographic proximity to home, make them a critical access point into higher education for Latinx students (Vega, 2017). The following are the primary factors influencing Latinx students and their decision to attend a community college: (a) limited guidance from high school personnel, (b) financial concerns, (c) family, and (d) seeing the community college as good place to begin their college education (Vega, 2017). Once at the community college, Latinx students have many barriers that interrupt, delay, or prevent them from transferring including the many years some have spent in developmental education. Crisp and Delgado (2013) found that at the national level students who place into a developmental English course are less likely to transfer to a 4-year institution.

Additional barriers include having limited financial aid resources (Alexander et al., 2007), poor quality of academic advising by advisors (Gard et al., 2012), challenges in developing relationships with faculty and staff (Nuñez & Elizondo, 2013), and personal challenges due to family responsibilities, in particular having dependents while being a full-time student (Dias, 2017). With a critical race theory lens applied to education, we see these as institutional barriers, rather than intrinsic barriers to the Latinx students themselves.

Experiences of Latinx Transfer Students at 4-Year Institutions

Andrade (2018) and Castro and Cortez (2017) published two prominent studies that focus on the Latinx community college transfer experience. Andrade (2018) describes how Latinx transfer students developed spatial awareness of comfort spaces where they selectively engaged in socioacademic, nonsocial, and nonacademic *moments of integration*—times during which students feel integrated into the social fabric on campus. Socioacademic moments of integration are those during which academic influence couples with elements of social integration to provide support and feelings of cultural belonging and safety. Moments of nonsocial or nonacademic integration were created in areas on campus where students can feel safe yet be on their own to self-reflect, recharge, and find peace—either within or without a specific academic context. These safe spaces, which include places like the library, cultural resource centers, parks, and so on allow Latinx students to gain social and cultural capital on campus. Institutional provision of these sorts of spaces and opportunities for these moments can positively affect student performance.

Castro and Cortez (2017) described how Mexican American community college transfer students made sense of their transfer experiences based on the intersection of their identities (race/ethnicity, social class, gender, age, sexuality, etc.). Most studies on Latinx transfer students at 4-year colleges and universities focus on the transitional experiences at their respective institutions (Cobian, 2008; Hagler, 2015; Rivera, 2007; Valenzuela, 2006). However, few studies have explored the post-transfer experience for Latinx students who successfully transfer from the community college to a 4-year college or university.

SSU

SSU was selected because it is highly ranked among public universities by *U.S. News and World Report* and is a leading destination for transfer students both within its home state and from around the country (U.S. News and World Report, 2019). This qualitative study described the post-transfer experiences of 10 Latinx community college transfer students along with eight university academic affairs personnel. The following section illustrates the themes that emerged corresponding to the third tenet of the transfer receptive culture—financial resources and academic support as it is was the most salient post-transfer element theme in the study.

Financial Resources

SSU provided limited financial opportunities for Latinx transfer students. However, it did offer two forms of scholarships for transfer students in general, one private and one public, both of which presented challenges. For example, SSU had no control over how the private scholarship was awarded; therefore, students who presented the most need may have been overlooked. However, the public scholarships presented a challenge in that there was a severely limited number of them awarded each academic year. In response to the limited financial resources, Latinx students used their aspirational capital and were motivated to do whatever it took to ensure they persisted, including working multiple jobs during the summer or working a part-time job during the academic year. Additionally, students' familial capital provided financial support as some parents or other family members were able to provide limited monetary assistance toward their student's needs beyond tuition, such as the purchasing of groceries and/or school supplies. Familial support highlighted how students' families valued education and overall well-being of students during their educational pursuits.

For an institution like SSU to be able to practice a transfer receptive culture for Latinx community college transfer students, it must be intentional in providing specific need-based financial resources to meet transfer student needs. These financial resources may be, but are not limited to, need-based scholarships, work-study opportunities that would give students the flexibility to work on campus, or stipends awarded to students who were pursuing research opportunities or graduate school preparation.

Academic Support

From the perspective of SSU personnel who worked with transfer students, the academic support offered to Latinx transfer students was limited in the type of opportunities it provided them to achieve at a high academic level. Students described getting the general academic support offered to every student, such as office hours with their teaching assistants and professors, tutoring, and use of the writing center. However, there were no academic services in place that specifically helped them with the academic transition from a community college to a 4-year college/university.

These students reacted to the lack of academic support by applying their navigational capital that consisted of gaining institutional knowledge to determine where they needed to go depending on their particular course of study.

Institutions like SSU would benefit from developing academic support better aligned with what Kiyama et al. (2017) describe as "culturally responsive communities of learners" (p. 186). These communities of learners build on students' lived experiences in which their cultural and social contexts are understood and integrated, power dynamics are minimized, and teaching and learning are equitably shared among the community. Knowledge developed at home by these students becomes a base from which content for these learning communities is developed. Some of these practices include recognizing students' experiences as worthy knowledge, encouraging them to share their knowledge in multiple ways, engaging them in critical dialogue, and engaging students in student-led discussions (Kiyama et al., 2018). These practices have the potential to increase community college transfer students' academic success, while building on and centering students as holders and producers of knowledge.

Social Support

There were two main types of nonacademic support available for transfer students. First, students were invited to events organized by the SSU Office of New Student Services to connect students to services on campus. Second, SSU had a Transfer Experience Center that provided social programming and opportunities to interact with faculty, staff, and transfer peers. Despite these programs set in place, none of the participants mentioned having knowledge of them.

These students had a hard time establishing a social network. Several of them had dependents and were not made aware of how to access institutional support. To compensate for the nonacademic support they needed, they used their navigational and social capital to use different spaces/environments on campus to develop relationships with people on whom they would later rely. Additionally, students' practice of familial capital showed the non-traditional ways students continued to pursue their academic goals while ensuring the well-being of their family members that depended on them. For example, on occasion, students with dependents in this study sacrificed by making the decision to live away from their child or younger sibling leaving them in the care of a family member or someone they trusted, to pursue their education. They did this hoping to be in a better economic situation when they graduated.

Academic and student affairs practitioners can use the community cultural wealth that students of color bring to assess, evaluate, and enhance transfer receptive initiatives from an asset-based perspective, meaning that they focus on the positive and complex lived realities that students bring to campus. Institutions like SSU can benefit from critically analyzing their own assumptions about who Latinx community college transfer students are and what type of challenges they may face (Castro & Cortez, 2017). The Latinx students who participated in this study represented different ethnic groups, immigration status, marital status, and so on and were part of different family structures and had different roles and responsibilities in addition to being students. These differing responsibilities brought with them a unique set of barriers and challenges they faced before and after they transferred to SSU. In addition, it is important not to consider all Latinx students as a homogenous community and assume they all face the similar challenges in their transfer process.

Receiving institutions must also do a better job at continuing to engage with students after they transfer. The more the institution purposefully reaches out to them post-transfer, the more opportunities they have to interact with other students and the institution. These actions can reduce the academic and non-academic challenges these students face. For example, this effort can be undertaken through diversity initiatives within academic affairs such as academic advising, collaborative learning, and mentoring. Finally, receiving institutions should develop partnerships with community organizations that offer social support services, in case students need additional social support that the college or university cannot provide directly.

Application of Community Cultural Wealth

Today, despite large numbers of Latinx students enrolling at community colleges, there is a considerable gap in educational attainment compared to other racial/ethnic groups (Bailey et al., 2005; Gándara et al., 2012). This study found that a transfer receptive culture for Latinx community college transfer student at SSU was limited to nonexistent. Thus, these students at SSU used their own aspirational, familial, navigational, and social capital to create the resources and strategies to negotiate the different physical and social environments to become successful. Although this study specifically focused on Latinx transfer students, we frame our recommendations based on the various types of capital for transfer students of color in general.

Aspirational Capital

Latinx students who participated in this study maintained high levels of motivation despite facing financial, academic, and nonacademic challenges to ensure their goal of completing their bachelor's degree. Student affairs and student success practitioners can build on students' aspirational capital to enhance their institution's transfer receptive culture by first acknowledging that community college transfer students are highly motivated to strive for their personal and academic goals. Being aware of the national statistic that the overall transfer and mobility rate was only 38% for the 2011 first-time cohort of students (Shapiro et al., 2018), practitioners need to acknowledge the aspirational and navigational capital students used even before they got to their institution and not dismiss transfer students as academically unmotivated.

Administrators and staff can also enhance or develop transfer-related practices that allow students to maintain their motivation by creating financial resources based on need. This would allow them to focus on their academics while being able to take full advantage of personal, academic, and professional development opportunities.

Often, community college students are stigmatized once they transfer to a 4-year college/university, which may have a negative impact on their overall academic adjustment (Laanan et al., 2010; Shaw et al., 2019).

One of the strongest sources of motivation for students with dependents is achieving their academic goals to put themselves in a position to be able to provide for their children or their family members. Practitioners at receiving institutions can enhance transfer policies and tap into aspirational capital through tailored programing and creating spaces where students feel that their children and family members are welcomed (Jain et al., 2011). Additionally, student affairs/student success practitioners should also look into extending housing policies that allow siblings and or other family members the opportunity to live in campus housing.

Familial Capital

Students who participated in this study practiced a commitment to the well-being of their family and community (Yosso, 2005). Staff and administration at receiving institutions can use familial capital by creating more family programing including workshops on "first-to-go," "what it means to be a transfer student," and "financial literacy," to name a few. These workshops should also be offered in other languages for parents whose native language is not English. Additionally, physical spaces for families must also be created within and inside the institution that reflect what familial capital represents—cultural knowledge, family histories, well-being of family members and community (Jain et al., 2011). For example, the institution can incorporate art and promotional signage that represent diverse student families as well as students that are beyond traditional age. This would provide students and their families an extension of home while creating a sense of belonging.

Conclusion and Recommendations

The goal of this chapter was to introduce higher education practitioners and leaders to theoretical frameworks centering the student of color in the transfer process. In particular, this chapter highlighted a study that used community cultural wealth and a transfer receptive culture to explore the post-transfer experience of Latinx students. As a significant number of students of color enroll at a community college with high aspirations to earn their bachelor's degree yet are not successful, this represents a call for transfer rates to be a much higher institutional priority for both community colleges and 4-year institutions. A transfer receptive culture at a 4-year institution must be more than simply granting transfer students admissions into a college or university where they rightfully belong, it should also include retention services that honor their community cultural wealth. The emphasis on a transfer receptive culture provides receiving institutions the opportunity to confront their assumptions of who community college students are and to eliminate potential institutional barriers these students face along the transfer journey. Recognizing the value of community cultural wealth highlights community college students' agency in navigating and negotiating their place in institutions of higher education.

Focusing on the third tenet of a transfer receptive culture, which emphasizes offering financial and academic support through opportunities targeted at nontraditional and reentry students, reveals that merely having transfer programing does not necessarily mean the institution is serving their transfer student community equitably. Placing the responsibility of finding the information and resources on the student and not on the receiving institution does not reflect a transfer receptive culture. The experiences of Latinx community college transfer students at SSU showed, despite the limited transfer receptive culture, that they used their aspirational, familial, navigational, and social capital to create resources and strategies to navigate the different environments at SSU to become successful.

We offer the following recommendations, some of which are also embedded in the preceding text, to assist educators and leaders at 4-year colleges and universities with developing a transfer receptive culture that acknowledges a student's community cultural wealth:

- Partner with resources that may already exist on your campus that are directed toward students of color, provided by students of color. For instance, turn to racial/ethnic student organizations and inquire if or how they approach transfer students in the transition from a community college to a baccalaureate-granting institution.
- Be mindful of students with dependents when planning social programming for transfer students of color. Make sure to include options for childcare or eldercare and also schedule events/programming at times that are considerate of daycare and school hours.
- Ask faculty who teach research methods courses in disciplines such as education or sociology if there are student assignments related to assessment or evaluation. As well, collaborate with institutional research professionals. Offer to create a student research team to assist with assessment of current transfer practices, polices, or programming. This way, institutions may have the opportunity to approach assessment or evaluation from a student-led perspective.
- Start a reading group with your staff regarding critical theories and/or student development theories and then analyze your current transfer resources and practices through the lens of that theory.

By using transformative frameworks such as community cultural wealth and a transfer receptive culture, both informed by critical race theory in education, we are able to view transfer students of color in a more asset-based manner rather than with a deficit vantage point. Rather than focusing on what transfer students of color may lack, a community cultural wealth/transfer receptive culture approach asks a practitioner to flip that question toward the institution and ask how the institution is lacking. Even if the campus is providing specific transfer services, the fundamental questions to ask are: Who accesses these resources, and how often? We end this chapter with additional questions to consider regarding transfer receptive discussions when discussing service to transfer students.

Discussion Questions

1. *Student assumptions.* What are your assumptions about transfer students of color regarding access, academic success, and retention? Do the institutional data on your campus support or detract from these assumptions? How can you educate others about the needs of transfer students of color on your campus?
2. *Building a transfer receptive culture.* What is one thing you would like to achieve by developing or enhancing support for a transfer receptive culture on your campus? How will you identify allies to assist you in developing this plan? Identify the challenges you will encounter and how you plan to address them.
3. *Creating change.* How can you enhance or change your practices based on a collaborative understanding of a particular theoretical framework?

References

Acevedo-Gil, N., Santos, R. E., Alonso, L., & Solórzano, D. G. (2015). Latinas/os in community college developmental education: Increasing moments of academic and interpersonal validation. *Journal of Hispanic Higher Education, 14*(2), 101–127. https://doi.org/10.1177/1538192715572893

Alexander, B. C., Garcia, V., Gonzalez, L., Grimes, G., & O'Brien, D. (2007). Barriers in the transfer process for Hispanic and Hispanic immigrant students. *Journal of Hispanic Higher Education, 6*(2), 174–184. https://doi.org/10.1177/1538192706297440

American Association of Community Colleges (2019). *2019 fact sheet.* https://www.aacc.nche.edu/wpcontent/uploads/2019/05/AACC2019FactSheet_rev.pdf

Andrade, L. M. (2018). Latina/o transfer students' selective integration and spatial awareness of university spaces. *Journal of Hispanic Higher Education, 17*(4), 347–374. https://doi.org/10.1177/1538192717701252

Bahr, P. R., Toth, C., Thirolf, K., & Massé, J. C. (2013). A review and critique of the literature on community college students' transition processes and outcomes in four-year institutions. In M. B. Paulsen (Ed.), *Higher education: Handbook of theory and research* (pp. 459–511). Springer.

Bailey, T., Jenkins, D., & Leinbach, T. (2005). *What we know about community college low income and minority student outcomes: Descriptive statistics from national surveys.* Community College Research Center. https://files.eric.ed.gov/fulltext/ED484354.pdf

Bernal, S., Herrera, A., Jain, D. (2019, February 13). *Transforming higher education through a transfer receptive culture.* Workshop facilitated at the annual meeting of the National Institute for the Study of Transfer Students, Atlanta, GA.

Bonilla-Silva, E. (2014, January 14). *The (White) color of color blindness: How race matters in a "post-racial" America.* Talk given at the Ralph J. Bunche Center for African American Studies at the University of California, Los Angeles, Los Angeles, CA.

Bourdieu, P. & Passeron, J. (1977) *Reproduction in education, society and culture.* SAGE.

Castro, E. L., & Cortez, E. (2017). Exploring the lived experiences and intersectionalities of Mexican community college transfer students: Qualitative insights toward expanding a transfer receptive culture. *Community College Journal of Research and Practice, 41*(2), 77–92. https://doi.org/10.1080/10668926.2016.1158672

Cobian, O. (2008). *The academic integration and retention of Latino community college transfer students at a highly selective private four-year institution.* (Unpublished doctoral dissertation). University of Southern California, Los Angeles, CA.

Crisp, G., & Delgado, C. (2013). The impact of developmental education on community college persistence and vertical transfer. *Community College Review, 42*(2), 99–117. https://doi.org/10.1177/0091552113516488

Crisp, G., & Nuñez, A. M. (2014). Understanding the racial transfer gap: Modeling underrepresented minority and nonminority students' pathways from two-to four-year institutions. *The Review of Higher Education, 37*(3), 291–320. https://doi.org/10.1353/rhe.2014.0017

Delgado, R., & Stefancic, J. (2017). *Critical race theory: An introduction* (3rd ed.). New York University Press.

Del Real Viramontes, J. R. (2018). *Exploring the cultural production of the transfer receptive culture by Latina/o/x community college transfer students at a predominantly White institution in Texas.* (Unpublished doctoral dissertation). University of Texas at Austin, Austin, TX.

Dias, T. W. (2017). Experiences of Latino community college students in overcoming barriers to persist. *Journal of Underrepresented and Minority Progress, 1*(1), 52–65. https://doi.org/10.5281/zenodo.1165454

Gándara, P., Alvarado, E., Driscoll, A., & Orfield, G. (2012). *Building pathways to transfer: Community colleges that break the chain of failure for students of color.* The Civil Rights Project/Proyecto Derechos Civiles. https://civilrightsproject.ucla.edu/research/college-access/diversity/building-pathways-to-transfer-community-colleges-that-break-the-chain-of-failure-for-students-of-color/Fullpaper-Building-Pathways-final-2-112b.pdf

Gard, D. R., Paton, V., & Gosselin, K. (2012). Student perceptions of factors contributing to community-college-to-university transfer success. *Community College Journal of Research and Practice, 36*(11), 833–848. https://doi.org/10.1080/10668920903182666

Giraldo, L. G., Huerta, A. H., & Solórzano, D. (2017). From incarceration to community college: Funds of knowledge, community cultural wealth, and critical race theory. In J.M. Kiyama & C. Rios-Aguilar (Eds.), *Funds of knowledge in higher education: Honoring students' cultural experiences and resources as strengths* (pp. 48–65). Routledge.

Gomez, S. T., & Santiago-González, C. (2016). PolyTransfer: A dynamic and collaborative approach to transfer student success. *Journal of College Orientation and Transition, 24*(1), 90–93. https://doi.org/10.24926/jcotr.v24i1.2907

Hagler, L. R. (2015). *Exploring the academic and social experiences of Latino engineering community college transfer students at a 4-year institution: A qualitative research study.* (Unpublished doctoral dissertation). California Lutheran University, Thousand Oaks, CA.

Harper, S. R. (2012). How higher education researchers minimize racist institutional norms. *The Review of Higher Education, 36*(1), 9–29. https://doi.org/10.1353/rhe.2012.0047

hooks, b. (2000). *Feminism is for everybody: Passionate politics.* South End Press.

Jain, D. (2010). Critical race theory and community colleges: Through the eyes of women. *Community College Journal of Research and Practice, 34*(1), 78–91. https://doi.org/10.1080/10668920903385855

Jain, D., Bernal Melendez, S. N., Herrera, A. R. (2020). *A critical race perspective of transfer: Transforming higher education through a transfer receptive culture.* Michigan State University Press.

Jain, D., Herrera, A., Bernal, S., & Solórzano, D. (2011). Critical race theory and the transfer function: Introducing a transfer receptive culture. *Community College Journal of Research and Practice, 35*(3), 252–266. https://doi.org/10.1080/10668926.2011.526525

Kiyama, J. M., & Rios-Aguilar, C., & Diel-Amen, R. (2017). Funds of knowledge as a culturally responsive pedagogy in higher education. In J. M. Kiyama & C. Rios-Aguilar (Eds.), *Funds of knowledge in higher education: Honoring students' cultural experiences and resources as strengths* (pp. 175–188). Routledge.

Laanan, F. S., Starobin, S. S., & Eggleston, L. E. (2010). Adjustment of community college students at a four-year university: Role and relevance of transfer student capital for student retention. *Journal of College Student Retention: Research, Theory & Practice, 12*(2), 175–209. https://doi.org/10.2190/CS.12.2.d

Ladson-Billings, G. (1998). Just what is critical race theory and what's it doing in a nice field like education? *International Journal of Qualitative Studies in Education, 11*(1), 7–24. https://doi.org/10.1080/095183998236863

Ladson-Billings, G., & Tate, W. F. (1995). Toward a critical race theory of education. *Teachers College Record, 97*(1), 47–68. https://doi.org/0161.4681.95/9701/047

Ledesma, M. C., & Calderón, D. (2015). Critical race theory in education: A review of past literature and a look to the future. *Qualitative Inquiry, 21*(3), 206–222. https://doi.org/10.1177/1077800414557825

Ma, J., & Baum, S. (2016). *Trends in community colleges: Enrollment, prices, student debt, and completion.* The College Board. https://trends.collegeboard.org/sites/default/files/trends-in-community-colleges-research-brief.pdf

Martín, L. (2014). *The hidden curriculum exposed: How one outreach program bridges cultural capital and cultural wealth for Latina/o community college transfer students.* (Unpublished doctoral dissertation). University of California, Los Angeles, CA.

McNair, T., Albertine, S., Cooper, M. A., McDonald, N., Major Jr., T. (2016). *Becoming a student-ready college: A new culture of leadership for student success.* Jossey-Bass.

Nuñez, A. M., & Elizondo, D. (2013). *Closing the Latino/a transfer gap: Creating pathways to the baccalaureate.* San Antonio, TX: UTSA Center for Research and Policy in Education. https://eric.ed.gov/?id=ED571016

Ornelas, A., & Solórzano, D. G. (2004). Transfer conditions of Latina/o community college students: A single institution case study. *Community College Journal of Research and Practice, 28*(3), 233–248. https://doi.org/10.1080/10668920490256417

Pérez Huber, L., Malagón, M. C., Ramirez, B. R., Gonzalez, L. C., Jimenez, A., & Vélez, V. N. (2015). *Still falling through the cracks: revisiting the Latina/o education pipeline.* UCLA Chicano Studies Research Center. https://www.chicano.ucla.edu/files/RR19.pdf

Rivas, M., Pérez, J., Alvarez, C., & Solórzano, D. (2007). *Latina/o transfer students: Understanding the critical role of the transfer process in California's postsecondary institutions.* UCLA Chicano Studies Research Center. http://www.chicano.ucla.edu/files/RR9_001.pdf

Rivera, R. (2007). *Latino community college transfer students in engineering: Transition experiences and academic success at a large research university.* (Unpublished doctoral dissertation). Arizona State University, Tempe, AZ.

Shapiro, D., Dundar, A., Huie, F., Wakhungu, P. K., Bhimdiwali, A., Nathan, A., & Young-sik, H. (2018, August 7). *Transfer and mobility: A national view of student movement in postsecondary institutions, fall 2011 cohort* (Signature Report No. 15). National Student Clearinghouse Research Center. https://nscresearchcenter.org/signaturereport15/

Shaw, S. T., Spink, K., Chin-Newman, C. (2019). "Do I really belong here?": The stigma of being a community college transfer student at a four-year university. *Community College Journal of Research and Practice, 43*(9), 657–660. https://doi.org/10.1080/10668926.201 8.1528907

Smith, W. A., Altbach, P. G., & Lomotey, K. (Eds.). (2002). *The racial crisis in American higher education: Continuing challenges for the twenty-first century.* New York Press.

Solórzano, D. G. (1998). Critical race theory, race and gender microaggressions, and the experience of Chicana and Chicano scholars. *Qualitative Studies in Education, 11*(1), 121–136. https://doi.org/10.1080/095183998236926

U.S. News and World Report. (2019). *2019 best colleges.* https://www.usnews.com/best-colleges

Valencia, R. R. (Ed.). (1997). *The evolution of deficit thinking: Educational thought and practice.* Routledge Falmer.

Valenzuela, Y. (2006). *Mi fuerza/My strength. The academic and personal experiences of Chicana/Latina transfer students in math and science.* (Unpublished doctoral dissertation). University of California, Irvine, CA.

Vega, D. (2017). Navigating postsecondary pathways: The college choice experiences of first-generation Latina/o transfer students. *Community College Journal of Research and Practice, 42*(12), 848–860. https://doi.org/10.1080/10668926.2017.1360219

Wassmer, R., Moore, C., & Shulock, N. (2004). The effect of racial ethnic composition on transfer rates in community colleges: Implications for policy and practice. *Research in Higher Education, 45*(6), 651–672. https://doi.org/10.1023/B:RIHE.0000040267.68949.d1

Yosso, T. (2005). Whose culture has capital? A critical race theory discussion of community cultural wealth. *Race, Ethnicity, and Education, 8*(1), 69–91. https://doi.org/10.1080/1361332052000341006

PATHWAYS, TRANSITIONS, AND SUPPORT

5

A GUIDE FOR CREATING A TRANSFER-AFFIRMING CULTURE AT 4-YEAR INSTITUTIONS TO INCREASE THE ENROLLMENT OF COMMUNITY COLLEGE TRANSFER STUDENTS

Stephen J. Handel

This chapter is written primarily for undergraduate admission and enrollment leaders at 4-year institutions who are supportive of enrolling more students from one or more of the nearly 1,200 community colleges that dot the American landscape. In addition, those of you who are not members of this relatively small but influential community will still be able to translate insights and applications from this unique context to other functions in the higher education ecosystem that impact transfer students.

This chapter is for leaders who appreciate that predicted demographic shifts in the U.S. college-going population make the prospect of admitting more transfer students not only a strategic enrollment opportunity but also—for at least for some 4-year colleges—an absolute necessity; leaders who are willing to embrace the unique challenges that come with reviewing the credentials of community college transfer students; and, finally, leaders who are willing to advocate for transfer students, a constituency not well understood by faculty, senior administrators, and boards of trustees.

In my 3-decade career as an academic counselor, student affairs professional, articulation officer, outreach officer, policy analyst, and admissions and enrollment leader (most recently as the senior undergraduate admissions officer for the University of California [UC] system), I have yet to see an article addressing transfer admissions from the perspective of the 4-year institution. While my knowledge is hardly encyclopedic, I have noticed so few books, monographs, articles, or other resources that examine transfer in any depth that the lack of professional guidance on transfer admission seems a missed opportunity. I hope this chapter spurs others to dive into this important subject.

College admission is hardly ignored by the public. Much of the widely available literature about higher education in America consumed by members of the public is around this topic, especially students and their families who are or will be involved in college choice. These readers have a keen interest in the ways that students are reviewed for admission at the first-year level. When I served as the chief admissions officer for the UC system, I received hundreds of complaints from applicants, their parents, and their local political representatives about a process they viewed as biased, unfair, unworthy, unintelligible, hurtful, out-of-touch, incoherent, or all of the above. Regarding our process for admitting transfer students, however, I received only a handful of complaints.

The popular press, always sympathetic to individual grievances, however implausible, regularly reflects this bias toward first-year admission to the detriment of any regular treatment of transfer admission. The interest expressed for admission at the first-year level—by applicants, parents, the news media, and politicians—even when negative, still served a positive purpose: highlighting important aspects of the process, creating a public space for a discussion of the ways in which colleges and universities admitted these students, and allowing colleges and universities to improve the transparency of a process the public often views as sinister or frightening. I was irked that the public rhetoric around college admission almost never addressed how colleges and universities reviewed transfer applicants. For those of us who wished to advance transfer issues in a similar way—if only to make students aware that a pathway existed to the 4-year degree other than the traditional one—the opportunities were never numerous; interest never as intense.

Equally concerning was the lack of interest in this topic generally held by leaders at other 4-year colleges and universities. (I do not include my former UC colleagues. While the transfer process in California is not perfect, the Master Plan for Higher Education, adopted in 1960, righted the transfer ship in a way some states are still struggling to master.) The disinterest of 4-year institutions is not reflected by the number of transfer students they enroll, but, in my opinion, by how they treat those they admit, especially after they admit them.

A few years ago, I read that a prominent and elite 4-year institution had publicly announced the admission of 13 transfer students for its 2017–2018 class (Hotchkiss, 2018). Although the press coverage seemed disproportionate to the handful of students that the institution admitted, I was momentarily struck with the thought that the firmament that is elite college admissions had shifted overnight.

It had not.

The press announcement indicated that these students would begin as sophomore (second-year) students, although some students might begin as juniors or be required to enter as first-year students; in any event, student standing would be determined after faculty and college deans evaluated the students' transfer credit.

This announcement is instructive because it characterizes a couple of problems with transfer admissions in the United States, neither unique to this institution. First, these students will begin their careers at this university as sophomores or juniors or first-year students. Pity the poor community college sophomore or junior who transfers to this institution only to emerge as a first-year student. Second, the institution's faculty and college deans will establish the transfer students' standing *after* their credit was evaluated. The implication is that these students were asked to decide to attend this institution before an official evaluation of their credit transfer was completed and their academic standing was confirmed.

While criticizing the rich and powerful may be satisfying, no admissions leader should feel smug about this elite institution's intentions. Those 13 transfer students are attending one of the best universities on the planet, an institution that provides an extraordinary liberal arts education and significant financial support. Upon graduation—and it should be emphasized that this institution graduates just about every student it admits—these transfer students will be thrust into a world of achievement, of influence, and, yes, of privilege.

They are going to be better than fine.

The moral of this story is *not* how an elite institution treats its incoming transfer students. Rather, it is how the rest of the nation treats them. Many 4-year colleges and universities carry on some of the same practices that this elite college does, but are in no position, academically, financially or otherwise, to make up for those shortcomings.

Of course, the admission process in 4-year institutions is better understood by the general public and education policymakers. Most Americans have and do traditionally identify the starting point of "college" in that space. In contrast, the nation pays much less attention to the admissions process in community colleges although these institutions enroll 43% of all undergraduates in the United States (American Association of Community Colleges, 2018). For many Americans, that statistic is rarely compelling since community college may be *a* college, but it is simply not *the* college many people attended (or wished they had).

Fortunately, the argument about which kind of college is authentic or legitimate is starting to lose meaning. The Great Recession, which brought extraordinary increases in tuition, made the American consumer a better higher education shopper. Families and their offspring who would not have considered enrollment in a community college are leveraging their limited college fund dollars by committing to the transfer process (Spencer, 2018). The market is a brutal leveler, especially for colleges and universities that have priced themselves out of the market.

The biggest levelers may be yet to come. Nathan Grawe (2018), author of *Demographics and the Demand for Higher Education*, predicted that by 2030, the 4-year sector will lose as many as 280,000 students from its current high level. Many colleges, especially regional institutions without national reputations, will be scrambling to fill seats. Reduction in the number of students who will be graduating from high school has already begun to manifest itself in the Midwest and Northeast. At the same time, the National Clearinghouse regularly reports that undergraduates are less and less interested in staying at a single institution. Its data reveal that over one third of undergraduates enroll at more than one 4-year institution before graduating (Shapiro, 2018). There are also the inevitable downstream effects of COVID-19, which are yet to be determined.

These trends will boost the relevance and importance of student transfer. Of course, community colleges will also be competing for students. However, I believe these institutions will be insulated somewhat for two reasons (even if this observation does not hew closely to Grawe's 2018 analysis). First, the relatively low cost of attending a community college makes them a bargain in a growing buyer's market. Second, as the income divide in the United States continues to express itself in the shrinking numbers of individuals in the middle class, community colleges will remain a less expensive point of entry for individuals who might not otherwise be able to pursue postsecondary education.

The logic here is that if an increased share of this reduced number of high school graduates starts at community colleges, 4-year institutions will need increasingly to entice those students to transition to their institutions to earn a baccalaureate degree. There is no lack of interest on students' part. As researchers have documented elsewhere, most first-time community college students want to transfer and earn a baccalaureate degree (Brint & Karabel, 1989; Dougherty, 1994; Handel, 2013a, 2013b; Handel & Williams, 2012). That interest is underappreciated by 4-year institutions today. One must believe, however, that as 4-year institutions increasingly depend on a stream of community college students for tuition revenue, the need to survive may supersede the historic lack of interest in community college transfers.

Transfer Admission and Enrollment Basics

Every capable admissions and enrollment officer knows the kinds of processes and procedures that are needed for success: Recruit qualified applicants that represent the diversity of your community or region; develop an application process that provides essential academic performance information such as transcripts, test scores, and letters of recommendation; review all applications in an authentic and timely way; and send admission notices in advance of the decision date for transfer applicants. I do not mean to minimize the effort involved in developing such processes—they are essential and important, requiring skill and very hard work. However, the propensity for an institution to be successful in admitting more transfer students is not dependent on the transactional qualities of a traditional admissions process, assuming a capable staff and a leader at the helm who understands the demand of undergraduate admissions generally.

What is more essential about transfer admission—the way it differs from your process for admitting first-year students—is the broader vision required. Plenty of institutions assume transfer students will automatically beat a path to their door. (Spoiler alert: They will not.) To entice transfers, institutions need to devote more attention to long-term planning and less on meeting immediate enrollment targets. If the goal to increase transfer enrollment is only tactical—more applications are needed because your first-year admission process fell short this year—there will not be as much success as if a long-term strategy for recruiting and serving transfers were followed.

The Top 10: A Transfer-Affirming Culture

I have described the importance of what I call a transfer-affirming culture in other places and recommend you consider those references and the work of others who advance similar constructs to bolster transfer student academic success (Handel, 2011; Handel & Herrera, 2003). The construct itself is not a difficult one. Strategy is stressed over tactics, inter-institutional partnership over institutional provincialism, consultation over sovereignty, and data over instinct.

1. Make Your Case for Transfer at the Highest Levels

Increasing the number of transfer students enrolling at your institution requires the support of senior campus leaders, which may not be automatically forthcoming. Most leaders are familiar with first-year students and the achievement test scores they bring that are used to draw comparisons with other institutions. Transfer students are an under-recognized constituency and are rarely used as measures of institutional success. You will need to demonstrate not just that an unserved market of transfer students who wish to enroll at your campus exists, but that thoughtful and sustained investment can bring these students to your institution—students who will typically thrive and complete their educational objectives.

Ensure your rationale is compelling and rooted in the mission of the institution. Some postsecondary education leaders argue that they need more transfer students because the number of high school graduates is drying up. Making that case is understandable, but that argument is not persuasive to the transfer students themselves. They want to know how you are committed to their unique educational needs, not simply that you are trying to hit an enrollment target.

2. Engage Your Faculty

Transfer admission is a two-way partnership of respect and understanding among each institution's mission, vision, and goals. Nowhere is this partnership more critical, yet most often ignored, than in the relationship between the faculty of 2-year and 4-year institutions. Admission requirements, articulation agreements, and degree expectations are controlled by the expertise of the faculty and their engagement in the academic enterprise.

The long-term health of any transfer partnership depends on the degree to which your faculty are engaged in this work. Regular dialogue is required between and among faculty members at 2- and 4-year institutions. As a leader, you need not take responsibility for the outcome of such discussions, but you must arrange them. These kinds of "disciplinary dialogues" or "alignment conversations" (regarding curricular alignment—or lack thereof) also frame the interaction in ways that support transfer students and reduce the kind of institutional provincialism that almost always works against transfer students in the form of lost credits, the need to repeat courses post-transfer, or a general distrust of students who originate at open-access institutions.

3. Take Your CEO and Your Faculty Leaders to a Community College—and Invite the Press

Once your CEO and other institutional leaders, such as those who oversee the faculty senate, have adopted your strategic plan (and ideally appropriated some dollars along with it) you and your president/chancellor need to initiate a meeting with the leadership team at the community college, community colleges, and/or community college district from which you wish to recruit your students. Carve out a day for this and ensure that the CEO and faculty leaders of your institution and the community college(s) have plenty of time to meet one-on-one. Don't shy away from tough questions. Are both institutions committed to serving students? The only way you can know is if you embrace the totality of your two-way commitment with the community college.

If your president/chancellor has never set foot on the local community college campus, expect that your invitation will be politely accepted but not acted upon. If you haven't engaged in regular outreach to your potential institutional partner, developed a steady enrollment of transfer students, and made rigorous follow-up in the form of reports on student completion and success outcomes—you may have to make several calls. Be prepared to be the better partner. You will need to give more initially to get more in the long run.

4. Double-Down on Articulation Agreements

Along with your chief academic officer and the leadership of your academic/faculty senate, you now need to develop an agreement with the academic leadership at the community college about how credit will transfer between the institutions. Referred to as *articulation agreements*, these "understandings" can come in various forms: course-to-course equivalencies, program-centered agreements that accept blocks of courses in preparation for specific elements of the degree (i.e., general education), or a blanket agreement that makes transparent all courses across both institutions. The key goal here is to develop agreements that guide students in preparing well for their success on your campus. In other words, how will the courses completed at the community college ensure the transfer students you admit have a satisfactory academic experience at your institution and eventually complete a degree?

At the start of these discussions with one or more community colleges, there may be a bit of academic jockeying for position. Faculty may ask what courses are deemed "worthy" of transfer? Which ones are "equivalent" to the ones your institution offers?

Individual faculty members are understandably partial to their courses, sometimes to the detriment of similar courses offered elsewhere. These kinds of discussions at the start of partnership work can potentially derail otherwise productive interactions and reflect little more than institutional provincialism. Substantive and sometimes difficult conversations about inter-institutional course rigor, equivalencies, and transferability certainly should not be avoided. On the contrary, the only point of articulation is to ensure that students are well prepared academically to make a successful transition from one institution to the other. But those important debates can only happen if you first establish a partnership and the type of articulation agreement(s) that is to be pursued.

In that vein, the first priority is to engage the chief academic officers of both institutions to develop a blueprint for developing an articulation agreement. (See also chapter 12 in this volume.) Such a blueprint could be as simple as an agreement that all courses will be eligible for transfer between the two institutions, provided that the content or learning outcomes are shown to be largely similar. Another approach is to accept the general education framework as developed by the community college as acceptable in partial or complete satisfaction of the 4-year institution's general education requirements. For more complicated articulation agreements, such as those that link specific skills and knowledge gained at the lower-division level with upper-division competence (i.e., licensed or clinical-based areas such as engineering and nursing), standards from discipline-based accrediting agencies can serve as an important reference.

At this point, if you are concerned that the negotiation of articulation agreements is a challenging, perhaps even tedious, exercise full of academic land mines, endless delays, and unexpected costs, recognize that is the reality. Many attempts to expand transfer have foundered in this area of work. To stay focused and motivated, remember to ask: How will this articulation agreement prepare students for success at my institution and what mechanisms are used to assess their effectiveness in preparing students for academic success?

5. Set Enrollment Targets

Develop a specific enrollment target. However, a mistake that many institutions make is conflating the first-year student enrollment target with the transfer student target. There is a certain logic in this (it's called the bottom line), but it serves neither transfer students nor your embryonic partnership with one or more community colleges well. As I have written elsewhere (Handel, 2007), some 4-year institutions enroll transfer students as backfill for an unsuccessful first-year student recruitment effort which, over time, only satisfies the lucky students who were admitted.

Transfer students admitted at the back end of the admission process will undercut your strategic plan. These students will arrive on your campus not as honored new students, but as individuals for whom you will need to accommodate on a distracting, often irritating, *ad hoc* basis. Do you have housing for these "just-in-time" students? Is there financial aid of any sort to support them? Is your curriculum aligned appropriately so that they can make sustained progress toward a degree? While meeting your enrollment target will help the bottom line, it won't advance your long-term transfer agenda. Your community college partners will have no idea from year to year what to expect from you.

6. Intrude—Politely—on Prospective Applicants

Tell potential students in concrete terms what it will take to be admitted to your institution: courses, grades, units completed, test score requirements. Focus on general education or major preparation or both. Establish processes that ensure new students have satisfactory writing and quantitative reasoning skills so they will be successful upper-division students at your institution. The techniques applied here are not different than those you use for recruiting first-year students at local or regional high schools. Building a steady stream of well-prepared and interested recruits requires your outreach team to build a relationship with both prospective applicants and the institutions themselves. Regular visits are important. Students most often have questions at times other than when your staff is physically on the community college campus. Plan to build a rapport which allows your partners regular access to insights about your institution. The need for more detailed information, especially regarding the transferability of coursework, makes the need for sustained communication vital to the success of your efforts.

7. Make Allies of Community College Faculty, Counselors, Advisors, and Other Student Affairs/Student Success Professionals

Community college faculty and advisors can be your greatest allies; a legitimate and authentic extension of your outreach efforts. These professionals are going to reach many more prospective students than you can ever hope to engage. They can also turn away many prospective students. In general, they will treat you well if you keep them apprised about the transfer issues that matter most to their students. You can do no worse—though most 4-year institutions make this mistake repeatedly—than to fail to inform them of changes to your admission requirements, major curricular changes, and articulation agreements so that their students can make appropriate adjustments. Community college faculty and advisors understand that it is your institution's prerogative to adjust the terms of your relationship. What they will not accept, however, are arbitrary changes communicated without concern or consideration for their students.

8. Collect Data and Freely Give It Away

How successful are your first-year students as measured by retention, persistence, and completion rates? Do you notice any special adjustment issues at the beginning of the new school year for these students? Are some groups of students more susceptible to departure than others? Are the reasons for these departures related to academic preparation issues, financial concerns, availability of housing, or other issues? Have members of the faculty brought to your attention gaps in skills or knowledge of first-year students, perhaps necessitating the need to talk with local high schools about how they are preparing students for college? Have you, in turn, provided local high schools with the expectations of your faculty about how much reading and writing new students will be asked to complete when they arrive on your campus? What data do you provide to high schools about the success of their students at your institution, the majors they enter, or the special talents they bring to your institution?

I suspect you have answers for all these questions for first-year students. You may, however, have few or no answers for your transfers.

These are precisely the sorts of questions you will need to address, although the conversations will be with your community college colleagues. Colleges and universities lacking a strategic transfer plan (which is probably the majority) will often neglect this important component. Leaders at 4-year institutions hardly dismiss the importance of data that demonstrate the successes of their first-year students, but they seem to disregard that importance for transfer students. Having such data not only informs the effectiveness of your outreach effort but also is vital for informed discussion around your articulation agreements.

For example, if transfer students appear to struggle in upper-division math courses, have relevant faculty members described the correct level of lower-division math necessary for success? Is there a disconnect between what is assumed to be taught in the community college classroom and what is expected in your institution's mathematics courses? Only by tracking the success of transfer students and sharing this information with relevant faculty at all levels of the educational pipeline can these questions be answered.

9. Reorient Your Orientation Program

I asked the assistant vice provost for transfer partnerships at one of America's most successful transfer-receiving institutions about the importance of orientation programs in helping students get started on the right foot at a new institution. After describing all the important characteristics of a first-rate orientation, he added: "At many four-year institutions, freshman orientation lasts two or three days, but transfer orientation lasts only a few hours. What's wrong with this picture?" (College Board, 2011, p. 26).

His lament was powerful. While almost all administrators in higher education support the need for strong orientation programs, that so few transfer orientations measure up to the quality of the institution's first-year offerings is another indication of our misperceptions about the needs of these students. There seem to be three common objections or excuses:

1. "These students are already in college; they do not need to be oriented again." This may be true for some students but certainly not for all. Starting at a new institution obligates that institution to welcome all its students with information and insight that will help ensure students' academic success. If the average

completion rates of most 4-year institutions' transfer students were higher, we might be able to escape the need for a solid orientation program, but the facts tell a different story.

2. "We don't want to disadvantage our transfer students in the summer who often must work or have other responsibilities during that time." Understanding that many transfer students must work in the summer to pay for college expenses is understandable. Why not offer the orientation in phases? Perhaps institutions could offer an online version that could be taken at the student's convenience, followed by in-person gatherings closer to the start of the academic year? In fairness, the same argument could be made for first-year students. They too need to work during the summer, but we don't allow that reality to become an excuse for missing comprehensive and longer orientation initiatives.

3. "Transfer students are more mature, much more focused on a purpose; they already know what they are doing and why they are here." This thought assumes transfer students have made an appropriate choice of major and also assumes that they cannot still be "undecided," which we know is not the case. These general presumptions undercut our services to transfer students. We cannot honor the diversity of background, thought, circumstances, and educational preparation of first-year students without addressing this with the transfer population, as well. Institutions across the country have come up with a variety of formats that do not unduly burden transfer students, but which communicate the importance of a good start by developing a first-rate orientation program. Examples can be found in the case studies included in this volume and in its accompanying online compendium.

10. Lead the Way

Strengthening your institution's commitment to transfer students comes from leadership at all levels, but especially from rank and file employees, whether these individuals are administrators in the admissions office or disciplinary teaching faculty. In my experience, a focus on transfer students is most likely to come from individuals who oversee the admissions and enrollment platform of the 4-year institution. Of course, there are transfer advocates in all quarters—politicians, policymakers, community college leaders, and community-based organizations. Ideally, as we make the case elsewhere in this book—chief academic officers are hopefully encouraging your CEO or board of trustees/directors to enroll more transfer students from community colleges. Admissions and enrollment leaders have both the vision and on-the-ground skills to know how this work might be conducted. Part of the reason is the result of their expertise in recruiting, evaluating, admitting, and enrolling first-year students. This chapter has not dealt largely with the transactional implications of transfer precisely because enrollment professionals already have the requisite knowledge and skills to partner with their academic colleagues. Having such expertise provides your institution with the perspective needed to think strategically about serving transfer students.

My guidance here is based on 2 decades of work in a public 4-year institution that was committed to enrolling large numbers of students from community colleges. Professionals with similar experience will offer other insights, and I make no claim that my advice is definitive or exhaustive. Nevertheless, I am confident that the advice offered here is a good starting point for how to leverage the talents of enrollment management professionals to move the institution forward both to admit more transfer students from community colleges and to increase their academic success outcomes.

Recommendations

1. Before embarking on a plan of advocacy for increased transfer student enrollment, ensure that your strategic plan takes account of the unique advantages and challenges facing your institution's transfer students.
2. Ensure that your transfer strategic plan is bolstered by the best available evidence regarding the benefits—and challenges—of enrolling more students from community colleges. Great intentions are often defeated by *moderate* resistance, either anticipated or unanticipated, from one or more campus constituencies that often prevents a relaunch of the initiative for many years.
3. Engage faculty throughout the institution in this effort, as not only pivotal partners in the effort but also skilled instructors and researchers who can inform, test, and evaluate your plan rigorously.
4. Assess who your "allies" are in this effort early in the planning stages; reach out to potential critics early to gauge their concerns and objections and to involve them collaboratively in developing new initiatives for transfer students.

Discussion Questions

1. In what ways would greater enrollment of community college transfer students serve your institution?
2. What aspects of your campus would be uniquely attractive to community college transfer students? In what ways could those elements be enhanced or expanded?
3. Of the "Top 10" elements described here, which ones would be the easiest to implement at your institution? Which ones would be the most challenging?

References

American Association of Community Colleges. (2018). *Fast facts*. Author.
Brint, S., & Karabel, J. (1989). *The diverted dream: Community colleges and the promise of educational opportunity in American, 1900–1985*. Oxford University Press.

College Board. (2011). *Improving student transfer from community colleges to four-year institutions: The perspective of leaders from baccalaureate-granting institutions.* The College Board.

Dougherty, K. J. (1994). *The contradictory college: The conflicting origins, impacts, and futures of the community college.* State University of New York.

Grawe, N. D. (2018). *Demographics and the demand for higher education.* John's Hopkins University Press.

Handel, S. J. (2007, September/October). Second chance, not second class: A blueprint for community college transfer. *Change: The Magazine of Higher Education, 39*(5), 38–45. https://doi.org/10.3200/chng.39.5.38-45

Handel, S. J. (2011). Increasing higher education access and success using new pathways to the baccalaureate: The emergence of a transfer-affirming culture. *Proceedings of the 1st Annual 1st International Australasian Conference on Enabling Access to Higher Education,* Adelaide, Australia, December 6, 2011.

Handel S. J. (2013a, September 23). Two-year students have long had four-year dreams. *The Chronicle of Higher Education.* https://www.chronicle.com/article/2-Year-Students-Have-Long-Had/141787

Handel, S. J. (2013b, Winter). Community college students earning the baccalaureate: The good news could be better. *College and University, 89*(2), 22. https://search.proquest.com/docview/1496068779

Handel, S. J., & Herrera, A. (2003). Access and retention of students from educationally disadvantaged backgrounds: Insights from the University of California. In L. Thomas, M. Cooper, & J. Quinn (Eds.), *Improving retention rates among disadvantaged students* (pp. 33–51). Trentham Books.

Handel, S. J., & Williams, R. A. (2012). *The promise of the transfer pathway.* The College Board.

Hotchkiss, M. (2018). *Princeton offers admission to 13 students in reinstated transfer program.* Office of Communications, Princeton University. https://www.princeton.edu/news/2018/05/09/princeton-offers-admission-13-students-reinstated-transfer-program

Shapiro, D. T. (2018). Student transfer and mobility: Pathways, scale, and outcomes for student success. In M. A. Poisel and S. Joseph (Eds.), *Building transfer student pathways for college and career success.* University of South Carolina: National Institute for the Study of Transfer Students and the National Resource Center for the First-Year Experience and Students in Transition.

Spencer, K. (2018, April 5). Middle-class families increasingly look to community colleges. *The New York Times.* https://www.nytimes.com/2018/04/05/education/learning/community-colleges-middle-class-families.html

6

MAKING FINANCIAL AID WORK FOR TRANSFER STUDENTS

Jason Taylor

The price of college for students and families has increased dramatically over the past several decades. Over the past 10 years, in-state tuition at public 4-year colleges has increased at a rate of 3.1% per year (College Board, 2018a), in part because state funding to higher education has decreased over time (State Higher Education Executive Officers Association, 2018). On average, these students will pay about $10,230 for tuition and fees. Accompanying this trend in increased tuition is the increase in aid. College Board (2018b) data also show that total federal, state, and institutional aid has increased 42% between 2007–2008 and 2017–2018. This amounts to approximately $241 billion, of which undergraduates received 76%. On average, this means that undergraduate students received about $14,790 per *full-time equivalent (FTE)*, typically defined as the equivalent of a 15-credit hour course load in 2017–2018 (College Board, 2018b). These figures underscore the significance of student financial aid in the American higher education system.

Another salient feature of the American higher education system is transfer and mobility. As this book illustrates, transfer is a complex and multifaceted phenomenon. There is not one single definition of *transfer*, although as Taylor and Jain (2017) argue, much of the transfer literature focuses on 2-year to 4-year transfer, or vertical transfer. Additionally, this book focuses primarily on vertical transfer as well as considers transfer more broadly, including simply enrolling concurrently at more than one institution. This also aligns with the expanded definition of *transfer* laid out by this volume's editors.

This chapter considers the intersection of financial aid and transfer and mobility in higher education, both of which are complex systems and phenomena. The first section briefly introduces readers to differences in federal, state, and institutional aid. The second section reviews how aid influences student success and how students use aid, with a focus on transfer students. The third section considers the intersection of aid with transfer and assesses how federal, state, and institutional aid influences and impacts students who transfer and are mobile. This section also illustrates how many existing aid policies and practices disadvantage transfer students. The chapter concludes with recommendations on how to improve financial aid to better support transfer students.

Student Financial Aid

The system of student financial aid in American higher education is complex, involving the federal government, state governments, local governments, higher education institutions, the private sector, and students and families. Even in early colonial colleges, students relied on financial assistance to attend college. As Fuller (2014) notes, "The American system of higher education continued the tradition of sponsorship, charity, and patronage established by European universities" (p. 45). The contemporary system of financial aid has clearly evolved since early colonial colleges, but the model of discounting college prices through aid has not changed. Indeed, this history is reflected in the modern system of higher education financing. The tuition model in the United States is what Johnstone and Marcucci (2011) characterize as up-front tuition and fees. Among international financing models, up-front is among the most common models whereby students are required to pay tuition and fees to enroll in college.

In order to pay tuition and fees, students receive public financial aid from three critical sources: the federal government, state governments, and institutions. Students receive financial assistance from private sources as well (e.g., private scholarships or family resources), but the focus of this chapter is on resources distributed to students from public and institutional resources. The following is a brief review of federal aid, state aid, and institutional aid.

Federal Financial Aid

The federal financial aid given directly to students primarily takes two forms: grants and loans. To be considered for either type of federal aid, students are required to complete the federal Free Application for Federal Student Aid (FAFSA). Grant aid is primarily available through the Pell Grant program and the Federal Work-Study program, both of which are means-tested programs and available to students based on their demonstrated financial need. The other primary federal program is federal student loans, which include Federal Stafford Loans and Parent PLUS Loans. These loans are broadly available to all students. They replaced the Federal Perkins loans, which were discontinued in 2017. The Pew Charitable Trusts (2015) estimated that in 2013, the federal government spent $31.3 billion on Pell grants, $12.2 billion on veteran's educational benefits via the G.I. Bill, and $1.6 billion on other federal financial aid grants. The federal government also facilitates over $100 billion in federal student loans each year to help students finance college. This combined amount represents a significant investment of federal money distributed directly to students, including transfer students, to help them pay for college.

State Financial Aid

Like federal aid, most states distribute aid directly to students through state-funded aid programs. According to the National Association of State Student Grant and Aid Programs (NASSGAP) annual report, states spent about $11 billion on grant aid in 2016–2017 (NASSGAP, 2018). About 76% of grant aid was need-based aid, while the remaining 24% was non-need based. NAASGAP reports that 46% of all grant aid to undergraduates is based exclusively on need, 17% is based exclusively on merit, and 37% is based on both need and merit. All 50 states have at least one state aid program (Education Commission of the States, 2019), but as described in the next section, these aid programs are often targeted toward a traditional student who is entering college immediately after high school, which may exclude transfer students.

Institutional Financial Aid

Institutional aid plays a critical role in students' financing of college, but the amount of aid varies based on the type of college that students attend. Institutions currently award approximately $60 billion in grant aid to students (which includes tuition discounting), an increase of about 24% in the past 5 years (College Board, 2018b). This amount represents about 44% of all grant aid given to students and 26% of total financial aid to undergraduate students (College Board, 2018b).

The amount of institutional aid varies considerably by the type of institution a student attends. For example, among full-time students, institutional aid represents 31% of all sources of grant aid at public 4-year institutions, and 10% at public 2-year institutions (College Board, 2018b). Among full-time students at private institutions, institutional grants represent 74% of all grant aid at private nonprofit 4-year institutions students, and 15% at for-profit private institutions (College Board, 2018b).

Like federal and state aid, institutional aid plays a critical role in students' financial aid packages. However, the purpose of institutional aid differs from much federal and institutional aid, because as McPherson and Schapiro (2002) argue, the role and purpose of institutional aid has shifted over time. Rather than using aid as a strategy to eliminate price as a factor in students' choice of whether and where to go to college, many institutions use institutional aid in their self-interest as an enrollment management strategy rather than toward a collective good (McPherson & Schapiro, 2002). That is, institutions primarily use aid to compete for students rather than to reduce the price for the neediest students.

Financial Aid and Student Success

Decades of literature have established an empirical foundation showing the relationship between financial aid and college choice, access, and success (e.g., Angrist et al., 2014; Castleman & Long, 2013; Dynarski & Scott-Clayton, 2013; Heller, 1997). However, the literature includes conflicting results about the influence of financial aid on student success. A comprehensive review of the influence of different types and sources of aid is beyond the scope of this chapter, but it is important to highlight Scott-Clayton's (2015) synthesis of evidence on the effectiveness of financial aid. Her review and synthesis of literature led to five important conclusions. First, she argued that net price influences college access and college choice. That is, the amount of money that students must pay, after considering grants and other discounts, influences student decisions about where they go to college (e.g., 2-year, 4-year, selective, nonselective) and if they stay in college. Second, Scott-Clayton argued that aid program complexity influences the effectiveness of aid. The landscape of financial aid is incredibly complex and individual aid programs (e.g., state aid, Pell, etc.) vary in their complexity; research suggests that these complexities influence the effectiveness of different aid types. That is, a well-intended aid program that is complex may confuse students and work against student access and success. Third, research suggests that students need more than just information about aid, they need proactive help in applying for aid and navigating the aid process (Scott-Clayton, 2015). Although aid is available to students from many sources, research shows that simply providing more information to students and families is insufficient. Rather, students and families need hands-on and individual assistance from experts to navigate the complex financial aid systems. Fourth, Scott-Clayton noted that financial aid programs have different incentives and these incentives influence outcomes. For example, financial aid programs might include GPA or enrollment requirements (e.g., full versus part time), which serve as incentives to drive the desired student choices and behaviors. Fifth, Scott-Clayton argued that loans, although unpopular, are an important college access mechanism. That is, several studies show how loans can and have helped students access and remain in college, despite the fact that they have incurred additional debt.

The scholarship on financial aid clearly suggests that financial aid matters for students, and this applies to transfer students as well. For example, Crisp et al. (2009) found that financial factors, including financial aid, were significant predictors of community college student success, including a predictor of transfer. Research also suggests that students from lower socioeconomic status (SES) transfer at lower rates relative to higher SES students, particularly to elite institutions (Dougherty & Kienzl, 2006; Dowd et al., 2008), and some evidence suggests the equity gap in transfer access to elite institutions has widened in recent decades (Dowd & Melguizo, 2008). This body of literature illustrates that financial aid impacts all students, but it also specifically impacts transfer students.

Accessing and Using Aid

Research shows there are differences in students' access to financial aid, and research on transfer students' aid suggests there are differences in aid access between transfer students and non-transfer students. Only a few studies examine differences in aid type and amount based on transfer status, but one study by Fernandez and Fletcher (2014) used data from the National Center for Education Statistics' Baccalaureate and Beyond (B&B) study to examine differences in aid among bachelor's degree graduates who transferred from a community college and those who did not transfer. Overall, they found that transfer students across nearly all income levels, and at both public and private institutions, had larger average amounts of cumulative debt than students who remain at a single institution. One explanation for this is that a significantly larger percentage of transfer borrowers tended to be "independent" students (i.e., students who are not dependent on their parents' finances from the federal government's perspective) compared to non-transfer borrowers. For example, of independent students at public 4-year institutions, 58% were transfer students whereas only 26% were non-transfer students (Fernandez & Fletcher, 2014). Transfer students who borrowed also tended to work more hours per week while they were college students, which is logical if they were also more likely to be independent. However, Fernandez and Fletcher found no differences in the average dollar amount of loans based on the number of hours worked per week.

Fernandez and Fletcher (2014) also found that transfer students and non-transfer students at public institutions tend to complete the FAFSA at about the same rate—about 80% of transfers and 78% of non-transfers. Fernandez and Fletcher (2014) did not provide data on differences in Pell grants or state grants by transfer status, but they did assess differences in average institutional grants. What they found is that transfer students tend to enroll in institutions with small average institutional grants. Although the sample was limited to first-time, full-time students, they ran a regression analysis and found that even after controlling for other factors, transfer students were more likely to enroll in institutions with smaller institutional grant aid, suggesting that transfer students likely receive smaller amounts of institutional aid than non-transfer students. Overall, this research shows that transfer students are disadvantaged in terms of access to institutional aid and level of debt accrual.

Assessing Aid Policy for the Mobile Student

This section examines federal, state, and institutional aid from the perspective of how aid policies influence transfer students. Overall, financial aid policies at all levels were developed and mostly perpetuate an outdated model of higher education that advantages students who begin and finish college at the same institution.

Federal Aid

To put it mildly, federal aid is complicated. Hundreds of rules, processes, and procedures govern federal aid that make it challenging for students and families to understand, access, and use aid, as Goldrick-Rab's (2016) book *Paying the Price* clearly illustrates. As previously noted, the intersection of federal financial aid and transfer presents an even more complicated landscape. Because of this complexity, the following sections focus on salient issues in which federal financial aid impacts transfer: (a) federal aid eligibility limits, (b) midyear transfer, and (c) co-enrollemnt.

Federal Aid Eligibility Limits

Perhaps one of the most critical implications of federal financial aid for transfer students is that financial aid eligibility limits may result in transfer students exhausting their financial aid. For example, federal Pell grants are only available to students for up to the equivalent of 6 years. Similarly, federal subsidized and unsubsidized loans have lifetime limits that apply to all students. As undergraduates, dependent students are limited to $31,000 in federal loans and independent students are limited to $57,500 in total federal loans.

These limits all have relevance for transfer students because of the well-documented phenomenon of inadequate transfer articulation and credit loss. Researchers have documented how state policies do not adequately address the articulation of courses, particularly courses in technical programs (Ignash, 1997; Ignash & Kotun, 2005). The result of ineffective articulation policies is that many students' credits do not transfer. A recent study by the U.S. Government Accountability Office (2017) found that, on average, students lost 43% of their credits (an average of about 13 credits) when they transferred. Credit loss ranged from a low of 37% for students transferring from public to public institutions to a high of 94% for students transferring from private for-profit to public institutions. If transfer students must repeat classes or take new classes for a program at a new institution, they risk exhausting their financial aid eligibility. A related issue is the significant percentage of community college students that participate in developmental education. According to nationally representative data from the National Center for Education Statistics, 68% of beginning community college students participated in developmental education within 6 years of enrolling, taking an average of three remedial courses (Chen, 2016). This has relevance for financial aid because many community college transfer students likely took developmental education for several semesters and accessed federal financial aid. Given federal limits on Pell grants, loans, and the aid eligibility time frame, transfer students may have less federal aid resources available to them to complete a bachelor's degree if they participated in developmental education.

Midyear Transfer

Perhaps one of the most complicated issues for transfer students is midyear transfer, that is, when a student transfers from one institution to another in the middle of an academic year. Midyear transfer involves procedural hurdles for students such as sending FAFSA information to a student's new institution, but a midyear transfer has several implications for students that are often not very clear.

As federal financial aid availability—particularly grants and loans—is based on an individual institution's cost of attendance (COA), it is likely that the amount of federal aid available to students will change if they transfer midyear. If the COA is higher at the new institution, the student may have more aid available to them, but if the COA is lower at the new institution, the amount of aid will likely decrease. If the amount of aid decreases, this could negatively impact students' ability to pay bills or follow through with financial commitments made at the beginning of the year (e.g., pay a lease that was signed for 1 year). As research by Kelchen et al. (2017) shows, the COA can vary greatly even within a very small geographic area. This variation is due in part to different tuition rates, but institutions can also calculate living costs in different ways. Thus, even midyear transfer within the same geographic area could mean a significantly different financial aid package.

If a student has a federal loan and they transfer from College A to College B in the middle of year, College A reports to the National Student Loan Data System (NSLDS) that the student is no longer enrolled, which could trigger a repayment timeline. College A and NSLDS do not know that the student is now enrolled in College B, and the burden is on the student to contact the loan servicer to request deferment of payment until that student completes the degree.

A related issue is that if a student has taken out a federal loan and they stop attending one institution, the institution will contact the student about exit counseling for federal student loans. It is unlikely that the student will notify an institution about their intent to transfer, so an institution likely assumes the student simply left the institution and therefore contacts the student about loan exit counseling.

Another implication of midyear transfer relates to potential unintended negative consequences. Research shows that many students transfer or they temporarily stop-out because of personal reasons (U.S. Department of Education, 2017), and their transfer or stop-out may be due to reasons they cannot control. In some cases, this enrollment disruption may prompt a student to leave an institution before the semester ends, with the intention to enroll at a new institution at the start of the next semester. The federal policy Return of Title IV Funds (R2T4) requires that federal aid must be returned if students do not complete at least 60% of the semester (U.S. Department of Education, 2018). That is, an institution might disburse aid at the beginning of the semester, but if the student does not complete at least 60% of the semester, that student would need to return aid dollars to the institution. This policy applies to any student but could have unintended consequences if students withdraw for personal reasons yet intend to transfer to another institution. For example, students may spend their financial aid dollars before they complete 60% of the semester, yet because of unforeseen circumstances, could be forced to pay money back to their college upon withdrawal. This could leave students in debt and/or could prevent them from receiving aid at the institution to which they transfer.

A final implication of midyear transfer is the extent to which some federal aid is not portable, mainly the Federal Work-Study program. Federal Work-Study aid is distributed to institutions, and then institutions allocate this aid to eligible students. So, for example, if a student qualifies for and uses work-study at their first institution and then transfers to a new institution within the same year, they may not be eligible for aid at the new institution if the new institution has exhausted its work-study funding.

Co-enrollment

Enrollment in more than one institution (co-enrollment) is a form of transfer because ultimately, students will likely transfer credits from one institution to the other.

However, as previously noted, the federal financial aid system was designed for and works best for students who begin and finish at one institution. Indeed, federal financial aid requires that students be degree-seeking in order to be eligible for aid, and federal policy indicates that students can only be degree-seeking and receive federal aid from one college. The law does accommodate students who enroll at more than one institution, but it requires cooperation between two institutions in the form of a consortium agreement, and the agreement may be a process that the student must initiate. The U.S. Department of Education's Federal Student Aid Office's handbook notes that

> a consortium agreement can apply to all FSA programs. Under a consortium agreement, students may take courses at a school other than the home school and have those courses count toward the degree or certificate at the home school. A student can only receive FSA assistance for courses that are applicable to the student's certificate or degree program. (U.S. Department of Education, 2018, p. 34)

For students to co-enroll in an institution other than their "home" institution (i.e., the degree-seeking institution) and receive federal financial aid, the institutions must have a consortium agreement. Federal policy allows for a blanket agreement that can apply to all students or a separate agreement for each student. In regions where there are multiple institutions, co-enrollment can be a common phenomenon. Crisp (2013) found that 14% of traditional-aged beginning community college students (she limited her analysis to traditional-aged students) co-enrolled at some point within their first 6 years of college.

State Aid

Although state aid represents a healthy proportion of students' financial aid, it is difficult to assess how state aid influences transfer students because there are 50 different policy contexts. Apart from one report (Long, 2005), there is little existing research on the relationship between state aid and transfer students. As we will describe, a few states have specific aid programs for transfer students, but in other states, transfer students would be eligible for existing state-aid programs in the same ways that non-transfer students are eligible. However, some existing state-aid policies are designed in a way that could disadvantage transfer students. For example, state-aid programs in Mississippi, New Mexico, South Carolina, and other states require students to attend full time to be eligible for state aid (Education Commission of the States, 2019). However, community college students and prospective transfer students are likely to enroll part time (Cohen et al., 2014), so it is likely that state-aid policies restricting eligibility to full-time status will disproportionately affect prospective and current transfer students.

Another state-aid design component that could disadvantage transfer students is whether aid eligibility is restricted based on the time that a student graduated high school. According to Education Commission of the States (2018), many state-aid policies are not linked to a high school graduation date, but some have eligibility restrictions based on high school graduation. For example, Arkansas' Academic Challenge Scholarship requires students to have graduated within 18 months to be eligible, Georgia's HOPE scholarship requires students to have graduated high school within 7 years to be eligible, and Indiana's 21st Century Scholars program requires recipients to have graduated from high school within 1 year to be eligible. These time restrictions could disproportionately influence transfer students for two reasons. First, community colleges serve many adult students who do not go to college immediately after high school (Cohen et al., 2014). Age restrictions will exclude these students and transferring to a 4-year institution will be more expensive simply because an individual decided not to attend college immediately after high school. Second, as has already been established, community college students and prospective transfer students are likely to attend part time, which extends their time to a bachelor's degree. This extended time to degree may disqualify students for a state aid program if it extends beyond the time frame established in the eligibility requirements.

These two examples illustrate ways that existing policies indirectly affect transfer students, but there are some direct ways in which transfer students are affected by state-aid policies. Most notably, many state-aid policies do not specifically incentivize students to transfer. However, a few states do have state-aid programs that are targeted specifically toward transfer students (Long, 2005). For example, Maryland's Hope Community College Transfer Scholarship is a state need-based and merit-based grant program targeted toward community college students who complete an associate degree at a Maryland community college and transfer to a public or private nonprofit 4-year Maryland university (Maryland Higher Education Commission, 2019). The grant provides up to $2,000 per year, and students can receive the award for up to 3 years or six semesters. Students must maintain full-time enrollment and a GPA of 2.5 in order to requalify for the grant. Although there are not many state-aid programs like Maryland's, these programs are promising and address critical affordability concerns experienced by many community college transfer students.

Institutional Aid

As noted previously, institutional aid represents the largest proportion of financial aid distributed to students—44% according to the College Board (2018b). However, as Fernandez and Fletcher's (2014) research demonstrates, it is likely that transfer students benefit less from institutional aid than non-transfer students. This is explained, in part, by an institutional strategy that uses aid to compete for and attract students coming directly from high school. Unlike first-time students, transfer students are not necessarily attractive to many 4-year institutions because they do not contribute to institutional rankings such as *U.S. News & World Report* rankings (Morse et al., 2019). Transfer from a low-price community college to a high-price 4-year university can be a significant financial lift. We do not have good evidence on how much institutional aid is directed to potential transfer students. However, there are examples of institutions that offer financial incentives to transfer students to help reduce the cost burden.

One example is the Community College Transfer Scholarship Program offered by Stephen F. Austin (SFA) State University in Texas. The scholarship is automatically awarded to all admitted community college transfer students if they meet a certain GPA requirement and community college credit requirement. Students receive $1,000 per year if their community college GPA is between 3.0 and 3.49, and they receive $2,000 if their GPA is 3.5 or higher. Students must also complete 45 transferrable community college credits. The GPA and credit parameters will likely exclude some community college transfer students, but the transfer scholarship offers prospective community college transfer students a financial incentive to transfer to a 4-year university. Another important feature of the scholarship program is that it is available to students if they transfer in the fall or the spring.

Iowa State University (ISU) offers a scholarship like SFA, although there are some important differences. The scholarship is a need-based and merit-based scholarship that varies between $500 and $2,000. Like SFA, students must have completed 45 transferrable credits with a minimum GPA of 3.0. ISU's scholarship differs from SFA's in that the scholarship is competitive and not automatically awarded to students. ISU also restricts the scholarship to students who enroll full time at ISU.

Institutional aid and scholarships suffer from some of the same weaknesses that admissions processes do, particularly at selective institutions or 4-year institutions that are not open access. That is, early application deadlines in late fall or early spring will exclude students who might want or need to transfer at a later point during the academic year. Research suggests that many students transfer for personal reasons (U.S. Department of Education, 2017), so it is likely that many students would miss admission and scholarship deadlines and not have access to these scholarships. Further, some institutions have priority admission deadlines and the availability of scholarships is limited to students who meet those priority deadlines. This can further restrict institutional aid from prospective transfer students who have not yet decided to transfer or who just do not yet know they need to or want to transfer.

Revamping Aid to Support the Mobile Student

This last section of the chapter offers recommendations for how the financial aid system could be changed to better support students who transfer and students who are mobile. Some recommendations in the following list are more easily implemented than others, but they are all solutions that can better accommodate the realities of the many mobile students in American higher education. The recommendations begin at the institutional level and include those that are most easily addressed and implemented by institutional leaders. Following the institutional-level recommendations are recommendations at the federal and state levels. Although institutional leaders may not be able to directly implement these recommendations, they should be aware of what changes are needed at the federal and state levels to better support mobile students. And they should be able to advocate for these changes to federal and state lawmakers.

Recommendations Related to Institutional Aid

- *Create transfer-specific institutional aid scholarships.* This recommendation encourages 4-year institutions to create specific scholarships for community college transfer students, like the previous examples from SFA and ISU. Transfer student scholarships offer a financial incentive for students to transfer and signal to prospective community college transfer students that they are welcome at the 4-year institution. However, institutions also face difficult choices in designing scholarship eligibility criteria because these criteria can systematically disadvantage some transfer students. Institutions should consider establishing broad criteria with no GPA caps and apply scholarships automatically so transfer students do not have to navigate another application process as they transfer to a new institution.

- *Offer a late admission and scholarship deadline specifically for transfer students.* Many students transfer because of personal reasons, and the timing of their decision to transfer does not always align well with early admission and scholarship deadlines. Institutions need to create a late admissions and scholarship deadline, ideally in the summer, for which only transfer students are eligible. This would provide more flexibility to transfer students and support the financial feasibility of transfer for many students who pursue both vertical and lateral transfer pathways. A late admission and scholarship deadline would also create the need for other late deadlines such as housing, registration, orientation, advising, and work-study opportunities; transfer students should not lose access to other critical services just because they do not have the luxury of planning their transfer almost a year in advance. This change would also require institutions to plan and reserve residence hall space, seats in courses for late admits, and work study funds and opportunities, for example.

- *Create an aid package guarantee for transfer students.* An aid package guarantee for transfer students could work by institutions promising to match the institutional aid package of students' prior institution. This guarantee would require 4-year institutions to validate transfer students' institutional aid at the 2-year institution, so it would require a partnership with the 2-year institution and perhaps an extra administrative step. However, a guarantee would reassure and signal to students that they can transfer and complete a bachelor's degree without paying a financial penalty in the form of lost institutional aid.

- *Develop and offer financial aid support services for transfer students.* As highlighted in this chapter, the financial aid process is messy and complex. Prospective transfer students do not just need more information about financial aid, they need support applying for and navigating the financial aid process. Thus, 4-year and 2-year institutions need to partner to develop and offer financial aid support services for transfer students prior to transfer. Ideally, these services should be offered on both 2- and 4-year campuses and proactively help students complete the FAFSA, apply for institutional aid (if applicable), apply for external scholarships, and navigate other barriers to paying for college.

As previously noted, there are several issues with the structure of federal aid that disadvantage transfer students who are mobile. The following recommendations address federal financial aid. They are offered to institutional leaders who should advocate for these policy solutions to their federal policymakers:

- *Reconceptualize the federal aid system to accommodate transfer and mobile students.* This recommendation is broad in that it prompts a reform to the entire federal aid system and will require calling for direct actions by policymakers to change laws. The existing system was developed on the assumption that students would begin and complete college at one institution. This supposition manifests itself in the current financial aid structure whereby individual institutions assess and award federal aid locally. However, over the course of a students' collegiate career, about half will attend more than one institution. Any changes to federal aid must first require policymakers and reformers to reconceptualize the system so it is not based on one single institution, but rather a collection of institutions. That is, policymakers need to understand and must begin from the assumption that students do not just attend one institution during their undergraduate career or even within 1 year of their undergraduate career.

- *Create state or regional entities that are responsible for federal aid assessment and disbursement.* This solution would centralize the assessment and disbursement of federal financial aid among large numbers of institutions at either a state or larger regional level. This is a student-focused solution that would reduce steps for students as they navigate multiple institutions during either a midyear transfer or if they decide to co-enroll. This recommendation would have trade-offs, including reducing some institutional autonomy, and it would be a massive change in federal aid practices. Similarly, it would require coordination among institutions and a centralized agency. However, it could greatly benefit students by streamlining processes and institutional bureaucracy. It would address issues related to notification of student transfer and consortium agreements, for example. Although many students transfer across state lines or outside of a major geographic region, it is likely that many students transfer within state or in a nearby geographic region.

- *Create exemptions to federal financial aid eligibility for students who lose credits.* Students should not be penalized for losing credits, and federal regulations could be created that allow students an exemption to federal financial aid eligibility limits if they lose a significant number of credits because of inadequate articulation policies. These exemptions could include an extension of the maximum Pell grant, an increase in the maximum federal loan limits, and an increase in the maximum time frame. Implementation of this change at the campus level would likely require collaboration between (a) transfer admissions counselors who would need to establish criteria around credit loss and automatically assess credit loss for transfers and (b) the financial aid office that would need to adjust federal financial aid eligibility.

Changes to financial aid at the state level have the potential to impact students in a significant way, perhaps more so than changes at the federal level. The following list includes recommendations for state financial aid. Similar to the federal aid recommendations, these recommendations are offered to institutional leaders who should advocate for these policy solutions to their state policymakers:

- *Assess and modify existing aid programs to ensure they do not negatively influence transfer students.* Many existing state-aid programs were not designed with the transfer student in mind. State-aid policies that restrict eligibility to students who only enroll full time or who recently graduated high school likely disadvantage students who transfer. States should assess how these policies influence transfer students and either eliminate these eligibility requirements or create new provisions that better accommodate transfer students. For example, if students transfer and must move from full-time to part-time enrollment, a part-time transfer exemption could be created so students are not unintentionally harmed by transferring.
- *Create transfer-specific state-aid programs.* Similar to the examples provided in this chapter, if states are committed to increasing vertical transfer and not penalizing transfer students, they should invest in reducing the price for students who often encounter 4-year tuition prices that are two or three times higher than the tuition they pay at a community college. The challenge with creating a transfer-specific aid program is establishing eligibility parameters around which students are worthy of a transfer scholarship. Advocates for these policies should aim for broad inclusion/eligibility criteria so as to not systematically disadvantage some students over others.
- *Discount tuition for students who co-enroll.* Many students enroll at more than one institution, which means they pay different tuition prices. States could develop policies that subsidize students and/or institutions for any lost tuition revenue so that students would not have to pay two different tuition prices.

Conclusion

As the price of college continues to increase for students and families, it is more important than ever for institutions to help students meet their financial need. Transfer students are no exception and face specific challenges that 2- and 4-year institutions need to address in order to affirm their commitment to transfer students. This chapter provides institutional leaders an assessment of these challenges and offers some concrete, transfer-friendly solutions to help support transfer students.

Discussion Questions

1. Why is financial aid important to transfer students, and how does financial aid impact student success?

2. What institutional, state, and federal policies create barriers for transfer students?

3. What specific policy changes can institutional leaders make and/or advocate for at the institutional, state, and federal levels?

References

Angrist, J., Autor, D. & Hudson, S. (2014, December 31). *Leveling up: Early results from a randomized evaluation of post-secondary aid.* (NBER Working Paper No. 20800). National Bureau of Economic Research.

Castleman, B. L., & Long, B. T. (2013). *Looking beyond enrollment: The causal effect of need-based grants on college access, persistence, and graduation* (NBER Working Paper 19306). National Bureau of Economic Research.

Chen, X. (2016). *Remedial coursetaking at U.S. public 2- and 4-year institutions: Scope, experiences, and outcomes* (NCES 2016-405). U.S. Department of Education: National Center for Education Statistics. http://nces.ed.gov/pubsearch

Cohen, A. M., Brawer, F. B., & Kisker, C. B. (2014). *The American community college* (6th ed.). Jossey-Bass.

College Board. (2018a). *Trends in college pricing.* College Board.

College Board. (2018b). *Trends in student aid.* College Board.

Crisp, G. (2013). The influence of co-enrollment on the success of traditional-age community college students. *Teachers College Record, 115*(10), 1–25. http://www.tcrecord.org.ezaccess.libraries.psu.edu/library/Content.asp?ContentId=17156

Crisp, G., Nora, A., & Taggart, A. (2009). Student characteristics, pre-college, college, and environmental factors as predictors of persisting in and earning a STEM degree: An analysis of students attending a Hispanic serving institution. *American Educational Research Journal, 46*(4), 924–942. https://doi.org/10.3102/0002831209349460

Dougherty, K. J., & Kienzl, G. (2006). It's not enough to get through the open door: Inequalities by social background in transfer from community colleges to four-year colleges. *Teachers College Record, 108*, 452–487. http://dx.doi.org/10.1111/j.1467-9620.2006.00658.x

Dowd, A. C., Cheslock, J., & Melguizo, T. (2008). Transfer access from community colleges and the distribution of elite higher education. *Journal of Higher Education, 79*(4), 442–472. https://doi.org/10.1080/00221546.2008.11772110

Dowd, A. C., & Melguizo, T. (2008). Socioeconomic stratification of community college transfer success in the 1980s and 1990s: Evidence from HS&B and NELS. *The Review of Higher Education, 31*, 377–400. https://doi.org/10.1353/rhe.0.0004

Dynarski, S. & Scott-Clayton, J. (2013). *Financial aid policy: Lessons from research* (NBER Working Paper No. 18710). National Bureau of Economic Research.

Education Commission of the States. (2019). *50-state comparison: Need- and merit-based financial aid.* https://www.ecs.org/50-state-comparison-need-and-merit-based-financial-aid/

Fernandez, C., & Fletcher, C. (2014). *Transfer students, financial aid, and a new perspective on undermatching.* Trellis Company.

Fuller, M. B. (2014). A history of financial aid to students. *Journal of Student Financial Aid, 44(1),* 4. http://publications.nasfaa.org/jsfa/vol44/iss1/4

Goldrick-Rab, S. (2016). *Paying the price: College costs, financial aid, and the betrayal of the American dream.* University of Chicago Press.

Heller, D. E. (1997). Student price response in higher education: An update to Leslie and Brinkman. *The Journal of Higher Education, 68*(6), 624–659. https://doi.org/ 10.2307/2959966

Ignash, J. (1997). *Results of an investigation of state policies for the A.A.S. degree.* Illinois State Board of Higher Education.

Ignash, J. M., & Kotun, D. (2005). Results of a national study of transfer in occupational/technical degrees: Policies and practices. *The Journal of Applied Research in the Community College, 12,* 109–120. https://eric.ed.gov/?id=EJ719987

Johnstone, D. B., & Marcucci, P. N. (2011). *Financing higher education worldwide: Who pays? Who should pay?* Johns Hopkins University Press.

Kelchen, R., Goldrick-Rab. S., & Hosch, B. J. (2017). The costs of college attendance: Trends, variation, and accuracy in institutional living cost allowances. *The Journal of Higher Education, 88*(6), 947–971. https://doi.org/=10.1.1.689.2259

Long, B. T. (2005). *State financial aid: Policies to enhance articulation and transfer.* Western Interstate Commission of Higher Education.

Maryland Higher Education Commission. (2019). *2+2 transfer scholarship.* Author. https://mhec.maryland.gov/preparing/Pages/FinancialAid/ProgramDescriptions/prog_2_plus_2.aspx

McPherson, M. S., & Schapiro, M. O. (2002). Changing patterns of institutional aid: Impact on access and education policy. In D. E. Heller (Ed.), *Condition of access: Higher education for lower income students* (pp. 73–94). Praeger Publisher.

Morse, R., Brooks, E., & Mason, M. (2019, September 8). *How U.S. news calculated the 2020 best college rankings. U.S. News and World Report.* https://www.usnews.com/education/best-colleges/articles/how-us-news-calculated-the-rankings

National Association of State Student Grant and Aid Programs. (2018). *48th annual survey report on state-sponsored student financial aid.* Author.

The Pew Charitable Trusts. (2015). *Federal and state funding of higher education: A changing landscape.* Author.

Scott-Clayton, J. (2015). The role of financial aid in promoting college access and success: Research evidence and proposals for reform. *Journal of Student Financial Aid, 45*(3), 7–22. https://ir.library.louisville.edu/jsfa/vol45/iss3/3

State Higher Education Executive Officers Association. (2018). *State higher education finance FY 2017.* Author.

Taylor, J. L., & Jain, D. (2017). The multiple dimensions of transfer: Examining the transfer function in American higher education. *Community College Review, 45*(4), 273–293. https://doi.org/10.1177/0091552117725177

U.S. Department of Education. (2017). *Table 7.2. Percentage of 2003-04 beginning postsecondary students who reported various reasons for transferring from their first institution, by student and institutional characteristics: 2006.* National Center for Education Statistics. https://nces.ed.gov/datalab/tableslibrary/viewtable.aspx?tableid=4292

U.S. Department of Education. (2018). *Federal student aid handbook, 2018-2019* (Vol. 2). Author.

U.S. Government Accountability Office. (2017). *Students need more information to help reduce challenges in transferring college credits.* Author.

7

THE NEED FOR A PRIOR LEARNING ASSESSMENT REVOLUTION TO SUPPORT TRANSFER STUDENT SUCCESS

Kathy Silberman and Rose Rojas

If you always do what you always did, you will always get what you always got.

—Unknown

More than a third of students attend multiple higher education institutions before landing at a transfer destination from which they will graduate with a bachelor's degree, and of those who transfer, over half will do so more than once (Shapiro et al., 2015). According to a 2016 Lumina Foundation report, one in five Americans of working age has some college credit but no degree. Because most college students balance a combination of family responsibilities, work, and schoolwork, students often take longer than initially expected to finish or never complete a college degree. To attract transfer students and help them reach their goals, colleges and universities must acknowledge and address this extraordinary student mobility within the context of degree completion. One currently underutilized transfer strategy is prior learning assessment (PLA).

Defining *Prior Learning Assessment* and Its Benefit for Transfer Students

PLA refers to the postsecondary evaluation of learning that takes place outside of a traditional classroom or online college course setting to determine if the learning experience is at college level, equivalent to coursework offered, and should be awarded incoming credit. This credit may be applied as elective credits or to meet general education or major requirements, either of which can reduce the number of remaining credits a student needs to complete a degree. Historical evidence indicates that World War II veterans earned college credit for military experience (Fain, 2012), and the Council for Adult and Experiential Learning (CAEL) was established in the early 1970s (Klein-Collins & Wertheim, 2013). Although PLA clearly is not a new process, many institutions have yet to develop a timely, clear intake and evaluation process to efficiently deliver the benefits to students.

PLA evaluates what the student has learned, not where the student has learned it or from whom. Advocates of credit through PLA emphasize that students can demonstrate mastery of the learning outcomes for specific courses or groups of courses. This mastery, when demonstrated through an appropriate mechanism and assessed by expert faculty, should be awarded credit for prior learning (Adult Learning Work Group, 2015). The traditional definition of *transfer* impedes student access by focusing solely on transfer credits instead of holistically meeting the learner "where they are" in their educational journey. Through carefully developed, faculty-approved assessment methods and recognition, institutions can create diverse and dynamic pathways that build upon a student's previous knowledge and learning while the students matriculate seamlessly into their transfer destination.

Common types of PLA include college-level standardized examinations, such as Advanced Placement (AP) and College Level Examination Program (CLEP), military training and service, and professional certifications. Less common types, especially at institutions that have not (or not yet) invested the time, effort, and resources to develop a comprehensive PLA program, include institutional and departmental examinations, sometimes known as "challenge" exams, and portfolio assessment to evaluate evidence of college-level learning (see Table 7.1).

Building the Case for PLA

Transfer students are particularly poised to benefit from PLA, as they move from one institution to another for a variety of reasons, accruing credit in segments and aiming to complete a credential. The conventional view of transfer is that students move from 2-year institutions to 4-year institutions as they progress toward a bachelor's degree, which is the case for many. A 2018 National Student Clearinghouse study (Shapiro et al., 2018) found that over 1 million students out of 2.8 million in the 2011 cohort transferred to a different institution within 6 years. Nearly 60% of the students who started at a 2-year institution transferred to a 4-year institution. While this is indeed a common pattern among transfer students, many are moving in different directions, such as from one 2-year institution to another, or from 4-year institutions to 2-year institutions through reverse transfer arrangements, taking summer courses, or because of other financial or academic reasons. And, of course, the editors of this book are arguing for a much more comprehensive definition and understanding of what constitutes the *transfer experience*—namely, the entirety of the educational experience up to, including, and after the actual transfer admissions, acceptance, and articulation process.

TABLE 7.1

Types of Prior Learning

Common types of prior learning include, but are not limited to, the following:

Prior Learning Type	Description
Transfer Credit	Not historically categorized as prior learning because this refers to "traditional" transcript evaluation of collegiate coursework completed in a college setting. May be cataloged at an institutional or statewide level and may include coursework from regionally and nonregionally accredited institutions
Standardized Exams	Common examples include: AP, CLEP, International Baccalaureate (IB), Excelsior/UExcel, Cambridge International Exams, ACT/PEP, DSST (formerly known as DANTES, owned and administered by Prometric)
Military Credit/Training and Service	Noncollegiate military training and service, often evaluated by the American Council on Education (ACE), which publishes credit recommendations for application to formal instructional programs to support military-connected students (National Guard members, reservists, active duty personnel, and veterans)
Corporate Articulation and Workforce Training (Licenses, Certifications, and Other Credentials)	Noncollegiate corporate training, often evaluated by ACE and the National College Credit Recommendation Service (NCCRS), which publish credit recommendations for application to formal instructional programs
Challenge Exams	Challenge exams or customized exams offered by some colleges to verify learning achievement—could be current course final exams or other tests developed by academic departments
Portfolio Assessments	Individualized student portfolio assessments conducted by individual institutions or a third party like CAEL's LearningCounts (national online PLA service)

Student mobility, sometimes called *churn, transience,* or *swirling,* occurs when students change institutions, drop out, or move out and then back into an institution for any period or reason. These terms, used to describe student movement between institutions, define *transfer* as "any change in a student's institution of enrollment irrespective of the timing, direction, or location of the move, and regardless of whether any credits were transferred from one institution to another" (Shapiro et al., 2018, p. 6).

Among these transfer students, but not exclusively, are adult learners who are active in the workforce or military and are seeking higher education for retooling, reskilling, or upskilling in their careers. PLA is especially valuable for adult learners because it allows them to earn credit for what they already know, have done, and can do, and it recognizes their skills and knowledge. It may also reduce costs and students' time-to-degree completion. This value builds confidence, increases positive outcomes, and enhances their ability to connect time spent in the classroom with their professional worlds (CAEL, 2018). Additionally, PLA gives students a path toward the broader benefits of baccalaureate attainment, which go beyond just vocational benefits. Higher levels of education are associated with a well-informed society, better health behaviors, and increased civic participation (Baum et al., 2013).

There are many definitions of the *nontraditional* or *adult learner*, but researchers generally consider age (typically 25 or older) to be the defining characteristic of nontraditional students, along with some or all of the following characteristics: delayed enrollment into postsecondary education, attending college part time, working full time while enrolled in college, being financially independent, having dependents other than a spouse, being a single parent, and/or lacking a standard high school diploma. From 1995–1996 to 2015–2016, at least 70% of undergraduates possessed at least one nontraditional characteristic (Radford et al., 2015). Structured program plans for traditional approaches such as 2+2 transfer models, dual and concurrent enrollment programs, and in-person classroom instruction typically do not address nontraditional needs.

Learner disillusionment with higher education due to rising costs, achievement gaps, and increased employer demands also calls for a more fluid, affordable model to support access and mobility for all. A 2016 Public Agenda research brief reported a "surprising shift" in national public opinion on the importance of higher education in relation to success in the workforce. More than 2,000 Americans, 18 years and older, were surveyed. Between 2009 and 2016, the percentage of people surveyed that believed a college education is necessary for career success fell from 55% to 42%, a notable change considering a steady increase in this belief from 2000 to 2009. Likewise, there was a 14% increase in respondents who said there are "many ways to succeed in today's work world without a college degree" (Public Agenda, 2016, p. 1). Public uncertainty about the value of a degree coupled with increased attention to "21st-century competencies," including knowledge, skills, and abilities (Carnevale et al., 2013, p. 22) provides a perfect opportunity for PLA. Awarding transfer credit for industry-recognized credentials allows students to build on what they know instead of starting from scratch on a degree. Credit awarded for their prior learning can accelerate their time to completion and strengthen or broaden the skills they bring to the workplace.

PLA Principles Are Similar to Those of Transfer Articulation

A strong commitment to transfer articulation embraces the principle that learners should not be required to repeat competencies already achieved. Additionally, seamless transfer is supported by a thorough and professional evaluation of learning, regardless of the modalities used by the source institution to deliver the course material. The same principles apply to PLA.

Two documents are particularly helpful for reference when reviewing articulation policy, both of which present PLA as an integral part of student transfer. The first is the "Joint Statement of the Awarding of Transfer Credit," written by the American Association of Collegiate Registrars and Admissions Officers (AACRAO), ACE, and the Council for Higher Education Accreditation (CHEA). The statement addresses the general principles of transferring and articulating credit (AACRAO et al., 2017). The second is the "Transfer Student Bill of Rights," presented as Appendix A within AACRAO's *A Guide to Best Practices* (2017), which identifies the basic rights of all transfer students. These resources encourage institutions to align transfer policies with their academic missions, make balanced decisions about awarding credit without focusing only on accreditation status, and, in AACRAO's words, "sustain academic quality in an environment of more varied transfer" (p. 3).

Another standard of articulation is that the evaluation of courses submitted by one academic institution (sending institution) for transfer to another academic institution (receiving institution) is based on the content of the course as presented in the sending institution's course description and learning objectives/competencies. PLA can employ comparable tools and standards developed or selected by faculty as content experts to evaluate other forms of college-level learning based on the learning itself rather than the source.

The transfer articulation process should be efficient, predictable, and sensitive to student needs according to the aforementioned joint statement (AACRAO et al., 2017). These practices contribute to a smooth transition from one educational experience or institution to the next. Similarly, developing a comprehensive and structured credit-through-PLA program will improve the intake process by increasing access and supporting credit and learner mobility.

National Workforce and Civic Needs

A strong workforce is vital to our nation's economic prosperity, and it has become more critical than ever that our workforce acquires advanced skills and postsecondary credentials, but in 2015, only 46% of all young adults in the United States had completed an associate degree or higher, and 39% had completed a bachelor's degree or higher (Kena et al., 2015). While 18 of the 30 fastest-growing occupations between 2016 and 2026 will require some type of postsecondary education for entry (U.S. Bureau of Labor Statistics, 2017), the United States ranks 13th among countries in global postsecondary attainment (Lumina Foundation, 2019).

To help postsecondary institutions meet the needs of an educated and credentialed workforce, PLA should be expanded with a focus on assisting working adults wanting to advance in their careers. By using PLA to boost momentum in completing a credential, skilled workers can enter the workforce faster to meet the growing need and projected demand. This situation is beneficial to both students and employers. Students who earn a college degree will earn over $830,000 more during their lifetimes than those with only a high school diploma (Daly & Bengali, 2014), and PLA can help more Americans earn their degrees. Educated citizens help preserve state and federal government funding through increased taxes (on increased income) and less dependence on social services (Baum et al., 2013).

PLA Supports Student Success

The first major multi-institutional study on PLA's effect on student success, reported in 2010 by CAEL, included 62,000 adult learners across 48 postsecondary institutions (Klein-Collins, 2010). This study yielded several important findings. Students with PLA credit are 2.5 times more likely to graduate than their peers without PLA credit—regardless of race/ethnicity, age, financial aid status, or gender. Students with PLA credit also tend to earn higher grade point averages and demonstrate higher persistence rates and a shorter time-to-degree completion.

The study also found that 56% of students awarded credit via PLA earned a postsecondary degree within 7 years, while only 21% of non-PLA students earned a degree. More specifically, 13% of students awarded credit via PLA earned associate degrees, and 43% earned bachelor's degrees. However, among students not awarded credit via PLA, only 6% achieved an associate degree, and 15% achieved a bachelor's degree (Klein-Collins, 2010).

In addition to assisting a general overall student population, awarding credit via PLA was found to support specific subpopulations. For instance, adult learners who were awarded credit through PLA completed degrees at a rate 2.5 times higher than traditional students. Veterans are another subpopulation benefiting from PLA, as two thirds (67%) of students with military service histories earned PLA credit compared to only two fifths (40%) of students coded as nonmilitary. Particularly noteworthy was the finding that Latinx students awarded credit via PLA earned bachelor's degrees at a rate nearly eight times higher than that of Latinx non-PLA awarded students (Adult Learner Work Group, 2015). In a follow-up study that focused on Latinx students' experiences with PLA, the authors stated, "Latinx students were more likely to earn PLA credit in the area of foreign language" (p. 2) and "Both institutional representatives and Latinx students discussed PLA as a practice that empowers [them] and validates [their experience]" (Klein-Collins & Olson, 2014, p. 4).

Challenges

PLA has the potential for far-reaching benefits for a huge swath of the transfer student population. However, many institutions seem reticent to fully embrace and develop PLA procedures and policies. In the following section, we enumerate and address several of these concerns.

Concerns About Impact on Accreditation

Despite all of PLA's benefits and its longevity in higher education, many institutions assess prior learning from only a limited scope of sources and allow only limited applicability of credit. Many institutional stakeholders hesitate to implement PLA or widen the scope of PLA due to potential implications to their accreditation status;

however, accreditors recognize that each institution is responsible for determining its policies and practices about the award of credit.

In the research brief, "Holding Tight or at Arm's Length: How Higher Education Regional Accrediting Bodies Address PLA" (CAEL, 2014), the role of regional accrediting organizations in shaping institutional PLA policies and practices was explored. CAEL found that all regional accrediting bodies address experiential or PLA in their policies or guidelines and state that prior experiential learning is comparable to institutionally provided learning experiences. There are notable differences between the accreditors' approaches, however. Some of the accreditors' policies emphasize institutional decision-making (e.g., Higher Learning Commission, Southern Association of Colleges and Schools Commission on Colleges), while others are more prescriptive (e.g., Middle States Commission on Higher Education and New England Association of Schools and Colleges).

According to the Accrediting Commission for Schools-Western Association of Schools and Colleges and the New England Association of Schools and Colleges transfer credit policy, PLA policies should encompass learning attained in extra-institutional settings in addition to accredited postsecondary institutions. In deciding upon the award of credit for extra-institutional learning, institutions may find the services of the ACE's College Credit Recommendation Service helpful. One of the service's functions is to operate and foster programs to determine credit equivalencies for various modes of extra-institutional learning. Similarly, the Middle States Commission on Higher Education provides guidelines for transfer and experiential learning and their respective implementations. The evaluation of learning is based on outcomes, using valid measures such as third-party review by qualified reviewers and recommendations from organizations experienced with such evaluations (e.g., ACE, CAEL).

Transfer Credit Bias

While an institution can apply PLA decisions toward degrees and credentials, when the student transfers credit earned through PLA, it may be denied at the receiving institution based on the origin of the credit. Policies and practices that have been in place for many years should be regularly reviewed to ensure they reflect and adequately serve today's population of mobile learners. Increasingly, students attend multiple institutions (regionally and nationally accredited) before graduating. The ability to transfer credits has taken on added importance because there are so many more of these mobile students and the nature of institutions they attend varies more widely. To attract transfer students and help them attain their goals, public institutions must develop ways to support this student mobility and must thoughtfully manage the broader implications—particularly when many students bring nationally accredited coursework to the table.

Typically, postsecondary institutions evaluate transfer credit and PLA from its source, using their own institutional standards. They do not automatically accept a sending institution's evaluation of credit. Therefore, the contributors of this chapter suggest that 2-year and 4-year institutions have the same authority when they are acting as receiving institutions. Just as community colleges and universities develop articulation agreements to align curriculum and help students maximize transfer applicability, collaboration on PLA outcomes would be helpful to transfer students as they move from one institution to the next.

Students who attempt to transfer from nationally accredited institutions (e.g., the Accrediting Council for Independent Colleges and Schools [ACICS]) or institutions with "specialized" or "programmatic" accreditation (e.g., American Bar Association, American Dental Association, Commission on Dental Accreditation, National League for Nursing, etc.) into regionally accredited institutions are often excluded through traditional transfer policies and practices. This problem is expected to grow with an increase in postsecondary school closures nationwide. According to an article in the *Chronicle of Higher Education*, "How America's College-Closure Crisis Leaves Families Devastated" (Vasquez & Bauman, 2019), an analysis of federal data shows that, in the last 5 years, more than 1,200 college closures (an average of 20 closures per month) displaced about half a million students. Among the contributing factors were falling enrollment and increased enforcement of programmatic accreditation and standards to protect students from fraudulent conduct at some institutions. In recent years, the U.S. Department of Education's recognition of the ACICS as an accrediting agency has fluctuated (recognition revoked in 2016 and restored in 2018 while federal review continues). The 2016 action against ACICS impacted more than 245 career-oriented colleges, most of them for-profit institutions, many of which closed their doors. These closures plunge students into an unexpected crisis that can derail their higher education pursuits and often leave them in debt.

Higher education can help keep students on the path to graduation by increasing access through evaluation and recognition of all types of credit. Transferability of credit between regionally and nationally accredited institutions continues to be an unresolved issue. Schools routinely evaluate prior learning, including academic coursework, from other similarly accredited institutions because of long-standing, consistent curricular standards. The inter-institutional comparability of the coursework is ensured by quality assurance processes based on peer review. However, students attempting to transfer from non-regionally accredited institutions like the Accrediting Commission of Career Schools and Colleges or the Accrediting Council for Continuing Education and Training have complained of denial of transfer credits based solely on their sending institution's accreditation—without their coursework ever having been evaluated. Certainly, the receiving institution may consider the sending institution's type of accreditation when deciding which credits to accept from transfer students; however, in most cases, receiving institutions base decisions on whether to even evaluate the credit solely on accreditation status. By automatically ruling out coursework from non-regionally accredited institutions, colleges and universities are disregarding a student's academic record and potential. It is counterproductive practice for institutions to assume students with inapplicable credit and unrecognized college-level learning will always be willing to backtrack, or even start over, on a degree program. The full impact of these policies and practices both on students' lives and college/university enrollment may never be determined unless institutions collect or track data specific to non-transferable credits.

Negative Perception of Prior Learning From External Sources

Many colleges and universities undervalue what incoming students bring with them, in terms of viable credit, if they don't have traditional transfer credit on a college or university transcript that is evaluated and deemed directly equivalent. Methods and types of college-level learning other than articulated traditional transfer credit are rarely, if at all, discussed with students during the matriculation process. Degrees often require internships and other field-specific, practical experience. However, institutions are often less accepting when students have otherwise parallel prior learning from sources other than colleges and universities and are trying to apply it to a degree program. This is a missed opportunity for students and institutions; evaluating these external sources of prior learning using the same standards as field experience in an academic program (e.g., classroom experience required for a teacher education course) would increase access and momentum for students, and enrollment for institutions.

There is a need to shift from the traditional view that college credit can only be earned in a traditional or online learning environment to create various access points for pathways to a degree or certificate. Furthermore, institutions must move away from narrowly defining *prior learning* as learning a student has acquired outside of a formal college course. Prior learning within a framework that facilitates student and academic mobility should include all types of demonstrated college-level learning for which credit can be awarded. Demonstrated learning is differentiated from work or life "experience" obtained in noncollegiate settings.

Effective use of PLA requires shared responsibility. Students with college-level courses in high school, military experience, corporate training, or professional certification may have verifiable college learning but may not realize they can earn college credit for it, so it is important for admissions, advisement, and other enrollment services staff to ask students questions that help reveal the potential for credit for prior learning. If there is potential, institutions should provide clear instructions on the administrative processes involved and be able to explain potential outcomes to students. Likewise, students need to be empowered and forthcoming about prior learning experiences they think may qualify for assessment and follow through with the institution's evaluation process. Students who plan to transfer after prior learning is assessed at one institution should become familiar with both institutions' PLA policies because prior learning may be evaluated, transferred, and applied differently at different institutions.

Because implementation of PLA has implications for not only students but also multiple areas of the institution (e.g., admissions and records, advising, instruction faculty, student services, business services), there is a need to build broad, cross-institution/campus communication, buy-in, and support for PLA. However, there are several misconceptions about PLA that still exist, such as the following: PLA is a way for students to "buy credit," students who are awarded PLA credit are not prepared for more advanced study at a college or university, PLA will decrease enrollment in certain classes, and PLA students have low success rates. Other concerns about implementation include inconsistent offerings, lack of institutional awareness and promotion, risks that an expansion of PLA would outweigh the benefits, and the difficulty of making changes to long-standing business practices. Therefore, it is vital to collect and share data from institutions that regularly assess prior learning and supporting organizations, such as CAEL. Using data and research to help address these concerns and benchmark progress can yield additional data to support growth for PLA. For example, the 2010 Klein-Collins study presented data dispelling a common concern from faculty and administration that students awarded credit through PLA will take fewer courses from the institution. Contradictory to this belief, students awarded credit via PLA persisted from year-to-year at a higher rate than students without PLA and completed, on average, nearly 10 more credit hours (separate from the credit awarded via PLA) at their college or university. CAEL's website (cael.org) hosts a significant amount of research from a variety of authors to address concerns and misconceptions about PLA.

Recommendations to Revolutionize PLA at Your Institution

If institutions are going to help their students maximize the benefits they can receive from PLA, there are several potential steps they can make toward this reality. In this section, we provide some recommendations—some of which may be low-hanging fruit—with which institutional decision-makers can engage.

Analyze the Current PLA Infrastructure

Although most colleges and universities have mechanisms in place for assessing learning gained outside the institution, that fact is not always well known within the institution and among the various stakeholders. Therefore, a strategic first step in building a sustainable infrastructure is to conduct an audit to assess awareness, perceptions, and knowledge of PLA within the organization. An inventory tool (see Table 7.2), is provided to assist with this effort. The inventory is designed to help institutions begin the dialogue about improving access, momentum, and degree completion utilizing PLA. Policy, process, resources, and reporting are examined using this inventory tool. Additionally, the audit will help institutions understand their strengths, weaknesses, opportunities, and threats related to PLA. By going through this exercise, key stakeholders can identify gaps readily before embarking on the pursuit of PLA—avoiding common strategy execution missteps and pitfalls like wasted time, frustration, lost momentum, and lack of engagement. Most postsecondary institutions will realize that their organization is not equipped currently to implement PLA effectively, efficiently, and successfully, so it is important to establish the necessary conditions first for PLA to thrive.

Engage Faculty and Staff

Because students may be unaware that they can receive credit for their learning outside the collegiate setting, it will be necessary to increase communication about PLA policies and practices among internal constituencies that work with students.

TABLE 7.2
PLA Inventory: A Self-Assessment Worksheet for Institutions

The following inventory is designed to help institutions audit their PLA practices and stimulate dialogue about improving access, momentum, and degree completion through PLA. Consider the following PLA-focused services, policies, business practices, and partnerships listed within a five-step process to implement and/or expand PLA:

Step One: Discuss and document the current state of the action items in the inventory.
Step Two: Determine institutional priorities and goals among the action items in the inventory, and delineate any preliminary or follow-up tasks necessary for successful implementation.
Step Three: Assign tasks to appropriate and invested personnel at your institution.
Step Four: Assess progress (throughout and after step three), then report results to your university or college community.
Step Five: Reassess goals and develop a plan for continued progress.

PLA Services for Students	○ Oversight and location for PLA are established. ○ Brochures, online information, and so on, are available and easily accessible to students seeking PLA options and staff who are in direct contact with students who PLA may benefit. ○ PLA application materials are shared with students during the matriculation process. ○ Equivalencies established through PLA methods are available online and are regularly maintained and updated. ○ Advising personnel and/or faculty inform students about PLA opportunities during first-year orientation and other workshops and meetings for incoming students. ○ A portfolio-building course is offered for credit. ○ Workshops are scheduled at various times to inform students about PLA possibilities. ○ Prospective students are invited to campus to meet with faculty/staff and learn about PLA options. ○ The fee structure is reviewed and revised as needed to include different types of PLA. Fees charged for assessment are based on the services performed in the process rather than the credit awarded. ○ There is a system for accepting and transcribing PLA quickly and in a timely manner.
Institutional PLA Policies, Practices, and Assessment Standards (Adapted from CAEL's Key Assessment Standards)	○ Formal PLA policies are listed in the official catalog and publicized to students. ○ Evaluation processes, systems, and/or pathways are in place to ensure that learning is of high quality and aligned to transparent, assessable learning outcomes, and that the credit has the potential to be applied toward a degree or certificate (not just toward elective credits). ○ Clear policies and related guidelines for assessing transfer credit and PLA evaluation requests are developed by faculty and shared with staff.

(Continues)

TABLE 7.2 (*Continued*)

	○ PLA training workshops and professional development opportunities are regularly provided to personnel who assist students with PLA requests. ○ PLA evaluations are conducted by designated trained personnel. ○ Baseline data are collected on PLA and its outcomes for students and shared with key stakeholders. ○ PLA decisions are documented on students' transcripts. ○ Credit or competencies are awarded only for evidence of learning, not for experience or time spent. ○ Assessment is integral to learning because it leads to and enables future learning. ○ Assessment is based on criteria for outcomes that are clearly articulated and shared among constituencies. ○ The determination of credit awards and competence levels are made by appropriate subject matter and credentialing experts, and any denial of credit has a clear and valid explanation. ○ Assessment advances the broader purpose of equity and access for diverse individuals and groups. ○ Institutions proactively provide guidance and support for learners' full engagement in the assessment process. ○ Assessment policies and procedures are the result of inclusive deliberation and are shared with all constituencies. ○ All practitioners involved in the assessment process pursue and receive adequate training and continuing professional development for the functions they perform. ○ Assessment programs are regularly monitored, evaluated, and revised to respond to institutional and learner needs.
Inter-Institutional and Industry Partnerships and Collaboration	○ Ongoing collaboration occurs among statewide transfer partners to work toward alignment and transferability of PLA decisions. ○ Institutional policies related to PLA at 2- and 4-year colleges in the state are jointly monitored. ○ Exam score credit equivalencies (for CLEP, AP, and similar exams) are annually reviewed to support alignment of credit awarded. ○ Industry training and/or certification programs are considered for PLA along with opportunities to onboard employees as students pursuing further education. ○ PLA is included in discussions regarding partnerships between institutions and industry and explored as a strategy to recruit students and/or increase momentum toward degree completion.

Faculty and staff may be equally unaware of PLA's benefits and availability, especially at institutions with newly implemented or improved PLA services. Faculty engagement in the development, implementation, and expansion of PLA is paramount for this infrastructure to be successful. Because faculty play a central role in effective PLA implementation, institutions must involve faculty in the design, development, delivery, and evaluation of any PLA program. Therefore, there will be a need to develop strategies specifically for faculty participation and engagement. Successful practices include building a PLA knowledge base among faculty, providing ongoing training and professional development, and incentivizing faculty to participate in PLA training and to serve as an evaluator. Sharing positive results from PLA, such as an increase in retention, degree completion, and time to completion, may foster interest among faculty who are critical or not aware of PLA.

While faculty are the drivers of assessment, PLA staff and areas such as advisement, admissions, enrollment services, and marketing should take the lead on promoting PLA services to students and guiding them through the process. Multiple areas such as academic affairs, student affairs, student success, and marketing and outreach must partner on the creation of a robust, sustainable PLA model.

Onboard Students Onto Guided Pathways Using PLA Methods

The national movement toward a guided pathways approach as a strategy to improve student momentum and degree completion, reduce college debt, and prepare for in-demand careers easily dovetails with PLA services. One of the design principles of a guided pathways model is to simplify choices for students, requiring them to select a program of study early in their college experience. As students progress through their programs, intensive support services are provided to support timely degree completion (Jenkins, 2014). One of the first support services for students with prior learning can be to build a bridge to college by using PLA as part of the initial student transition into the institution. In addition to potentially providing a head start on a degree, credit awarded through PLA may help a student decide which program to pursue in the first place. Alternately, awarding PLA credit toward general education or beginning major courses may allow the student some extra "room" within the degree to fine-tune interests and career goals into a realistic plan. Therefore, it is essential to include prior learning in early advising, orientation, and enrollment conversations with incoming students to identify potential credit opportunities from a variety of sources. This should include coursework from other institutions, international credit, college credit earned in high school, and any other sources of prior learning.

Institute a PLA Center for New and Reentry Students

PLA services are often limited in scope and implemented in multiple departments within an institution, which can be problematic for students trying to find information. For example, a typical scenario may include the following steps: The student asks an advisor about how their prior learning can be applied to a degree; the advisor refers the student to an academic department or admissions for evaluation; the student pays a fee for assessment; the student orders proof of the prior learning (e.g., certification, examination) to be sent to the institution for evaluation; the student goes back to the advisor or admissions to find out how the credit applies. These steps are not necessarily clearly defined, nor do they take place in a specific order. Furthermore, while students are going through this process, they may be delaying course registration in the hope that some requirements may be met through PLA, or by selecting courses to meet requirements they later learn would have been met through PLA. In the absence of an institution's "ownership" of PLA, the process and policies involved are left unclear and cumbersome.

In contrast, centralization of the PLA function facilitates ease of use for students, advisors, and faculty and creates more coherence and standardization of academic decisions involving PLA. Imagine a "PLA center" model with personnel focused on developing (or improving) the infrastructure needed to facilitate the intake of PLA assisting students with all types of PLA opportunities (e.g., standardized exams, portfolios, military credit) before enrollment. A centralized department for PLA would also serve as an appropriate setting for the evaluation of traditional transfer credit as well, which could shift some admissions and records functions to personnel who would develop a repository of evaluated learning. Channels of communication with faculty would be set up (or strengthened), streamlined, and documented to base decisions on new learning sources, anything not previously evaluated, on the faculty's academic standards.

A center like this would look different at institutions of various sizes, enrollment services models, and financial and human resources capacities. While its primary focus would be different than some typical "transfer centers," there is no reason why the two functional areas could not coexist in the same setting with shared personnel.

Expand Institutional and Statewide Policy to Include Multiple Methods for Awarding PLA Credit

Whether transfer credit resides on its own or under a PLA umbrella, institutions must integrate PLA into transfer policy and practice conversations (institutional and statewide) due to the impact on student and credit mobility. Therefore, another valuable and recommended step in the process is to establish a statewide PLA task force with representatives from community college and baccalaureate-granting institutions. Such a task force would be responsible for coordinating statewide PLA communication and policy discussions tailored to the needs of transfer students. This structured collaboration can be achieved by adopting solutions and business processes built on transparency, standards, and trust. Some suggested task force objectives could include the following:

- Provide greater consistency and transparency of PLA policy and its impact on transfer that help students, staff, and faculty more easily navigate PLA.
- Standardize military credit through the implementation of the ACE recommended credit for military service and provide clear communication to students about how their military experience may apply toward a degree program.
- Facilitate statewide agreement and acceptance of new and existing exams such as AP, CLEP IB, and DSST.

- Review institutional policies and practices to expand PLA access and equity in all its forms through policy changes.
- Keep transfer on the forefront by analyzing restrictive (institutional and statewide) policies prohibiting the use of PLA credit toward degree requirements.
- Identify PLA activities and opportunities where costs can be shared across multiple organizations, such as joint training of PLA advisors or faculty assessors.
- Analyze data to understand trends, particularly related to the use of specific methods of PLA and application to specific degree programs or areas of study.

Establish a Baseline Data Report

Baseline data on PLA—both aggregate and disaggregated by various populations—should be collected and used to set target goals. Outcomes should be shared and discussed with key stakeholders regularly. Suggested research questions could include:

- What are the characteristics of PLA students as compared to students who do not present any PLA?
- Does PLA credit impact degree completion?
- How does persistence compare for students with PLA credit and students without PLA credit?
- Do students with PLA credits have a different time-to-degree than students without PLA credit?
- Do the benefits of PLA credit vary by sociodemographic characteristics (age, gender, race/ethnicity, education level, and military service)?
- Is there a difference in the level of satisfaction with their postsecondary experience between students who do and do not have PLA credit?

A recommended list of data sets to emulate is included in the report, "Fueling the Race to Postsecondary Success" (Klein-Collins, 2010). CAEL collected data from participating institutions on both transfer students and first-time students. Institutions were asked to include the following:

- Matriculation data
- Degree goal and credits needed for that degree (where available)
- Number of transfer credits from other institutions
- Number of PLA credits accepted as transfer credits
- Number of PLA credits earned through a given academic year
- Number of PLA credits earned through an academic year by PLA method (where possible)
- Number of non-PLA credits earned through an academic year, total and by school year
- Degrees earned

- Date degree earned
- Cumulative GPA
- Student demographics: gender, race/ethnicity, age at time of enrollment
- Financial aid status
- Military status

Conclusion: Make It Happen

Institutional policies that support the blanket denial of transfer and PLA credits create barriers to inter-institutional mobility. The failure to consider potentially equivalent courses, even on a case-by-case basis, denies any acknowledgment of individual student achievement and impedes academic progression. Programs of study should allow students to build on their previously established foundation of coursework or prior knowledge rather than force them to redo it. Such policies delay time-to-degree completion and help drive up the cost of postsecondary education. Consequently, some students give up.

Finding any postsecondary institution that would not support ideas of providing access, fostering retention, and increasing completion at their institutions would be virtually impossible. Modernizing PLA practices and policies to meet current students' needs can help revolutionize higher education by impacting all these goals. PLA could be, arguably, one of the most underutilized student success strategy at many of today's institutions. While PLA, in one form or another, appears in every college catalog, many institutions have a long way to go in providing the proper procedures, policies, personnel, marketing, and buy-in necessary for it to reach its potential. Recommended implementation and expansion steps should focus on the following key areas: (a) faculty and staff engagement and development; (b) student outreach and support; and (c) infrastructure, policies, and processes.

Recognizing the potential of PLA within our institutions and building, or expanding, on it could be a key to reaching increased attainment goals and greater learner satisfaction. As transfer advocates and colleagues, we should openly discuss matters affecting transfer with a focus on collaboration to facilitate academic credit, and learner mobility. This collaborative advocacy for the transfer of PLA credit can contribute significantly to larger, collective efforts supporting credential and degree completion. As previously noted, PLA is no longer a new concept, and the time has come to make the promise of PLA become a reality. Transfer access should be for all, regardless of where students begin the path toward completion or how they attained college-level learning.

Discussion Questions

1. Acceptance of transfer and PLA credit are always the prerogative of the receiving institution. Are your institution's prerogatives regarding transfer and PLA credit based on the principles of equity, access, and inclusivity?

2. How can (or does) your institution create equitable access for transfer students with varied sources of prior learning and origin of credit?

3. Is your institution open to redressing long-standing policies and traditional practices in the evaluation of students' prior learning?

4. How can higher education institutions in your state partner to ensure an equitable evaluation process and transferability of credit for students?

5. Does your institution evaluate prior learning/coursework from non-regionally accredited institutions? Is this coursework comparable to other sources of prior learning outside of the traditional classroom at regionally accredited institutions?

6. What institutional policies and practices exist that impede the acceptance and application of PLA credit and non-regionally accredited coursework?

7. In addition to the challenges identified in the chapter, what other difficulties might individuals encounter in pursuit of an institutional PLA strategy?

8. What proportion of your students could be considered nontraditional or post-traditional transfer students, and is your institution positioned to help these students benefit from PLA?

References

Adult Learning Work Group. (2015). *A proposal for the Illinois Prior Learning Assessment Alliance.* Northern Illinois Regional P-20 Network. http://www.niu.edu/p20network/_pdfs/9.9.15-meeting-materials/PLA-Policy-Paper-9.2.2015.pdf_

American Association of Collegiate Registrars and Admissions Officers. (2017). *A guide to best practices: Awarding transfer and prior learning credit.* https://www.aacrao.org/resources/transfer-articulation

American Association of Collegiate Registrars and Admissions Officers, Council for Higher Education Accreditation, & American Council on Education. (2017, October 2). *Joint statement on the transfer and award of credit.* https://www.acenet.edu/news-room/Pages/Joint-Statement-on-the-Transfer-and-Award-of-Credit.aspx

Baum, S., Kurose, C., & Ma, J. (2013, October). *How college shapes lives: Understanding the issues. College Board.* https://files.eric.ed.gov/fulltext/ED572549.pdf

Carnevale, A., Smith, N., Strohl, J. (2013). *Recovery: Job growth and education requirements through 2020.* Georgetown University Center for Education and the Workforce McCourt School of Public Policy. https://cew.georgetown.edu/cew-reports/recovery-job-growth-and-education-requirements-through-2020/

Council for Adult and Experiential Learning. (n.d.). *Ten standards for addressing learning.* https://www.cael.org/ten-standards-for-assessing-learning

Council for Adult and Experiential Learning. (2014). *Holding tight or at arm's length: How higher education regional accrediting bodies address PLA.* https://www.cael.org/pla/publication/holding-tight-or-at-arms-length-how-higher-educational-regional-accrediting-bodies-address-pla

Council for Adult and Experiential Learning. (2018). *Linking public workforce systems and community colleges through prior learning assessment: Learnings from a national pilot project.* https://www.cael.org/workforce-and-economic-development/publications

Daly, M. & Bengali, L. (2014). *Is it still worth going to college?* Federal Reserve Bank of San Francisco Economic Research Department. http://www.frbsf.org/economic-research/files/el2014-13.pdf

Fain, Paul. (2012, May 7). College credit without college. *Inside Higher Ed.* https://www.insidehighered.com/news/2012/05/07/prior-learning-assessment-catches-quietly

Jenkins, D. (2014). *Redesigning community colleges for student success: Overview of the guided pathways approach.* Community College Research Center, Teachers College, Columbia University. https://pasadena.edu/student-success/docs/DavisJenkins-CCRC-Guided-Pathways-Overview-Revised.pdf

Kena, G., Musu-Gillette, L., Robinson, J., Wang, X., Rathbun, A., Zhang, J., Wilkinson-Flicker, S., Barmer, A., & Velez, E. D. V. (2015). *The condition of education 2015* (NCES 2015-144). U.S. Department of Education, National Center for Education Statistics. https://nces.ed.gov/pubsearch/pubsinfo.asp?pubid=2015144

Klein-Collins, R. (2010). *Fueling the race to postsecondary success: A 48-institution study of prior learning assessment and adult student outcomes.* Council for Adult and Experiential Learning.

Klein-Collins, R., & Olsen, R. (2014). *Random access: Examining the Latino student experience with Prior Learning Assessment.* Council for Adult and Experiential Learning.

Klein-Collins, R., & Wertheim, J. B. (2013). Growing importance of prior learning assessment in the degree-completion toolkit. *New Directions for Adult and Continuing Education, 2013*(140), 51–60. https://doi.org/10.1002/ace.20073

Lumina Foundation. (2016). *A stronger nation.* https://www.luminafoundation.org/files/publications/stronger_nation/2016/A_Stronger_Nation-2016-Full.pdf

Lumina Foundation. (2019, July 11). *The economic imperative for increasing attainment.* https://www.luminafoundation.org/facts-and-figures

Public Agenda. (2016). *Public opinion on higher education.* https://www.publicagenda.org/pages/public-opinion-higher-education-2016

Radford, A. W., Cominole, M., & Skomsvold, P. (2015). *Demographic and enrollment characteristics of nontraditional undergraduates: 2011-12. Web tables.* (NCES 2015-025). National Center for Education Statistics. https://nces.ed.gov/pubsearch/pubsinfo.asp?pubid=2015025

Shapiro, D., Dundar, A., Huie, F., Wakhungu, P. K., Bhimdiwali, A., Nathan, A., & Youngsik, H. (2018, July). *Transfer and mobility: A national view of student movement in postsecondary institutions, fall 2011 cohort* (Signature Report No. 15). National Student Clearinghouse Research Center.

Shapiro, D., Dundar, A., Wakhungu, P. K., Yuan, X., & Harrell, A. (2015, July). *Transfer and mobility: A national view of student movement in postsecondary institutions, fall 2008 cohort* (Signature Report No. 9). National Student Clearinghouse Research Center.

U.S. Bureau of Labor Statistics. (2017). *Career outlook, projections of the labor force.* https://www.bls.gov/careeroutlook/2017/article/projections-laborforce.htm

Vasquez, M. & Bauman, D. (2019, April 4). How America's college-closure crisis leaves families devastated. *The Chronicle of Higher Education.* https://www.chronicle.com/interactives/20190404-ForProfit

8

THE JOURNEY OF A TRANSFER STUDENT INTO A COMPETENCY-BASED DEGREE PROGRAM

Michelle Alvarez, Tess Diver, and Jamie Holcomb

Competency-based education (CBE) presents a nontraditional and potentially accelerated pathway to degree completion for transfer students seeking to complete a journey that may have been halted, rerouted, or re-envisioned by the learners themselves (Kelly & Columbus, 2016). The Competency-Based Education Network (C-BEN) defines *CBE* as follows:

> Competency-based education combines an intentional and transparent approach to curricular design with an academic model in which the time it takes to demonstrate competencies varies and the expectations about learning are held constant. Students acquire and demonstrate their knowledge and skills by engaging in learning exercises, activities and experiences that align with clearly defined programmatic outcomes. Students receive proactive guidance and support from faculty and staff. Learners earn credentials by demonstrating mastery through multiple forms of assessment, often at a personalized pace. (C-BEN, n.d., para. 1)

CBE has existed since the 1970s; however, it wasn't until the late 1990s that universities such as Western Governors University (WGU) began to offer CBE degree programs (McDonald, 2018). The number of CBE degree programs increased from just 20 in 2012 to 500 programs and growing in 2017 (Lumina Foundation, 2017a). CBE has been posited by former U.S. Department of Education Secretary Ted Mitchell as "the single-most important innovation in higher education" (Lumina Foundation, 2017a, p. 4), and its growth represents its clear alignment to meeting learner and workforce needs. The alignment to workforce needs tends to appeal to students currently in the workforce seeking to transfer to a highly relevant degree program to advance their career. Two student scenarios are included in this chapter to illustrate the benefits and challenges of the CBE transfer experience.

A survey conducted by Lurie et al. (2019) identified 57 institutions in the United States that offer 512 CBE degree programs. However, 430 of the 501 respondents to this survey reported they were exploring CBE or in the process of implementing it (Lurie et al., 2019). The development of CBE programs is centered on developing competencies and assessing students' mastery of them. Competencies describe the knowledge, skills, and abilities a student must be able to demonstrate at the end of the degree program, often written as a "can do" statement and are developed in collaboration with subject matter experts in industry (C-BEN, 2017). Competencies are also aligned to frameworks such as the degree qualifications profile (DQP), C-BEN's quality framework for CBE programs, and Bloom's taxonomy, which mirrors traditional course development (C-BEN, 2017). The quality of CBE is ensured with the use of frameworks such as these, collaboration with experts in the subject matter, and development of rigorous assessments (Lumina Foundation, 2017b). When transcribed, a student receives a "mastery" grade for each competency, which looks like Figure 8.1 and Table 8.1.

The key differences between a traditional degree program (offered face-to-face or online) and a CBE degree program include how students are graded, the emphasis on the credit hour, and delivery and support mechanisms. Some of the potential differences are listed in Table 8.1. It is important to note that within the context of the CBE movement, advancements are being made every day.

CBE can be implemented within a degree program by embedding competencies into traditional courses, revising traditional degree programs to include competencies aligned with credit hours, or by offering a CBE degree program that uses direct assessment. *Direct assessment* is defined by the U.S. Department in Title 34: Education, Part 668, Subpart A of §668.10:

> Direct assessment of student learning means a measure by the institution of what a student knows and can do in terms of the body of knowledge making up the educational program. These measures provide evidence that a student has command of a specific subject, content area, or skill or that the student demonstrates a specific quality such as creativity, analysis or synthesis associated with the subject matter of the program. Examples of direct measures include projects, papers, examinations, presentations, performances, and portfolios. (U.S. Government Publishing Office, 2006, para. 2)

Figure 8.1. Sample competencies and the course-based transcript.

CBE-DF5   Can recognize the economic, legal, and social issues surrounding the use of information
CBE-ESR1 Can recognize and articulate the ethical and moral implication of an issue

Course	Title	CRD	GRD	GRDPT
SPRING 2019				
COM-126	Intro to Mass Communication	3.00	MA	0.00
ECO-201	Microeconomics	3.00	MA	0.00

TABLE 8.1

Comparing Traditional Education and CBE

	Traditional	*CBE*
Assessment Model	Grades represent average performance in a course	Students demonstrate mastery of competency (Dragoo & Barrows, 2016)
	Students meet course outcomes at different levels represented by grades, must meet at least 60% threshold (Irakliotis & Johnstone, 2014; Lumina Foundation, 2017b)	Must master (prove learning) competencies to pass (Kelly et al., 2016; McDonald, 2018)
	Course outcomes	Competencies (knowledge, skill, ability) (Lumina Foundation, 2017b)
	Transcript with name of course and grade	Transcript lists competencies and second transcript lists courses to which they are equivalent (AIR, 2016)
Delivery and Support Mechanisms	Face-to-face, online	Offered largely or totally online (Dragoo & Barrows, 2016)
	Lectures, discussions, labs, textbooks or courseware within a course	Videos, projects, open education resources, flexible and personalized (Lumina Foundation, 2017b)
	Assessment includes exams or projects within a course (Lumina Foundation, 2017b)	Field authentic assessments, relevant to the workforce, are designed to determine mastery of competencies (Lumina Foundation, 2017b)
	Semester or term-bound	Term structure varies to allow students to progress at their own pace (Lumina Foundation, 2017b)
	Faculty, instructor, academic advisor	Coach, assessment reviewer, curriculum designer (Lurie et al., 2019)
Emphasis on credit hour versus skills acquired	*Time* is defined by the credit-hour (Lumina Foundation, 2017b).	Self-paced so time to degree completion can be reduced (AIR, 2016).

This chapter focuses on the direct assessment model of CBE—as it is a more complex pathway for transfer students. The chapter examines a general overview of CBE students and their journey through a transfer process to include onboarding, advising, mentorship, orientation, and instructional models.

Actualizing a direct assessment CBE program presents many challenges for a traditional institution. Dragoo and Barrows (2016) noted, "Implementing CBE was complex, requiring intricate adaption of administrative processes in the traditional academic system where time is fixed (e.g., quarter/semester) with progress demonstrated in courses, to a CBE system with progress denominated in competencies" (p. 77). The regulatory environment can also be a challenge. Lurie et al. (2019) found that of the 501 institutions responding to their survey, 14% had no interest in implementing CBE. These institutions cited federal student aid and accreditation regulations as top reasons for their response.

Developing a CBE degree program assumes that students are interested in that program, but in one example, McDonald (2018) found that traditional students on one campus were not interested in a self-paced CBE program. McDonald indicated that the campus moved from a direct assessment type model for CBE to developing competency-based credit courses that were an option offered within the degree program. The lack of interest by traditional-aged students is not surprising as CBE tends to appeal to adult learners in the workforce. Furthermore, there is also an assumption that a self-paced degree option could decrease time to degree completion. Dragoo and Barrows (2016) note that the lowering of the cost of a degree requires students to move more quickly through degree requirements. Student pace is very dependent on the motivation of the individual student, which could also lengthen time to degree completion.

One strength of CBE also poses one of its greatest challenges. The customization of competencies by each institution results in a lack of shared currency and impacts transfer credit options. Traditional higher education often has both accreditor requirements and institutional policies that limit the number and types of credit that can be transferred in to a degree program. This is compounded by transcripts that include credits with a grade similar to MA (Mastered) with equivalent courses and competencies. As a result of this customization, many institutions may not accept the transfer of CBE programs into a traditional degree (Baker, 2015). Now that we have explored CBE holistically, we will now look at CBE from the student perspective.

The CBE Transfer Student

The pathway to success for transfer students often is not clear or easily navigated. Students transfer from institution to institution for a variety of reasons; however, not all educational models can meet the diverse needs of the wide spectrum of learners pursuing higher education today. The lure of CBE for transfer students lies in its self-paced, ultra-flexible model and potentially accelerated time to completion, allowing learners to move ahead "based on what they know and can do, rather than time spent in class" (Lumina Foundation, 2017a, p. 2). For transfer students, this is particularly attractive as they often have school loan debt from multiple schools at degree completion. Rivers and Sebesta (2016) noted that at Texas A&M University, "Transfer students entered the CBE program with an average of 87 credits" (p. 1).

An additional benefit for transfer students is that CBE programs are often offered at a lower cost, which can help reduce or limit the amount of debt at graduation (Laine et al., 2015). These attributes make CBE an attractive option for many established learners seeking change.

The changing landscape of higher education, which now encompasses a large adult learner population, has encouraged institutions to consider alternate pathways to a degree such as CBE to meet the needs of these learners (Rivers & Sebesta, 2016). Many transfer students are part of this adult learner population due to an extended amount of time out of school. We will now explore CBE through the lens of the transfer student experience. This journey will cover the student experience from admissions through the onboarding process in their first year of enrollment at a new institution. In particular, potential barriers and policy considerations are investigated to highlight opportunities for institutions to better prepare for this population.

The Journey Begins

Support for the CBE student begins with a strong understanding of the student population—students' needs, their strengths, and their goals. Many CBE students are working adults with prior learning experiences that may include attendance at one or more institutions of higher learning or significant workforce experience (Laine et al., 2015). Kelchen (2015) examined data for nine institutions that enroll a large number of CBE students and found that the CBE model tends to appeal to female adult learners 25 years and older. The CBE learning experience is appealing to the working adult because it ensures that time dedicated to learning is maximized. This enables students to advance at a pace that reflects their knowledge and skills (Laine et al., 2015).

That said, students may bring with them assumptions or understandable anxieties about the CBE experience and the ways will differ from their prior learning experiences, the cost, and its transferability to the receiving institution. The exploration of specific transfer experiences into a CBE program will shed light on the challenges experienced and the supports necessary to complete a successful transfer from one program to the other. One of the most important areas to be considered in supporting CBE transfer students is the examination of policies and practices that encompass the transfer experience. The U.S. Department of Education (2018) outlined a need for higher education to "[e]nable academic and career mobility, including through common sense transfer-of-credit policies" (p. 7). Transfer credit policies have a significant impact on the experience of any student, but can be particularly important when working with competency transcripts and equivalencies.

To help illustrate challenges in the transfer process, two transfer student scenarios, those of Liling and Adrian, will be examined. These two scenarios include a student transferring from traditional experiences (credit hours) to CBE (Liling) and a student transferring from one CBE experience to another (Adrian). The scenarios are based on actual student experiences, but names and some details are changed to protect the anonymity of the students. The scenarios are provided to illustrate the unique challenges to be considered in the CBE transfer process. As CBE expands in popularity, more students may seek out this type of learning experience and make a transition from traditional learning models to the streamlined, personalized pathways of CBE, which makes understanding the transfer process so important.

Liling's Transfer Experience

Liling is a single mother who works rotating shifts as an office assistant in a 24-hour urgent care facility. She often has to decide whether to spend time with family, work extra shifts, complete assignments for her courses, or attend social events. Childcare is a challenge to coordinate for Liling because of her shift work. She is limited to small increments of time in which to complete her studies. She is self-motivated, and her supervisor has encouraged her to finish her degree, which is a requirement for advancement and management opportunities. Many of her coworkers have long assumed she has a bachelor's degree, which has motivated her to pursue competencies and move quickly. She completed some credits toward an associate of arts degree 10 years ago but stopped pursuing her education with the addition of family responsibilities. She is now attempting to transfer these credits to a competency-based bachelor's degree program at her local college.

Liling is transferring to an institution that has worked with the regional accreditor to allow a block credit transfer to satisfy associate degree requirements. Students who meet these criteria can then begin work on their CBE bachelor's degree. After evaluation of her transcript, Liling is informed that the competency-based degree program at the institution will not accept individual transfer credit from her previously attended credit-based program. Liling has completed only some credits of an associate degree. She has not satisfied the block transfer policy and is told by the admissions representative that she has to restart her associate degree within the CBE direct assessment program. Liling must now consider whether to begin her degree program again in the CBE program or return to her previous coursework to finish her credit-based associate degree and transfer these credits in as a block in order to start her bachelor's degree. The variables she must consider are time, cost, and ease or difficulty in meeting program expectations, all which are challenging for adult learners in her situation.

To support students like Liling, institutions should consider the following policies and practices:

- Clear policies regarding the number and types of transfer credits permitted
- Individualized transfer options that are not restricted to block transfer only
- Timely, realistic, and personalized consultation in regard to student transfer options
- Clear timelines for students regarding the evaluation process of previous coursework

Adrian's Transfer Experience

Adrian is 29 years old and has been pursuing a college education on and off over the last 6 years. Because of this, he accumulated a significant amount of school loan debt from multiple institutions, which is now a large contributing factor to his decision-making. He has taken on-campus courses but found that the structured format did not fit with his active social and work obligations. Based on his previous traditional experience, he opted for CBE. Both his work experience and relevant competencies achieved in his CBE coursework led to new opportunities for Adrian. He secured a position in management, which afforded him full benefits, including tuition reimbursement. His new employer has a CBE partnership with a specific provider that offers employee reimbursement for a specific business degree program that is aligned with the organization's goals. Adrian's manager would like him to start this new degree program at the beginning of the fiscal year in 2 weeks. Adrian was informed by the new institution that any competencies he would like to transfer in must be mastered or completed by the admissions deadline. This transfer timeline is challenging for Adrian as he is accustomed to working at a flexible pace. This process forced him to condense his learning into 2 weeks while maintaining his day-to-day work schedule and outside obligations. Adrian was able to fit this work into his busy schedule, and within 2 weeks he mastered the in-progress competencies. His institution was able to provide him with a competency transcript, which he then presented to the new institution for evaluation.

To support students like Adrian, institutions should consider the following policies and practices:

- Clear communication with business partners about deadlines and transfer requirements
- Individualized transfer options that allow for flexibility in transferring to/from a CBE program

As evident in the examples of Liling and Adrian, institutional policy needs to define the conditions of transfer while keeping in mind the impact on the student experience. Having clear policies and procedures in place up front decreases the challenges students face in the transfer process. As noted in the preceding transfer scenarios, obstacles in the transfer process are real and tangible. Because of this, institutions must consider carefully ways to streamline the transfer process and the translation of competencies to credit for students. This might encompass a block credit option or the use of prior learning assessment. The continual evolution of students, student needs, and workforce partnerships make the transfer process an iterative one that must be revisited often.

Onboarding for CBE Transfer Students

After an investigation into the CBE transfer experience from the perspectives of Liling and Adrian, the next important step is to explore what happens after transfer students are accepted and ready to start classes.

When onboarding transfer students into a CBE program, institutions must identify the outcomes of successful onboarding from a student experience perspective. These student-based outcomes serve as a guide against which every process, system, and interaction in the onboarding experience should be measured and either amplified or eliminated. For instance, there are two outcomes to be considered for students transferring into a CBE program: (a) include developing a sense of belonging to the institutional community (i.e., "Am I helping each student integrate into the CBE learning community?") and (b) building confidence and a growth mind-set (i.e., "Am I developing each student's capacity to be a self-directed learner?").

The next section will explore outcomes and their associated interventions.

Extended Advising Model and CBE

The more connected students feel to the institution and the more academically and socially connected they are, the more likely they are to persist (Lopez & Jones, 2017). This is especially critical for transfer students, like Adrian, who have attended several institutions prior to enrolling in a CBE program. There are a number of factors that influence a student's connectedness and belonging to the institution:

- Social relationships with peers both inside and outside the classroom
- Relationships with faculty and staff inside and outside the classroom
- Community engagement
- Social activities, in person or online, synchronous or asynchronous (Lopez & Jones, 2017)

Opportunities for transfer students to engage within their community can be intentionally designed and implemented in either the traditional classroom or online environment. For example, offering online events, clubs, organizations, and groups that are designed specifically to introduce transfer students within CBE programs to each other and to members of the broader student body and institution can greatly assist in the development of a sense of belonging.

An additional component of creating a successful transition to the CBE experience is the leveraging of an extended advising model that continues beyond the CBE onboarding experience. Historically, academic advisors serve both a student support and administrative function within the institution, playing a key role in student satisfaction and persistence (Kot, 2014). Transfer students entering a CBE program may benefit from this extended advising model which encourages self-efficacy and self-directed learning (Kimsey-House et al., 2011).

Within CBE programs, and particularly critical for transfer student success, the advising model may be extended to include elements of coaching such as goal-setting, personal transformation, fulfillment, balance, and understanding the learning process. In this extended model, advisors build trust and openness, identify the transfer students' values and goals, help them persist through obstacles, and cocreate the next right-size learning challenge (Kimsey-House et al., 2011). Because CBE programs are often self-paced, the role of the academic advisor/coach is critical to engaging students in critical thinking and reflection, fostering independent learning and the ability to stay on track to graduation.

For example, an advisor may ask Liling the following questions based on her personal challenges with time management, values, and motivators:

- Where does your CBE coursework fall in your daily/weekly priorities?
- What space do you need to create (physically, mentally, and logistically) to do this work?
- Who in your network can support you?
- What is one resource that would be most helpful but you haven't pursued?
- What is one thing you can do tonight/this week to make progress on your highest priority immediate and longer-term goals?

The advisor would find a convenient time to connect with Liling, and together they would develop a plan to help her meet her goals.

As another example, an advisor may ask Adrian a different set of questions based on his career focus, his expectations about the degree program, and his values. These questions are designed to create openness and transparency in the relationship so that, together, Adrian and his advisor can overcome obstacles to keep him on track toward degree completion. The following questions are not exclusive to work with CBE transfer students and are broadly applicable to other student populations:

- How do you see yourself applying what you've learned here to your personal or professional life?
- What do you expect of yourself? How would you define *success*?
- What accountability plan will feel most motivating for you?
- How will it feel when you accomplish this?

By encouraging students to share openly, dig deeper, and engage in creative problem-solving, Liling and Adrian may experience an increase in their growth mind-set and confidence as their advisor helps them *learn how to learn* in the CBE model. As illustrated, this type of personalized coaching may be especially important for transfer students in CBE programs who question their capability to earn a degree after several attempts at previous institutions and who need to be self-directed.

Peer Mentorship for CBE Students

Another natural extension of the support model in CBE programs is mentorship. One type of mentor, a peer mentor, provides practical advice based on personal experiences to a student mentee who shares common characteristics or is enrolled in a similar program (Beltman & Schaeben, 2012). In one study conducted at a university in California, mentored students reported a significantly greater increase in integration and connection to the university (Yomtov et al., 2017). This study determined that "students with mentors felt significantly more connected to the university, perceived significantly more support at the university, and felt significantly more like an active part of the university than students without a mentor" (Yomtov et al., 2017, p. 38). A peer mentorship intervention strategy may be especially critical for the CBE transfer student's successful integration to the institution. Through a peer mentor, CBE transfer students may learn strategies to stay on track in the self-directed learning experience, to navigate the learning environment, and to connect to other students to build connections. Peer mentors may also support CBE transfer students in becoming self-directed learners by fostering ability and potential and building resilience and confidence to navigate the institutional systems more easily and make the most of their CBE experience. As nontraditional learners increasingly seek engagement and connection within their institutions of higher learning (Meuleman et al., 2015), CBE transfer students benefit from building relationships with mentors inside their program and institution (Lopez & Jones, 2017). For example, matching Liling with a peer mentor enrolled in the same degree program and sharing her challenges of balancing work, family, and school provides a perspective on what it takes to succeed in her CBE program. Adrian, on the other hand, may connect with a peer mentor who has experienced a CBE program and shares his desired career field. This relationship provides Adrian with networking opportunities and advice that he can use throughout his CBE program.

Advisors and mentors provide support, guidance, motivation, and information, all of which serve an important role in helping Liling and Adrian successfully transfer into their new CBE program. This mentorship is especially critical for transfer students who may have attended several institutions previously and, like Adrian or Liling, encountered challenges in making the transition to a new learning model. By building relationships and offering personalized support, mentors can have a positive impact on student engagement, student satisfaction, feelings of support, academic skills and performance, and retention (Kramer et al., 2018).

Personalized Orientation for CBE Students

Creating a successful transition to the institution also encompasses orienting CBE students to their new surroundings and institutional expectations so they can thrive in this self-directed model. Traditionally, entrance orientation covered "topics in regard to college readiness, learning strategies, self-discipline, time management, self-efficacy, technological skills, and expectation setting" (Muljana & Luo, 2019, pp. 31–32). This traditional orientation experience often demands that students complete the experience in one sitting or iteration and rapidly absorb information that may not be relevant at the time of delivery but is designed to serve all students. For CBE transfer students looking for a flexible, self-paced, personalized experience, the entrance orientation should be carefully designed to meet their needs. Some considerations when designing a successful orientation experience for these students include the following:

- Providing content that is relevant and specific to the CBE program and personalized for each learner's unique needs and experiences

- Delivering content in the same learning modality or experience as the CBE program (self-paced, individualized)
- Extending access to content to be available when needed

For example, the institution may want to ensure that every new CBE transfer student receives information about the learning experience, academic expectations, support services, and technology requirements for the CBE learning environment. Students may opt into content that is relevant to their unique experiences, needs, and interests. Liling may be interested in getting math tutoring, finding family-friendly events, and brushing up on her study skills. Adrian, on the other hand, may opt for information around financial literacy and activities aligned with his career goals. Personalizing the orientation experience enables students to opt into personally relevant content, while simultaneously receiving information the institution feels is critical for every student.

Orientation historically takes place prior to the first day of class but, in a CBE learning model, this may not meet the needs of every student. Extending access to orientation content allows students to connect with it *when they need it.* For example, Liling may not need math tutoring until her second term, but with extended access to orientation, she can return for a refresher or engage with relevant content. This "just-in-time" response focuses precisely on what the student needs at that particular time in her/his educational development process. This process is an approach that is increasingly expected by today's consumers (Phelps, 2017) and subsequently impacts students' expectations within their learning environment. By embracing a personalized and accessible orientation experience, all CBE transfer students get the information they want and need in a format that works for them.

Introducing Students to the CBE Learning Model

Many students transferring into CBE, like Liling, will have had no previous exposure to this sort of learning model. One must build this assumption into the early learning experiences and programming for transfer students. Many will have had a traditional learning experience that included regulated homework, deadlines, tests and assessments, a schedule of some sort, a traditional teacher and classroom of peers, and an experience resulting in a clear letter grade as a measurement of mastery. Furthermore, even though a student like Adrian may have had prior CBE experience, models vary from institution to institution. As a learning model, CBE is entirely different than its traditional counterpart with a self-paced schedule (Wang, 2016), project-based learning—a faculty member or reviewer that provides feedback on each competency, and success measured in mastery, which must be achieved before attempting further progress in one's program. This must be described and explained in full for students transferring into a CBE experience. Not knowing what expectations are or what a new experience will be like can create insecurity and anxiety in learners that can impact confidence and self-efficacy (Jobe et al., 2018).

In addition, this model requires an understanding of adult learning theory, which focuses on learning that (a) is relevant to life experiences and prior knowledge; (b) is self-directed, putting adult learners in the driver's seat; (c) is pragmatic in nature, offering real-world value and application of skill learned; (d) encourages critical thinking and reflection, and (e) offers experience-based learning opportunities when possible (Yarbrough, 2018). As highlighted earlier, many CBE students are adult nontraditional learners. Content must include the emphasis of key skills students will need to leverage to find success within a CBE program from start to finish. Skills like time management and communication are especially important for CBE transfer students as they foster both independent learning and the ability to create successful connections.

Content alone, however, will not ensure student success. As with many early programs, students like Liling and Adrian may benefit from a high-touch faculty model, especially in the early months of their academic journey. This model may incorporate the following (with the understanding that institutional structures vary):

- Extensive communication opportunities (either asynchronous or synchronous)
- Robust, supportive, and action-based feedback that encourages students to take advantage of relevant institutional resources
- The encouragement of students to make connections with peers in their program

After students' coursework is successfully transferred and they are accepted to the institution, a comprehensive onboarding experience helps ensure transfer students have not only the tools they need but also holistic wraparound support from day one. Faculty teaching courses within the student's first year of enrollment may serve in the additional roles of coach and mentor, along with their academic responsibilities.

Recommendations

This chapter examined CBE and the transfer process associated with it. We explored the journey of two CBE students moving through the transfer process including onboarding, orientation, and personalized support. The key takeaways from the chapter should include the following strategies to improve the experience for students transferring into a CBE degree program:

- Identify who the students are that transfer into the CBE program—their values, needs, expectations, and challenges.
- Audit to ensure transfer-student friendly policies and procedures are in place.
- Develop onboarding experiences to engage transfer students entering a CBE program whose previous experiences differ from other students.
- Extend advising to include elements of coaching designed to help students learn how to learn in the CBE model.
- Provide peer mentorship opportunities to support students as they transfer into a CBE program.

- Provide a relevant and personalized autonomous orientation experience that extends access to content into the first year of enrollment.
- Introduce a high-touch faculty model in the student's first-year courses.

CBE holds promise for transfer student success, and institutions must be prepared to support students that transfer from or into CBE programs.

As noted earlier, CBE is growing quickly and in a state of continual development, which enables it to remain relevant for both workforce and learner needs. With this understanding, higher education must continually revisit the transfer process as more learners turn to CBE for its career relevancy and the highly tangible nature of the skills gained by students. As more students embrace this type of learning, we must continue to push for more flexibility and transparency in the transfer process to enhance rather than inhibit the student experience.

Discussion Questions

1. Why do you think some of your students would be interested in CBE degree programs?
2. What policy and procedures should be considered to support students who transfer to or from a CBE degree program?
3. What strategies can be used to create a successful onboarding experience for students transferring from a traditional degree program (credit) to a competency-based degree program?

Acknowledgment

A special thanks to Christian Devoe, executive director for Competency-Based Education and Transfer Credit Operations in the Office of the Registrar at Southern New Hampshire University for his contributions to the case scenarios.

References

Baker, R. B. (2015, June). *The student experience: How competency-based education providers serve students*. American Enterprise Institute for Public Policy Research. https://www.luminafoundation.org/files/resources/the-student-experience.pdf

Beltman, S., & Schaeben, M. (2012). Institution-wide peer mentoring: Benefits for mentors. *The International Journal of the First Year in Higher Education*, 3(2), 33–44. https://www.10.5204/intjfyhe.v3i2.124

Competency-Based Education Network. (n.d.). *Competency-based education*. https://www.cbenetwork.org/competency-based-education/

Competency-Based Education Network. (2017). *Quality framework for competency-based education programs*. https://www.cbenetwork.org/wp-content/uploads/2018/09/1st_button_CBE17016__Quality_Framework_Update.pdf

Dragoo, A., & Barrows, R. (2016). Implementing competency-based education: Challenges, strategies, and a decision-making framework. *Journal of Continuing Higher Education, 64,* 73–83. http://dx.doi.org/10.1080/07377363.2016.1172193

Irakliotis, L., & Johnstone, S. (2014). Competency-based education programs versus traditional data management. *EDUCAUSE Review Online.* https://er.educause.edu/articles/2014/5/competencybased-education-programs-versus-traditional-data-management

Jobe, R. L., Lenio, J., & Saunders, J. (2018). The first year: Bridging content and experience for online adult learners. *Journal of Continuing Higher Education, 66,* 115–121. http://dx.doi.org/10.1080/07377363.2018.1469074

Kelchen, R. (2015). *The landscape of competency-based education enrollments, demographics and affordability.* https://www.luminafoundation.org/files/resources/competency-based-education-landscape.pdf

Kelly, A. P., & Columbus, R. (2016). *Innovate and evaluate: Expanding the research base for competency-based education.* American Enterprise Institute for Public Policy Research.

Kelly, M. A., Hopwood, N., Rooney, D., & Boud, D. (2016). Enhancing students' learning through simulation: Dealing with diverse, large cohorts. *Clinical Simulation in Nursing, 12*(5), 171–176. https://doi.org/10.1016/j.ecns.2016.01.010

Kimsey-House, H., Kimsey-House, K., & Sandahl, P. (2011). *Co-active coaching: Changing business, transforming lives.* Nicolas Brealey Publishing.

Kot, F. C. (2014). The impact of centralized advising on first-year academic performance and second-year enrollment behavior. *Research in Higher Education, 55*(6), 527–563. https://doi.org/10.1007/s11162-013-9325-4

Kramer, D., Hillman, S. M., & Zavala, M. (2018). Developing a culture of caring and support through a peer mentorship program. *Journal of Nursing Education, 57*(7), 430–435. https://doi.org/10.3928/01484834-20180618-09

Laine, R., Cohen, M., Nielson, K., & Palmer, I. (2015, October). *Expanding student success: A primer on competency-based education from kindergarten through higher education.* National Governor's Association Paper. NGA Center for Best Practices. https://files.eric.ed.gov/fulltext/ED570497.pdf

Lopez, C., & Jones, S. J. (2017). Examination of factors that predict academic adjustment and success of community college transfer students in STEM at 4-year institutions. *Community College Journal of Research and Practice, 41*(3), 168–182. https://doi.org/10.1080/10668926.2016.1168328

Lumina Foundation. (2017a). *How competency-based education may help reduce our nation's toughest inequities.* https://www.luminafoundation.org/wp-content/uploads/2018/01/how-cbe-may-reduce-inequities-1.pdf

Lumina Foundation. (2017b). *Understanding competency-based education toolkit.* https://www.ecs.org/wp-content/uploads/CBE-Toolkit-2017.pdf

Lurie, H., Mason, J., and Parsons, K. (2019). *Findings from the 2018 national survey of postsecondary competency-based education.* https://www.air.org/sites/default/files/National-Survey-of-Postsec-CBE-2018-AIR-Eduventures-Jan-2019.pdf

McDonald, N. A. (2018). A private, nonprofit university's experience designing a competency-based degree for adult learners. *The Journal of Continuing Higher Education, 66,* 34-45. http://dx.doi.org/10.1080/07377363.2018.1415632

Meuleman, A.-M., Garrett, R., Wrench, A., & King, S. (2015). "Some people might say I'm thriving but . . .": Non-traditional students' experiences of university. *International Journal of Inclusive Education, 19*(5), 503–517. doi: 10.1080/13603116.2014.945973

Muljana, P. S., & Luo, T. (2019). Factors contributing to student retention in online learning and recommended strategies for improvement: A systematic literature review. *Journal of Information Technology Education: Research, 18*, 19–57. http://www.jite.org/documents/Vol18/JITEv18ResearchP019-057Muljana5043.pdf

Phelps, S. (2017, January 27). Mind the customer expectation gap. *Forbes Magazine.* https://www.forbes.com/sites/stanphelps/2017/01/27/mind-the-customer-expectation-gap/#4b051c2a7cb7

Rivers, C., & Sebesta, J. (2016, July 11). Competency-based education and predictive analytics: Learning from transfers. *EDUCAUSE Review Online.* https://er.educause.edu/articles/2016/7/competency-based-education-and-predictive-analytics-learning-from-transfers

U.S. Department of Education. (2018). *Rethinking higher education.* https://www.insidehighered.com/sites/default/server_files/media/White%20Paper%20on%20Rethinking%20Higher%20Education%2012.19.18.pdf

U.S. Government Publishing Office. (2006). *Electronic code of federal regulations (e-CFR) Title 34: Subtitle B Chapter VI Part 668 Subpart A §668.10.* https://www.ecfr.gov/cgi-bin/text-idx?c=ecfr&sid=c6dbf7953117d4ce6c48087ad7c495d5&rgn=div8&view=text&node=34:3.1.3.1.34.1.39.10&idno=34

Wang, J. (2016, January 6). Here is what we learned. [Blog post]. *Competency Works.* Aurora Institute. https://www.competencyworks.org/higher-education-2/we-did-research-on-the-student-perspective-on-competency-based-education-here-is-what-we-learned/

Yarbrough, J. R. (2018). Adapting adult learning theory to support innovative, advanced, online learning—WVMD model. *Research in Higher Education, 35*, 1–15. https://files.eric.ed.gov/fulltext/EJ1194405.pdf

Yomtov, D., Plunkett, S. W., Efrat, R., & Marin, A. G. (2017). Can peer mentors improve first-year experiences of university students? *Journal of College Student Retention: Research, Theory & Practice, 19*(1), 25–44. http://dx.doi.org/10.1177/1521025115611398

9

REVERSE-CREDIT TRANSFER FOR POST-TRADITIONAL TRANSFER STUDENTS

Leading Disruptive Innovation

Debra D. Bragg and Heather N. McCambly

In 2012, an innovation to improve transfer was launched by the Lumina, Kresge, and Bill & Melinda Gates Foundations, eventually attracting three more philanthropic funders: Helios Education Foundation, Greater Texas Foundation, and Strada. Seeking to boost college completion in the United States, the foundations coined the catch phrase Credit When It's Due (CWID) for a 16-state reverse transfer or, what our research team believes is more accurately labeled, reverse-*credit* transfer initiative. Our research team also chose to use the term *reverse-credit transfer* to distinguish this form of transfer from *reverse transfer*, defined by Townsend and Dever (1999) as students physically returning to universities to enroll in community colleges, including after they earned a baccalaureate degree.

CWID encouraged states to modify transfer policies and practices to authorize associate degrees for students who transfer to a 4-year college or university before completing sufficient credits to attain a 2-year degree. By facilitating the transfer of credit earned at the receiving institution back to the community college, students can attain their associate degrees after transferring. By authorizing the transfer of credits back to the community college, this innovation recognizes credit mobility in a way not previously recognized in many state transfer and articulation policies.

By 2017, CWID yielded approximately 16,000 college students who were awarded associate degrees through the adoption of reverse-credit transfer policies and practices by higher education systems and institutions (Wheatle et al., 2017). Seeking to understand this phenomenon, our research team gathered quantitative and qualitative data to document college degree attainment resulting from reverse-credit transfer policies and practices. A key interest of our team was in describing how these policies and practices would address the needs of the nation's increasingly diverse college student population, particularly historically underserved students.

From this perspective, reverse-credit transfer can be considered a form of disruptive innovation (Christensen et al., 2015) because of its focus on expanding an existing market, in this case the associate degree market, by reforming transfer policies and practices in a way that enables more students to benefit. A disruptive innovation takes existing products and increases their perceived value and quality through market expansion (Christensen et al., 2015). Whereas more research is needed to fully address the question of reverse-credit transfer program impact on student outcomes, it is already clear that students who chose to forego the associate degree in pursuit of baccalaureate degrees are taking advantage of this credentialing option in ways not previously possible.

Another feature that aligns reverse-credit transfer with disruptive innovation has to do with the perceived value that the associate degree has to society and the labor market. Associate degrees typically yield less value in the labor market than baccalaureate degrees because, in large part, they are associated with 2 rather than 4 years of study (Carnevale et al., 2011). Although reverse-credit transfer does not completely disrupt this norm, it suggests there may be value to students to secure the associate degree even after they transfer, especially when students fail to complete the baccalaureate degree. Because the economic payoff for an associate degree is substantially greater than for a high school diploma, and because students who do not complete a baccalaureate degree but who complete an associate degree attain economic benefits from the 2-year credential (e.g., see Belfield, 2013), it makes sense to enhance options for transfer students to attain the associate degree en route to the baccalaureate.

Another important lens for our research recognizes the relationship between reverse-credit transfer and degree attainment for America's increasingly diverse college students. As a form of disruptive innovation, the CWID network encourages participating states and institutions to extend their work to other states through modeling implementation and dissemination to spread promising practices and confront detrimental assumptions about college attendance by underserved student groups (Taylor & Bragg, 2015). Recognizing that degree attainment is integrally tied to students' upward social mobility suggests that transfer itself is also fundamentally about social justice (Rosenberg & Koch, chapter 3, this volume). From this perspective, reverse-credit transfer may play a role in overcoming systemic, structural barriers and biases in higher education that propagate differential access to and completion of college credits and degrees by minoritized college student populations.

CWID advances the notion that higher education reform is needed to implement and sustain improved outcomes for degree attainment. By restructuring transfer to allow for the implementation of reverse-credit transfer policy and practice, we increase the pathways by which students can achieve a successful outcome. Whereas the approaches to implementation of reverse-credit transfer vary from state to state, our research shows some states strengthened the capacity of their higher education systems and institutions to support students who move between and among colleges and universities by implementing reverse-credit transfer (Taylor & Jain, 2017). This development is important because multiple institutional attendance patterns are increasingly common among college students, and possibly more so for racially minoritized students (Soler et al., 2018).

Looking at data from the last 20 years, the National Student Clearinghouse estimates that more than 31 million higher education students have accumulated some college credits but no credential in the form of a certificate or degree. Perhaps as many as 1.2 million of these students left college after having completed 2 years of full-time attendance (Shapiro et al., 2014), suggesting a high likelihood of transfer if these students return to college. Undoubtedly some of these students may be potential beneficiaries of reverse-credit transfer. Students who attend college and transfer but do not attain degrees are more likely to be members of underserved student populations than students who pursue traditional college paths (Taylor & Jain, 2017), again suggesting that new transfer patterns involving credit mobility need to be studied and scaled when results show positive outcomes for diverse college learners.

We associate evolving college enrollment and transfer patterns with students who we designate as post-traditional transfer students because these students' characteristics and behaviors demonstrate movement in and out of college, sometimes participating in college in ways that appear counter to (or at least neutral to) vertical transfer and upward progression to degree completion. We acknowledge that our definition of *post-traditional transfer students* draws on prior conceptual work of Excelencia in Education! (Santiago, 2013) and the National Association of Student Personnel Administrators (Smith, 2013) who argue many students enrolled in college today do not fit the label of "nontraditional," which focuses primarily on age. Looking at today's transfer students, students' demographic characteristics, including racial and ethnic identity, gender identity, as well as age, and other attributes are integrally linked to college attendance. As such, we argue *nontraditional* is an outdated conception of transfer identity that should be replaced with the term *post-traditional transfer students* to better represent current student identities and attendance patterns. We contend that higher education systems and institutions that do not consider the ways transfer pathways are evolving run the risk of misunderstanding how transfer is working. They may also reproduce inequities in college access and outcomes for historically underserved students while advantaging White middle- and upper-income students who dominate traditional baccalaureate attainment.

For post-traditional transfer students, the inadequacies of the transfer function that yield inequities in college outcomes may also extend beyond college to employment. Post-traditional transfer students who amass college credits but do not secure degrees are left without a tangible marker to demonstrate the skills and knowledge they mastered in their college education (Bragg et al., 2011). Adding to this concern, these students may also experience student debt that further diminishes the full marketplace value of college completion with recognized credentials (associate and baccalaureate degrees). Employers may be disadvantaged as well, as they struggle to secure qualified employees who reflect the diversity of their customers and constituencies. By better accounting for students' mobility and progression toward degrees, CWID seeks to reform transfer policies and practices in ways that produce more equitable outcomes.

Contributing to our understanding of transfer reform, the implementation of CWID benefited from lessons learned in Project Win-Win, led by the Institute for Higher Education Policy. Project Win-Win focuses on assisting community college students who have left college but who are very close to completion of their associate degrees (Adelman, 2013; Wheatle et al., 2017). Like CWID, Project Win-Win reforms institutional policies and practices to make degree completion more possible by reforming communications, advising, and graduation policies to make associate degree completion possible for community college students who are close to the associate degree finish line.

Another initiative that is closely aligned to CWID and Project Win-Win is called Quality Collaboratives, led by the Association of American Colleges & Universities (AAC&U) (Humphreys et al., 2015). Quality Collaboratives examined structures and processes that contribute to transfer student success using frameworks aligned with student proficiencies and course outcomes. The AAC&U team sought to advance equity in the transfer process by examining the way it functions in selected community colleges and by reframing transfer in terms of student learning assessment, thereby challenging traditional sources of credit. Infrastructures intended to legitimize transfer are particularly prone to leaving student populations historically underserved by higher education uncertain of their options to navigate systems and institutions. For example, students who are the first in their family to attend college, many of whom have limited financial resources, do not understand the complexities of the transfer process and are therefore disadvantaged by a heavily rules-driven system that does not provide adequate advising to ensure that students can participate successfully. The Quality Collaboratives sought to find avenues for deconstructing historical transfer systems by looking at how transfer partners can reassess their criteria and relationships around what students have and need to learn.

Noting the complimentary nature of these various transfer reforms, some of which deliberately recognize the needs and aspirations of post-traditional transfer students, in this next section we delve more deeply into what our research team learned by studying how states affiliated with the CWID network implemented reverse-credit transfer from 2012 to 2017.

Reverse-Credit Transfer Implementation

CWID states chose different policy instruments with which to implement reverse-credit transfer. Some states passed legislation, while others made changes to statewide transfer and articulation agreements, and still others chose less formal routes encouraging change through institution-level routines. Among the CWID states, Colorado, Florida, Maryland, Michigan, Missouri, Oregon, Tennessee, and Texas passed legislation on reverse-credit transfer, generally encouraging reform but holding short of prescribing implementation protocols or performance requirements (Anderson, 2015a, 2015b). By 2015, five more state legislatures passed laws on reverse-credit transfer, again encouraging institutions to adopt this transfer reform without prescribing implementation. Even so, this state legislation was seen as an unfunded mandate in some CWID states, creating concern for the means by which higher education institutions would respond and engage in the reform. To realize the potential to broaden and scale transfer reform, higher education leaders must demonstrate the will to change even when capacity limitations exist. Our research on reverse-credit transfer policy showed states did not mandate a specific model or particular approach to implementation, but state legislation did create momentum to propel state and institutional leaders to engage with reverse-credit transfer policies and practices more expeditiously than in states without formal legislation (Taylor & Bragg, 2015). In fact, state leaders tended to express appreciation for laws to motivate institutions at both the 2-year and 4-year levels to buy in to reverse-credit transfer reform.

Critical Dimensions of Reverse-Credit Transfer

The following critical dimensions emerged in our research on reverse-credit transfer in 15 CWID states: (a) student identification, (b) consent, (c) transcript exchange, (d) degree audit, and (e) degree conferral and advising (Taylor & Bragg, 2015). These dimensions reflect core policies and processes pertaining to the implementation of reverse-credit transfer programs, and each is described briefly in the following list:

1. *Student identification*: The first dimension focusing on student identification refers to general eligibility criteria for reverse-credit transfer, including criteria used to identify students who are potentially eligible to participate. These criteria vary across states, systems, and institutions, but they tend to address various aspects of eligibility, such as residency requirements and the minimum number of credits needed at the 2- and 4-year levels to qualify for consideration of an associate degree. The criteria also vary in restrictiveness versus expansiveness, with more students being potentially impacted when the reverse-credit transfer criteria are restrictive. For example, policies with higher residency requirements or higher cumulative college credit cutoffs will eliminate more potentially eligible students than policies that set lower limits (McCambly & Bragg, 2016).

2. *Consent*: The second dimension is consent, referring to the ways in which consent is acquired from students to ensure that they have been given the opportunity to assess reverse-credit transfer as an option. The ability of students to get the information they need to make informed decisions about participation is very important especially ensuring federal, state, and institutional laws and administrative rules are followed. To this end, the Family Education Rights and Privacy Act requirements tend to require that students decide to

participate by actively consenting—operationalized as "opt-in" rather than "opt-out"—to ensure that students have control over their transfer experience. Methods that institute consent procedures at the point of admission to the community college and/or university levels are evolving in the 15 CWID states, with states such as Hawaii and Texas capitalizing on admissions processes governed by single higher education systems, therefore allowing for more expansive opt-in methods.

3. *Transcript exchange*: Transcript exchange, the third dimension, refers to the ways in which transcripts and/or course data are transmitted from the community college to the 4-year institution prior to a degree audit (discussed more fully in the next list item). States in CWID have experimented with and adopted several different technologies to support electronic transcript exchange, with state higher education agencies, state or regional higher education systems, community colleges, and universities investing in varied technologies having to do with transcripts, advising, data sharing, and so forth. Our research showed technology investments to have a sizable impact on the scope and pace of implementation as well as scale. Whereas technology investments took longer to implement than using existing processes due to the need to identify, test and adopt new technology, once these investments were implemented, states could move toward scaling statewide more readily than states without such investment.

4. *Degree audit*: The fourth dimension of degree audit determined whether a student's combined collection of courses as evidenced in community college and university transcripts add up to meet the requirements for a reverse-credit associate degree. As noted previously, some states and institutions utilized new technologies to automate degree audits, sometimes moving from simulations to actual live implementation to ensure the accuracy of technology-driven audit routines. These efforts have been especially important in states that were auditing an ever-growing volume of students who sought the reverse-credit transfer option (Taylor & Bragg, 2015). Often, these technologies require the sharing of student-level data in real time, which expedites data use for the purposes of auditing transcripts.

5. *Degree conferral and advising*: The fifth dimension is degree conferral. In reverse-credit transfer, the community college confers the degree and notifies the 4-year institution when students have attained the associate degree. Degree conferral may be associated with the option of attending commencement and other celebratory events held by community colleges. Our research suggests some students value these culminating experiences for themselves as well as their families, while others do not take part. Our research has also shown that students who do not complete the associate degree requirements benefit from advising to help them understand what is lacking in their college education to complete the associate degree. In some cases, college advisors confer with students on courses that they can take to obtain the associate degree en route to the baccalaureate degree.

Looking at these five dimensions, we see how higher education systems and institutions are changing to implement various policies and processes pertaining to reverse-credit transfer. These dimensions include student eligibility criteria; student consent to transcript review and degree conferral; institutional transmittal of transcripts, records, and data; methods by which course equivalencies are determined, including using competency (versus credit) attainment upon mastery; formulating and reforming transfer and articulation agreements; and improving data sharing and research. These changes seek to impact the ways reverse-credit transfer is deployed over both the short- and long-term, but they also have implications for how transfer happens beyond the reverse-credit transfer context.

The Broader Transfer Reform Landscape

As noted earlier, CWID represents one of the most recent initiatives to improve transfer. However, it does not operate in isolation from other transfer reforms, nor is it alone in terms of the conclusions it draws about the necessity to improve transfer for post-traditional college students. By implementing reverse-credit transfer, lessons should be learned to improve other transfer policies and practices. This perspective is one our team explored in our research agenda, and we share qualitative results in the following section.

Transfer and Articulation Agreements

Reverse-credit transfer policies and practices operating statewide or interinstitutional, including 2+2 and 3+1 agreements, may strengthen transfer and articulation agreements between community colleges and universities and contribute to more comprehensive changes in the transfer function. Reverse-credit transfer may impact these agreements and lead to other, potentially larger reforms by intentionally changing transfer and articulation agreements to optimize transfer for more students, including post-traditional transfer students. Institutions adopting these reforms may be better positioned to facilitate the movement of students between and among institutions without the students' losing credit. Although not universally in favor of reverse-credit transfer, many students expressed confidence in being able to transfer credits needed to progress toward completion of their college degrees (Eden & Taylor, 2018).

Course or Learning Equivalencies

System and institutional learning outcomes assessment initiatives related to transfer use can help experts, academic groups, faculty committees, and other personnel to align curricula and course equivalencies and make transparent how students attain course credits toward their degrees. Evolving efforts to convert college curricula from credit-based to competency-based (referring to demonstration of the mastery of learning in terms of knowledge and skills at the students' own pace [Girardi, 2017] that was evident in the Hawaii system) represent what we deemed as some of the most forward-thinking ways of considering how transfer may work in the future. When competencies become more transparent and aligned to tangible outcomes, then transfer students, particularly post-traditional transfer students who tend to engage in part-time attendance, can benefit by having their competencies more readily recognized toward degree attainment.

Transfer Course/Credit Blocks

State- or system-wide efforts establishing general education transfer course or credit blocks toward specified transfer degrees are emerging in some CWID states, such as Colorado and Missouri. These states are evaluating the way the transfer block idea may still be able to apply to students who reverse transfer credits back to the community college. As originally conceived, transfer blocks guarantee the credits that students complete by taking certain course sequences or meeting general education requirements at one institution—usually a community college—for certain requirements at a 4-year institution. For example, a student who completes all general education requirements at a community college might, upon transfer to a 4-year school, have their general education requirements considered complete, even if the general education requirements were slightly different at the 4-year institution.

Transfer blocks are intended to reduce the guesswork in course and credit transfer and enable students to progress from institution to institution to attain credits that qualify them for their degrees. However, students who transfer to 4-year institutions before completing their associate degree often do not qualify. Determining how course credits may be applied in lieu of a student's meeting the transfer-block requirement is under consideration in many CWID states as is the evaluation of the extent to which transfer blocks are being used and how benefits from them, as originally conceived.

Pathways Initiatives

System or institution level efforts organize and communicate curricular pathway options to students through advising, intentional communications, classroom instruction and other pedagogical endeavors, and learning outcomes' assessment (Bailey et al., 2015). To this end, Wyner et al. (2016) authored a "transfer playbook" to apply lessons from their research to help community colleges and universities improve transfer policy and practice at the institutional level. This publication reports on the transfer-related strategies that institutions with especially high transfer-student success rates have implemented, pointing to the need to prioritize transfer, create clear pathways, and reinforce advising processes.

Moreover, some CWID states have endeavored to create transfer pathways built on efforts with "guided pathways" and "career pathways" to assist students to transfer in general education and the liberal arts and sciences but also in career-technical education and adult education (Clagett, 2015). Generally, these various pathways initiatives help students map out their programs of study from start to finish so that they can see how their course-taking needs to be optimized to secure college credentials in a method that is as efficient as possible (without credit loss). Beginning by carefully planning the students' college experience, including advising on what programs of study to pursue, pathways approaches help students understand and navigate the college curriculum. Interestingly, the guided pathways approach heavily emphasizes full-time student enrollment, which complicates and potentially diminishes the value of this approach for post-traditional transfer students who are more likely to attend college part time and intermittently than traditional college-goers.

Lessons Learned From CWID

Seemingly straightforward, the conferral of associate degrees to transfer students who have matriculated to a 4-year college or university, such as occurs through CWID, is a surprisingly complex endeavor. Some CWID states found that they had to engage in substantial self-study to implement a robust reverse-credit transfer program. This process of self-study led some states to redefine various aspects of their transfer and articulation function beyond what was initially expected, including investing in system-wide and interinstitutional relationship and partnership building. These changes suggest leadership for the purpose of changing policy is important to transforming higher education institutions, as well as systems, in ways that may better meet the needs of post-traditional transfer students.

Transfer reforms that recognize the need for transfer function to be malleable and responsive rather than rigid and bureaucratic are emerging through CWID and other initiatives mentioned in this chapter. In the increasingly outcomes-focused, performance-based environment in which CWID is operating, higher education practitioners need to be able to learn from one another about how to implement and scale new and evolving transfer policies and practices, including sharing lessons about how to situate reverse-credit transfer in larger transfer reform agendas. The integration of research from the start of CWID reinforced the importance of gathering and using data and evidence to ensure that students remain the constant focus of decisions about to improve transfer. Some of the important lessons CWID state and institutional leaders shared with our research team are discussed in this section (Bragg & the CWID research team, 2016).

First, many states intentionally used CWID as a test bed for transfer reform. No doubt, they were interested in reverse-credit transfer, but their focus on improving the overall transfer function was ever-present in thinking about how the higher education system could benefit from reform. For example, recognizing that advancements in technology would allow systems and institutions to more easily and efficiently access student records, perform student record audits, and share student information was viewed as necessary to operationalize reverse-credit transfer but also a highly consequential benefit for transfer writ large. Contrary to naysayers who claim CWID is mostly about gaming the system for the sake of boosting college completion rates (see, e.g., Strahler, 2015), state leaders reported a range of intentional and unexpected spillover benefits. With respect to planning, states used CWID funds to update outdated technologies and procedures to accurately track transfer student attendance and were surprised to learn about curriculum misalignment that contributed to these tracking problems. Existing transfer agreements that were thought to be working well were not as functional as expected, and these misalignments were addressed. In so doing, CWID brought to light concern about a wider array of policies and practices that may have been creating barriers and contributing to diminished transfer student outcomes, especially for students who demonstrate post-traditional attendance patterns.

Second, experience with reverse-credit transfer highlighted for states and institutions the importance of communications, active networking, targeted technical assistance, and focused professional development. Without adequate supports to help reform and sustain change, it is very difficult to reform any higher education function but especially a function as complex as transfer. To this end, states such as Missouri, Ohio, and Tennessee used media campaigns, including social media, to advance communications about reverse-credit transfer policy and practice within their systems and institutions. Some recommended communications with other CWID state systems and institutional leaders to facilitate cross-state policy borrowing that can reduce inefficiencies and grow impact; however, our research team has not studied state adoption of reverse-credit transfer policies and practices outside of the CWID network.

Third, as higher education continues to reform at the state and institutional levels and changes in leadership at all levels occur, offering ongoing professional development and technical assistance is important, including professional development and technical assistance approaches that deliberately link reverse-credit transfer to broader transfer reform agendas operating at the institution, system, and state levels. Also important is deeper knowledge of historic and present systemic and structural barriers which impede post-traditional transfer students from securing college degrees through vertical transfer or other emerging paths. Linking research to these reforms is a strong interest for many of the states participating in CWID to ensure that reforms are student-focused, for both majority and marginalized students.

Fourth, as noted previously, the CWID states implemented reverse-credit transfer in very different ways, varying their approaches to policy and practice to address their own specific needs. Whereas some states devoted most of their CWID resources to technological improvements designed to automate the reverse-credit transfer process, other states used their resources to convene working groups, conduct professional development, and offer technical assistance for institutions with more limited or no investment in technology. Still other states saw the value in adopting technology and offering support for practitioners involved in the change, implementing a hybrid approach that meant spreading resources across these functions. Reflecting on these decisions, state leaders tended to think they made the best decisions for their circumstances. They felt they had launched CWID in ways that moved the critical dimensions mentioned earlier (student identification, consent, transcript exchange, degree audit, and degree conferral and advising) along in appropriate ways for their own contexts and therefore advanced the state's transfer reform agendas (Taylor & Bragg, 2015; Taylor & Jain,, 2017).

Fifth, some state leaders reported that community colleges and universities with long-standing positive transfer relationships wherein campus leaders know and value a strong working relationship to advance transfer tended to prioritize reverse-credit transfer while institutions that appeared to place more limited value on transfer tended to make less time to engage. Some campuses that valued transfer were also ones that recognized that students who stand to benefit from reverse-credit transfer are the post-traditional transfer students. These students, including racial and ethnic minority students, first-generation students, low-income students, and nontraditional age (adult) learners, are represented in increased numbers on many community college and university campuses and are increasingly identified as important to a diverse campus learning environment.

However, state leaders observed that many institutions having more limited experience with transfer continued to show less interest in reverse-credit transfer, preferring to continue their focus on transfer on traditional student populations. Leaders of some of these institutions expressed concern for stretching limited resources for transfer to now include reverse-credit transfer, particularly when manual degree audits and other time-consuming processes were required. These institutions tended to see reverse-credit transfer as competing for resources with the traditional transfer function, downplaying the value of transfer to the campus mission.

Sixth, while most states focused exclusively on liberal arts and sciences programs of study that have been the primary focus of state transfer and articulation policies, leading to associate of arts (AA) and associate of science (AS) degrees, as CWID continued to evolve over the years, some state leaders expressed greater interest in including career-technical education programs that confer associate of applied science (AAS) degrees in their reverse-credit transfer initiatives. Readily admitting that the initial focus of CWID was on AA and AS degree programs, several state leaders spoke about enveloping more programs and institutions in reverse-credit transfer in their states. For example, in states conferring applied baccalaureate degrees at the 4-year college level and increasingly now at the community college level, it makes sense to consider the expansion of reverse-credit transfer to include AAS degree programs. As AAS students progress to the upper-division level, they may experience some of the same challenges as other transfer students who are benefiting from reverse-credit transfer. Designing pathways that optimize options for students no matter their associate degree program provides greater flexibility and expanded options for post-traditional transfer students.

Seventh, virtually all state leaders acknowledged that their systems have limited capacity to measure student transfer experiences and outcomes, with some states noting they had attempted to implement new measurements without fully preparing institutions to gather the data. Only a few states became fully functional in measuring student participation in reverse-credit transfer, and our team recognized that these differences in measurement complicated and potentially invalidated our ability to do cross-state comparisons. Based on the data collection by our team, only modest consistency exists in some of the most critical terminology and measurements for reverse-credit transfer and in some cases more generally for transfer by the end of the

5-year grant period. These concerns extend to such fundamental measures as who is considered a transfer student, what "transfer" means, and what outcomes it has for students, especially those who follow paths other than vertical transfer.

Finally, an eighth lesson relates to the quality of transfer data in terms of tracking transfer student participation and degree conferral, including reverse-credit transfer. In most states, the data required to measure reverse-credit transfer had to be added to existing data systems, and many states lacked capacity to do this work without technical assistance from our research team. Moreover, new measures such as credits earned prior to transfer, credits accepted by institutions receiving transfer students, credits attributed back to associate degrees after transfer, and total accumulated credits and transfer grade point average over a student's entire college career are important to operationalize. Yet, much of this data is not collected or is collected but not by using standardized methods, which affects data quality and measurement of impact of reverse-credit transfer and any other transfer reform. For example, our research team found cases where transfer students received more credits from receiving institution than the total number of credits they had earned prior to transfer. These patterns may represent inadequate transcripts for students who attend multiple institutions or any number of other errors, but this finding points to the importance of improving transfer documentation that understandable, transparent, and portable so that students, institutions, and systems are able to use the information to advance their plans.

Implications for Future Policy and Research

As of 2018, 6 years after the launch of CWID, transformation of state and institutional transfer policies and practices is ongoing, with each CWID state establishing its own plans for growing implementation and ensuring sustainability. Indeed, today's transfer policies and practices need to be more student-focused and intentionally directed at interinstitutional and system-wide relationships that support a diversity of transfer pathways. Strengthened partnerships between 2- and 4-year institutions become possible with improved data sharing and research that allows the institutions to learn and improve in meeting students' needs. Improved communications among higher education leaders and practitioners is essential to facilitate transfer pathways that meet the needs of post-traditional transfer students. These students deserve policies and practices that improve transfer and contribute to greater economic and social advancement. Transfer reforms that prioritize key values like transparency, recognition of a diversity of approaches to student learning and credit attainment, and adaptable inter-institutional relationships that serve an increasingly diverse transfer students are what is needed most.

Higher education systems and institutions that meet the needs of post-traditional transfer students are bound to flourish. To implement meaningful change, recognizing that transfer students are increasingly diverse and therefore require more advising is not enough, although good advising is certainly a positive step. We must also analyze and further accommodate post-traditional transfer students' participation patterns as transfer reforms continue to advance. The goal should not be to teach transfer students to work in an outdated system but to transform the system so that it more readily serves the transfer students of today and tomorrow. Transformative changes needed to truly benefit post-traditional transfer students can be identified by listening to the students and understanding their experiences through firsthand accounts. Quantifying matriculation patterns by student subgroups is important, but it is insufficient to understand and act upon without qualitative data that reflects the nuanced personal experiences of the students.

Extending from the last point, our future research on transfer has expanded to the vertical transfer function through a Gates Foundation research project called High-Performing Transfer Partnerships. In this research, we are studying how community colleges and 4-year institutions partner to support higher student transfer rates, particularly for minoritized and low-income students who make up a high proportion of post-traditional transfer students. Our research focuses on identifying and sharing promising policies and practices pertaining to transfer partnerships that produce more equitable student outcomes than other pairs of institutions within states. Looking at four CWID states, a series of studies examines the implementation and impact of transfer partnerships on degree attainment, paying close attention to institutions that form and sustain alliances yielding higher degree completion for racially minoritized students (see, e.g., Blume & Meza, 2019; Yeh & Wetzstein, 2019). Through this work, we are extending lessons from reverse-credit transfer to broader transfer policies and practices throughout the United States to better meet the evolving needs of post-traditional transfer students.

For leaders who are just getting started with reverse-credit transfer initiatives, we recommend reviewing the set of guiding principles for implementation set forth by the CWID research team. Taylor (2017) provides guidance on a comprehensive set of strategies that new leaders should consider in planning, implementing and sustaining reverse-credit transfer at the system and institutional levels. These recommendations begin by encouraging leaders to gain a full grasp of their state's policy context to understand what policy mechanisms, including funding, can be deployed in the implementation process. Leaders also benefit from understanding how reverse-credit transfer aligns with other transfer and articulation efforts, a point made earlier in this chapter, so that reforms build toward a common goal rather than competing or contradicting other transfer activities. At the system and institutional levels, technology to support reverse-credit transfer should be assessed for potential enhancements needed to audit transcripts and confer degrees. Considerations also need to be given to data and research to document how the reform is happening and what impact it has on students, including their educational experiences and degree attainment. Broader changes in cultural, leadership as well as faculty and student engagement should also be monitored to understand how transfer is changing over time.

A set of evidence-based resources that evolved from CWID appears on the website of the Community College Research Initiative at the University of Washington (www.washington.edu/ccri/research/transfer/). There is a set of "data notes" presenting a brief description of research as well as evidence-based policy and practice recommendations, such as the guiding practices for reverse-credit transfer previously mentioned. Research reports, journal articles, and lengthier briefs are also linked on this website, along with state profiles for all 16 CWID states. In addition, the CWID transfer page also presents 10 data notes on high-performing transfer partnerships that offer related research and evidence-based practices that may be beneficial to the implementation of reverse-credit transfer.

Institutional Reflection Questions

1. What is the incidence of student transfer without the associate degree? That is, how many transfer students matriculate from your institution or to your institution prior to attaining the associate degree?
2. What higher education system and institutional policies and practices exist that would facilitate or impede the conferring of associate degrees via reverse-credit transfer?
3. What proportion of your students could be considered "post-traditional transfer students," and how could these students benefit from reverse-credit transfer policies and practices?
4. What other transfer reforms are taking place that should be considered in conjunction with the implementation of reverse-credit transfer? How can these reforms be aligned and possibly integrated to create a synergistic approach to improve transfer outcomes?
5. How can higher education institutions that are predominantly 2-year and 4-year partner to ensure more equitable student outcomes for racially minoritized students and other historically underserved by the transfer function of higher education?

References

Adelman, C. (2013, October). *Searching for our lost associate's degrees: Project Win-Win at the finish line.* Institute for Higher Education Policy. http://www.ihep.org/sites/default/files/uploads/docs/pubs/pww_at_the_finish_line- long_final_october_2013.pdf

Anderson, L. (2015a). *Reverse transfer: The path less traveled.* Education Commission of the States. https://www.ecs.org/clearinghouse/01/18/77/11877.pdf

Anderson, L. (2015b). *Reverse transfer: What is the best route to take?* ECS Promising Practices in Education. Education Commission of the States. https://www.ecs.org/wp-content/uploads/12112.pdf

Bailey, T., Jaggars, S. S., & Jenkins, D. (2015). *What we know about guided pathways.* Columbia University, Teachers College, Community College Research Center. http://ccrc.tc.columbia.edu/media/k2/attachments/What- We-Know-Guided-Pathways.pdf

Belfield, C. (2013). *The economic benefits of attaining an associate degree before transfer: Evidence from North Carolina.* Community College Research Center, Teachers College. https://ccrc.tc.columbia.edu/media/k2/attachments/economic-benefits-associate-degree-before-transfer.pdf

Blume, G., & Meza, E. (2019). *Identifying effective and equitable institutions for transfer students: Exploring the contribution of the pair multilevel modeling.* Community College Research Initiatives, University of Washington. https://www.washington.edu/ccri/files/2019/02/HPTP_DataNote10.pdf

Bragg, D. D., Cullen, D. P., Bennett, S., & Ruud, C. M. (2011). *All or nothing? Mid-point credentials for college students who stop short of credential requirements.* Office of Community College Research and Leadership, University of Illinois. https://occrl.illinois.edu/docs/librariesprovider4/cwid/all_or_nothing.pdf?sfvrsn=c58fb289_4

Bragg, D. D., and the CWID Research Team. (2016, May 2). *What we've learned, what we still need to know: Insights from the Credit When It's Due (CWID) Research Meeting in Salt Lake City.* Community College Research Initiatives, University of Washington. https://s3-us-west-2.amazonaws.com/uw-s3-cdn/wp-content/uploads/sites/158/2018/08/23173614/RB-What-We%E2%80%99ve-Learned-What-We-Still-Need-to-Know-Insights-from-the-Credit-When-It%E2%80%99s-Due-CWID-Research-Meeting-in-Salt-Lake-City.pdf

Carnevale, A., Rose, S., & Cheah, B. (2011). *The college payoff: Education, occupations, lifetime earnings.* Center on Education and the Workforce, Georgetown University. https://www2.ed.gov/policy/highered/reg/hearulemaking/2011/collegepayoff.pdf

Christensen, C. M., Raynor, M. E., & McDonald, R. (2015). What is disruptive innovation? *Harvard Business Review, 93*(2), 44–53. https://hbr.org/2015/12/what-is-disruptive-innovation

Clagett, M. G. (2015, December). *A guide for the development of aligned career pathways systems.* Jobs for the Future. https://s3.amazonaws.com/PCRN/docs/A-Guide-for-the-Development-of-Aligned-Career-Pathways- Systems.pdf

Eden, C-L., & Taylor, J. (2018). Reverse credit transfer and the value of the associate's degree: Multiple and contradictory meanings. *Community College Journal of Research and Practice,* 1–17. http://dx.doi.org/10.1080/10668926.2018.1556358

Girardi, A. (2017, October). *Paving the way: Remaking entry for postsecondary success.* Jobs for the Future. https://eric.ed.gov/?id=ED588450

Humphreys, D., McCambly, H., & Ramaley, J. (2015). *The quality of a college degree: Toward new frameworks, evidence, and policies.* Association of American Colleges & Universities.

McCambly, H. N., & Bragg, D. D. (2016). *Reforming transfer to meet the needs of "post-traditional" transfer students: Insights from Credit When It's Due.* Community College Research Initiatives, University of Washington. https://s3-us-west-2.amazonaws.com/uw-s3-cdn/wp-content/uploads/sites/158/2018/08/23173616/RB-Reforming-Transfer-to-Meet-the-Needs-of-%E2%80%9CPost-Traditional%E2%80%9D-Transfer-Students.pdf

Santiago, D. (2013). *Using a Latino lens to reimagine aid design and delivery.* Excelencia in Education! http://www.edexcelencia.org/sites/default/files/latinolens_excelenciawhitepaperfeb2013.pdf

Shapiro, D., Dundar, A., Harrell, A., Wild, J., & Ziskin, M. (2014). *Some college, no degree: A national view of students with some college enrollment, but no completion* (Signature Report No. 7). National Student Clearinghouse Research Center. http://nscresearchcenter.org/signaturereport7/

Smith, E. J. (2013, October 31). *Post-traditional learning amid a post-traditional environment.* https://www.naspa.org/rpi/posts/NASPA-post-traditional

Soler, M. C., Meza, E. A., & Bragg, D. (2018, March). Initial research on multi-institutional attendance patterns and racial equity. *Data Note 3.* Community College Research Initiatives, University of Washington. https://s3-us-west-2.amazonaws.com/uw-s3-cdn/wp-content/uploads/sites/158/2020/05/26231635/HPTPdatanote3.pdf

Strahler, S. R. (2015, October 17). How city colleges inflate graduation rates. *Crain's Chicago Business*. http://www.chicagobusiness.com/article/20151017/ISSUE01/310179995/how-city-colleges-inflates-graduation-rates

Taylor, J. L., & Bragg, D. D. (2015, January). *Optimizing reverse transfer policies and processes: Lessons from twelve CWID states*. Office of Community College Research and Leadership, University of Illinois at Urbana-Champaign.

Taylor, J. L., & Jain, D. (2017). Multiple dimensions and meanings of transfer: The transfer function in American higher education. *Community College Review, 45*(4), 273–293. https://doi.org/10.1177/0091552117725177

Townsend, B. K., & Dever, J. T. (1999). What do we know about reverse transfer students? In B. K. Townsend (Ed.), *Understanding the impact of reverse transfer students on community colleges*. (New Directions for Community Colleges, No. 106, pp. 5–13). Jossey-Bass. http://dx.doi.org/10.1002/cc.10601

Wheatle, K., Taylor, J., Bragg, D., & Ajinkya, J. (2017). *The potential for degree reclamation: A path to reclaiming the nation's unrecognized students and degrees*. Institute for Higher Education Policy. http://www.ihep.org/sites/default/files/uploads/docs/pubs/potential_degree_reclamation_final.pdf

Wyner, J., Deane, K., Jenkins, D., & Fink, J. (2016). *The transfer playbook: Essential practices for two- and four-year colleges*. The Aspen Institute. http:// ccrc.tc.columbia.edu/media/k2/attachments/transfer-playbook-essential-practices.pdf

Yeh, T. L., & Wetzstein, L. (2019). *The dynamic nature of transfer partnerships: Catalysts and barriers to collaboration*. Community College Research Initiatives, University of Washington. https://s3-us-west-2.amazonaws.com/uw-s3-cdn/wp-content/uploads/sites/158/2019/01/16042701/HPTP_DataNote8.pdf

STATE HIGHER EDUCATION SYSTEM INFORMATION PROVISION TO PROMOTE TRANSFER STUDENT SUCCESS

Angela Bell

State higher education systems can contribute to transfer as a means for student success through provision of information and analytics to both system and institution leaders and practitioners. While much of the dynamic around transfer student success occurs at individual institutions, state systems frequently construct the policy framework and develop the expectations and resources that are the context in which institutional transfer practice takes place. The transfer literature regarding state systems traditionally focuses on articulation and credit acceptance policies. However, only a few studies have shown that these state level efforts play a positive role in whether students transfer to a baccalaureate program or improve the likelihood of success and time to degree after transfer (Taylor & Jain, 2017).

Fortunately, other tools exist that state higher education systems can employ to improve the student transfer experience and help institutions manage the large role that transfer and multi-institutional attendance play in campus planning and decision-making. In an era when data-informed decision-making is an expectation rather than an aspiration, state systems can provide critical support for the transfer information needs of their campuses. This, in turn, enhances institutions' ability to effectively plan, make decisions, and implement initiatives around student transfer.

Furthermore, state systems often have access to more comprehensive data than institutions themselves, as well as the ability to deploy new analytic techniques and tools efficiently for the whole system. These state systems are uniquely positioned to advance the analytic capacity of all institutions in service to improving system outcomes. With the growing prevalence of student transfer and multi-institution attendance, higher education must move beyond viewing transfer as a problem to solve. Rather, the imperative should be to regard transfer as a tremendous opportunity for increasing degree attainment and upward mobility, hence the need to support transfer comprehensively and strategically as an integral part of a larger student success ecosystem. This chapter describes how one public statewide higher education system, the University System of Georgia (USG), is working to meet this challenge. Given that "public university systems educate approximately three-quarters of the nation's students in public, 4-year higher education and a significant proportion of students seeking 2-year degrees" (National Association of System Heads, 2019, para. 3), state systems have the reach and should use their resources to ensure the transfer process functions optimally to support student achievement.

State Higher Education Governance, Policy, and Student Transfer

In every U.S. state save one, institutional transfer practice occurs within a state context that includes some type of centralized higher education governing or coordinating association. (The state of Michigan has no such body.) While the nature and strength of the state-level entities vary by state, the general trend has been for these organizations conceptually to foster rational development of postsecondary capacity, increase efficiency, and meet public priorities, including student success (McGuinness, 2016). At a high level, state higher education organization functions usually are some combination of activities like planning for postsecondary education in the state as a whole, state finance policy, provision of information to guide policymaking, regulation of institutions, administration of state-level services such as financial aid, and governance of systems and institutions (National Center for Public Policy and Higher Education, 2005). Also, in the last 2 decades, organizations have increasingly focused on increasing educational attainment in the state. These organizations and their leaders have a dual obligation to citizens and lawmakers on the one hand and their constituent institutions on the other hand to develop and articulate a broad public agenda around higher education and to advance the public good (Tandberg et al., 2018). As student transfer has become increasingly common, fostering seamless transfer has become a focus of both citizens and lawmakers and therefore an object of state agency action. Transfer policy and initiatives are part of broader advocacy efforts for students by state higher education executive officers on several fronts such as affordability, efficient pathways to completion, campus safety, and so on (Holly, 2018).

Although state legislation largely was not employed as a tool to facilitate student transfer and articulation until the 1970s (Kintzer & Wattenbarger, 1985), today most states have policies or legislation designed to improve how transfer functions. According to an analysis by the Education Commission of the States (2016), 36 states have a common general education core curriculum that fosters seamless transfer, 16 states have common course numbering, and 36 states have a transfer associate degree. While these transfer-friendly practices could have been enacted as either system policies or state legislation, the work of executing them indubitably occurred within state agencies or system offices in collaboration with institutions. And yes, research on the effectiveness of these transfer policies in promoting student success suggests that transfer policies alone are not sufficient. Three national studies found no effect of transfer policies on the likelihood of student transfer from 2-year to 4-year institutions (Taylor & Jain, 2017). Also, Roksa and Keith (2008) found that state articulation agreements did not in and of themselves improve bachelor's degree outcomes including completion and time and credits to degree. Studies within individual states have had mixed results (Taylor & Jain, 2017).

In contrast with these mixed-policy outcomes, research has found that the existence of a statewide transfer guide is a predictor of *vertical transfer*, defined as mobility from a 2-year to a 4-year institution (LaSota & Zumeta, 2015). This finding suggests that transfer agreements, while necessary and desirable, are not enough. Proactive communication of these agreements to students makes the difference. These transfer guides, which provide information to students and advisors, often are created by state higher education agencies or systems. This is consistent with literature on functions of state systems noting their role in collection and use of data for accountability toward the state's agenda as well as for decision-making (McGuinness, 2016). While this type of information about institution articulation agreements and policies has shown positive outcomes, the rise of better postsecondary student-level data systems, and research and analysis based on them, has revolutionized approaches to improving student success. The field has moved from only using data retrospectively to report on outcomes and progress toward goals to utilizing new data sources and more real-time data to inform decision-making, build predictive models, and target students for interventions. Thus far, using data to promote student success is most common in predictive models of applicant yield, student retention and completion, and early warning systems within a single institution. At the system level, the USG is engaged with all its campuses in several data-driven initiatives to advance student success, such as the Gardner Institute's Gateways to Completion process, which leverages historical data on student gateway course success and longer-term outcomes to drive course redesign. Innovative data analysis for supporting transfer student success has been less common, perhaps in keeping with less focus in general on student success efforts beyond the first year.

In the transfer space, an important advancement has been building on the foundation of interinstitutional articulation guides and course equivalencies and coupling this with institution degree audit software to build inter-institutional degree audit Web portals. These allow students to know exactly how the credits they have accrued thus far will be applied toward completing a particular academic program at another institution. Owens and Knox (2014) detail how this innovation was developed in the State University of New York (SUNY) system to support transfer policy and then led to other information and policy innovations. Innovations like this are critical given research findings that building the knowledge of students as well as the knowledge and capacity of advisors is important to improving not only acceptance of transfer credit but also application of that credit toward students' program of study (Hodara et al., 2017). Against this backdrop of transfer policy research and the growing use of data to support student success, this chapter presents the USG's approach to increase availability and use of information to support student transfer success.

Theoretical Construct

This chapter draws on a theoretical framework employed by Owens and Knox in their chapter in the book *Building a Smarter University* (Lane, 2014). The chapter details how the SUNY system developed a system-wide degree-audit tool to support transfer policy and how this tool then shaped the development of reverse transfer policy and system course equivalencies. The authors draw on previous policy instrument studies that differentiate between substantive and procedural instruments (Eliadis et al., 2005). While substantive instruments aim to change behavior in the delivery of goods and services (e.g., regulation, grants, registration, reporting, etc.), procedural instruments are tools that "ensure support for agency action" (Owens & Knox, 2014, p. 162) and aim to affect implementation without "predetermining the results of substantive implementation activities" (p. 162). While noting previous research on information use as a procedural instrument, the SUNY study focuses instead on *administrative capacity*, which they define as the sum total of tools an agency possesses to implement policy including leadership, planning, management, and autonomy (Boschken, 1988; Milio, 2007; Owens & Knox, 2014). This current chapter focuses on information as a form of administrative capacity and how information developed at the USG supports the implementation of its student transfer policy. This is consistent with transfer policy literature that emphasizes the importance of building the knowledge and capacity of advisors and students across all transfer policy contexts (Hodara et al., 2017). This chapter expands on that literature to highlight the power of increasing information available to enhance transfer success for not only students and advisors but also institution and system decision-makers and planners.

The USG Context

The USG enrolled over 328,000 students in fall 2018 in 26 public postsecondary institutions organized into four sectors: four research universities, four comprehensive universities, nine state universities, and nine state colleges. Importantly for student transfer, most of the state colleges previously were classified as 2-year colleges but have all since begun to award bachelor's degrees. Removing the one state college that only offers bachelor's degrees, 71% of the degrees conferred in 2017–2018 at state colleges were sub-baccalaureate. State colleges in the USG function somewhat like community colleges in other states and serve as access institutions for the system. Their strong transfer mission is evidenced by 84% of associate degrees conferred in 2017–2018 being associate of arts (AA) or associate of science degrees intended for transfer, as opposed to the associate of applied science degrees, which are less likely to facilitate transfer. The Technical College System of Georgia (TCSG), a separate public system of 22 institutions, conversely does not offer AA degrees.

The USG has a robust transfer policy. To facilitate seamless transfer, USG policy mandates a 42-hour core curriculum, fully transferable between system institutions. This core includes 18 hours of major-specific lower-division classes, which are also transferable if the student stays in the same major upon transfer. In addition, as an outgrowth of the Governor's Complete College Georgia initiative that launched in 2011, the number of TCSG general education courses that are guaranteed for transfer as core curriculum credit was expanded and now stands at 28 (USG, 2012). Common course numbering exists across the USG for about 150 of the most common core curriculum classes including the courses guaranteed for transfer from the TCSG. Finally, all USG institutions are required to have a chief transfer officer to facilitate transfer within the USG, respond to concerns about transfer of the core curriculum, and work to develop procedures that minimize transfer problems (USG, 2018a). This position tends to be someone in the office of the chief academic officer, registrar, admissions, or enrollment management.

Both transfer magnitude and the tracking of transfer in system reporting illustrate how transfer is integral to the system fulfilling its mission for the state. The system's Semester Enrollment Report shows that transfers accounted for 26% of all undergraduates entering institutions as new students in fall 2017 and 7% of all undergraduates (USG, 2017). That information has been published since 1975—when 29% of new undergraduates and 10% of all undergraduates were transfer students (USG, 1975). The declining numbers of USG students that are transfers is a function of the previously noted addition of select bachelor's degree programs to all state colleges as well as nine institutional consolidations since 2013. Both policy changes resulted in broader availability of bachelor's degree programs across the state, which reduces the need for students to transfer to pursue their desired academic program.

The centrality of transfer to the USG also is shown by explicitly accounting for its contribution to institutional retention and graduation outcomes at least back to 1991. Retention and graduation rate reports provide separate figures for students retained or graduated at their initial institution as well as the success rate including students who have transferred and been retained or graduated at any system institution. For example, the system 6-year bachelor's graduation rate for fall 2011 full-time, first-time freshmen (elsewhere referred to in this volume as "first-year students") completing at their initial institution was 50%. Including students' completion at any USG institution increases that rate by 8 percentage points to 58% (USG, 2018b). Both the graduation rates themselves and the increase in success provided by transfer have increased over time.

Transfer Information to Support Decision-Making and Student Success

As suggested by the data points in the preceding section, the USG has explicitly tracked the enrollment of new transfer students and examined how transfer increases system outcomes. Publishing this information illustrates both the contribution of transfer as well as the value placed on transfer as a means of success in the system. Nationally, it is common for other state system websites to provide this type of information. The federal government has recently moved to including the contribution of transfer to student success in its IPEDS survey. While these types of information are valuable for accounting more accurately for all types of students, they have limited utility for practitioners. This chapter now turns to system provision of further information about transfers to support decision-making and student-success initiatives. Increasingly, the USG incorporates information about transfers into all planning and student initiatives.

Historical Provision of Information

The USG has long provided reports that track the annual volume of students transferring into each USG institution from other individual USG institutions, all non-USG Georgia institutions combined, and all out-of-state institutions combined. These data are based on the comprehensive transfer history data the USG collects every term for each student. In addition, the report provides for each intra-USG sending and receiving institution combination, the average GPA and median credit hours earned before transfer, the first term after transfer, and 1 year after transfer. Sector aggregates are also provided. The reports provide valuable information to campuses about how they fit into the larger transfer ecosystem in the state, and how their former students are faring at USG receiving institutions overall and at specific receiving institutions and sectors. The reports also allow them to compare this success with other similar USG institutions. Institutions have also noted that they use the changes over time in transfer student outcomes to gauge the success of changes in practice, such as how they advise students prior to transfer.

These types of state system reports are common according to canvassing of state system research leaders at national meetings. State systems also commonly provide information about demographic characteristics of transfer students; this can be helpful in assessing equity gaps in transfer dynamics. The USG does not currently provide this demographic information in public reports. This omission is not the result of a formal decision, but a function of our transfer data reporting still being less mature than reporting on first-time freshmen and few or no requests for this level of granularity in public reporting. However, the USG does provide this information directly to campuses as described in the following text and integrates it into the transfer analytics addressed later in this chapter. (The Mississippi Institutions of Higher Learning interactive data portal is an example of this type of visualization: www.mississippi .edu/research/IDP_Xfer.asp)

In addition to aggregate information about transfer students, the USG has, since 2009, provided each institution with a student-level file of their students who transferred to another USG campus during an academic year along with demographic information, the student's declared major upon transfer, and courses with grades in each term of the year following transfer. This detailed look at student success after transfer, and the ability to tie it back to student experience prior to transfer, enables a campus to identify where there may be problems in preparing students for transfer. For example, being able to see that many students who transfer later struggle in upper-level courses in a particular subject area points directly to the need for redesign of introductory courses. Institutions can also integrate these data with information on their campus about the student's use of services such as transfer advising to assess the impact of these offerings. More recently, as the completion agenda has intensified, the USG has created new versions of the aggregate transfer reports that show, again for each system sending and receiving institution combination, the share of transfer students who persist 1 year after transfer and graduate within 4 years of transfer. This report helps highlight not just outcomes for sending institutions but also places the spotlight on receiving institutions in terms of their success with incoming transfer students. Some other state systems (e.g., City University of New York, Oregon Higher Education Coordinating Commission, State Council of Higher Education for Virginia) provide similar information, including comparing graduation rates for transfer students and native students at the same class standing as incoming transfers.

The USG also carries out or facilitates periodic in-depth examinations of transfer dynamics related to specific policy questions. For example, the USG provided extensive longitudinal outcome data to a system state college (through a FERPA compliant agreement) to support its analysis of the success of entering students that enroll in instructional sites co-located with system research and comprehensive universities and then later transfer to these universities. The state college instructional sites aim to provide more geographically dispersed access points to the system, smooth transfer from the state college to the universities, and raise bachelor's completion rates. Analysis to date has compared outcomes at the partner universities of the students who transfer from the state college co-located sites, the state college's traditional residential campus, and other system schools. These analyses have led to changes at one of the instructional sites: (a) including partner university personnel in orientation; (b) efforts to increase the state college students' participation in university activities and courses; (c) promoting completion of the associate degree before transfer; and (d) a robust reverse transfer program. Also, work is underway to bolster the less well-developed partnership with the other university by moving the state college instructional site physically onto the campus of the university. This is an example of the system office providing information to its campuses to support their evaluation of innovations to improve the outcomes of transfer students in the state.

Another example of this type of in-depth analysis has been performed at the system itself to evaluate the 2012 policy change referenced previously that increased the number of courses at the TCGS guaranteed acceptance as core curriculum credit at USG institutions. Internal USG data as well the state's longitudinal data system, called GA-AWARDS (Georgia's Academic and Workforce Analysis and Research Data System), were used to compare subsequent course outcomes for students who took the transferable core courses either at a technical college or a USG institution. The findings were as follows:

- Both groups of students, those starting at TCSG and USG, performed worse in the subsequent, higher-level courses than in the transferable introductory courses. This is perhaps expected given that the subsequent courses are more advanced.
- TCSG transfer students were more likely than native USG students to withdraw from those higher-level courses.

- TCSG transfer students, however, who completed the subsequent course, performed better than their native USG peers, despite having lower prior academic indicators.
- TCSG transfers who earn lower grades in the transferable course or who wait longer after transfer to take the subsequent courses perform less well in the subsequent course.
- TCSG students appear to be advised into different follow-up courses based on their grade in the transferable course. These findings are important to validate the appropriateness of the articulation of the TCSG courses but also offer opportunities for improving the success of TCSG transfers. The results have contributed to system office leadership maintaining the articulation policy despite concerns from some quarters about whether the TCSG courses are as rigorous. The results have also been presented at system-wide academic discipline meetings to allay similar concerns and justify current policy. System office access to data on course success, both at TCSG and USG institutions, and aggregation of outcomes across the system, which provides adequate sample size for analysis, are key for assessing the success of the articulation policy change. These analyses are critical for system office and campus leaders to understand the impact of the system transfer policy and provide valuable information that increases institutional ability to better implement that policy, advise students, and improve outcomes.

A System Approach to Transfer Analytics

The reports and analyses discussed thus far are valuable contributions to both leaders and practitioners in their work with transfer policy and success initiatives. Conversations with other state research personnel and exploration of their websites suggest this type of work is a common contribution of state system offices. However, the use in higher education of information to guide decision-making and planning has changed dramatically in recent years. The culture of data-informed decision-making has increased demand for accessible and actionable information, compelling visual formats, and advanced analytics including statistical analysis and predictive models (Baldasare, 2018). While analytics is not a silver bullet for the many challenges facing higher education, it is viewed as an organizational innovation with "the potential to . . . improve student learning and success, reduce costs, improve effectiveness, and promote the innovation of individual institutions and the higher education industry" (Foss, 2014, p. 188). However, to realize the promise of analytics, tremendous data preparation work is required along with a blend of skills and competencies not commonly found in one organization, much less one division (Gagliardi, 2018). These realities led in 2014 to a partnership between the USG and the University of Georgia's (UGA's) Carl Vinson Institute of Government (CVIOG), a service unit with the mission of providing resources to state and local governments to improve their functions. The goal of the partnership was to combine system data and institutional research expertise with CVIOG's multidisciplinary approaches to data to create better information for decision-making and student success efforts. This project has risen to the call that systems need to facilitate the sharing of expertise across constituent institutions to carry out innovative analytical work (Cohen-Vogel, 2018) and from its inception had an explicit focus on understanding system transfer dynamics and their contribution to system student success. It also illustrates the potential for systems to leverage the analytic capacity at one of its research universities to benefit the entire system.

As the project began, its stated goal was to enhance system office decision-making through provision of innovative analytics around USG student body composition, the pipeline of first-time freshmen, the progression of undergraduate students over time, and transfer patterns. This project, importantly, embraced as co-equal subjects of analytics both first-time freshmen and transfer students. One cannot understand the functioning of the system and its contribution to the state without intentionally accounting for the fact that over one fourth of entering undergraduate students are transfers. Thus, through more sophisticated analytics, the USG/CVIOG collaboration sought to elucidate the patterns of student transfer in the system as well as how these contributed to the system mission of providing statewide access and success.

Figure 10.1 details the steps involved in this system-level analytics project. The first task was overcoming the challenge that USG student data collected from institutions was warehoused in term-by-term data tables that were not optimized for analysis of the inherently longitudinal nature of student progression. As a result, CVIOG reformatted all student records beginning in 2002 into a database that contained a row for each student for each term they were enrolled and includes data on student

Figure 10.1. Analytics project processes.

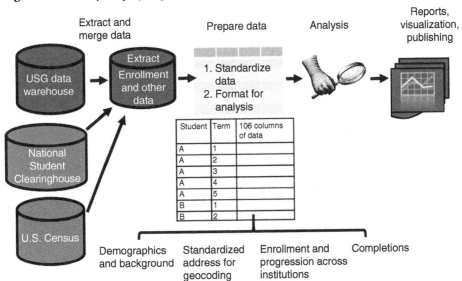

background, enrollment, courses taken and outcomes, and, ultimately, credentials conferred. This shift from data organized around institutions and terms to student progression over time was critical. Background information includes student permanent address at time of matriculation, which was geocoded to analyze student origins geographically and provides the data link enabling a merge with U.S. Census data at a very granular level. The Census data provide information about students' communities of origin which subsequent analyses have shown are important predictors in student outcomes including transfer. And critical to the subject of this book, analysts on the project submitted all USG student records to the National Student Clearinghouse so that information about transfer even beyond the USG could be included in the longitudinal dataset. The data preparation alone for this project took over half a year for a full-time analyst. The intensive work involved in this necessary step points to why most institutions cannot engage in this type of work and the value of a state system leveraging its resources to carry out the data preparation one time for all system institutions.

After the creation of the massive longitudinal dataset, the project shifted to analysis. A unique contribution of CVIOG is its multidisciplinary research team. They brought to the table analysts with expertise in demography, geographic information systems, data science, and data visualization. These approaches along with subject matter expertise from system campuses in institutional research, student success, and enrollment management were critical to pushing beyond traditional analyses. But perhaps most critical to the success of the project was the value added by visualization. We have been able to provide more data in accessible and interactive formats that has proved more useful to decision-makers than standard tabular or graphical presentations.

Visualizing Transfer as a Mechanism to Expand Access

One goal of the USG is to provide educational opportunity to the entire state of Georgia. And while the 26 institutions of the USG span the state, much of the geographic coverage of the state depends on the more numerous, less selective, and hence more accessible state colleges and universities. The research universities are all located in the northern half of the state and only two of the four comprehensive institutions are in the southern part of the state. This raises the question of whether all parts of the state have access to the state's more selective institutions with their broader curricular offerings and mixed research and teaching mission. The ability for students to transfer from access-mission institutions is part of the means of providing access to these more selective institutions, but historical data reporting had not highlighted the success of this pathway. The USG/CVIOG collaboration, however, was able to cast light on this question via visualizing student origins on heat maps and deliberately contrasting the origins of first-time freshmen with transfer students.

For example, the maps in Figure 10.2 show the origins of in-state students matriculating to the Georgia Institute of Technology. On the left are origins of first-time freshmen, and on the right are origins of transfer students. While the scale of

Figure 10.2. Georgia Institute of Technology origins of first-time freshmen and transfer students.

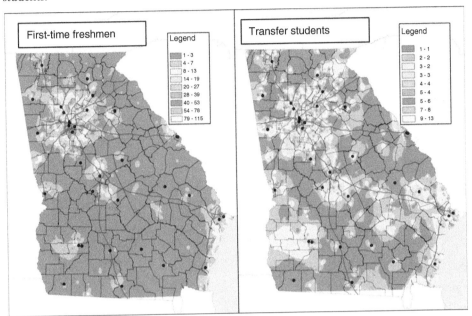

the maps differs, the maps make it very easy to see that although this highly selective school disproportionately enrolls first-time students from the metropolitan Atlanta area, the origins of transfer students are more geographically dispersed relative to the first-time student population. Student transfer is a means by which the Georgia Institute of Technology can provide its highly sought-after programs more broadly to the population of Georgia.

Contrast this with similar maps for UGA in Figure 10.3. Here the origins of the first-time freshman population on the left are spread more evenly across the state. However, UGA transfers are disproportionately drawn from the counties in northeast Georgia close to UGA itself. Further research revealed that students strategically enroll in the less selective University of North Georgia (UNG), which has a campus near UGA, in order to participate in UGA culture and activities in anticipation of transferring into UGA. UNG, in turn, has a more geographically diverse freshman population and so, through UNG transfers, UGA has a broader reach across the state. Similar maps for the access-mission state colleges show that both their first-time freshman and transfer populations are largely from the institution's immediate geographic area. They are serving regional access needs for both populations. The insights for these institutions, while possible with tabular data, were more readily created and made accessible to leadership based on the system-level data preparation and analytic work. These analyses also illustrate that visualization can reveal dynamics that lead to further analysis, such as the interesting UGA transfer student origins.

Figure 10.3. UGA origins of first-time freshmen and transfer students.

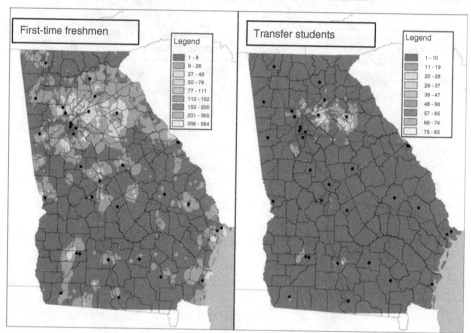

Visualizing Student Transfer Flows

Another important dynamic for system and campus leadership to understand is not only transfer's contribution to geographic service of the entire state but also the flows between system institutions and how those have changed over time. Institutions know from their own data where their transfer students come from and can utilize National Student Clearinghouse data to see to which institutions their students transfer. The USG is enhancing that institutional capability in a few ways. First, the USG carries out this origin/destination analysis once for the whole system, freeing up individual campus analysts to do other critical analytical work or, as is likely at smaller campuses with limited institutional research resources, provide analysis that would not be done at all.

Second, the USG combines this transfer information for all institutions into an interactive visualization so that not only analysts but also leaders can easily see what their campus's sending and receiving patterns are and how they change over time as well as how they fit into a larger state system transfer ecosystem. Figure 10.4 shows the chord diagram visualization prepared as part of the USG/CVIOG partnership. The method was adapted from a similar type of visualization illustrating population migration. The visualization shows the flows of students between the differently shaded sectors of schools with the width of the band connecting them indicating transfer volume. The user can interact with the diagram by clicking on sectors to reveal individual institutional flows or select years to see change over time.

Figure 10.4. Intrasystem student transfer flow chord diagram.

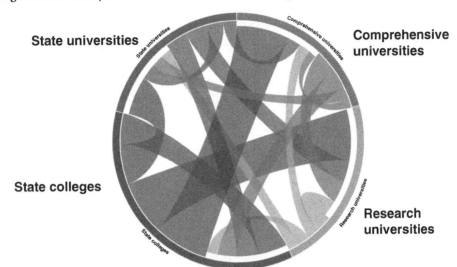

For example, a campus leader can easily see the year after the campus's transfer admissions policy changed that the number of students transferring into the institution from other USG institutions increased. Alternatively, a state college that added a new bachelor's degree in a particular year can see a reduction in the number of students transferring out of the institution. A receiving institution might see a drop in incoming transfers from that same state college and reach out to understand the driver of the decline. Institutions can also download the underlying data to analyze actual numbers.

At the same time, the system office is easily able to analyze the entire internal transfer ecosystem and how it has changed in response to system initiatives. One such initiative is institutional consolidations. Since 2013, in a proactive response to uneven population growth in the state as well as growing competition with other services for state appropriations, the USG carried out nine consolidations of system institutions. The aim of the consolidations is to provide postsecondary education more efficiently across the state, expand academic program offerings, and to reinvest administrative savings into the academic mission of the institutions. Data on transfer has played a role in the decisions to consolidate institutions as pairs of colleges where there is already a strong transfer relationship that would make them strong candidates for consolidation. But enrollment managers and chief business officers across the system have stated concern about how consolidations impact transfer flows to their institutions. This visualization provides an easy way to look at changes in transfer flows after consolidations. Analysis showed that campus consolidations reduce the number of students transferring *out* of the consolidated institutions and that while this changes the overall number of students transferring to other system institutions, it does not impact the shares of students transferring to individual institutions. This insight facilitates institutional planning for the likely impact on transfer flows of subsequent consolidations and broadens system comprehensive understanding of the impact of consolidation.

The chord diagram is innovative and allows rapid consumption of large amounts of information about the USG transfer ecosystem. This representation also allows analysts to interact with the data, asking and answering their own questions. Yet, it still provides only yearly snapshots of transfer flows. While useful in planning and policy impact analysis regarding transfer volume, the USG still needed a tool to understand how student transfer contributes to student success. Student progression is fundamentally a longitudinal process.

The analysts at the CVIOG developed interactive Sankey diagrams to capture how students flow between institutions over time and the relationship of transfer pathways to student completion. Figure 10.5 is an adapted image of the tool for illustrative purposes. A campus user can track a beginning cohort of students at any system institution and follow them from left to right through their next three enrollment statuses, whether that be transferring, graduating, or not enrolling. A significant portion of students at the access-mission state college shown here discontinue enrollment while a smaller portion proceed straight to graduation at that institution. The user can also see that a substantial share of students transfers to institutions A, B, and C. The user can then follow the next two statuses for these transfer students. The user can click to select just the students transferring into institution A, and the diagram adjusts to show more granular outcome information for only those students. The tool also has filters on student gender, race/ethnicity, age, and high school of origin to dig deeper into equity questions and easily compare student transfer outcomes for different populations.

Figure 10.5. Student transfer Sankey visualization.

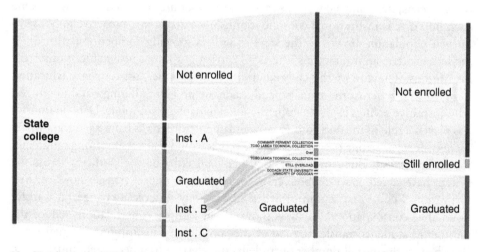

Note: Visualization by CVIOG using anonymized 2018 data from USG and the National Student Clearinghouse.

With this new Sankey transfer visualization, there is capability to understand long-term outcomes of transfer students and how outcomes differ across destination institutions. An advisor at this state college is equipped with empirical information to guide advisement of students seeking to transfer out. In this example, transferring to institution C is a pathway that historically has yielded higher chances of graduation than institution A. An advisor can utilize this to help a transfer student make informed choices. Similarly, an advisor at destination institution A is equipped with information about how students from this state college fare after transfer, which is actionable in a few ways. This information can lead to collaboration with the state college to improve the preparation of transfer students for entering institution A, to provide enhanced services to students transferring in from the state college, and perhaps yield outreach to institution C to better understand how its transfer practices result in higher completion rates.

This tool does not advise a student, nor does it prescribe a change or practice at an institution. Rather, the tool provides information to campus personnel that enhances their capacity to advise well and implement stronger transfer practices based on empirical information. This context is important in understanding the success of a campus's own students and the effectiveness of institutional practices.

The other critical system contribution is merging all these data one time for all system institutions, deploying it in an accessible, interactive visualization, and then making it available through a secure, Web portal. Most individual institutions lack either the capacity or the in-house expertise to undertake this significant effort. Also, the USG has provided multiple training opportunities for institution researchers and practitioners to become comfortable with using the visualization platform and to discuss use cases for the tools.

At the system level, administrators can more readily see the vital role transfer plays in the production of successful graduates. By pivoting from merely looking at whether beginning students finish to examining the myriad pathways of those who do and don't graduate, this tool provides ready insight into the role of transfer in larger student success dynamics. By focusing on outcomes for students who arrive at an institution as transfers, it also highlights our responsibility for all our students, not just those who entered as first-time freshmen.

In its graduation rate figures, the USG has long accounted for the reality that many students transfer to other system institutions to complete their degree. This inclusive perspective has been embraced only recently in federal graduation rate figures. But the USG/CVIOG analysis moves beyond that to emphasizing how critical transfer is in the myriad student success pathways that constitute our efforts to raise educational attainment. Complementary analysis of the term-by-term pathways of graduating students further highlights this contribution.

Among students who entered USG institutions from 2003 to 2008 and graduated within 4 years, 37% had transferred. But if we look at the individual enrollment patterns of these graduates, out of the 10,241 distinct term-by-term enrollment pathways, 7,833 or 76% of the unique pathways to success involved a transfer. The visualization here brings to life this diversity of student pathways involving transfer, as well as providing the more granular details that raise up centers of success that merit promotion across the system and highlight leaky pipelines that require intervention. This longitudinal, interactive Sankey diagram has been published recently to campuses on the USG data visualization portal; the work of realizing its potential to enhance practice and success is just beginning.

Recommendations

The USG system office was not positioned 5 years ago to make these analytical contributions. Lessons learned from the experience can assist other state systems similarly wanting to provide campuses information that will advance institutional capacity to enhance transfer as an integral component of student success.

- Support the application of data to investigate policy and practices to maximize transfer student success. Institutions commonly apply analytics to beginning freshman populations or all undergraduates. Student transfer is a unique phenomenon that requires separate, intentional analyses and different analytic approaches given its multi-institutional nature.
- Intensive analytical work requires focused resources ranging from personnel time and expertise to data visualization software. While the USG hired additional personnel in institutional research and business intelligence, the far greater contribution to these efforts has been the leveraging of existing system resources. By partnering with the CVIOG, a service unit at a system institution, the USG capitalized on the existence of an entity that already had talent in the multiple disciplinary approaches critical to this work as well as technology resources and licenses that were deployed for the project. Other state systems, and even individual institutions, will have similar existing expertise and technology resources on campus they can marshal to carry out this type of work rather than having to use external vendors. The partnership with CVIOG also benefited greatly from subject matter experts from system institutions. Their knowledge and experience contributed to the tools developed and leads to better campus buy-in on their use.
- Embrace analytical approaches outside of traditional institutional research. The contributions of demography, geography, and data science have been critical to being innovative in transfer analysis.
- Incorporate visualization. Visualization doesn't just make data attractive. It makes information accessible to a broader audience including leaders and practitioners and, if well done, facilitates insights about complex dynamics in less time. The mobility involved in student transfer lends itself well to visualization.
- Invest in user training. Providing sophisticated analytical tools is not sufficient. Providing training in a variety of formats including documentation, webinars,

STATE HIGHER EDUCATION INFORMATION PROVISION   *179*

and hands-on workshops can appeal to different users and help overcome the challenge that adoption and use of new information sources requires investment in time and energy. We find a critical need to teach not only about the information itself but also about how to apply it in campus processes. This challenge is ongoing for the USG as we continually seek to broaden use of the provided tools.

- Attend closely to student privacy. Providing campuses information about the progress of transfer students at other institutions requires FERPA-compliant data sharing agreements with campus users that restricts who can see the information and how they can use it. It also requires technology tools that can restrict access to sensitive information to specific users and automatically censor sensitive information in public displays.

Conclusion

Returning to the conceptual framework posed at the beginning of the chapter, the analytical tools the USG created are examples of information as a procedural instrument in support of system transfer policy and initiatives. The transfer data and analytics provided by the USG to system institutions enhance administrative capacity to carry out system policy to foster seamless transfer of students between institutions and support transfer to broaden access and success in the system. These state system offices have long used data collected from campuses for reporting and accountability or even for system-level policy analysis and initiatives. Some of this work has been transfer-focused, given that many state systems uniquely have the comprehensive multi-institution data to cast light on transfer dynamics. The work at the USG, however, is closing the loop in returning to campuses more granular, interactive, and visualized data that support transfer student enrollment management, pointing to the effectiveness of transfer practices, and fostering better advisement of transfer students. The USG provides information to campuses that raises administrative capacity to support the USG policy and structures intended to facilitate seamless transfer among institutions in support of a larger mission to promote student success.

In conclusion, information is a critical tool in raising the capacity of institutions to promote transfer student success and postsecondary attainment more broadly. System offices are uniquely positioned through their access to multi-institutional data to enhance the information to which campuses themselves have access and can leverage to improve practice. Strategic investment in analysis of transfer dynamics and provision of accessible, value-added information back to campuses fits well with state system office historic functions of aggregating data for both accountability and informing a statewide agenda. As transfer has become a more prevalent student pathway, the state system function of promoting the public good through focused attention to student success necessarily must embrace transfer as a critical component. The USG offers a positive case study in how a state system office can deploy its personnel, expertise, data, and technology resources to provide system and campus leaders and practitioners with actionable student transfer information that supports transfer policy and student success.

Discussion Questions

1. What transfer metrics or data exist, not referenced in this chapter, that should be considered for incorporation in institution- or system-level analytics to improve policy analysis and practice?
2. What are best practices for advising and otherwise supporting prospective or recent transfer students based on historical data that casts light on their chances for success?
3. How might an individual institution apply the example and recommendations provided here based on a state system to enhance information use in support of transfer student success?

References

Baldasare, A. Y. (2018). Pursuit of analytics and the challenge of organizational change management for institutional research. In J. S. Gagliardi, A. Parnell, & J. Carpenter-Hubin (Eds.), *The analytics revolution in higher education: Big data, organizational learning, and student success* (pp. 71–88). Stylus.

Boschken, H. L. (1988). Turbulent transition and organizational change: Relating policy outcomes to strategic administrative capacities. *Review of Policy Research 7*(3), 477–499. https://doi.org/10.1111/j.1541-1338.1988.tb00849.x

Cohen-Vogel, D. R. (2018). Higher education decision support. In J. S. Gagliardi, A. Parnell, & J. Carpenter-Hubin (Eds.), *The analytics revolution in higher education: Big data, organizational learning, and student success* (pp. 15–30). Stylus.

Education Commission of the States. (2016). *50-state comparison: Transfer and articulation policies.* https://www.ecs.org/transfer-and-articulation-policies-db/

Eliadis, P., Hill, M., & Howlett, M. (2005). *Designing government: From instruments to governance.* McGill-Queens University Press.

Foss, L. H. (2014). Integrating data analytics in higher education organizations: Improving organizational and student success. In J. E. Lane (Ed.), *Building a smarter university: Big data, innovation, and analytics* (pp. 187–209). State University of New York Press.

Gagliardi, J. S. (2018). The analytics revolution in higher education. In J. S. Gagliardi, A. Parnell, & J. Carpenter-Hubin (Eds.), *The analytics revolution in higher education: Big data, organizational learning, and student success* (pp. 1–14). Stylus.

Hodara, M., Martinez-Wenzl, M., Stevens, D., & Mazzeo, C. (2017). Exploring credit mobility and major-specific pathways: A policy analysis and student perspective on community college to university transfer. *Community College Review 45*(4), 331–349. http://dx.doi.org/10.1177/0091552117724197

Holly, N. (2018). The SHEEO and the public good. In D. A. Tandberg, B. A. Sponsler, R. W. Hanna, & J. P. Guilbeau (Eds.), *The state higher education executive officer and the public good: Developing new leadership for improved policy, practice, and research* (pp. 47–65). Teachers College Press.

Kintzer, F. C., & Wattenbarger, J. L. (1985). *The articulation/transfer phenomenon: Patterns and directions.* American Association of Community and Junior Colleges.

Lane, J. (2014). *Building a smarter university: Big data, innovation, and analytics.* State University of New York Press.

LaSota, R. R., & Zumeta, W. (2015). What matters in increasing community college students' upward transfer to the baccalaureate degree: Findings from the beginning postsecondary study 2003–2009. *Research in Higher Education, 57*(2), 152–189. http://dx.doi.org/10.1007/s11162-015-9381-z

McGuinness, A. (2016). *State policy leadership for the future: History of state coordination and governance and alternatives for the future.* Education Commission of the States.

Milio, S. (2007). Can administrative capacity explain differences in regional performances? Evidence from structural funds implementation in southern Italy. *Regional Studies 41*(4), 429–442. http://dx.doi.org/10.1007/s11162-015-9381-z

National Association of System Heads. (2019). *About NASH.* http://nashonline.org/about/

National Center for Public Policy and Higher Education. (2005, July). State capacity for higher education policy leadership. [Special supplement.] *National Crosstalk.* http://www.highereducation.org/crosstalk/ct0305/news0305-insert.pdf

Owens, T. L. and Knox, D. J. (2014). Unanticipated data-driven innovation in higher education systems: From student success to course equivalencies. In J. E. Lane (Ed.), *Building a smarter university: Big data, innovation, and analytics* (pp.159–183). State University of New York Press.

Roksa, J., & Keith, B. (2008). Credits, time, and attainment: Articulation policies and success after transfer. *Educational Evaluation and Policy Analysis, 30*(3), 236–254. http://dx.doi.org/10.3102/0162373708321383

Tandberg, D. A., Sponsler, B. A., Hanna, R. W., & Guilbeau, J. P. (Eds.) (2018). Introduction. In *The state higher education executive officer and the public good: Developing new leadership for improved policy, practice, and research* (pp. 1–11). Teachers College Press.

Taylor, J. L., & Jain, D. (2017). The multiple dimensions of transfer: Examining the transfer function in American higher education. *Community College Review, 45*(4), pp. 1–21. http://dx.doi.org/10.1177/0091552117725177

University System of Georgia. (1975). *Semester enrollment report.* https://www.usg.edu/assets/research/documents/enrollment_reports/qe_fall75.pdf

University System of Georgia. (2012, March 14). *Regents approve 17 general education courses for transfer to support complete college goals.* https://www.usg.edu/news/release/regents_approve_17_general_education_courses_for_transfer_to_support_comple

University System of Georgia. (2017). *Semester enrollment report.* https://www.usg.edu/assets/research/documents/ceu/SER_Fall_2017_1.pdf

University System of Georgia. (2018a). *Academic and student affairs handbook.* Section 2.4.9. https://www.usg.edu/academic_affairs_handbook/section2/C738/

University System of Georgia. (2018b). *USG by the numbers.* https://analytics.usg.edu/cognos/cgi-bin/cognos.cgi?b_action=cognosViewer&ui.action=run&ui.object=%2fcontent%2ffolder%5b%40name%3d%27Public%27%5d%2ffolder%5b%40name%3d%27Reports%27%5d%2ffolder%5b%40name%3d%27Academic%27%5d%2freport%5b%40name%3d%27Graduation%27%5d&ui.name=Graduation&run.outputFormat=PDF&run.prompt=true&CAMUsername=cognosguest&CAMPassword=R3adOnlyUs3r&CAMNamespace=BOROUD

11

TRANSFERRING COUNTRIES

International Perspectives and Student Immigration Issues

Jason Chambers, Karen Ramos, and Sarah Mackey

Transfer students with formal postsecondary (tertiary) education outside the United States are a unique population that merits further research. Higher education institutions are scrambling to enroll more international students, but what is being done to create a welcoming environment for them? Who are these students? Where do they originate? What unique challenges and barriers do international transfer students experience? How are they using support structures, and are those structures facilitating student success? This chapter will answer these questions by examining the transfer experience of nonimmigrant international students.

International Transfer Students: Who Are They?

Nonimmigrant international students are students seeking to enter the United States on a temporary basis for the purpose of receiving an educational degree. The typical U.S. visa classification for these students would be either an F-1 or J-1. For the purposes of this chapter, *international students* are defined by this visa classification. The recruitment of international students has become an attractive pursuit for many institutions of higher education seeking to diversify the student body, strengthen research capabilities, and expand revenue sources—to the extent that now many institutions are very dependent on this revenue (Armstrong, 2007; Cantwell, 2015). Beyond profits, college and university leaders seek to enroll a talented and diverse pool of international students by offering "an environment that encourages interaction and cross-cultural learning between its foreign and American students" (Weller, 2012, p. 23). Representing an increase of 40% over the past decade, recent figures reported by the Institution of International Education (IIE) indicate that over 1 million international students are currently studying in the United States. As such, international student enrollments constitute 5.5% of total higher education enrollment domestically, the highest percentage of total enrollment to date (IIE, 2018). However, the number of new international students has declined, and the percentage of students employed through their postgraduate optional work-study portion of their visa is up 3% annually to 22% of students. This statistic shows that there are fewer students in classes and international enrollment in educational coursework has flattened since 2015.

At present, the United States receives the highest number of international students in the world on a per capita basis primarily due to the number of well-known higher education institutions across the country. China has been the largest feeder for international students to the United States since 2008, followed by India and South Korea (Loudenback, 2016; Passos, 2015; Stephens, 2013). Students from the top two countries of origin, China and India, represent approximately 50% of the total enrollment of international students in the United States (IIE, 2018). The year 2017 marked the 11th consecutive year of reported expansion of nonimmigrant student visas in U.S. higher education. However, since 2016, new international student enrollments have decreased by 6.6%; approximately 30,000 fewer new students have enrolled in U.S. universities and colleges since 2015–2016 (IIE, 2018).

International enrollment professionals familiar with the international transfer student population understand that there are two distinct sources of transfer. Receiving institutions admit international students originating from not only institutions outside of the United States but also colleges and universities located within the United States. For the purposes of this chapter, we shall define these two groups in the following manner:

> *Domestic International Transfer Students (DITSs)*—Nonimmigrant international students transferring from higher education institutions *inside* the United States. These students are more familiar with the norms associated with higher education in the United States.
>
> *Foreign International Transfer Students (FITSs)*—Nonimmigrant international students transferring from an institution(s) *outside* the United States. These students benefit from orientation and support services that help to familiarize them with the structure of higher education in the United States.

From an enrollment management perspective, understanding the educational, cultural, and academic performance background of these students is important. DITS and FITS identification helps guide the development of institutional polices related to admission, credit transfer, and immigration services. Gaining access to higher education in the United States is a multistep process that extends beyond completing an online application. In general, after a student is admitted, finances, visa acquisition, and travel and living arrangements need to be arranged.

Current Trends in International Student Enrollment

Within the United States, current political factors are influencing international student enrollments. The 2017 political effort by the Trump administration to implement a travel ban (and the subsequent abortive attempt during the COVID-19 pandemic to deport international students if they were not enrolled in at least one in-person course) threatened recruitment plans to attract more international students (Choudaha, 2017). However, political forces and administrative policies have been threatening the stability of the international student market for decades. According to Armstrong (2007), "higher education in the United States is rapidly losing its global luster" (p. 134) due to discouraging immigration rules in the United States that instead open the doors to other English-speaking countries. Choudaha (2018) identifies various reasons for the declining interest in U.S. education, which include the increased cost of U.S. tuition, strict immigration policies, and a decrease in institutional financial aid for international students. In addition, prospective students are concerned that there are fewer opportunities for employment in the United States after graduating. Compounded by the "unwelcoming rhetoric of the Trump administration" (p. 3), he points to a concerning trend that seems to indicate that international students are seeking alternative destinations.

Canadian higher education is benefiting from the political situation in the United States. Harris (2017) claims that Canadian higher education institutions witnessed a recent spike in international applications provoked by the 2016 United States presidential election. According to the ICEF Monitor, a dedicated market intelligence resource for international education industry, international enrollment in Canadian higher education has increased a dramatic 20% from 2016 to 2017 and 40% since 2015. Canada's student visa program offers attractive pathways toward employment and permanent residency (ICEF Monitor, 2017). In addition, Australia and Japan are witnessing a double-digit percentage increase in international enrollment (ICEF Monitor, 2018). In sum, the political arena can quickly threaten the economic gains enjoyed by numerous institutions in the United States when international students choose to enroll elsewhere, but issues of rising costs of education and reduced employment opportunities after graduation are also significant driving factors in the slower growth of international enrollment.

Recommendations for U.S. institutions to combat noted declining trends are dependent on the size, international presence, and mission of the institution. Due to "uncontrollable factors" such as increased competition, strict immigration policies, and unfavorable political trends, Choudaha (2018) recommends that institutions of higher education develop "proactive outreach strategies" that help "support student success" (p. 8). To create a successful learning and living environment, for example, he recommends reinvesting a portion of the income generated from international student tuition by expanding services to this population and offering them new scholarship opportunities.

Admission

The likelihood that international transfer students will be admitted into U.S. institutions varies depending on the previous educational experience(s) presented within the application portfolio. DITSs hold an advantage in the transfer process assuming they have attended regionally accredited universities or colleges in the United States. Prior educational experiences within the United States frequently remove the international applicant's burden to prove English proficiency and increase the likelihood that receiving institutions will accept transfer credit. In order to enhance international enrollment, the removal of barriers to entry is a key strategy. For example, at the University of Cincinnati, if any transfer student successfully completes at least 30 semester hours (or 45 quarter hours) of college-level credit, these applicants are exempt from submitting high school transcripts for admission. Furthermore, if the student has earned a grade of C or better in a three-semester-hour course (or the equivalent on the quarter system) of introductory composition at their previous university or college, they are exempt from submitting any standardized English language test scores for admission such as the Test of English as a Foreign Language (TOEFL) or the International English Language Testing System (IELTS). The retrieval of official U.S. transcripts is often standardized and efficient. The National Student Clearinghouse and other organizations facilitate electronic delivery for many institutions' transcripts on behalf of the students.

The secure electronic delivery of academic records is not a global norm. Acquiring official original transcripts from other countries outside the United States can be quite burdensome. In many countries, registrars will only issue one transcript at the point of graduation. The registrars at some foreign universities may have policies that require a student to be physically present to receive an official transcript of earned coursework. This presents a challenge when U.S. institutions require a sealed and stamped original transcript submitted directly from the sending institution. In a transfer-friendly environment, records management personnel are equipped to authenticate and evaluate the documentation the student has "in-hand" rather than requiring official sealed documentation sent directly from the sending institution. International credential evaluation services such as World Education Services and Education Credential Evaluators offer training to records management personnel on verifying the authenticity of these documents. Institutional policies that can provide "in-house" authentication will remove barriers students may face during the application process. Certified credential evaluation associations such as the National Association of Credential Evaluation Services (NACES) or professional organizations like NAFSA: Association of International Educators are excellent resources for institutions concerned with developing admissions and credit transfer policies that maintain academic credibility and provide access and equity to international transfer students.

Standardized tests of English, such as TOEFL and IELTS, present numerous challenges for international students such as the expense of the exam as well as the expense and time spent traveling to limited testing locations abroad. Students also feel intimidated by these high-stakes standardized tests. Both the institution and the student benefit when educational leaders propose alternative policies to remove unnecessary admission barriers. For the DITS applicant, proof of English proficiency is in the academic transcript. At the University of Cincinnati, if the DITS population can prove success within the U.S. higher education system, they would not need to pursue standardized testing or obtain proof of graduation from high school.

FITSs, students who have never attended higher education institutions in the United States, have a very different admissions process than DITSs. Some standard transfer admissions practices require the FITS population to not only prove their English ability but also endure a grueling and lengthy process to determine the worthiness of their previous education. In general, while both international and domestic applicants report feeling anxious as they await the arrival of their decision letter, this period of anxiety is prolonged for the international transfer student. International enrollment professionals often face questions of how to compare a foreign transfer student educated abroad to a transfer student coming from a regionally accredited U.S. institution. Some institutions lack trained personnel to evaluate international transcripts. Admissions policies at these institutions dictate that applicants are required to submit their transcripts to a foreign credential evaluation company. These companies are usually vetted through the foreign credential evaluation accrediting organization NACES. Students must incur the cost of having their transcripts evaluated course by course, typically between $175 and $225 per record. These companies research the institutions and transcripts supplied by the student. The result is a professional evaluation that informs enrollment managers of the student's grade point average, semester hours (or quarter hours) earned, and equivalent letter grades for each course. These evaluations also describe the equivalent level of education attained, any earned degrees and the entrance requirements for the program of study. However, the time and costs required to secure this type of informative document are enough to turn many students away from applying. Delays are frequent in decision turnaround time. The process from point of application to evaluation may take 1 to 2 months assuming all the needed application materials are submitted on time.

International Credit Transfer

Comparing courses and credit earned at non-U.S. regionally accredited colleges and universities to that of the courses offered at U.S. institutions presents a unique set of challenges. Without specialized training, international enrollment professionals may find the evaluation process to be difficult and perplexing. For example, international records do not differentiate between lab and lecture courses. Sometimes academic terms are displayed as yearlong courses instead of by semesters or quarters. Lastly, some transcripts do not clearly indicate credit hours or hours appear to be excessive. Due to the diverse nature of the credits presented on international academic records, the process for granting credit is often inconsistent, unregulated, and unpredictable. Transfer students frequently discover that credit is recognized for coursework from abroad, but the awarded credits are inapplicable toward their desired degree in the United States.

Admission staff at institutions with inconsistent and undocumented credit transfer policies struggle to answer essential questions such as "If I transfer to your school, how long until I can graduate?" or "How many of these courses do I need to retake?" Institutions may witness a decrease in international enrollments if they have not established procedures to regulate the transfer of international credit.

The proactive concept of awarding "credit where it's due" is often fostered at institutions that value the educational experiences of non-native transfer students. Adhering to rigid and simplistic policies is detrimental to recruitment and retention. Sweeping policies, for example, insisting that no credit will be awarded if the sending institution is not regionally or nationally accredited is problematic for the FITS population. Aside from branch campuses of U.S. institutions that are located overseas, regional accreditation is rarely granted to colleges and universities outside the United States. Some reasons why most regionally accredited institutions will not accept a wider variety of transfer credit from institutions that lack accreditation include maintaining their own accreditation, loss of revenue when credit is transferred, and lack of staffing resources. McComis (2005) states,

> Accountability for transfer of credit is placed wholly upon sending institutions in that these institutions must demonstrate the equivalency of credit to a receiving institution. By setting standards which prohibit restrictive transfer-of-credit policies, an accrediting agency could also hold accountable receiving institutions for policies and practices related both to acceptance and denial of credit transfer. (p. 7)

U.S. institutional statements often cite desired values such as social responsibility, cultural competency, and the ability to effectively deal with a complex, diverse, and evolving global world. If U.S. universities are held to the same ideals that they expect to cultivate in their students, then these institutions should practice those ideals when developing international transfer credit policies.

International Articulation Agreements

Postsecondary U.S. institutional policies should support the student's development and progression toward obtaining a degree or credential. Articulation agreements between two institutions are contracts that spell out several aspects of collaborative agreements that usually involve research, student exchange, and/or credit transfer. Creating international articulation agreements with partner universities and colleges outside the United States is one way to create a seamless progression toward degree completion.

Articulation agreements benefit transfer students by creating a potentially stable and successful transfer environment. These agreements offer a guarantee between two institutions such that the amount of time needed to attain a degree is minimized. For articulation agreements that involve credit transfer, the contract should include a guarantee of an articulated curriculum that fosters a streamlined process for seamless transfer of credit from one institution to another.

In other words, an articulation agreement provides structure for recognizing a student's credit such that the credit award does not fluctuate when transfer occurs.

These agreements can be program specific (e.g., a chemistry major with a 2+2 articulation agreement) or institution wide. Institutional agreements tend to last longer than program-specific agreements due to less dependence on specific faculty and academic unit heads to maintain effectiveness and consistency.

Setting goals to internationalize the campus will affect the level of commitment toward creating international articulation agreements. Partnerships can succeed or fail depending on factors such as leadership, commitment level and expectations, language and cultural differences, academic freedom perspectives that vary with political constraints, balance of exchanging students and faculty, health and safety issues, clarification of roles for the institutions and individuals involved, and shifting priorities and goals (Van de Water et al., 2008). Building lasting relationships with key stakeholders at international institutions will affect a far greater number of students for many years to come.

Immigration Issues

All international students face the unique challenge of obtaining a nonimmigrant student visa to enter the United States for their education. After the events of September 11, 2001, the passage of the Patriot Act and the Enhanced Border Security and Visa Reform Act required stricter scrutiny of student visa approvals and enhanced monitoring of students currently on a student visa. As such, institutions are required to manage an extensive database, the Student and Exchange Visitor Information System (SEVIS), a program administered under the Department of Homeland Security. Institutions must capture critical data regarding each international student, including permanent and temporary addresses, citizenship and place of birth, sources of financial support, and dependent information where applicable. In a post–September 11, 2001, world, prospective international students themselves must also navigate a complex, expensive, and time-consuming process in order to obtain a Form I-20 (Certificate of Eligibility for Nonimmigrant Student Status) to apply for an initial F-1 student visa. This process involves no fewer than five stages in which students are required to pay over $500 in processing fees, obtain nearly a dozen documents, and appear for an in-person interview at a U.S. consulate or embassy (U.S. Department of State–Bureau of Consular Affairs, n.d.). Unsurprisingly, key findings from a survey by IDP Education USA (2018), in which over 2,900 prospective international students participated, indicate that the United States lags far behind other destination countries in perception of ease of visa requirements.

Completing this process does not guarantee that a student will receive a visa, and often students experience challenges that fall outside of their control. Factors that can contribute to student visa denials include the following:

- Timing of the application in the academic calendar
- Location. If a student's country of origin has a fraught political relationship with the United States, or a high visa overstay rate, the student may have more

difficulty obtaining a visa. This disproportionately impacts students from the developing world.

- Student financial resources (i.e., private family funds, government sponsorships, or institutional scholarships). A student from a low socioeconomic background is at a distinct disadvantage.
- English proficiency. Students with lower English proficiency often experience increased difficulty obtaining a visa.
- The reputation of the American institution. An admission offer by a prestigious institution may make the F-1 visa process easier.
- Existing stereotypes. Toutant (2009) provides the example of Jamaican students who have a difficult time in obtaining visas due to negative associations with crime and drugs.

Like the admissions process, students who have never attended higher education institutions in the United States (i.e., FITSs) have a different immigration process than students who are transferring from one U.S. institution to another (i.e., DITSs). These students must apply for their initial student visa at a U.S. embassy or consulate abroad in the process outlined in the previous paragraphs. While DITS are not required to obtain a new student visa to transfer between institutions, they must go through a different process in which they request that their SEVIS record be electronically transferred to their new institution. While institutions may differ slightly in protocol, the standard transfer process for DITSs is as follows:

- Students must first notify their current U.S. institution's international office of their intent to transfer and submit the necessary documentation to initiate this process. This documentation usually involves both an admissions letter to the students' new institution, and a standard "Transfer Out" form. On this form, students will indicate the receiving institutions SEVIS school code, along with requesting a transfer "release date"—the date by which they request that their record be released to their new institution. Students must maintain their status and continue attending classes while awaiting their transfer, and they cannot have more than a 5-month gap between their last day of attending classes at their current institution and the first day of attending classes at their new institution.
- Once a student's SEVIS record has been transferred by a designated school official (DSO), a new I-20 can be processed. The student's new institution will require the student to submit documentation including passport copies and proof of finances before issuing the new transfer pending I-20.

While this process is straightforward, complications can often arise, most commonly around travel and work authorization. For example, if a student requests a SEVIS transfer during summer vacation and leaves the United States before receiving a new I-20, when the student enters the United States at a port of entry with their previous institution's I-20, the SEVIS record will appear to Customs and Border Patrol officials as "deactivated." The student may then face additional questioning, referred to as "secondary inspection," or, in rare cases, be denied entry into the United States altogether.

In another common scenario, students may be unaware that their employment, whether on campus or authorized off campus, is tied to their active I-20 at their current institution. If students are employed on campus during the summer at their current institution and request a SEVIS transfer release date to their new institution on June 1, they must cease employment on that date. Continuing employment would constitute unauthorized work and, if disclosed, could result in the termination of the students' I-20. Unquestionably, an established transfer protocol along with clear communication between the student, the sending institution, and the receiving institution is critical, as failure to do so can result in negative and lasting consequences.

To conclude, an appreciation of the depth and complexity of students' pre-enrollment immigration experiences is integral to assisting international transfer students. Institutions interested in providing a welcoming environment to their international transfer students should be mindful of the frustrations and hurdles experienced due to the rigorous immigration process and be equipped to help students navigate the complexities of U.S. immigration regulation.

International Students: The Community College Choice

International students seeking higher education opportunities in the United States often select community colleges as the start of their educational journey. According to the latest Open Doors Report (IIE, 2018), there have been 96,472 nonimmigrant international students studying at associate degree–granting colleges in the United States since 2017. International community college students comprise 8.9% of the total international student population of all higher education institutions in the United States (IIE, 2018). The largest 2-year institution for international enrollment, the Houston Community College System, supports 5,982 international students (IIE, 2018). Many of these students, like their domestic counterparts, will transfer to an institution that grants baccalaureate degrees.

Despite the various barriers and challenges that studying in a foreign country poses, international student resilience and success is evident. Among the major racial and ethnic groups, foreign-born students experience greater success on several key indicators including persistence to graduation and transfer rates as compared to native-born students (Bailey & Weininger, 2002).

What attracts international students to the community college campus? The decision to attend a community college as opposed to a 4-year institution may be determined by several factors including the open-access mission, the lower costs than 4-year institutions, English language training opportunities, and small class sizes. The cost of ESL courses within community colleges is often less expensive than at a baccalaureate-level college or private intensive English courses. In addition to language learning, ESL courses offer a chance for international transfer students to receive informal counseling and peer learning from ESL instructors (Szelenyi & Chang, 2002).

Fostering a Welcoming Environment

To cultivate a welcoming culture for international transfer students, the receiving institution's enrollment management and academic advising plans should be inclusive of this population. The literature reflects that successful transition to a new institution for the domestic transfer student requires some mentoring and assistance to complete the transfer process. Adjustment to a new and possibly larger institution is a daunting task for many students (Townsend & Wilson, 2006). For the international transfer student, the challenge is even greater as cultural adjustments in addition to "psychological, academic and environmental challenges" are intertwined (Laanan, 2001, p. 5). Unfamiliar with transfer credit policies and accreditation issues within the United States, the international transfer student will require an even greater "hand hold" as described by Townsend and Wilson (2006, p. 450). Some transfer students will be coming from institutions where "it is easier to find out what to do and how to do it" (p. 452). Faculty and staff will have greater success integrating new international transfer students into the campus culture if proactive measures focused on international transfer student recruitment, advising, and retention are established in advance.

Much of the literature focuses on the challenges encountered by domestic transfer students such as transfer shock and the major transition from a community college to a large research university; however, very little examines the international transfer student adjustment process. The research of Jain et al. (2011), however, does suggest ways to develop an international "transfer receptive culture." Primarily, inclusion of international students should clearly be part of the institution's planning process. Special consideration and thought should be given to hiring culturally competent staff dedicated to serving not only the new incoming first-year international students but also the international transfer student population. In sum, the institution must value the diversity international transfers bring to the campus from their home institution abroad or from a different sending institution within the United States.

Another element to consider is the type of programming, literature, and staff training needed to make international transfer students feel welcome. Cultural factors and possibly second language requirements need to be considered when developing publications and outreach efforts to welcome new international students. For example, common institutional jargon should be clearly defined online and in print publications. What may seem obvious to a domestic student may not be apparent to international students transitioning to a new campus. For example, terminology such as *credit hour, grade point average, quality points, prerequisites, transcript evaluation, freshman, sophomore, junior, senior, faculty, college, school,* and even the most basic of terms such as *course* may have a very different meaning in the United States than in the student's home country. Cultural differences related to topics such as the concept of time, women in positions of authority, and negotiation and direct communication styles may need to be explained, reiterated, or stressed depending upon the student's original culture and/or prior experiences in the United States. Perceptions of academic integrity may vary between countries. To illustrate, plagiarism in the U.S.

culture is typically an unknown concept in some Asian academic cultures "in which the norm is to repeat back a textbook or a professor verbatim (without a citation) as a sign of respect to the source of knowledge" (Redden, 2007, para. 7).

Support programming designed especially with the needs of the international transfer student in mind, is essential to retaining this unique student population. International transfer students may feel uncomfortable if mixed-in as an after thought with traditional U.S. first-year students. Transfer students want to be recognized for their maturity and experience at the graduate and undergraduate levels. New transfer students are challenged to find friends on campus as other experienced college and university students "may have little interest in expanding their social groups" (Townsend & Wilson, 2006, p. 450). On a related note, while transfer students desire an orientation that contains some elements typical of a first-year orientation, they also desire separate sessions geared specifically with transfer student needs in mind (Townsend, 2008).

Intentional peer-to-peer programming that allows international transfer students to "develop a sense of belonging" (Jain et al., 2011, p. 259) is essential. Some institutions, for example, create communication frameworks whereby experienced third- and fourth-year students are trained to serve as mentors to new international students. Aware of what it feels like to live and learn in a new country or campus, study-abroad returnees may be interested in being matched with a new international transfer student to offer guidance during the first year on the new campus. Mentoring may occur in-person and online. At the University of Cincinnati, a student group called the International Partners and Leaders serves as a student network that meets to make new friends, learn about life at UC, and share their culture with one another (University of Cincinnati, n.d.). Educational leaders may want to employ social media to address the needs of international transfer students from the point of pre-application to enrollment and beyond as an efficient way of communicating vital information. Similarly, highlighting the academic or personal achievements of international transfer students in newsletters, online blogs, or in presentations is another way to demonstrate that the institution values the diversity of this unique population.

The development of a welcoming culture for international transfer students will not occur automatically. Intentionality is critical to facilitating the academic and social integration of this population. Larger institutions with a centralized international center are generally equipped with the staffing and resources to offer specialized programming and support services. There are measures, however, that smaller institutions can take to provide services without a centralized international hub. One suggestion for successful integration is to develop a nonresidential-based learning community for transfer students to facilitate small group interaction (Townsend & Wilson, 2006). Learning communities typically bring a diverse group of first-year students together on a weekly basis over the course of an academic term based on a shared academic interest. These learning communities, however, do not need to be restricted to first-year students. Mixing both domestic, international, first-year, and transfer students together offers numerous intercultural communication learning opportunities. Campus newcomers are often unaware of the services the institution has to offer such as academic support, financial aid, counseling, health, employment, student organizations, educational seminars, and community engagement activities. Learning communities designed specifically for new transfer students offer an opportunity for faculty, student affairs/student success representatives, and/or selected third- and fourth-year students to share information about campus resources.

Another suggestion at the departmental level is for faculty to host a welcome reception or welcome dinner for all transfer students. Considering the international transfer student population, perhaps campus event organizers may want to design the event with the countries of origin in mind. Many transfer students do not want to be housed with incoming first-year students. The campus student housing office may want to consider the allocation of a floor or wing reserved for paired transfer students (Townsend, 2008). Some international transfer students confirm their admission later in the cycle after learning about financial aid and the applicability of transfer credit. As a result, international students are sometimes the last to confirm their housing application. To welcome newcomers to campus and demonstrate a commitment to diversification of the student body, the housing office should have space reserved for international transfer students confirming later in the cycle.

Culturally Competent International Enrollment Professionals

The rapid internationalization of campuses within the United States has consequently produced a need for culturally competent staff and faculty. While there are many different definitions of *cultural competency*, the term referenced here refers to one's ability to accurately understand and adapt behavior when engaged with culturally distinct others (Deardorff, 2011). Educational leaders seeking to hire international admissions professionals cite cultural competency as important since these professionals are frequently the first point of contact for prospective international students. International enrollment professionals have daily contact with prospective students around the world seeking admission to degree-granting colleges and universities in the United States. Recruitment frequently involves travel to overseas territories. International enrollment professionals achieve successful outreach efforts by developing relationships with counselors, advisors, and agents from a multitude of different cultures. Qualities that define individuals who are culturally competent include flexibility, curiosity, respect, open-mindedness, the ability to tolerate ambiguity, sensitivity, empathy, cultural humility, a knowledge of other world cultures, and effective cross-cultural communication skills (Bennett, 2009; Deardorff, 2011; Lombardi, 2010; Sinicrope et al., 2007). Other factors include suspension of judgment, an appreciation of differences, a willingness to engage with those of other cultures, a tendency to question cultural stereotypes, an ability to comprehend the worldviews of others, and a desire to incorporate the positive aspects of other cultures into one's routine (Bennett, 2009; Deardorff, 2011; Sinicrope et al., 2007). According to Bennett (2009), the familiar lists of salient features that describe intercultural competency are an "excellent starting point for assessing" but in the end "no list fits all cultures, all contexts, all conditions" (p. 122). Without skilled culturally competent recruiters, U.S. institutions will be challenged to outpace other countries eagerly devoted to targeting the expansion of the international student market.

Sending recruiters overseas to meet with prospective students does not necessarily afford staff members the opportunity for the development of cultural competency. Merely experiencing another culture as a visitor, completing a course with international learning outcomes, or spending some time in another country is not adequate to sufficiently develop the cultural competency skills that are so highly desired and expressed in the core values of institutions of higher education (Bloom & Miranda, 2015). According to Deardorff (2011), self-growth necessitates the assessment of intercultural competence throughout the process over time, allowing individuals the opportunity to self-reflect on personal progress. By completing journal entries, blogging or writing positional papers, individuals seeking to move toward an ethnnorelative orientation make better sense of their interactions. Ethnorelative refers to a worldview orientation where one respects differing cultural values and attitudes. Individuals with an ethnorelative worldview orientation tend to be more open-minded and appreciative. In sum, intentional and deliberate efforts for self-improvement foster the development of intercultural competence (Deardorff, 2011).

Conclusion

International transfer students may originate from institutions of higher education within the United States or from institutions located beyond U.S. borders. In either case, these transfer students encounter unique challenges along the pathway to enrollment. Difficulties in obtaining transcripts, securing a student visa, traveling to test sites, and developing the ability to navigate a new campus culture are a few of the topics discussed. This chapter argues that simplified institution-wide transfer policies and articulation agreements will help to reduce barriers. Lastly, intentional cultivation of a transfer-friendly campus with culturally competent faculty and staff is essential if enrollment managers desire to grow or accommodate the international transfer student population.

Recommendations

In summary, institutions should take the following steps to foster a welcoming campus environment for international transfer students:

- Determine if international student admissions and transfer credit policies align with your institution's mission statement regarding internationalization of the campus (and if you don't have such a statement you should consider developing one if you hope to provide legitimate experiences for international transfers).

- Examine institutional policies and practices that allow for transfer credit pathways through formalized articulation agreements with institutions overseas or postsecondary U.S. institutions.
- Train culturally competent admissions representatives, staff members of the registrar's office, and academic advisors to understand the differing needs of international transfer students.
- Consider the unique needs of international transfer students. These needs include housing that places international transfer students with globally minded domestic and international students; a welcome reception or unique social gatherings for new international transfer students; campus amenities that are sensitive to people of other cultures (e.g., a prayer space or a communal vegan-friendly cooking area, etc.).
- Hire culturally competent staff and faculty members. Offer ongoing cultural competency training opportunities for international educators.

Discussion Questions

The development of institutional practices and policies conducive to improving international transfer student admission and retention rates requires awareness, motivation, and deliberate effort. International educators interested in developing new initiatives may want to consider asking themselves the following questions:

1. Is internationalization an integral part of our institution's mission statement?
2. Does my institution have documented international transfer credit policies that are clearly defined and communicated to key stakeholders? What is the current process for evaluating foreign credentials from postsecondary institutions overseas?
3. How can we reduce barriers to international transfer admission?
4. How does my institution define *cultural competency*? Are we considering cultural competency when hiring new staff and faculty?
5. What amenities do we offer to welcome international transfer students? Are there welcoming events and opportunities for students to share their own unique cultures?
6. To what extent are we perceived by our current international students to be "international student friendly"?

References

Armstrong, L. (2007). Competing in the global higher education marketplace: Outsourcing, twinning and franchising. *New Directions for Higher Education, 140,* 131–138. https://doi.org/10.1002/he.287

Bailey, T. R., & Weininger, E. (2002). Performance, graduation, and transfer of immigrants and natives in the City University of New York Community Colleges. *Educational Evaluation and Policy Analysis, 24*(4), 359–377. https://doi.org/10.3102/01623737024004359

Bennett, J. M. (2009). Cultivating intercultural competence: A process perspective. In D. K. Deardorff (Ed.), *The SAGE handbook of intercultural competence* (pp. 121–140). SAGE.

Bloom, M., & Miranda, A. (2015). Intercultural sensitivity through short-term study abroad. *Language and Intercultural Communication, 15*(4), 567–580. https://doi.org/10.1080/14 708477.2015.1056795

Cantwell, B. (2015). Are international students cash cows? Examining the relationship between new international undergraduate enrollments and institutional revenue at public colleges and universities in the US. *Journal of International Students, 5*(4), 512–525. https://files.eric.ed.gov/fulltext/EJ1066279.pdf

Choudaha, R. (2017). Three waves of international student mobility (1999–2020). *Studies in Higher Education, 42*(5), 825–832. https://doi.org/10.1080/03075079.2017.1293872

Choudaha, R. (2018). *A third wave of international student mobility: Global competitiveness and American higher education.* The Center for Studies in Higher Education. https://cshe .berkeley.edu/publications/third-wave-international-student-mobility-global-competitive ness-and-american-higher.

Deardorff, D. K. (2011). Assessing intercultural competence. *New Directions for Institutional Research, 2011*(149), 65–79. https://doi.org/10.1002/ir.381

Harris, K. (2017, September 3). *Foreign students flock to Canada as government struggles to get grads to stay.* CBC News. http://www.cbc.ca/news/politics/international-students-jump-1.4268786

ICEF Monitor. (2017, November). *Canada's international student enrollment surged in 2016.* http://monitor.icef.com/2017/11/canadas-international-student-enrolment-surged-2016/

ICEF Monitor. (2018, August). *Up and down the table: Growth trends across major international study destinations.* http://monitor.icef.com/2018/08/up-and-down-the-table-growth-trends-across-major-international-study-destinations/

IDP Education USA. (2018). *International student buyer behaviour research 2018.* https:// www.idp.com/partners/news-article-12/

Institute of International Education. (2015). 2015 *Open Doors report on international educational exchange.* https://www.iie.org/Why-IIE/Announcements/2015/11/2015-11-16-Open-Doors-Data

Institute of International Education. (2018). 2018 *Open Doors report on international educational exchange.* https://www.iie.org/Why-IIE/Events/2018/11/2018-Open-Doors-Press-Briefing-Washington-DC

Jain, D., Herrera, A., Bernal, S., & Solórzano, D. (2011). Critical race theory and the transfer function: Introducing a transfer receptive culture. *Community College Journal of Research and Practice, 35*(3), 252–266.

Laanan, F. S. (2001). Transfer student adjustment. *New Directions for Community Colleges, 114,* 5–13. https://doi.org/10.1080/10668926.2011.526525

Lombardi, M. R. (2010). Assessing intercultural competence: A review. *NCSSSMST Journal, 16*(1), 15–17. http://files.eric.ed.gov/fulltext/EJ930654.pdf

Loudenback, T. (2016, September 16). International students are now 'subsidizing' public American universities to the tune of $9 billion a year. *Business Insider.* http://www.business insider.com/foreign-students-pay-up-to-three-times-as-much-for-tuition-at-us-public-colleges-2016-9

McComis, M. (2005). *Transfer of credit: A policy agenda.* Accrediting Commission of Career Schools and Colleges of Technology. http://www.accsc.org/UploadedDocuments/Transfer %20of%20Credit%20Policy%20Agenda.pdf

Passos, S. (2015, June 2). How international students are subsidizing U.S. universities. *Splinter News*. http://splinternews.com/how-international-students-are-subsidizing-u-s-univers-1793848068

Redden, E. (2007, May 24). Cheating across cultures. *Inside Higher Ed*. https://www.insidehighered.com/news/2007/05/24/cheating-across-cultures

Sinicrope, C., Norris, J., & Watanabe, Y. (2007). Understanding and assessing intercultural competence: A summary of theory, research, and practice (Technical report for the Foreign Language Program Evaluation Project). *University of Hawai'i Second Language Studies Paper, 26*(1). https://scholarspace.manoa.hawaii.edu/handle/10125/40689

Stephens, P. (2013, September/October). International students: Separate but profitable. *Washington Monthly*. http://washingtonmonthly.com/magazine/septoct-2013/international-students-separate-but-profitable/

Szelenyi, K., & Chang, J. (2002). ERIC review: Educating immigrants: The community college role. *Community College Review, 30*(2), 55–73. https://doi.org/10.1177/009155210203000204

Toutant, L. E., (2009). *International graduate students, the F-1 visa process, and the dark side of globalization in post 9/11 American society* (Unpublished dissertation). University of California, Los Angeles, CA.

Townsend, B. K. (2008). "Feeling like a freshman again": The transfer student transition. *New Directions for Higher Education, 144*, 69–77. https://doi.org/10.1002/he.327

Townsend, B., K., & Wilson, K. B. (2006). "A hand hold for a little bit": Factors facilitating the success of community college transfer students to a large research university. *Journal of College Student Development, 47*, 439–456. https://doi.org/10.1353/csd.2006.0052

University of Cincinnati. (n.d.). *International Partners and Leaders (IPALs)*. https://campuslink.uc.edu/organization/uc-international-partners-and-leaders

U.S. Department of State–Bureau of Consular Affairs (n.d.). *Student visa overview*. https://travel.state.gov/content/travel/en/us-visas/study/student-visa.html

Van de Water, J., Green, M., & Koch, K. (2008). *International partnerships: Guidelines for colleges and universities*. American Council on Education.

Weller, J. D. (2012). *Improving the cultural acclimation of international students enrolled in American colleges and universities* (Doctoral dissertation). ProQuest no. 3518124.

PART THREE

TEACHING AND LEARNING

12

THE CHIEF ACADEMIC OFFICER'S ROLE IN TRANSFER STUDENT SUCCESS

Mark Canada

hief academic officers (CAOs) and provosts have good reasons to think—indeed worry—about college transfer. For many of us, transfer students make up a sizable portion of our student populations. According to a 2018 report from the National Student Clearinghouse Research Center, more than 1 million, or 38%, of the 2.8 million first-time students beginning college in 2011 transferred to another institution (Shapiro et al., 2018). Furthermore, the "birth dearth" the United States experienced after the 2007–2009 recession will leave the country with a much smaller pool of high school students for 2-year and 4-year institutions to recruit. Grawe (2018), citing figures from the Western Interstate Commission for Higher Education, predicts a 9% drop in enrollment in the late 2020s (and this prediction was made before the COVID-19 pandemic). In this highly competitive recruiting environment, we can expect to see in the Midwest and other regions institutions looking to transfer as a viable source of enrollment. Finally, and most importantly, transfer students face their own set of challenges when it comes to student success—and student success is (or ought to be) the raison d'être for all our institutions.

Many offices and individuals play a role in supporting transfer students, but success depends on leadership, and provosts are ideally positioned to provide this leadership. This chapter is written by a CAO especially for other CAOs and provosts serving at 4-year baccalaureate level transfer-receiving institutions. However, it also speaks to the essential contributions of other educators to the success of transfer students, especially faculty at both sending and receiving institutions who teach transfers and the chairs of academic departments serving large numbers of transfers.

While we have the potential to touch and shape much of the formative work around transfer, we often must operate through influence, not control, just as we must do in realms such as overall student success, promotion and tenure, and the like. As CAOs, we can use our unique position to cultivate a transfer-friendly culture, recognize faculty and staff who support transfer students, and jump-start transfer initiatives, particularly curricular change. Along the way, we should develop and leverage strong relationships with our counterparts at 2-year institutions; these fellow CAOs can be valuable partners in helping our shared students to persist and graduate.

At Indiana University Kokomo, where I am CAO, we employ several strategies described in the following section, and we have seen some positive developments in college transfer. Notably, fall-to-fall retention for transfer students under the age of 20 has increased from 59% in 2013 to 80% in 2018. We also have seen a slight increase in the number of transfer students coming from our main feeder schools—from 154 in 2013 to 170 in 2017. As is often the case, it is difficult or impossible to attribute these positive developments to specific initiatives, but the strategies described in the next section are worth considering as part of a holistic approach that CAOs can lead as they strive to attract, retain, and graduate more transfer students.

Identity Challenges

In some respects, transfer students may seem like ideal candidates for success. Because they have some college credit, they are closer to earning a degree than most students fresh from high school. Ideally, transfer students come to their new institutions with some degree of knowledge and experience that will help them succeed in the challenging college environment. These advantages often outweigh any disadvantages of being a transfer student, but the disadvantages present substantial challenges that provosts and CAOs should know and address. As part of my research for this chapter, I met with several of my institution's advisors, who shared specific challenges they have encountered in their work with transfer students and communicated with admissions staff at our institution. I also spoke to several transfer students about their own experiences and have drawn liberally from these conversations.

The first step provosts should take toward promoting transfer on their campuses is to identify these challenges. The most obvious challenge many transfer students face is related to the first advantage noted in the previous paragraph—that is, transfer students have earned some college credit, but "bringing in" that credit is not automatic. Students may assume, logically, that their success in completing, say, 15 credits for courses in composition, quantitative reasoning, history, biology, and psychology will mean that they are exactly 15 credits closer to a degree and they will not have to take what appear to be these same courses at their new institutions. Provosts know better; as much as we all would appreciate a system that allowed for seamless transfer of courses equal in content and rigor, we don't yet have such a system.

Indeed, some of our institutions make transfer difficult despite good intentions. Byzantine general education requirements (two of *these* courses or three of *those*, but only if *these* three don't include any one of *those* over there) are confusing enough for new students, but these idiosyncratic curricular requirements are particularly problematic for transfers. They increase the likelihood that these students will need to take additional courses (increasing time, expense, and the threat of prematurely exhausting their limited amount of eligible financial aid) to earn their degrees. If, for example, a receiving institution requires a particular type of math or composition or, for that matter, more credits for general education than the sending institution, students may not have completed the necessary general education requirements even if they were diligent in working through those requirements at their initial institutional home. Provosts probably have encountered at least a few examples of such specialized requirements over the course of their careers. Perhaps they have seen a general education curriculum that required *ancient* philosophy, *world* politics, or *applied* physics instead of general courses that introduce students to the basic components and approaches of these disciplines. The intentions behind these specific requirements may have been good (particularly at some distant time in the past), but the results become barriers to transfer students.

Similarly, faculty who take a "purist" approach when assessing credit coming from other campuses complicate matters. Faculty are right not to count, say, a studio sculpture course toward an art history requirement, since making art does not leave students with a better knowledge of the history of art. On the other hand, insisting that an art history course at the source institution cover exactly the same artists or themes as the one at the new institution seems excessive, particularly since many would argue that general education should expose students to general principles and "ways of knowing" rather than specific examples within the discipline. A transfer student I interviewed for this chapter explained that he had taken three writing courses at his previous institution and still had to take a writing course at his new institution. While we can imagine good reasons for "guarding the line," we also can understand the frustration that many transfer students feel, and we ought to be willing to look for ways to calm the too-often treacherous waters of college transfer.

Students often rely on advisors to navigate these waters. Strong, appropriate advising, then, can help to overcome this challenge; but fragmented, incomplete, or inappropriate advising can leave students adrift or even exacerbate problems. If students are interacting with two or more advisors at the sending institution, for example, they may receive conflicting or fragmented information about courses they will be able to bring into their new institutions. Even sound advising at the sending institution may not adequately prepare students for transfer, since this advising is, logically, oriented around that institution's curriculum. At community colleges, for example, the focus may be on 2-year degree completion rather than fulfilling requirements for the 4-year degree that students might seek in the future at another institution. Finally, at the point when students are moving from one institution to another, advisors at the new institution rely on advisors or registrar staff at the former institution for transcripts. Delays may mean that students cannot make good decisions about courses to take initially at the new institution, since their new advisors cannot know which of their earned credits will count toward their new degrees.

Communication can help identify some of these institutional barriers. Consider organizing a summit in which you and your counterparts at 2-year institutions—ideally staff from each institution's advising and admissions offices, as well as academic leadership—can discuss challenges and solutions. Deans and chairs can collaborate on pathways that advisors and admissions counselors can promote and explain to students at the 2-year institutions.

Students themselves present challenges, as well. Some try to enroll at their new institutions only weeks or days before the beginning of a semester, leaving little time for advisors and others at these institutions to assess their transcripts and other paperwork. Even those who enroll well in advance may not be sufficiently informed about articulation agreements that could facilitate transfer, shorten time to graduation, and save them money. In Indiana, 2-year students who declare their interest in a Transfer Single Articulation Pathway (TSAP) and complete the prescribed courses in any one of several disciplines, such as biology and criminal justice, are guaranteed the opportunity to earn a 4-year degree at our institution as long as they complete our prescribed courses, which can amount to no more than 60 credit hours. Of course, students who are not aware of TSAPs (and thus do not declare and take the right courses at their 2-year institutions) lose out on this opportunity.

Cultivate a Transfer-Friendly Culture

How should provosts use their formal and informal spheres of influence to address the specific challenges that their transfer students face? The most important strategy is to develop a transfer-friendly culture on their campuses. As in the case of the "culture of student success," a transfer-friendly culture can dramatically affect an institution's performance by normalizing supportive attitudes and key behaviors. In short, a culture of transfer recognizes the value of transfer students (both to the institution and in their own right) and prioritizes their success.

Cultivating any kind of culture is hard, and changing one entirely is even harder, so provosts should strive to be both deliberate and diligent in their efforts. Invest time in gathering information about the challenges transfer students face, as well as the strategies that advisors and others on your campus are using to support these students. Talk to some transfer students. (You may be very surprised by what you learn.) Your conversations with the people on the front lines will not only inform your future efforts to facilitate transfer and prioritize transfer students' success but also paint you a picture of the campus culture as it now stands. Are your advisors able to secure decisions from faculty on course equivalencies in a timely manner? Are they getting what they need from advisors and registrars at the main feeder institutions? Do they feel supported? How about the transfer students themselves? Do they find your institution a welcoming place to be? Were they able to bring in all or most of the credit(s) they earned at their previous institutions? Do they feel that your institution fully appreciates the challenges involved in successful transfer and acts commensurately? What would they change about the onboarding and the overall culture on your campus?

Once you have a sense of the current culture, you can target some aspects that need tweaking (or overhauling). You may hear that advisors are waiting a long time to get decisions from faculty or mixed messages about course equivalencies. Perhaps students are telling you that they found transfer onerous because of a host of idiosyncratic requirements at your institution, or that faculty seem indifferent to the challenges they face in making the transition to a new institution.

Changing the culture will necessitate communications with faculty, but these communications must be carefully crafted. After all, because of their roles and perspectives, administrators tend to worry about enrollment more than many faculty members do—and faculty know it. For this reason, calls to facilitate transfer may come across as mercenary money grabs. While attracting more transfer students will increase enrollment and promote the financial health of the institution, enrollment and financial health are not the only reasons—or even the best reasons—to facilitate transfer and support transfer students. As well, those reasons are not likely to resonate with many faculty.

A better strategy may be to lead with the important issues of access, diversity, equity, and success. Transfer students are, after all, human beings with goals, abilities, and, more to the point, challenges that make their progress more difficult than that of first-time college students. At my institution, for example, 18.5% of our transfer students in fall 2017 were attending part time (compared with only 2.5% of other students), and 36.5% of them were 25 years old and older (compared with 1% of other students). Given these numbers, we can assume that many have family and work obligations. The human side of transfer is likely to be lost in the day-to-day work that faculty are doing in their teaching, scholarship, and service. Indeed, unless they specifically request this information, they may never know which of their students came from other institutions. Transfer, in short, will be nothing more than an abstract concept unless someone, such as a provost or a distressed transfer student, makes it personal. One way to put a face on transfer is to connect faculty with the transfer students themselves, as well as the advisors who work with them. Another way is to organize a focus group with transfer students to include their voices, literally. Quote or paraphrase these students and advisors when you communicate with faculty. Even better, bring some transfer students and advisors to a meeting of the Faculty Senate, a relevant campus committee, or department meetings and let them tell their own stories in person.

This approach can help provosts build a culture of transfer among existing faculty. New faculty, staff, and administrators are an important ingredient in overall culture change, and here provosts wield a different kind of influence. Provosts decide who will serve as deans (who, in turn, decide who will serve as chairs, who, in turn, hire faculty and academic staff), and they have influence at all levels of hiring. In short, no one becomes a dean, chair, assistant professor, lecturer, adjunct instructor, member of the academic staff, or, in the case of centralized advising housed in academic affairs, advisor of an institution without the provost's approval.

Hiring and developing administrators, particularly chairs and deans, is especially important, since they often decide whether to accept specific transfer credits.

Additionally, they are often the people most likely to work directly with transfer students who are declaring majors in their units. At many institutions, chairs review individual transfer student transcripts to determine what will or will not count for equivalent status. The potential here for generosity, openness, and goodwill is enormous—but so is the potential for capriciousness and prejudice! Chairs must strive to be open, but also fair, consistent, and conscientious. A chair who is eager to welcome transfer students, guide them toward good decisions, and follow up with them as they progress—or don't progress—can make the difference between success and failure for many transfer students. One transfer student told me that the helpfulness of a chair made a dramatic difference in her positive transfer experience. Hiring transfer-friendly faculty is important, as well, as instructors are both the faces of the institution and the people with the most direct influence on students' success. Because they have the greatest influence on appointments of new faculty, transfer friendly or not, chairs play an indirect, but crucial role in this respect, as well.

Ideally, when approving job postings and interviewing candidates, provosts can screen for candidates with experience, awareness, and strategies that will promote the success of transfer students. This approach can help provosts identify strong candidates for chair and dean positions, but it will go only so far in the case of faculty searches, since most candidates for these positions, especially doctoral students completing graduate school, probably have little or no special expertise working with transfer students. This shortcoming could be exacerbated by the fact that the research institutions where they may have been teaching assistants probably did not have strong cultures of transfer. Still, it may be worthwhile to ask open-ended questions, such as "Tell me about your experience with college transfer," particularly since some candidates may be able to draw on their own experience as a transfer student to speak to challenges and strategies for overcoming these challenges.

Even if provosts cannot expect a pool of candidates with extensive experience with transfer, they can take care to craft the message that goes out to these candidates in ads and interviews. A provost, for example, might make a point of telling every faculty candidate, "More than a third of our students come to us from other institutions, and we work intentionally to promote their success through both teaching and advising." After hearing such a message, candidates who embrace the challenge of serving transfer students are more likely to accept a job offer than those who do not. Furthermore, those who do wind up accepting an offer come in with their eyes wide open; their minds have been primed for the culture of transfer, along with your institution's attendant strategies and resources, and they are more likely to contribute enthusiastically and effectively to your efforts.

A transfer-friendly culture can result in dividends that are intangible but powerful. One transfer student I interviewed told me he appreciated the climate on our campus, saying of the people he encountered, "They all knew who I was . . ." and adding that his advisor was "very sweet and very kind." A student-athlete pointed out that our institution helped arrange for him to room with a teammate who shared his values.

Reward Contributions to Transfer

Even for all of the converts you have created and the true believers you have recruited with the strategies previously described, supporting transfer students will take a back seat to research, course development, and committee service if your institution does not tie rewards to work for transfer. For junior faculty, aligning work with rewards is a crucial survival strategy. Indeed, the zero-sum math is familiar to any administrator who has tried to stack additional work on top of existing faculty workloads. Every hour spent on an institutional priority outside tenure guidelines is an hour taken away from work explicitly recognized in the guidelines. Provosts, of course, do not control tenure or promotion guidelines, but they can guide conversations. They typically meet with Faculty Senate leadership, and they have the strongest voice of anyone on the academic side of the institution. Besides, if they have been following the strategies previously described, they should have some new and existing faculty colleagues who value transfer work. Ideally, a few of them are thought leaders in their units. These faculty members can help to get transfer work into tenure and promotion guidelines.

Their best approach, as provosts can help them to see, is to promote this work as an *option*. Faculty rightly get nervous, even resistant, when administrators seem to be pushing to substitute a new priority for an existing one, particularly when the new one is something that seems external to faculty work and the existing one is teaching or research. Far less troubling is an *opportunity* to earn recognition for doing mission-critical work. Chances are, a sizable proportion of your faculty colleagues would welcome the opportunity to develop transfer-friendly curricula and pedagogy, contribute to initiatives supporting transfer students, and perhaps even help with recruiting these students. They just want to know that this work will count for something. Something as simple as adding a few transfer-related examples to a list of kinds of evidence that faculty can consider citing as demonstration of teaching or service can go a long way toward promoting this work on a campus. The following are just a few possibilities:

- Designed a success course for transfer students
- Served on an orientation panel for transfer students
- Used one-on-one conferences with students to assess prior learning at previous institutions

Providing options allows faculty who want to invest their time and energy into valuable work for transfer students to "count" this work when they apply for tenure.

Other forms of recognition can help drive home the point that the institution values work that helps transfer students succeed. For example, provosts can secure modest funds to launch annual awards for faculty and advisors whom transfer students have nominated for their outstanding support. If the campus has a newsletter, provosts can invite the campus community to contribute shout-outs for faculty, advisors, and others who have gone the extra mile for transfer students. These little

"Way to go!" messages not only provide positive reinforcement for those recognized but also say to everyone who reads them, "Our institution values work for transfer students."

Deploy Initiatives

These strategies for building a culture of transfer and rewarding those who are serving transfer students will help make the ground fertile for a variety of initiatives aimed at helping transfer students succeed. Some are administrative initiatives that require no formal approval and thus are under the direct control of the provost or fellow administrators. The most important of these initiatives is the development of a clear transfer pathway into your institution. Transfer students already have invested time and energy (and, in some cases, a lot of money) in their education; they want to know that they are on a direct pathway to a degree when they invest in completing their education at your institution. Individual institutions can set up articulation agreements with community colleges, such as the TSAPs previously described, and establish very clear degree pathways on their own campuses. In any case, ensure that all requirements are described clearly on your institution's website, and provide online tools so that students can track their own progress through these pathways.

Additional administrative initiatives can facilitate transfer in other ways:

- To build partnerships with source institutions, provosts can arrange for "Meet & Greet" events, summits, and meetings of discipline-based affinity groups. Such meetings provide valuable venues to troubleshoot minor problems, share major challenges, and develop broad-based solutions. Consider inviting your counterparts at 2-year institutions to help solidify positive relationships.
- To attract potential transfer students and help them get off to a strong start, schedule "Transfer Visit Days" where prospective transfer students can learn how many credits your institution will accept, meet with advisors, and so on. Have students submit transcripts in advance to leave plenty of time for transcript assessment. Work with your counterparts at 2-year institutions to help ensure strong attendance and to provide these students with the information they need.
- In consultation with your counterparts at 2-year institutions, arrange for one of your institution's advisors to have office space and hours on their campuses. Strive to integrate them into the advising centers at these institutions. There, they can communicate directly with potential transfer students about your institution's admission requirements, course equivalencies, and so on.
- To reduce complications associated with transcript review, set earlier deadlines for transfer enrollment. In addition, if possible, provide multiple start points for transfers.
- Consider expanding course offerings (evening and weekend courses, online courses, and 8-week sessions) in ways that will facilitate a student's progress

with consideration for their individual life circumstances. At my institution, online classes have proven especially popular among transfer students: 54.6% of our transfer students took at least one online class in fall 2018 (compared with 35.7% of other students), and 13.4% of these students took all classes online in fall 2018 (compared with 3.6% of other students).

- Consider building special programs tailored for transfer students and designed to promote their success. Along with other regional campuses of Indiana University, IU Kokomo participated in a grant-funded ABC (Associate + Bachelor's = Career) program, which froze tuition for transfer students who participated and placed a specialist in community colleges to offer guidance to students on these campuses. As a member of our institution's admissions team told me, this specialist can provide an initial evaluation of a student's transcript and answer questions, but, perhaps more importantly, can also look out for warning signs, such as low grades or a move from full-time to part-time enrollment. The ABC program, according to an interim report submitted to the granting agency, attracted a sizable number of students: 514 as of January 2018, nearly twice the initial goal of 270. Two thirds of these students were still enrolled and active at the time of the report (Buckman, 2018).

In most cases, provosts can collaborate with direct reports or fellow administrators to enact these changes in relatively short order.

Other administrative initiatives require broader participation—and, in some cases, faculty approval—and thus call for a different approach. For example, provosts may see value in providing orientations and summer bridge programs designed specifically and strategically for transfer students, establishing positions for transfer advisors, and developing faculty learning communities and workshops on serving transfer students, along with accompanying incentives for participation. Some may wish to consider offering an open-ended major, such as general studies, which can facilitate progress toward a degree for students with lots of disparate college credit. At my institution, 52.6% of the students who graduated with a general studies degree in 2017–2018 were transfer students. This last initiative may be a controversial one on some campuses; provosts and their faculty will have to decide whether they feel that a college major must involve some disciplinary expertise. Even if they do, they still could elect to develop an interdisciplinary major, rather than an open-ended one, and thus accommodate students with various credits while also requiring some disciplinary focus (e.g., see the bachelor of arts in interdisciplinary studies at the University of South Carolina at Columbia, developed in 1972 to accommodate transfer students).

Even on a campus with a strong transfer-friendly culture, it is crucial that provosts plan and act very strategically when pursuing these or other broad-based initiatives. Faculty and staff are famously (and justly) wary of administrative initiatives, and even a single misstep is potentially harmful to not only a transfer initiative but also future initiatives the provost wants to champion. As a result, a very promising transfer initiative can go down—in flames and on the record—as yet another "idea du jour" and become a chapter in the lore that primes faculty and staff for initiative fatigue. To avoid this fate, provosts should be intentional with each of the following steps:

- *Take a grassroots approach.* Faculty and staff are much more likely to embrace, support, and run programs they have been deeply involved in creating. Have lunch with some colleagues who have shown special interest in transfer, along with faculty and staff thought leaders, just to bat around some ideas about potential opportunities and challenges. Take advantage of campus walks to drop in on colleagues and have some informal conversations. Call some brainstorming sessions. Listen, listen, listen.

- *Empower faculty and staff to lead.* Once the conversation is well under way, you will need someone to turn the ideas into a plan, and that someone is not you (if you are a CAO). You may elect to give a charge to an existing committee, such as one leading work on student success in general or convene a new task force.

- *Show real interest.* People care what a provost thinks, so demonstrating your interest in the progress of the planning can be powerful. Talk informally with the members of the committee or task force from time to time and report—or let the chair report—on its progress to the rest of the campus community.

- *Balance autonomy with your involvement.* If you seem to be taking over the work of the committee or task force, it will no longer be a grassroots initiative. At the same time, if you keep too much distance, the work may stall or fizzle. Some informal check-ins with the chair and the occasional visit to a meeting can be very helpful in ensuring progress.

- *Provide deadlines.* A lot of useful and interesting thought can go into the challenges transfer students face and ways to address them. At some point, though, there needs to be a plan with action steps and assignments to people responsible for these action steps. To ensure that the committee or task force gets to this stage, schedule or three meetings when the group will report on its progress to you and set deadlines for a preliminary draft and final recommendations.

- *Follow through on recommendations.* This step is the most important. Countless faculty and staff members have had the experience of working diligently, perhaps over many months, on a plan that never becomes anything more than a plan. A provost who fails to follow through on recommendations alienates the people who invested time and energy into these recommendations *and* may start to develop a reputation as indifferent, feckless, or even incompetent. Before you even begin any of this work, work with your president/chancellor and chief financial officer to ensure that you will have the financial and political capital to enact all the sound recommendations you receive. Commit yourself to completing each step and check yourself often.

One type of initiative deserves special attention. As previously noted, a chief challenge for both the enrollment and the success of transfer students is curricular:

Students earn credits for courses taken at their previous institutions and then have trouble "bringing in" these credits when they transfer to new institutions. Launching an initiative that creates a more transfer-friendly curriculum, especially regarding general education, requires a very delicate touch. Because faculty control the curriculum, provosts depend on their willingness to make changes, and this willingness depends on the rationale for making them. Some of your faculty colleagues may have been heavily involved in designing the current curriculum, and some—even if they did not contribute to its current configuration—have a stake in it. To cite just one example, the English professor who believes in the value of American literature as part of well-rounded education (and really likes to teach the standard survey course) is likely to question a proposal to change a literature requirement from "one course in American literature and one course in world literature" to "one course in literature." Such a proposal is, after all, threatening on both philosophical and practical levels to someone who has spent years immersed in a discipline's specialty, one that has become intertwined with their own identity. This can be seen as no small threat, and provosts need to address it head-on by helping faculty to consider not only content and their own teaching preferences but also the institution's priority of student success. If requiring specifically *American* literature is impeding progress toward a degree for transfer students, it is counterproductive (and I make this point as a professor who specializes in American literature). A course with different content still helps students to learn the skills of literary analysis, consider universal themes of the human experience, and conduct research and make arguments. In short, allowing it to count toward a general education requirement achieves the major goals of general education while also facilitating college transfer for many students, ultimately probably leading to more college degrees.

The approaches just described—for cultivating a transfer-friendly culture and for jump-starting initiatives—can help provosts overcome this threat. For example, before calling on a curriculum or general education committee to consider curricular changes, provosts should work with advisors, as well as staff from the admissions and registrar's offices, to identify barriers the current curriculum presents to transfer students. Both data and anecdotes supported by data can be useful here. Here are some questions worth asking:

- Are transfer students taking longer to complete their degrees at your institution than they are at peer institutions?
- Can advisors point to actual situations in which transfer students they advised had to take a course practically identical to one they took at a previous institution?
- Are there certain courses that many transfer students have taken at major transfer sending schools, particularly community colleges, but that never qualify for transfer into your institution? What tweaks might your institution make (or ask the sending institutions to make) to make these courses eligible for transfer? For example, if your institution never accepts a certain math

course from a local community college because it includes no instruction in statistics, would the faculty at the community college consider integrating such instruction into the course and thus facilitating transfer into your institution?

Again, provosts should take care to frame these barriers as threats to real human beings striving to earn degrees that will positively and permanently transform their lives.

You may help by encouraging committee members to look for creative ways to accommodate these transfer students while still preserving the institution's values. For example, if your institution is an outlier because it requires a separate general education course in information literacy, perhaps it could eliminate this course, but integrate information literacy into another course, such as a first-year seminar college success course and/or gateway courses within majors (where the instruction could be more customized and thus presented in such a way that it is more relevant, meaningful, and valuable to the students in the course).

At my institution, we worked successfully with faculty to streamline our general-education program, ultimately making it more transfer friendly. Specifically, the associate provost, working with advisors, produced a report showing the barriers that our general education program was creating for transfer students, and the chancellor shared copies with every academic department. She and I attended department meetings where we spelled out the need for reform, answered questions, and addressed concerns. Later, a task force took up the task of revisiting general education requirements and developed a revised program that would retain the essential principles of general education while better serving transfer students (as well as incoming online students). The Faculty Senate approved this revised program, and it went into effect in fall 2019.

Curricular change is the most challenging form of change on the academic side of an institution, but it may make the greatest difference in the success of its transfer students. Provosts must be sensitive, strategic, and persistent if they want to see positive change.

Conclusion

Indeed, sensitivity, strategy, and tenacity are essential to success in general when it comes to leading change that will serve transfer students. By cultivating a transfer-friendly culture and rewarding those who support transfer, provosts create fertile ground for positive change. They then can begin planting seeds for specific initiatives, including curricular changes, that will facilitate transfer and promote the success of transfer students.

In short, through their formal and informal influence, provosts can collaborate with their faculty and staff colleagues to craft an environment that both attracts transfer students and supports them as they advance successfully toward their college degrees.

Recommendations

1. Identify challenges. Draw on the experience and expertise of advisors, admissions and registrar's staff, faculty, and others to determine what barriers transfer students encounter, as well as possible solutions.
2. Create a culture of transfer. Help faculty and staff see a seamless transfer system as a means to cultivating both access and success for a very large group of students. Strive for a culture that provides a personal touch to transfer students.
3. Reward those faculty and staff who support transfer. Look for ways to revise tenure guidelines. Establish awards and other forms of recognition.
4. Jump-start initiatives that facilitate transfer and support transfer students. Work with direct reports and fellow administrators to launch administrative initiatives. Employ a more nuanced, strategic approach to seed grassroots initiatives requiring broad-based participation and/or faculty approval.

Questions for Discussion

1. What challenges are your prospective transfer students facing?
2. What is the culture of your campus when it comes to transfer? Are faculty and staff aware of transfer students' situations and challenges, or are they laser-focused on first-time college students?
3. What kind of campus climate do your transfer students encounter when they come to campus? Do advisors and others make them feel confident and comfortable or intimidated and unwelcome?
4. What is your relationship with major source institutions, particularly community colleges? Do you know one another's challenges, curriculum, advising systems, and so on?
5. Is your institution's curriculum "friendly" to prospective transfer students, or does it consist of onerous and byzantine requirements that will impede or even repel them?

References

Buckman, C. (2018). *Third interim report to the Kresge Foundation: Implementation of the adoption and adaptation of the GSU (Illinois) dual degree program at Indiana University and Ivy Tech Community College—The ABC Program (250162)* [Unpublished report]. Indiana University–Kokomo.

Grawe, N. D. (2018). *Demographics and the demand for higher education.* Johns Hopkins University Press.

Shapiro, D., Dundar, A., Huie, F., Wakhungu, P.K., Bhimdiwali, A., Nathan, A., & Youngsik, H. (2018, July). *Transfer and mobility: A national view of student movement in postsecondary institutions, fall 2011 cohort* (Signature Report No. 15). National Student Clearinghouse Research Center.

13

MOMENTUM STOPPERS AND EQUITY BLOCKERS

The Implications of Gateway Courses for Students at Their Transfer-Receiving Institutions

Andrew K. Koch and Brent M. Drake

This chapter explores how transfer students fare in foundational, "gateway" courses they take after the point of transfer. The chapter is an extension of our previously published scholarship focused broadly on students enrolled in gateway courses (Koch, 2017a, 2017c, 2018; Koch & Drake, 2018, 2019). That scholarship shared outcomes in gateway courses both in aggregate and disaggregated by various common demographic classifications, but it did not include transfer standing. This chapter sheds light on what we believe is a long-standing but rarely discussed issue in higher education—the fact that students who transfer to a new postsecondary institution take gateway courses at their new college or university and they do not fare as well in them as many would believe.

Wang et al.'s (2017) scholarship does suggest that classroom experiences in gateway courses taken at the community college can play a pivotal role in developing transfer student momentum. This effect is particularly evident in math courses taken at the community college; successful completion early on in math at a community college is directly related to a higher rate of credential completion (Wang et al., 2017). While Wang et al.'s research has focused on how gateway course success at the community college can lead to higher credential attainment for students in the science, technology, engineering, and mathematics (STEM) fields, it is applicable to other subjects as well. That shared, Wang et al.'s research is focused only on community college transfer-bound students in gateway courses. We have discovered no published research looking at transfer student performance in gateway courses in transfer-receiving institutions.

We share findings drawn from a sector-spanning, 36-institution data set on "DFWI rates"—the combined rates of D grades, F grades, W grades for any form of withdrawal formally listed on a transcript, and I grades for incompletes or the equivalent thereof on a transcript—for transfer students enrolled in eight specific foundational-level "gateway" courses at the institution to which they each transferred. Four courses are from the STEM fields—college algebra, calculus, general biology, and general chemistry. Three are courses in the humanities and social sciences—English composition, U.S. history, and general psychology. The last is a course required for all business majors—principles of accounting.

For purposes of this chapter, we are drawing on the definition for *gateway courses* provided by Koch and Rodier (2014) and Koch (2017b) and used in the nonprofit John N. Gardner Institute for Excellence in Undergraduate Education (Gardner Institute) course redesign efforts (Gateways to Completion) over the past 7 years. In accordance with that body of scholarship and work, *gateway courses* are defined as courses that are:

- *Foundational:* These courses may be noncredit-bearing developmental or remedial education courses that often serve as "gateways to the gateway courses" themselves. They are also, and more commonly, college credit-bearing courses—generally at the lower-division level.
- *High risk:* Course risk levels are identified by the rates at which D, F, W, and I grades are earned across sections of the course(s). Note that there is no set threshold or rate; what constitutes a "tolerable" rate must be defined in local institutional contexts.
- *High enrollment:* These courses are identified by the number of students enrolled within and/or across course sections. Some institutions have a few sections of a course with each enrolling hundreds of students. Others have much smaller section sizes but offer many sections of that course. As with the "high-risk" designation, there is no set rate or threshold since context matters. All institutions, whether they enroll 400 or 40,000 undergraduates, have high-enrollment courses. What constitutes high enrollment at one institution differs from another, but the courses are a near universal feature in U.S. higher education.

As supported by the data we share and buttressed by other forms of our previous scholarship in the following discussion, gateway courses serve as a pivotal academic hurdle for students. But the deleterious implications associated with courses are disproportionately borne by students who have been historically underrepresented and/or underserved by higher education in the United States. In many disciplines, this is defined by race/ethnicity and family income (Koch, 2017a, 2017c, 2018; Koch & Drake, 2018, 2019). In the STEM fields in particular, where females are grossly underrepresented, this also includes gender (Weston et al., 2019).

This chapter, the first of our efforts to examine transfer students and gateway course outcomes, considers race/ethnicity, family income, and transfer standing as part of our overall analysis. We use the data available to us to answer the following three questions about transfer students in gateway courses at the institutions to which they transferred—also known as the transfer-receiving institution.

1. Do transfer students have lower or higher DFWI rates when compared to their non-transfer counterparts in the courses?
2. Do transfer students of color as defined by federal race/ethnic classification have higher or lower DFWI rates when compared to both the average DFWI rates for transfers in the courses and the DFWI for their White transfer counterparts in the courses?
3. Do transfer students from low-income families/backgrounds have higher or lower DFWI rates when compared to their non-low-income transfer counterparts in the courses?

The findings lead us to conclude that gateway courses serve as "momentum stoppers"—academic experiences that can derail baccalaureate degree aspirations—and "equity blockers"—academic experiences that deter just outcomes in a variety of academic disciplines by preventing students of color and students from low-income backgrounds from continuing in a particular field of study. But before delving into the findings that support our conclusions, we first must share a bit about our method.

Brief Methodological Overview

The data for this study are drawn from a convenience sample of 36 institutions that agreed to work with the Gardner Institute on processes to redesign their undergraduate experiences—especially the first college year and/or gateway courses. While the sample is limited by the fact that these are all institutions that have been willing to participate in broader undergraduate education redesign projects conducted by the Gardner Institute, it does have the benefit of providing a broad array of institutional types. There are 26 public institutions and 10 independent (private) institutions in the sample. Two of the independent institutions are proprietary (for profit). The remaining 34 institutions are not for profit. Additionally, by Carnegie classification, the sample comprises seven associate colleges, six baccalaureate colleges, 14 master's colleges and universities of all size classifications, and nine doctoral universities of all research activity classifications.

As a part of participation in the undergraduate education redesign processes in which they were engaged, the institutions each submitted a large set of de-identified student and course data. This included data on introductory courses across the curriculum. Those institutions were asked to use the definition for *gateway courses* provided earlier in this chapter to select the courses on which they would focus their redesign efforts. Most frequently, faculty and staff chose courses fitting the following eight course types: principles of accounting, college algebra, general biology, introductory college calculus, general chemistry, general psychology, English rhetoric and composition, and introductory U.S. history. We are choosing to focus on these eight courses in this chapter simply because the institutions chose to focus on them for their redesign efforts.

The institutions submitted data on these courses spanning the 2005–2006 through 2015–2016 academic years—with the earlier academic year ranges allowing for analysis of 4-, 5-, and 6-year graduation rates in other studies not discussed in this chapter. The full data file, consisting of over 1.2 million records, contained the following:

- *Course data:* course type, instructor type, mode of instruction, course number, section, initial grade, final grade
- *Student registration data:* enrollment, retention, degree completion, student classification, degree type, academic program (classification of instructional programs/CIP codes), credits, credits source
- *Student demographic data:* race/ethnicity, gender, first-generation status, entry term, birth date, high school location, high school GPA, prior degrees, GED status
- *Financial aid data:* Pell grant eligibility and recipient status, Free Application for Federal Student Aid (FAFSA) filing date, grant award status

For the purpose of this study, the data were limited for each institution to the academic year prior to their implementation of any efforts associated with the gateway course redesign process in which they were involved—also known as the baseline year data. Applying this method, the baseline years for the gateway course data ranged between 2012–2013 and 2014–2015 for the 36 institutions involved in the study.

We used the baseline data to calculate a DFWI rate for each institution by course. The DFWI rate is the percentage of DFWI grades of the total grades awarded in the course. We then calculated the mean DFWI rate for a course from the institutions' individual DFWI rates. We wanted to know how aggregate DFWI rates in a specific course were similar or different to other courses in other disciplines—such as college accounting compared to college calculus—rather than knowing how DFWI rates in calculus at a specific institution differed from those outcomes at the other 30-plus institutions in the data set. As a result, we did not factor in or weight DFWI rates by institutional enrollment in a specific course.

We also decided not to factor in course enrollments at a specific institution. Had we factored in institutional course enrollments in the DFWI rates—in other words, weighted the DFWI rates by the institutional enrollments in a given course—we would have skewed the data toward a few institutions with the largest student populations in a specific course. This would potentially inflate or deflate the DFWI rate issue based on outcomes at a few institutions in the data set that were much larger than the majority of the institutions in the study.

As Table 13.1 shows, not all 36 institutions offered or provided data for all eight course subject areas we examined in this chapter. In the case of principles of accounting, 32 institutions provided data; 33 provided general biology data; 31 provided general chemistry data; 34 provided English composition/writing data; 32 provided

TABLE 13.1

Rates of D, F, W, and I Grades in Gateway Courses by Transfer and Non-Transfer Classifications

A. Course	B. Number of Institutions	C. Total Number of Students Across the Courses	D. Average DFWI Rate All Students	E. Non-Transfer, First-Year DFWI Rate	F. Transfer DFWI Rate	G. Non-Transfer, Upper-Level DFWI Rate
Principles of Accounting	32	18,217	30.1%	36.3%***	25.3%***	28.5%***
General Biology	33	24,636	29.7%	34.8%***	29.8%***	24.7%***
General Chemistry	31	20,987	29.4%	32.1%***	27.5%***	28.5%***
English Composition	34	96,258	22.8%	23.5%***	23.6%***	22.5%***
History (U.S. Survey)	32	27,666	25.1%	29.8%***	21.2%***	17.2%***
Math—Algebra	34	55,075	34.8%	34.6%***	38.2%***	31.5%***
Math—Calculus	32	13,253	34.6%	34.9%***	41.5%***	40.0%***
General Psychology	34	91,108	25.3%	28.4%***	22.3%***	20.2%***

*$p < 0.05$, **$p < 0.01$ *** $p < 0.001$

data on U.S. history; 34 provided algebra data; 32 provided data for calculus I; and 34 provided data on general psychology.

We disaggregated the data for these eight courses by race/ethnicity and family income status, as well as by transfer-student standing. Transfer-student standing is used to indicate whether a student did or did not transfer into the institution where they took the gateway courses we examined. What follows are the questions we used to guide this analysis for the eight previously mentioned courses and both the aggregate and disaggregated findings.

Questions and Findings

Three main questions about transfer student performance in gateway courses guided our research for this chapter. Each of these questions forced us to make choices about the population to which we would compare the transfer students. The three questions and the logic framing our analysis—our comparison population "choices"—follow:

1. *Do transfer students have lower or higher DFWI rates when compared to their non-transfer counterparts in the courses?* We further divided this by comparing transfers to two non-transfer populations: non-transfer, first-year students and non-transfer, upper-level students. We defined *non-transfer, first-year students* as any student enrolled in the courses who was not a transfer and had earned fewer than 30 earned credits at the time they were enrolled in the considered courses. We defined *non-transfer, upper-level* students as any student who was enrolled in the courses, and who had earned 30 or more credits at the time they were enrolled in the courses. This definition allowed us to compare transfer student performance in these courses to a largely new student population (non-transfer, first-year students) with whom they shared "new to the institution" transition characteristics. The approach also allowed us to compare the transfers to non-transfer, upper-level students with whom they often shared academic standing—that is, sophomore/second-year, junior, or senior standing.

2. *Do transfer students of color as defined by federal race/ethnic classification have higher or lower DFWI rates when compared to both the average DFWI rates for transfers in the courses and the DFWI for their White transfer counterparts in the courses?* Given that the previous question allowed us to compare transfers to non-transfers, for purposes of this second question—a question focused on race/ethnicity—we decided to hold transfer student classification as constant. For this reason, we did not compare transfer students of color to non-transfer students of color. Such a study has merit—it is just beyond the scope of what we were able to consider in this chapter given our two other questions and chapter length considerations.

3. *Do transfer students from low-income families/backgrounds have higher or lower DFWI rates when compared to their non-low-income transfer counterparts in the courses?* As with the transfer question focused on race, we decided to limit our examination of the relationship between family income and transfer DFWI

rates strictly to transfer students. In other words, we are comparing low-income transfer students to the non-low-income transfer student counterparts in the courses. We used Pell grant eligibility as the determinant as whether a student was or was not a low-income transfer student—with Pell-eligible transfers being classified as low-income and non-Pell-eligible transfers being classified as non-low income.

Statistical Significance—Method, Findings, and Thoughts

We are adding content on statistical significance here, because, as supported by the outcomes reported in Tables 13.1, 13.2, and 13.3, the method is identical and the findings are essentially consistent for all three "slices" of the data. In this research, we compared group differences in percentage rates. For this reason, we use a Pearson's chi-square test to determine if the differences in DFWI rates were respectively independent of the students' transfer, race/ethnicity, and Pell status.

With a few exceptions, nearly all the between-group differences in DFWI rates found in each this chapter's three tables are statistically significant when compared to the other outcomes on the table row on which the rates are displayed. Many are significant at the $p < .001$ level. The only non-statistically significant outcomes were (a) the differences in DFWI rates in English composition by transfer student race/ethnicity displayed in Table 13.2 and (b) the differences in DFWI rates in both chemistry and algebra by transfer student Pell eligibility displayed in Table 13.3.

We have included this section about statistical significance here, because many readers will rightly wonder about whether the differences we display in our tables are "statistically significant." Without that evidence, some readers might be inclined to disregard this chapter and its findings. That would be a mistake—both for methodological and societal reasons.

The societal reason these data are important cannot be discounted. As educated citizens and scholars, we acknowledge that race- and income-based inequality are complex and deeply rooted social issues. Garcia et al. (2018) note that these issues are often "not readily amenable to quantification" (p. 151). Garcia et al. continue, noting that numbers are rarely if ever "neutral and they should be interrogated for their role in promoting deficit analyses that serve" dominant—frequently White and/or more affluent interests (p. 151). Further, they explain that data "cannot speak for itself"—that it must "be informed by the experiential knowledge of marginalized groups" (p. 151). Whereas most of the differences we report are, in fact, statistically significant, the meaning of the few that are not, as well as those that are significant at lower levels—such as $p < .05$ as opposed to $p < .001$—should not be dismissed. For example, just because the number of Native Americans transfers in English courses is too small to make their DFWI rate difference finding statistically significant when compared to other race/ethnicity groups, we should not dismiss the finding. In fact, the higher DFWI rate coupled with the lack of statistical significance is very meaningful—it speaks to how the legacy of extermination and forced removal manifests itself today in small Native American enrollment numbers and higher failure rates in courses.

TABLE 13.2

Rates of D, F, W and I Grades by Course and Selected Race/Ethnicity Designations for Transfers

A. Course	B. Number of Institutions	C. Number of Students Across the Courses	D. Average Transfer DFWI Rate	E. African American Transfer DFWI Rate	F. Native American Transfer DFWI Rate	G. Latinx Transfer DFWI Rate	H. White Transfer DFWI Rate
Principles of Accounting	26	5,740	25.3%	35.6%***	**57.7%***	35.3%***	24.0%***
General Biology	29	5,802	29.8%	**37.8%***	31.2%***	33.8%***	27.2%***
General Chemistry	26	6,325	27.5%	43.6%***	**55.7%***	35.2%***	25.6%***
English Composition	29	5,753	23.6%	19.4%	**24.5%**	23.1%	20.7%
History (U.S. Survey)	27	2,532	21.2%	**43.1%***	24.5%***	22.3%***	18.1%***
Math—Algebra	28	4,674	38.2%	**54.7%***	50.0%***	37.9%***	33.3%***
Math—Calculus	26	4,278	41.5%	45.0%*	**48.9%***	46.0%*	38.2%*
General Psychology	26	7,609	22.3%	**40.6%***	26.8%***	26.4%***	17.8%***

*$p < 0.05$, **$p < 0.01$ ***$p < 0.001$
Note. Bold numbers indicate the highest DFWI rate for each respective course.

TABLE 13.3

Rates of D, F, W and I Grades by Course and Pell-Eligibility Statuses for Transfers

A. Course	B. Number of Institutions	C. No. of Transfer Students Across the Courses	D. Average Transfer DFWI Rate	E. Pell-Eligible Transfer DFWI Rate	F. Non-Pell-Eligible Transfer DFWI Rate
Principles of Accounting	26	5,740	25.3%	30.9%***	22.3%***
General Biology	29	5,802	29.8%	33.4%*	29.4%*
General Chemistry	26	6,325	27.5%	27.2%	28.2%
English Composition	29	5,753	23.6%	23.6%***	18.0%***
History (U.S. Survey)	27	2,532	21.2%	25.9%***	16.5%***
Math—Algebra	28	4,674	38.2%	36.7%	35.5%
Math—Calculus	26	4,278	41.5%	41.8%***	33.0%***
General Psychology	26	7,609	22.3%	27.0%***	16.3%***

*$p < 0.05$, **$p < 0.01$ ***$p < 0.001$

Question 1: Comparing Transfer Students' DFWI Rates to Those of Non-Transfer Students

Transfers Compared to Non-Transfer, First-Year Students
As shown in Table 13.1, in five out of the eight courses—principles of accounting, general biology, general chemistry, U.S. history, and general psychology—transfer students have lower DFWI rates than non-transfer, first-year students. (See Table 13.1, column F for transfer and column E for non-transfer, first-year students.) The exceptions to this are the two math courses—college algebra and calculus I—and English composition. In those three cases, transfer DFWI rates exceed those of the non-transfer, first-year students in the courses—although in English composition the difference is only one-tenth of a percentage point (23.6% for transfers compared to 23.5% for non-transfer, first-year students).

The fact that transfers earn lower DFWI rates in five courses could be the result, in part, because they have "done college before"—a common refrain about transfer students, especially from those who argue that transfers need not be treated any differently than non-transfer students. But understanding what this really means is important. This could very well be a case of many transfer students not only having been in college before but also having taken these exact courses before. The failure of many institutions to award credit for prior learning may mean that the lower DFWI rate is a byproduct of transfer students having to retake courses that they already successfully passed at a previous postsecondary institution—thereby wasting money and prolonging time-to-degree. There are also many other plausible reasons for this finding; further study, especially transcript analysis, is merited here.

The differences in math also merit discussion and an attempt at explanation. In college algebra, transfers have a 3.6 percentage point higher DFWI rate—38.2% for transfers compared to 34.6% for non-transfer, first-year students. This constitutes a 10.4% higher rate of D, F, W, and I grades for transfers when compared to their non-transfer, first-year counterparts in the course. In calculus, transfers have a 6.6 percentage point higher DFWI rate—41.5% for transfers compared to 34.9% for non-transfer, first-year students. This represents an 18.9% higher rate of D, F, W, and I grades in calculus when comparing transfers to their non-transfer, first-year counterparts in the course.

The math differences in particular lead us to wonder if the lack of success has to do with, at least in part, the delay between when transfer students last took a math course, either in high school or at the transfer-sending institution, and when they took the same course as transfer students at the receiving institution. Presumably, most first-year students had taken at least 3 years of college preparatory mathematics courses—some 4. Simply stated, transfer students who may be many years removed from high school may have much larger gaps in time and perhaps also gaps in amount of preparation, between when they last took a math course and when they took it again at the transfer-receiving institution.

These gaps in time really matter. Students commonly report that knowledge gleaned in a particular course is rapidly lost once the course has ended. These self-reported perceptions are backed up by research (Conway et al., 1991; Kamuche & Ledman, 2011). In short, the more time that elapses between when a student takes a course and the next time they take a related course in the same subject area, the more knowledge from the previous course is forgotten.

This forgotten knowledge is exacerbated by anxiety—in the case of algebra and calculus, math anxiety. A growing body of research suggests that students who experience anxiety in a specific subject—particularly those who see themselves as otherwise successful students—are subconsciously motivated to forget subject matter in that subject as a coping mechanism to defend against memories that threaten their self-concept (Aronson et al., 1999; Sherman & Cohen, 2006; Tajfel & Turner, 2004). This phenomenon, known as "motivated forgetting" (Ramirez, 2017), may lead students to fail to encode threatening course content (Appel et al., 2011), reduce their interest in the field of study associated with the course (Cheryan & Plaut, 2010), or even disassociate all together with the field of study associated with the course (Major et al., 1998; Nussbaum & Steele, 2007; Osborne, 1997; Osborne & Walker, 2006; Schmader & Major, 1999).

We were not able to conduct transcript analysis for the transfer students in our examination since there were no available data of this kind from the sending institutions. However, the body of scholarship we reference in the previous paragraph gives us reason to believe that one of the reasons transfers do not do well in math courses at the receiving institution is because they had not taken math in the 1 or more years prior to transferring.

This hypothesis is applicable to more than just transfer students. It merits noting that non-transfer, upper-level students also have higher DFWI rates in calculus when compared to their non-transfer, first-year counterparts. Non-transfer, upper-level students have a 40.0% DFWI rate in calculus, which is 5.1 percentage points (14.6%) higher than the 34.9% DFWI rate that non-transfer, first-year students have in the course. These findings suggest that for both upper-level, non-transfer students and transfer students, math anxiety may lead to postponement of math taking. That postponement can be associated with increased forgetting of content which, in turn, is associated with higher rates of failure in the course.

Transfers Compared to Non-Transfer, Upper-Level Students
Previously, we introduced the phrase "non-transfer, upper-level students." For purposes of our research, we define *non-transfer, upper-level students* as non-transfer students who had 30 or more earned credits when they were enrolled in the course in consideration. This means they were at "sophomore-level" standing or higher. When compared to non-transfer, upper-level students, transfers have lower DFWI rates in only two courses: principles of accounting and general chemistry. (See Table 13.1, columns F for transfer and G for non-transfer, upper-level students.). Non-transfer, upper-level students have the lowest DFWI rate in five of the eight

courses considered. The three exceptions are the aforementioned calculus outcomes, where non-transfer, first-year students have the lowest DFWI rate of all groups considered, and the accounting and general chemistry courses where transfers have the lowest DFWI rate of all the groups considered.

The calculus outcome merits additional discussion. First-year students who place into calculus are generally the most "math-ready" student population. After all, they placed into calculus as an incoming first-year student and presumably did so based on placement tests, standardized test scores, and/or previous grades. Thus, one should not be surprised by the fact that they have the lowest DFWI rate in the course. This "lowest rate" should not be celebrated, however, as it still represents over a third of all students in the course (34.9%).

The fact that transfers have lower DFWI rates in accounting and general chemistry than non-transfers of all types—both first-year and upper-level—also merits some consideration. We believe that these outcomes may be the by-product, at least in part, of the receiving institution's perception that accounting and general chemistry courses at the sending institutions were inferior, thereby resulting in the transfer students being required to retake the course at the receiving institution. The perceived inferiority of the sending institution's version of the course may be the result of prejudice but not actual evidence. As noted by Holzer and Baum (2017), community college "students have particular difficulty transferring into other programs and to institutions because the credits they have earned are frequently not accepted" (p. 160). Considering this issue, the lower DFWI rates in these two courses could be more of a byproduct of transfers essentially being forced to retake courses at the receiving institutions that they have already passed at their previous sending institutions. Further research on course-taking patterns for transfer students in these fields—and others like them—is warranted to see if what we suggest is, in fact, supported by transcript evidence.

Question 2: Comparison of Transfer DFWI Rates by Race/Ethnicity Classifications

As supported by the data displayed in Table 13.2, *transfer students of color*—for purposes of our research defined as being students from African American, Native American, or Latinx race/ethnicity groups—almost always have a DFWI rate that exceeds the course average as well as the average for their White counterparts. (See Table 13.2, columns D, E, F, and G.) In four courses—general biology, U.S. history, college algebra, and general psychology—African Americans have the highest DFWI rates when compared to both the course average DFWI rate for transfers and the DFWI rate for transfers from all other race ethnicity groups we considered for this analysis. In the other four courses—principles of accounting, general chemistry, English composition, and calculus—Native Americans have the highest DFWI rate when compared to both the course average DFWI rate for transfers and the DFWI rate for transfers from all other race ethnicity groups we considered for this analysis. These rates are highlighted in bold.

The differences are striking in many instances. For example, in U.S. history, African American students have a DFWI rate that is 21.9 percentage points (103.3%) higher than the course average for transfers and 25.0 percentage points (238.1%) higher than that of White transfer students in the course. In general chemistry, Native American students have a DFWI rate that is 28.2 percentage points (102.5%) higher than the course average for transfers and 30.1 percentage points (117.6%) higher than White transfer students in the course.

These findings are consistent with other scholarship we have produced to date (Koch, 2017a, 2017b; Koch & Drake, 2018, 2019). Sadly, we must point out here the same point we made in those other publications—the race- and income-based inequity that is a part of the history of the United States continues in gateway courses. This study allows us to add that even being a transfer student—a student who has "done college before" and arguably did it successfully based on the student's ability to gain admission at the transfer-receiving institution—does not mitigate race- and income-related inequitable outcomes in gateway courses.

Question 3: Comparison of Transfer DFWI Rates by Income (Pell) Classifications

Table 13.3 shows that, like the students from the race/ethnicity groups in Table 13.2, transfer students who are eligible to receive a Pell grant—the federal grant for students from families from the nation's lowest income backgrounds—on average do worse in the courses we examined when compared to both their transfer peers from more affluent (non-Pell) families as well as the overall course DFWI rate average for transfers. Students who are Pell-grant eligible have a DFWI rate higher than the course average for transfers in five of the eight courses included in this study—principles of accounting, general biology, U.S. history, calculus, and general psychology. These differences range between 0.3 percentage points (0.7%) higher in calculus (41.8% Pell-eligible transfers compared to 41.5% for transfers in aggregate) to 5.6 percentage points (22.1%) higher in accounting (30.9% Pell-eligible compared to 25.3% for transfers in aggregate). (See Table 13.3, columns D and E.)

The differences are even more striking when comparing Pell-eligible transfers to their non-Pell-eligible transfer peers in the same courses. With the exception of general chemistry, where Pell-eligible transfers have a DFWI rate that is 1.0 percentage point lower than their non-Pell transfer peers (27.2% for Pell-eligible transfers compared to 28.2% for non-Pell-eligible transfers), Pell-eligible transfer students always have higher DFWI rates than their non-Pell-eligible transfer counterparts. The differences range between 1.2 percentage points (3.4%) higher in college algebra (36.7% for Pell-eligible transfers compared to 35.5% for non-Pell-eligible transfers) to 9.4 percentage points (57.0%) higher in U.S. history (25.9% for Pell-eligible transfers compared to 16.5% for non-Pell-eligible transfers), as shown in Table 13.3, columns E and F.

While the differences are not as large as those seen for many of the race/ethnicity groups in Table 13.2, they do suggest that students from families with greater financial capital (non-Pell-eligible transfers) have an advantage in gateway courses over their peers who come from less affluent and privileged backgrounds (Pell-eligible transfers). This finding is consistent with previous research on outcomes in gateway courses for students irrespective of their transfer or non-transfer status (Koch, 2017b; Koch & Drake, 2018, 2019).

Summary and Conclusions

Race/ethnicity, family income, and transfer status matter in the gateway-course passing rates detailed in this chapter. However, transfer status on its own does not mean a student is more likely to earn a D, F, W, or I grade in all of the courses we examined. The fact is, when it comes to transfers and DFWI rates in gateway courses, the outcomes frequently depend on the race/ethnicity and family-income status of the students considered.

As seen in the findings associated with our first question (Do transfer students have lower or higher DFWI rates when compared to their non-transfer counterparts in the courses?) transfers have the highest DFWI rates in only three of the eight courses considered in our analysis when compared to their non-transfer, first-year counterparts. The differences are particularly acute in math—where "motivated forgetting" and math anxiety may be factoring into the lower course-passing rates exhibited by transfers when compared to the non-transfer, first-year counterparts. The fact that transfers have lower DFWI rates in five courses when compared to their non-transfer, first-year counterparts could, in part, be explained by the fact that credit for coursework at previous institutions was not accepted at their receiving institutions. Thus, their lower DFWI rates could be due, in part, to their repeating courses they may have previously taken and mastered elsewhere.

Transfers have the highest DFWI rates in six of the eight courses considered in this study when compared to their non-transfer, upper-level counterparts. The two courses where their DFWI rates are lower are accounting and general chemistry. We believe the lower rates in these two courses can also be explained, at least in part, because transfer students may have taken comparable versions of these courses before at their transfer-sending institutions but their transfer-receiving institutions did not accept the credits. Thus, unlike their non-transfer counterparts—even upper-level, non-transfer counterparts—they had a "leg up" on earning a good grade in the course before they had mastered the content at their sending institution. Admittedly, this assumption is just that—an assumption. It should be verified with another study that examines the transcripts of transfers to see if they are, in fact, repeating these courses.

The findings associated with our second question (Do transfer students of color as defined by federal race/ethnic classification have higher or lower DFWI rates when compared to both the average DFWI rates for transfers in the courses and the DFWI for their White transfer counterparts in the courses?) were disturbing but, based on previous analyses we have conducted, on gateway course outcomes, not surprising. In short, *transfer students of color*—for purposes of this chapter defined as African

American, Native American, or Latinx race/ethnicity groups—almost always have a DFWI rate that exceeds the course average as well as the average for their White counterparts. In several cases, the DFWI rate differences for students from specific race/ethnicity come close to or even exceed double that of the course average and/or White comparison groups.

Analysis associated with our third question (Do transfer students from low-income families/backgrounds have higher or lower DFWI rates when compared to their non-low income transfer counterparts in the courses?) yielded results similar to those associated with the race/ethnicity findings. While the differences were not as extreme as the race/ethnicity comparisons associated with question 2, we found that transfer students who are eligible to receive a Pell grant—the metric we used to determine whether a student fit into the "low-income" or "non-low-income" categories—on average do worse in the courses we examined when compared to both their transfer peers from more affluent (non-Pell) families as well as the overall course DFWI rate average for transfers.

There are three items that strike us most about the answers to our three questions. The first is the fact that transfer students perform better than their non-transfer, first-year counterparts in many courses and do better than their non-transfer, upper-level counterparts in two courses. If, as we suspect, this has something to do with transfers repeating courses for which they previously earned credit at their sending institutions, then the credit acceptance and placement practices at many institutions merit examination. The academic performance of transfers is not an issue. But the fact that transfers outperform both groups of non-transfer students in two of the eight courses we examined—specifically principles of accounting and general chemistry—and that they are doing better than non-transfer, first-year students in three additional courses beyond the two already mentioned in this sentence—specifically general biology, U.S. history, and general psychology—makes us wonder if transfers are unnecessarily repeating courses and, as a result, taking longer to earn their baccalaureate degrees. Further analysis looking at demographics such as age and gender, as well as transcript analysis from the sending institutions, would shed more light on this issue.

The second item that troubles us is the challenge that transfer students appear to have with math—especially when compared to the non-transfer, first-year students enrolled in the same courses. This challenge is not unique to transfer students. Non-transfer, upper-level students also have significantly higher DFWI rates in calculus when compared to their non-transfer, first-year peers (see Table 13.1). This finding suggests that institutions need to consider employing math support strategies for students "who have done college before" if they have not had a math course for several years. Efforts such as math bridge programs, corequisite support efforts, and course-embedded support come to mind.

Last, but arguably most significant of all items in our analysis, is the fact that race/ethnicity and family income are the best determinants of whether or not a transfer student is going to succeed in a gateway course at the institution to which they have transferred. By this we mean that if a student is not White, and/or if a student comes from a poor family, that student is much more likely to not succeed in the eight gateway courses we examined for this study. Think about that for a moment. These are students who successfully navigated postsecondary education at another college or university. They successfully transferred into a new institution with the intent to earn a degree. And they did not succeed in gateway courses at the institution to which they transferred. This is disturbing for two reasons.

First, based on prior research we conducted (Koch & Drake, 2018, 2019), we know that students who do not succeed in even one gateway course are appreciably less likely to be retained at the institution where they took the course. We also know from Adelman's 1999 publication *Answers in the Tool Box*, and his 2006 follow-up work, *The Toolbox Revisited*, that students who earned D, F, W or I grades in 20% or more of their foundational-level courses were the least likely to finish a degree—not just at the institution at which they earned these grades, but at any institution anywhere over the 8-year time period considered in each of his respective studies. While we have not yet conducted an analysis of the retention and graduation implications of the DFWI rates for transfer students in this data set, if their retention outcomes are similar to those found in the other analyses of gateway course outcomes we have conducted, then we have reason to believe that transfer students who do not succeed in gateway courses at their transfer-receiving institution are at particularly high risk of attrition. Failure in gateway courses at the transfer-receiving institution may help explain, at least in part, why only 13% of students who start in a community college with the expressed intent of transferring to obtain a baccalaureate degree have actually earned that degree 6 years later (Shapiro et al., 2017). In short, lack of success in gateway courses at the transfer-receiving institutions can be a tremendous baccalaureate degree attainment momentum blocker.

The second reason why these race/ethnicity and family income findings for transfer students in gateway courses troubles us has to do with the overall representation of students of color and students from low-income families in the community college sector. Approximately 40% of first-time, first-year students start their college experience in community colleges (Doyle, 2009; National Center for Education Statistics, 2015; Shapiro et al., 2015; Shapiro et al., 2016). Over two fifths (42%) of those students are from low-income families (National Center for Public Policy and Higher Education, 2011). From a race/ethnicity standpoint, over two fifths of Latinx (42.6%) students, nearly one third of African American (31.3%) students, nearly two fifths of Native American students (39.3%), and nearly one out of every three (29.4%) students who identify as belonging to two or more race/ethnicity groups start their collegiate experience in community colleges (The Chronicle of Higher Education, 2018). In other words, some of the largest concentrations of students of color and low-income students begin their postsecondary experience in the community college sector. Jenkins and Fink (2016) found that while lower-income students who started at a community college were just as likely as higher-income students to earn associate degrees or certificates, they were *less* likely to earn baccalaureate degrees than their more affluent community college transfer counterparts. While there are many reasons for this, gateway course performance at the transfer-receiving institution cannot and should not be overlooked. Based on what we found in our own exploration of existing research, transfer performance at their receiving institutions is barely discussed. It needs to be, however, as there are tremendous equity-blocking implications at work here.

And this brings us to, arguably, the most critical implication of our study. Simply stated, if left unchecked, current conditions and passing rates in gateway courses for transfer students—particularly those from low-income and historically underrepresented race/ethnicity groups—will exacerbate an already bleak transfer student baccalaureate degree completion scenario. As Grave (2018) unambiguously points out, "Over the next 15 years, persistent trends in immigration, migration, and differential birth rates coupled with the recent acute birth dearth will markedly alter the college-age population" (p. 18). In other words, the very sample populations that historically constitute large portions of community college enrollments, and that do not do well in the gateway courses at transfer-receiving institutions in our study, will constitute the growing majority of the college-going population in both the 2- and 4-year sectors.

Educators can shrug their shoulders and yearn for the "golden age" when "better students" made teaching "a breeze." But such a reaction would be unwise, ill informed, and, ultimately, self-defeating. It would also mask the harsh reality: that for decades a more affluent and privileged college-going majority has masked failure rates among other populations. In the process of masking these rates, educators were blinded to structural racism and classism at work in gateway courses, the plight of transfer students, and the broader undergraduate experience of which transfer and gateway courses are a part.

In the contemporary era—a period during which public skepticism about the value of a college education seems to be increasing at almost the same speed with which state funding for postsecondary education is decreasing—gateway course failure rates can no longer be ignored or viewed as a badge of distinction and rigor. To do so would reward outcomes that clearly are inequitable. It would ignore the weight of the evidence about who does and does not succeed in undergraduate education broadly and gateway courses in particular and disregard the growing body of evidence about pedagogical and policy practices that can alter these outcomes.

It is beyond the scope of this chapter to discuss the strategies and policy changes that can be employed to help the 21st-century student demographic learn and grow in and through the courses that comprise the transfer experience. The study also is limited by the data set with which we were working. We may have created more questions than we answered. However, it is well within the scope and confines of this chapter to end by noting that, for the betterment of both the transfer-sending and transfer-receiving institutions, the communities they serve, and, ultimately, the transfer students themselves, we hope that readers will not ignore the weight of this evidence and that they will make gateway courses in general and transfer student success in gateway courses in particular a primary place for action and agency.

Recommendations

Based on our work within this chapter, and the scholarship we used to write it, we recommend the following approaches for institutions seeking to learn more about and continuously improve transfer student success in gateway courses:

1. Conduct an institutional analysis to examine how transfer students perform in courses that they take at various stages of their transition into the transfer-receiving institution.
2. Once the "gateway courses" at transfer-receiving institutions are identified, conduct transcript analysis for transfers from primary sending institutions to see what, if any, pre-transfer course taking and content mastery patterns emerge.
3. Bring together faculty, advisors, and academic leaders associated with gateway courses at the primary transfer-sending and transfer-receiving institutions to discuss the evidence collected as part of recommendations 1 and 2.
4. When and where possible, conduct recommendations 1, 2, and 3 as part of an intentional self-study and course redesign process—one that helps all involved parties learn about what is actually going on in their courses and programs of study for the transfer students who take them and subsequently supports faculty and staff as they adopt and adapt evidence-based course redesign strategies that can yield more equitable outcomes for transfer students and all other students in the gateway courses examined.

Questions to Consider

Based on our work within this chapter, and the scholarship on which we drew to write it, we recommend institutions consider the following questions as they seek to learn more about and continuously improve transfer student success in gateway courses:

1. Does your institution collect and analyze data on the performance of transfer students in gateway courses? If yes, are those data and/or their analysis sufficient? If no, why not?
2. If the institution does collect and analyze the data on transfer performance in gateway courses, how is it shared with faculty at the transfer-sending and/or transfer-receiving institutions?
3. If data are shared with faculty from the transfer-sending and transfer-receiving institutions, are those faculty supported in their efforts to interpret and apply the data to their teaching efforts? If yes, are the goals for those receiving the data clearly identified and understood? If no, why not?
4. Who else, in addition to and in concert with faculty, should be involved in efforts to improve transfer outcomes in gateway courses? How would you go about doing this?

5. How might you combine efforts to improve teaching, learning, and success for transfer students in gateway courses with other teaching and learning improvement efforts underway at the institution?
6. How might you combine efforts to improve teaching, learning, and success for transfer students in gateway courses with efforts such as reaffirmation of accreditation, program review, strategic planning, performance-based funding, general education review, and other broader institutional efforts?

References

Adelman, C. (1999). *Answers in the tool box: Academic intensity, academic patterns, and bachelor's degree attainment.* U.S. Department of Education.

Adelman, C. (2006). *The toolbox revisited: Paths to degree completion from high school through college.* U.S. Department of Education.

Appel, M., Kronberger, N., & Aronson, J. (2011). Stereotype threat impairs ability building: Effects on the test preparation of women in science and technology. *European Journal of Social Psychology, 41*(7), 904–913. https://doi.org/10.1002/ejsp.835

Aronson, J., Lustina, M. J., Good, C., Keough, K., Steele, C. M., & Brown, J. (1999). When White men can't do mathematics: Necessary and sufficient factors in stereotype threat. *Journal of Experimental Social Psychology, 35,* 29–46. https://doi.org/10.1006/jesp.1998.1371

Cheryan, S., & Plaut, V. C. (2010). Explaining underrepresentation: A theory of precluded interest. *Sex Roles, 63,* 475–488. https://doi.org/10.1007/s11199-010-9835-x

The Chronicle of Higher Education. (2018). *Almanac of Higher Education 2018-19.* https://www.chronicle.com/specialreport/The-Almanac-of-Higher/214

Conway, M. A., Cohen, G., & Stanhope, N. (1991). On the very long-term retention of knowledge acquired through formal education: Twelve years of cognitive psychology. *Journal of Experimental Psychology: General, 120*(4), 395–409. https://doi.org/10.1037/0096-3445.120.4.395

Doyle, W. R. (2009). Impact of increased academic intensity on transfer rates: An application of matching estimators to student-unit record data. *Research in Higher Education, 50,* 52–72. https://doi.org/10.1037/0096-3445.120.4.395

Garcia, N. M., López, N., & Vélez, V. N. (2018). QuantCrit: Rectifying quantitative methods through critical race theory, *Race Ethnicity and Education, 21*(2), 149–157.

Grave, N. D. (2018). *Demographics and the demand for higher education.* Johns Hopkins University Press.

Holzer, H. J., & Baum, S. (2017). *Making college work: Pathways to success for disadvantaged students.* Brookings Institution Press.

Jenkins, D., & Fink, J. (2016). *Tracking transfer: New measures of institutional and state effectiveness in helping community college students attain bachelor's degrees.* Community College Research Center, Teachers College, Columbia University. http://ccrc.tc.columbia.edu/publications/tracking-transfer-institutional-state-effectiveness.html

Kamuche, F. U., & Ledman, R. E. (2011). Relationship of time and learning retention. *Journal of College Teaching and Learning, 2,* 25–28. https://doi.org/10.19030/tlc.v2i8.1851

Koch, A. K. (Ed.). (2017a). *Improving teaching, learning, equity, and success in gateway courses* (New Directions for Higher Education, no. 180). Jossey-Bass.

Koch, A. K. (2017b). It's about the gateway courses: Defining and contextualizing the issue. In A. K. Koch (Ed.), *Improving teaching, learning, equity, and success in gateway courses* (New Directions for Higher Education, no. 180, pp. 11–17). Jossey-Bass.

Koch, A. K. (2017c). Many thousands failed: A wakeup call to history educators. *Perspectives on History, 55,* 18–19.

Koch, A. K. (2018). Big inequity in small things: Toward an end to a tyranny of practice. *National Teaching and Learning Forum, 27*(6), 1–5. https://doi.org/10.1002/ntlf.30169

Koch, A. K., & Drake, B. M. (2018). *Digging into the disciplines I–Accounting for failure: The impact of gateway courses in accounting, calculus, and chemistry on student success.* John N. Gardner Institute for Excellence in Undergraduate Education.

Koch, A. K., & Drake, B. M. (2019). *Digging into the disciplines II–Failure in historical context: The impact of gateway courses in history, accounting, and chemistry on student success.* John N. Gardner Institute for Excellence in Undergraduate Education.

Koch, A. K., & Rodier, R. (2014). *Gateways to completion guidebook.* John N. Gardner Institute for Excellence in Undergraduate Education.

Major, B., Spencer, S., Schmader, T., Wolfe, C., & Crocker, J. (1998). Coping with negative stereotypes about intellectual performance: The role of psychological disengagement. *Personality and Social Psychology Bulletin, 24,* 34–50. https://doi.org/10.1177/0146167298241003

National Center for Education Statistics. (2015). *Enrollment and employees in postsecondary institutions, fall 2014; and financial statistics and academic libraries, fiscal year 2014: First look (provisional data).* Author. https://nces.ed.gov/pubs2016/2016005.pdf

National Center for Public Policy and Higher Education. (2011). *Affordability and transfer: Critical to increasing baccalaureate degree completion.* Policy Alert. ERIC Clearinghouse. http://www.highereducation.org/reports/pa_at/PolicyAlert_06-2011.pdf

Nussbaum, A. D., & Steele, C. M. (2007). Situational disengagement and persistence in the face of adversity. *Journal of Experimental Social Psychology, 43*: 127–134. https://doi.org/10.1016/j.jesp.2005.12.007

Osborne J. W. (1997). Race and academic disidentification. *Journal of Experimental Social Psychology, 89,* 728–735. https://doi.org/10.1037/0022-0663.89.4.728

Osborne, J. W., & Walker, C. (2006). Stereotype threat, identification with academics, and withdrawal from school: Why the most successful students of colour might be most likely to withdraw. *Education Psychology, 26,* 563–577. https://doi.org/10.1080/01443410500342518

Ramirez, G. (2017). Motivated forgetting in early mathematics: A proof-of-concept study. *Frontiers in Psychology, 8*(2087). https://doi.org/10.3389/fpsyg.2017.02087

Schmader, T., & Major, B. (1999). The impact of ingroup vs. outgroup performance on personal values. *Journal of Experimental Social Psychology, 35,* 47–67. https://doi.org/10.1006/jesp.1998.1372

Shapiro, D., Dundar, A., Huie, F., Wakhungu, P.K., Yuan, X., Nathan, A., & Hwang, Y. (2017, September). *Tracking transfer: Measures of effectiveness in helping community college students to complete bachelor's degrees* (Signature Report No. 13). National Student Clearinghouse Research Center.

Shapiro, D., Dundar, A., Wakhungu, P. K. Yuan, X., & Harrell, A. (2015). *Transfer & mobility: A national view of student movement in postsecondary institutions, fall 2008 cohort* (Signature Report 9). National Student Clearinghouse Research Center. https://nscresearchcenter.org/signaturereport9/

Shapiro, D., Dundar, A., Wakhungu, P. K., Yuan, X., Nathan, A. & Hwang, Y. (2016, November). *Completing college: A national view of student attainment rates—fall 2010 cohort* (Signature Report No. 12). National Student Clearinghouse Research Center. https://nsc researchcenter.org/signaturereport12/

Sherman D. K., & Cohen G. L. (2006). The psychology of self-defense: Self-affirmation theory. *Advances in Experimental Social Psychology, 38*, 183–242. https://doi.org/10.1016/ s0065-2601(06)38004-5

Tajfel, H., & Turner, J. C. (2004). The social identity theory of intergroup behavior. In J. T. Jost & J. Sidanius (Eds.), *Key readings in social psychology. Political psychology: Key readings* (pp. 276–293). Psychology Press.

Wang, X., Wang, Y., Wickersham, K., Sun, N., & Chan, H. (2017). Math requirement fulfillment and educational success of community college students: A matter of when. *Community College Review, 45*, 99–118. https://doi.org/10.1177/0091552116682829

Weston, T. J., Seymour, E., Koch, A. K., & Drake, B. M. (2019). Weed-out classes and their consequences. In A. Hunter & E. Seymour (Eds.), *Talking about leaving revisited: Persistence, relocation and loss in undergraduate STEM education* (pp. 197–243). Springer.

14

TEACHING FOR INSPIRATION

Approaches to Engaging Transfer Students in Gateway Courses

Stephanie M. Foote

No pedagogy which is truly liberating can remain distant from the oppressed by treating them as unfortunates and by presenting for their emulation models from among the oppressors. The oppressed must be their own example in the struggle for their redemption.

—Freire, *Pedagogy of the Oppressed*, 1970, p. 54

Higher education is considered a vehicle for upward social mobility, yet for transfer students, particularly those entering through 2-year institutions, the likelihood that they will persist to the point of transfer and ultimately experience the gains in social and cultural capital associated with earning a baccalaureate degree is limited at best (Shapiro et al., 2017). While there are many barriers to transfer student transition and success (Fink & Jenkins, chapter 2, this volume; Foote et al., 2015; Shapiro et al., 2017), gateway courses are one of the main but frequently overlooked pathways for transfer students. Specifically, when these courses are developed with consideration to both the subject matter and the unique asset-based (rather than deficit-based) identities of the students in the course, they have the power to be liberating, and in turn, transformational learning experiences.

Gateway courses, once termed *barrier courses*, are, by definition, often foundational (lower-division or developmental courses that serve as a pathway to credit-bearing courses); high risk (courses that yield higher rates of D, F, W, or Incomplete grades); and have high enrollments within, as well as across, sections (as defined by the institution) (Koch, 2017). Success in gateway courses is important because students who fail these courses frequently do not persist in higher education, and it is often the most vulnerable students (those who identify as first generation, low income, or are from underrepresented minority populations) that disproportionately earn DFWI grades in gateway courses (Adelman, 1999; Koch, 2017; Koch & Drake, chapter 13, this volume).

The challenge of designing or redesigning gateway courses to become environments that are inclusive, engaging, and inspiring can be daunting for faculty, particularly because nationally, many of these courses are taught primarily by part-timers or adjuncts (Ran & Xu, 2017). These contingent faculty often lack departmental or institutional support and in many instances are simply trying to stay afloat as they, themselves, try to navigate their own institutional barriers (Ran & Xu, 2017). Even in the best circumstances, faculty teaching gateway courses may struggle finding the balance between coverage of content and using pedagogical approaches that focus more on inspiring students to "do, think, and value what practitioners in the field are doing, thinking, and valuing" (Caulder, 2006, p. 1361). Moreover, since transfer student identities may not be obvious in the classroom, determining who those students are and creating environments that are truly inclusive of and responsive to them, especially in high-enrollment gateway courses, can be a formidable task. Despite the challenges associated with this work, the significance of designing courses where all students—and, in particular, transfer students—can be successful has never been more important (Rosenberg & Koch, chapter 3, this volume; Koch & Drake, chapter 13, this volume). Faculty should undertake course design or redesign with the goals of creating equitable outcomes, student engagement, and inspiration in mind. This process will benefit all students—not only transfer students but also first-year students, historically underrepresented/underserved students, and upper-level non-transfers who may have put off taking these courses.

Transfer Students and Influences on Their Transition and Success

While many different approaches exist to engaging transfer students in the classroom, this chapter focuses on those pedagogies that are responsive to aspects of transfer student identity and development, as well as those that can be applied across a range of disciplines. Before exploring these pedagogies, one must gain a deeper understanding of the transfer students in gateway courses and the influences on their transition and success. Both institutional enrollment and historical course data can provide valuable information on the number of transfer students, their prior institution(s), their performance in courses at the college or university, and retention at the institution. While these data are all important, a more nuanced understanding of transfer students can be gained by gathering information from the students enrolled in gateway course(s). For example, asking students reflective questions can help faculty better understand who their students are while illuminating aspects of motivation and mind-set that could influence students' engagement and performance in our course(s). Consider asking questions such as the following:

- What are your expectations for the course?
- In what areas do you feel most challenged and most confident, based on what you know about the course or your prior experience in this particular subject or discipline?
- What are your strengths as a learner?

Responses to these questions can also help faculty avoid making assumptions about students and their needs, which is particularly important because transfer students are often examined in the aggregate or as a monolithic group and without attention to the nuances in their individual transfer experiences.

Student and adult development theories can also provide context for and understanding of the various identities and intersections of identities that are evident in the transfer students. For example, transition theory (Goodman et al., 2006) can help faculty understand how transfer students experience transition, as well as the situational factors that influence their experience. Other theories that focus on cognitive structural and psychosocial development—as well as social identity development theories with roots in modern social movements—provide faculty with context that can be used to design classroom approaches that are truly responsive to their students. For example, cognitive structural theories can help faculty as they consider teaching students ways to approach learning at the college level that provide the requisite support and challenge to help them progress to more advanced and deeper forms of learning that are described in this chapter. Psychosocial theories examine "the content of development" (Patton et al., 2016, p. 283), and, as such, provide faculty with insight into the types of issues students experience at a particular moment.

Evidence-Based Pedagogies to Inspire and Engage Transfer Students

What does it mean to inspire transfer students in gateway courses? What does that look like? In many ways, teaching to engage and inspire transfer students simply looks like good teaching. However, the specific pedagogies and approaches that are described in the following section have been chosen specifically because they (a) are evidence-based and effective; (b) help create inclusive learning environments (inclusive of various identities and learner needs); and (c) can be used in courses in a variety of disciplines, as well as courses taught in different modes and modalities. While these pedagogies are not exhaustive—there are many more interdisciplinary and disciplinary approaches from which to choose—they do offer faculty a place to begin as they consider how they might design their gateway course(s) to engage and inspire transfer students.

Significant Learning and High-Impact Learning Experiences

Fink (2013) describes significant learning experiences as those that consider both process and outcome and represent learning that is central to the lives of students.

In other words, to be significant, these experiences must engage students in their learning. Students learn about themselves and others and, through that process, they often undergo changes in interests and values (Fink, 2013). Through the experiences detailed in the six categories in Fink's taxonomy (2013), students learn how to learn and ultimately become self-directed learners. Well-designed courses, then, induce significant learning by engaging in students challenging active learning experiences. These courses are taught by faculty who demonstrate care for their discipline and their teaching as well as for their students—and these faculty interact with students, providing them timely feedback (Fink, 2013). For transfer students, some of the most significant learning experiences are those that involve "working harder than they thought they could to meet an instructor's standards or expectations" (Fauria & Fuller, 2015, p. 39), as well as opportunities to contribute to class discussions, and tutor other students, formally or informally (Fauria & Fuller, 2015). While these types of experiences can be beneficial for all undergraduate students, the impact on overall grade point average is greater for transfer students than their non-transfer peers (Fauria & Fuller, 2015).

Significant learning experiences can come in many different forms in gateway courses but incorporating high-impact practices (HIPs) in these courses is particularly promising for transfer students (Finley & McNair, 2013). HIPs are "teaching and practices that have been widely tested and have been shown to be beneficial for college students from many backgrounds" (Association of American Colleges & Universities [AAC&U], n.d., para. 1). HIPs include first-year seminars and experiences, common intellectual experiences, learning communities, writing-intensive courses, collaborative assignments and projects, undergraduate research, diversity/global learning, ePortfolios, service-learning/community-based learning, internships and capstone courses and projects (AAC&U, n.d.).

Overall, the outcomes and benefits from participation in HIPs are wide reaching and include gains in student persistence and GPA, increases in critical thinking and writing, greater appreciation for diversity, and enhanced student engagement (Brownell & Swaner, 2010; Kinzie, 2012; Kuh, 2008). For transfer students, participation in multiple HIPs can have a significant impact on learning and success (Finley & McNair, 2013). The incorporation of HIPs can help communicate the utility of concepts and ideas in gateway courses, which is important to all students, but is particularly important to transfer students who often struggle to find utility in their academic course work (Foote et al., 2015).

Critical Compassionate Pedagogy and Reflective Teaching

Critical compassionate pedagogy encourages faculty to be critical of "institutional and classroom practices that ideologically place underserved students at disadvantaged positions, while at the same time be self-reflexive of their [faculty] actions through compassion as a daily commitment" (Hao, 2011, p. 92). The notion of being critical and compassionate in the classroom, specifically in gateway courses, is important to the success of all underserved students, including transfer students.

Critical compassionate pedagogy is based in the concept of compassionate communication (Rosenberg, 2003), which has four foundational components:

1. *Observation*—Observe without judgment. How do my transfer students engage in class?
2. *Feeling*—Express feelings. Is it challenging to meet the needs of the transfer students in my class?
3. *Need*—Connect feelings and needs. What types of pedagogies can I use in my class to meet the needs of my transfer students?
4. *Request*—Open channels for communication. Are you experiencing challenges with the assignments in this class? (Adapted from Hao, 2011)

While this form of pedagogy has been applied to work with first-generation students, critical compassionate pedagogy lends itself to engaging all underserved students, including transfer students, in gateway courses because it fosters both self-reflection and action.

Similarly, reflective teaching (RT) engages instructors in a process of self-evaluation with the goal of continuous improvement (Brookfield, 2017). Specifically, in the RT process, instructors examine pedagogical approaches as well as the alignment of these approaches with their personal beliefs about teaching and learning and identify areas for potential improvement (Poorvu Center for Teaching and Learning, n.d.). This process, which occurs during the course and after it ends, is action-oriented, meaning the instructor looks for ways to mediate challenges or issues in a class. RT includes four lenses that "correlate to processes of self-reflection, student feedback, peer assessment, and engagements with scholarly literature" (Miller, 2010, p. 1). RT can be applied to create gateway courses that are responsive to the nuanced needs of transfer students. When faculty are actively engaged in RT, they are more likely to be aware of their teaching and the impact of that teaching "from as many vantage points as possible" (Miller, 2010, p. 1).

Metacognition and Active Learning

Commonly referred to as thinking about one's thinking, metacognition involves becoming aware of and taking control of one's knowledge and understanding. From a teaching and learning perspective, students who are metacognitive are aware of gaps in their understanding and they make changes in their thinking and learning—often seeking out resources or strategies that will help them fill these gaps (Girash, 2014). Students who are metacognitive are also more likely to plan, monitor, and evaluate strategies they use to learn and adapt these strategies based on the specific learning environment and/or subject (Steiner & Foote, 2017). While not a concept specifically designed to engage transfer students, metacognition can be particularly important for these students because, as a flexible approach to learning, students can use various metacognitive strategies depending on the specific task. Faculty can also employ various metacognitive teaching approaches to help foster deeper learning among all students in their gateway courses.

Active learning in gateway courses can take many different forms, ranging from think-pair-share to peer teaching but, ultimately, active learning involves students in doing things and thinking about the things they are doing (Bonwell & Eison, 1991). For transfer students, specifically students in STEM majors, active learning experiences can contribute to their "transfer-related motivational attributes" that speak to their potential success in STEM-transfer (Wang, 2016, p. 52). To ensure active learning is both meaningful and produces deeper understanding of concepts and ideas for all students, faculty should provide context before engaging students in a learning experience and, following the experience, offer an opportunity for reflection (Fink, 2003). Some examples of active learning are considered "small teaching," or short activities or in-class assignments (e.g., minute papers, think-pair-share, and polls) designed with the intent to briefly engage students in reflection on a specific question or idea.

For transfer students, metacognitive teaching and learning strategies and active learning provide deeper, more critical thinking skills applicable in various other settings, academic and nonacademic. While these forms of thinking and learning are important for all students, they are particularly important to transfer students who are seeking the utility in their course work, particularly in the gateway courses they are required to take after they transfer.

Other Considerations: Are Transfer Student Seminars Gateway Courses?

While there is a wealth of research and practice literature about first-year seminars (Greenfield et al., 2013; Koch et al., 2005; Upcraft et al., 2005) and the impact of participation in these courses on first-year student retention (Boudreau & Kromey, 1994; Davis, 1992; Fidler, 1991; Schnell & Doetkott, 2002–2003; Wilkie & Kukuck, 1989), less is known about the structure and outcomes of transfer student seminars. A 2010 national survey of chief academic officers at 4-year institutions on student success and retention efforts, revealed that 25.3% of 357 institutions had a dedicated seminar for transfer students, and the combined enrollment in those courses for all institutions reporting, was 55.9% of the transfer population (Barefoot et al., 2012). A search for transfer student seminars revealed a variety of approaches and content, although all appeared to be focused on creating a positive transition experience for transfer students. While transfer student seminars are not ubiquitous examples of gateway courses, at institutions where a seminar is offered for transfer students, there might be opportunities to (a) create dedicated student learning communities that link the seminar with a general education and/or major course (e.g., Kennesaw State University's *Flourishing at KSU* transfer student learning community; see Foote & So, 2016) or (b) offer dedicated sections of general education courses with common assignments and activities (e.g., Stockton University's transfer seminars; Foote & Grites, 2017). Other transfer student seminars, like the Students in Transition (STS) seminar at Rutgers University, focus on helping transfer students make a successful transition to the university while developing essential skills such as goal setting, learning styles, career services, time and life management, academic planning, and habits of effective students (R. Diamond, personal communication, November 26, 2018). Ultimately, these courses should be targeted specifically to the transfer student population; be systematic in approach, which can include using many of the aforementioned approaches to course design and pedagogy; and be inclusive.

Next Steps

As faculty begin to implement the pedagogies described in this chapter, they should be aware that innovation in the classroom does not always result in immediate, positive outcomes. Specifically, multiple attempts and revisions to specific teaching approaches are often necessary to produce differences in student outcomes in gateway courses. Thus, faculty must commit to continuous improvement and to gathering and evaluating evidence to help them understand what is working, and conversely, what is not working in their course(s). Through the scholarship of teaching and learning (SoTL), faculty systematically examine student learning, reflect on learning goals, find innovative evidence-based teaching practices that align with learning goals in their gateway course(s), identify methods to evaluate changes in student learning, and ultimately share what is learned through this process. Huber (2013) describes SoTL as an approach to teaching that "views classrooms (and other learning spaces) as sites for inquiry, innovation, and knowledge-building" (para. 3). A key aspect of SoTL, like disciplinary research, is that the results of these efforts should be shared publicly (through publications or presentations) to help advance teaching at the college level (Huber, 2013). Faculty embarking on this work will also need departmental and institutional support in the form of development activities and recognition through annual evaluation, promotion, and tenure processes. Finally, faculty teaching gateway courses should become advocates for transfer students, both within and beyond their courses by partnering with academic affairs staff, faculty development staff, student affairs and enrollment services staffs, and academic advisors to share information and resources that can foster transfer student transition and success.

Recommendations for Action

1. Create faculty allies by providing faculty teaching gateway courses detailed institutional profiles and characteristics of transfer students as well as their academic performance compared to non-transfer students, engaging faculty in conversations about programs and services aimed at supporting transfer student transition, and inviting faculty who were transfer students or are transfer allies to identify as such (with buttons, stickers, or signs on their office doors). While not focused on classroom pedagogy, when faculty are more aware of who transfer students are and the resources available to support them, they are more likely to be inclusive of and responsive to transfer students in their gateway courses.

2. Provide institutional-level support and development for faculty teaching gateway courses to allow them to learn about evidence-based teaching practices and apply them in gateway courses. One approach could involve creating an institution-based course-redesign institute that would allow faculty time and resources to intentionally redesign all or part of their gateway courses.

3. Identify ways to recognize and reward faculty who engage in innovative teaching practices through annual evaluations and the promotion and tenure processes. While faculty should be encouraged to use evidence-based teaching approaches, formal recognition of this work is critical to creating sustained change in gateway courses.

4. Promote SoTL in gateway courses and recognize it as a valid form of teaching-based inquiry. Similar to recognizing teaching innovation through annual review, promotion, and tenure, SoTL should be both encouraged and recognized as a form of scholarship to empower faculty who want to make sustained improvements to teaching and learning and to share their work broadly.

Questions to Consider

1. How can faculty be more aware of transfer students and their nuanced needs in gateway courses?
2. What other pedagogies and practices, particularly from specific disciplines, can be applied in gateway courses to create equitable outcomes for transfer students and for all student populations?
3. How can innovative teaching be recognized and supported in gateway courses?
4. Do transfer student seminars exhibit outcomes like other historically high failure rate gateway courses? If so, how should they be redesigned and taught? How do they compare to first-year seminars?

References

Adelman, C. (1999). *Answers in the toolbox: Academic intensity, academic patterns, and bachelor's degree attainment.* U.S. Department of Education.

Association of American Colleges & Universities. (n.d.). *High-impact educational practices.* http://www.aacu.org/leap/hip.cfm

Barefoot, B. O., Griffin, B. Q., & Koch, A. K. (2012). *Enhancing student success throughout undergraduate education: A national survey.* https://static1.squarespace.com/static/59b0c486d2b857fc86d09aee/t/59bad33412abd988ad84d697/1505415990531/JNGInational_survey_web.pdf

Bonwell, C. C., & Eison, J. A. (1991). *Active learning: Creating excitement in the classroom.* (ASHE-ERIC Higher Education Report No. 1). The George Washington University, School of Education and Human Development.

Boudreau, C. A., & Komrey, J. D. (1994). A longitudinal study of retention and academic performance of participants in freshman orientation courses. *Journal of College Student Development, 35,* 444–449.

Brookfield, S. (2017). *Becoming a critically reflective teacher.* Jossey-Bass.

Brownell, J. E. & Swaner, L. E. (2010). *Five high-impact practices.* Association of American Colleges & Universities.

Caulder, L. (2006). Uncoverage: Toward a signature pedagogy for the history survey. *The Journal of American History, 92*(4), 1358–1370. https://doi.org/10.2307/4485896

Davis, Jr., B. N. (1992). Freshman seminar: A broad spectrum of effectiveness. *Journal of the Freshman Year Experience, 41*(1), 79–94.

Fauria, R. M., & Fuller, M. B. (2015). Transfer student success: Educationally purposeful activities predictive of undergraduate GPA. *Research & Practice in Assessment,* 10, 39–52.

Fidler, P. P. (1991). Relationship of freshman orientation seminars to sophomore return rates. *Journal of the Freshman Year Experience, 3*(1), 7–38.

Fink, L. D. (2003). *Creating significant learning experiences: An integrated approach to designing college courses.* Jossey-Bass.

Fink, L. D. (2013). *Creating significant learning experiences: An integrated approach to designing college courses* (2nd ed.). Jossey-Bass.

Finley, A., & McNair, T. (2013). *Accessing underserved students' engagement in high-impact practices.* Association of American Colleges & Universities. http://www.aacu.org/assessinghips

Foote, S. M., & Grites, T. J. (2017, February). *Maximizing transfer student transitions and success in the classroom.* Presentation at the 15th Annual Conference of the National Institute for the Study of Transfer Students, Atlanta, GA.

Foote, S. M., Kranzow, J., & Hinkle, S. (2015). Focusing on the forgotten: An examination of the influences and innovative practices that affect community college transfer student success. In S. J. Jones & D. L. Jackson (Eds.) *Examining the impact of community colleges on the global workforce* (pp. 94–124). GI Global.

Foote, S. M. & So, C. J. (2016). Fostering self-authorship in the transfer student experience through the development of a learning community. In S. J. Handel & E. Strempel (Eds.), *Transition and transformation: Fostering transfer student success* (pp. 39–50). University of North Georgia Press, National Institute for the Study of Transfer Students.

Freire, P. (1970). *Pedagogy of the oppressed.* Continuum.

Girash, J. (2014). Metacognition and instruction. In V. A. Benassi, C. E. Overson, & C. M. Hakala (Eds.), *Applying science of learning in education: Infusing psychological science into the curriculum* (pp. 152–169). http://teachpsych.org/ebooks/asle2014/index.php

Goodman, J., Schlossberg, N. K., Anderson, M. L. (2006). *Counseling adult students in transition: Linking theory with practice* (3rd ed.). Springer.

Greenfield, G. M., Keup, J., R., & Gardner, J. N. (2013). *Developing and sustaining successful first-year programs.* Jossey-Bass.

Hao, R. N. (2011). Critical compassionate pedagogy and the teacher's role in first-generation student success. In *Faculty and first-generation college students: Bridging the classroom gap together* [Special Issue] (New Directions for Teaching & Learning, no. 127, pp. 91–98). Wiley. https://doi.org/10.1002tl.460

Huber, M. (2013). *What is the scholarship of teaching and learning?* https://teachingcommons.stanford.edu/teaching-talk/what-scholarship-teaching-and-learning-mary-huber

Kinzie, J. (2012). *Fostering student learning and success: The value of high-impact practices.* http://www.d.umn.edu/vcaa/sem/kinzieHO2012%283%29.pdf

Koch, A. K. (Ed.). (2017). It's about the gateway courses: Defining and contextualizing the issue. In *Improving teaching, learning, equity and success in gateway courses.* (New Directions for Higher Education, no. 180, pp. 11–17.) Wiley. https://doi.org/10.1002/he.20257

Koch, A. K., Foote, S. M., Hinkle, S., Keup, J., & Pistilli, M. (2005). *The first-year experience in higher education: An annotated bibliography* (4th ed.). University of South Carolina, National Resource Center for the First-Year Experience and Students in Transition.

Kuh, G. D. (2008). *High-impact educational practices: What they are, who has access to them, and why they matter.* Association of American Colleges & Universities.

Miller, B. (2010). *Brookfield's four lenses: Becoming critically reflective.* https://valenciacollege.edu/faculty/development/courses-resources/documents/brookfield_summary.pdf

Patton, L. D., Renn, K. A., Guido, F. M., & Quaye, S. J. (2016). *Student development in college: Theory, research, and practice.* Jossey-Bass.

Poorvu Center for Teaching and Learning. (n.d.). *Reflective teaching.* http://poorvucenter.yale.edu/ReflectiveTeaching

Ran, F. X., & Xu, D. (2017). *How and why do adjunct instructors affect students' academic outcomes? Evidence from two-year and four-year colleges.* https://ccrc.tc.columbia.edu/media/k2/attachments/how-and-why-do-adjunct-instructors-affect-students-academic-outcomes.pdf

Rosenberg, M. B. (2003). *Nonviolent communication: A language of life* (2nd ed.). Puddle-Dancer Press.

Schnell, C. A., & Doetkott, C. D. (2002–2003). First year seminars produce long-term impact. *Journal of College Student Retention, 4*(4), 377–391. https://doi.org/10.2190/nkpn-8b33-v7cy-l7w1

Shapiro, D., Dundar, A., Huie, F., Wakhungu, P.K., Yuan, X., Nathan, A. & Hwang, Y. (2017, September). *Tracking transfer: Measures of effectiveness in helping community college students to complete bachelor's degrees* (Signature Report No. 13). National Student Clearinghouse Research Center.

Shapiro, D., Dundar, A., Wakhungu, P. K., Yuan, X., & Harrell, A. (2015). *Transfer and mobility: A national view of student movement in postsecondary institutions, fall 2008 cohort* (Signature Report, 9). National Student Clearinghouse Research Center.

Steiner, H. H., & Foote, S. M. (2017, May 13). Using metacognition to reframe our thinking about learning styles. *Faculty Focus.* https://www.facultyfocus.com/articles/teaching-and-learning/using-metacognition-reframe-thinking-learning-styles/

Upcraft, M. L., Gardner, J. N., & Barefoot, B. O. (2005). *Challenging & supporting the first-year student: A handbook for improving the first year of college.* Jossey-Bass.

Wang, X. (Ed.). (2016). Upward transfer in STEM fields of study: A new conceptual framework and survey instrument for institutional research. In *Studying transfer in higher education: New Approaches to enduring and emerging topics* [Special Issue]. (New Directions for Institutional Research, 170, 49–59.) Wiley. https://doi.org/10.1002/ir.20184

Wilkie, C., & Kukuck, S. (1989). A longitudinal study of the effects of a freshman seminar. *Journal of the Freshman Year Experience, 1*(1), 7–16.

15

DIGITAL LEARNING FOR TRANSFER STUDENTS

From Definition to Applicable Possibilities

Susannah McGowan

To believe that change is driven by tech, when tech is driven by humans, renders force and power invisible.

—Jill Lepore, in Cohen (2017)

This chapter synthesizes recent work I conducted with my Gardner Institute colleagues as part of a planning grant funded by the Bill & Melinda Gates Foundation in 2016–2017 examining the role of digital learning as a vehicle for student success, faculty development, and the transfer experience. This chapter will expand on possibilities for digital learning environments to support and build on students' transfer experiences in the context of their learning. Specifically, this chapter will consider the following questions:

1. How do digital environments prepare transfer students to enter their academic experiences?
2. Where do digital technologies support students in facilitating a smooth transition into the learning expectations and spaces set forth for them?
3. Given the needs of transfer students and the transfer pathway, what tools or environments enable and facilitate this transition?

Based on an extensive literature review and multiple conversations with experts in student success and learning technologies, the emphasis in any definition regarding *digital environments* remains on the learning—both in digital and face-to-face contexts—and setting transfer students up to learn effectively from the moment of transition through to graduation.

Examining Digital Realms of Transfer

In 2016–2017, my Gardner Institute colleagues and I were asked by the Gates Foundation to develop a proposal to explore transfer student success issues and the role "digital learning" could play in student success and faculty development. The Gates Foundation provided resources to explore these two areas offering an opportunity to consult with many stakeholders both in transfer and digital realms. To investigate these two areas, we conducted a literature review as well as an environmental scan of current institutions that work in digital learning spaces. We coordinated three webinars to seek input from a group of 22 stakeholders in higher education—each with a specialization around student success, educational technology, or a blend of the two. This exploration project culminated in a final meeting in May 2017 with multiple productive conversations that revealed thinking on the research questions and developing common definitions around *digital learning* and what it affords the transfer student experience.

Early in the project, it was clear the funder focused on the digital learning environment as a place of "acceleration," meaning the proliferation of digital tools and courseware for students equates to the speed with which they could enter college, progress through college, and graduate. Our early inclination to address the purpose of a digital learning environment for transfer students was not really about acceleration but more about helping important stakeholders understand the capabilities of digital environments. In chapter 2 (this volume), Fink and Jenkins identified one institutional barrier for transfer students was a lack of clear information about transfer requirements available from institutional websites. Citing four studies relating to website usability, the two main barriers to information were accessibility and applicability to transfer students seeking information. If the online information available for transfer students is opaque, how will students then be able to navigate the digital learning environment once they enter a new institution? We felt it was important to clarify the purpose of digital tools in order to mitigate against further "transfer shock" (Hills, 1965) students experience when entering new institutional culture, new student culture, and a new digital environment culture.

The Drive Toward a Workable Definition of *Digital Learning*

There are multiple factors that might explain the transfer shock experience for students; yet the focus for this project asked important questions around the role of digital environments in terms of transfer students' needs and development of their academic capabilities. Do digital learning environments exacerbate the transfer shock, or could they mitigate against it? The project focused on defining *digital learning environments* for faculty, students, and staff and how to effectively leverage digital learning environments for transfer students.

In compiling our literature review, we found *digital learning* was a ubiquitous term with varying emphases on tools that were perceived to accelerate learning (Means et al., 2014) afforded as result of the use of those tools (Linder, 2016; Lovett et al., 2008; Veletsianos & Shepherdson, 2016). When searching for one definition of *digital learning*, we discovered that the term encompasses "distance learning," "online learning," "distance education," "online education," "digital education," "educational technology," "web-based instruction," and "technology-enhanced learning"; each yielding its own breadth of studies. Walker et al. (2012), in their survey of technology-enhanced learning in higher education, defined *digital learning* as "any online facility or system that directly supports learning and teaching" (p. 2). Digital systems should be in service to the learning and teaching processes in place. We wanted to encapsulate that into a definition that would make sense to administrators, faculty members, and students.

The working definition of *digital learning* for the purposes of our project resulted in the following:

> Digital learning (DL) is learning that occurs within an environment combining student-centered design and tools to support learning and teaching. DL environments engage students in the discipline, foster problem-solving processes, encourage self-assessment and reflection, develop analytical and communication skills including critical reading and persuasive writing, and prepare students to live, work and meaningfully contribute in an increasingly digital world by nurturing digital fluency for all students—especially those from historically underrepresented and underserved groups.
>
> The design of the environment should be a vehicle for the application of evidence-based, active learning strategies. A DL environment leverages software tools to enhance delivery, and measure outcomes of quality curated digital content and credentials. Digital learning occurs when courseware, open educational resources, social collaboration and dialogue platforms, or other technology-based systems and tools are applied to strengthen the teaching and learning processes. (McGowan & Koch, 2017, p. 3)

This definition works for all students, yet the explicit emphasis here is on developing meaningful, curated, applicable environments for transfer students so as to engage them from the moment they do an internet search for how to transfer to any given institution to the moment they choose courses and then use the tools as part of their learning experience. The literature and the conversations yielded the need for a definition that allowed for breadth, depth, and an emphasis on the notion of the digital in service to students as opposed to servicing acceleration. The definition outlines five key themes in which to consider institutional digital environments and how transfer students navigate through them. The five themes are: learning, progress, employability, transparency, and design.

Learning

It is crucial to point out that the heart of the definition focused on research conducted on how students learn (Ambrose et al., 2010; Bransford et al., 1999) and how students learn when active pedagogies complement traditional instruction (Freeman et al., 2014; Nilson & Goodson, 2017). Freeman et al. (2014) consolidated much of the literature proving active learning strategies were beneficial to student learning while current studies focus on the benefits for learning and creating a sense of community (Eddy & Hogan, 2016) as integral to all students, especially for underrepresented student groups. Building a sense of community, especially in the first-year courses within these active learning research studies, is particularly critical for transfer students in order to maintain motivation and momentum (Wang, 2017); "The sense of confidence as learners that students gain from engaging in active learning and doing well academically helps them gain momentum in their field" (Fink & Jenkins, p. 41, this volume). When transfer students (or all students) engage in the process of applying skills and integrating their understanding, they are capable of being more engaged in their course of studies.

Progress

Building on that momentum, developing mechanisms for students to see and document their academic progress is crucial to maintaining motivation. In this sense, a digital learning environment should enable a centralized location of student work and the feedback received on that work. Related to this, one of our project stakeholders, an associate vice chancellor at a large public institution, discussed the role of technology in assessment purposes,

> [S]tudents [should] have real-time and self-assessment-based ways to determine their level of success and progress toward completion. I always think about the root of the term *assessment* as "to sit down beside"—that sense of accompanying the learner in her or his learning journey is important. (D. Pointer Mace, personal communication, April 25, 2017).

Within this statement, the digital environment should support the learning journey of the student by providing a record of progress and feedback.

Employability

The notion of fluency supports the inherent employability factor of having students work and gain experience through learning in digital environments. What instructors ask them to accomplish within a given virtual learning environment, blog, discussion board, or even composing an email contributes to the transferable skills students will be asked to perform in any given career due to the multitude of project management and collaboration tools available in any workplace. The implication for transfer students is any digital learning space should encourage them to think and develop the skills best suited for multiple career opportunities.

Transparency

Inherent in this part of the definition is the need for transparent and accessible digital tools to support students, to help them progress through a system that records their work, and to provide essential resources that are not extraneous or distracting from the learning experience. Another project stakeholder, an associate dean for graduate studies as a small regional institution, emphasized the theme of simplicity in how software tools should work together to enhance delivery and organization,

> It seems to me if you're going to use digital tools, the key would be to start with really simple tools, not hard to learn and not hard to use, not profound and then ramp it up or build it up as the program progresses. It's not necessary [to think] of one tool that solves all issues. (B. Eynon, personal communication, April 25, 2017)

Design

Finally, the tools chosen for inclusion within any digital learning environment should support the teaching and learning processes. In other words, the chosen tools support goals, assessments, and chosen activities for student learning. "Like any successful course, the blended modality requires intentional design components to ensure a well-structured learning environment" (Linder, 2016, p. 3). The work of teaching and learning in digital contexts involves creating new environments for learning or, as Brigid Barron describes it, a "'learning ecology' or a set of contexts found in physical or virtual spaces that provide opportunities for learning" (Greenhow et al., 2009, p. 248). The emphasis here remains on learning as a result of carefully designed contexts.

The five overarching themes represented in this definition include the transparency of how tools are used and a respect for processes that can be enabled by technology, not accelerated. Additionally, digital learning environments should foster the development of particular disciplinary skills, they should be judiciously chosen for the purpose of student learning, and they should encompass a variety of tools that support teaching and learning. The starting point for this definition recognized the nuanced understanding of what a digital learning environment could afford beyond acceleration. As one of our stakeholders noted, "developing a learning environment for students to learn how to be a student, how to play college, how to succeed and who or what will help them get there" (MJ Bishop, personal communication, April 4, 2017) should be the main goal of any digital learning environment.

How Can Digital Environments Better Prepare Transfer Students to Access Learning in a Digital Environment?

In May 2017, we used the working definition as the basis for conversations regarding potential recommendations we would make to the funder. If within our *digital learning* definition, we value authentic learning, transparency, and the learning process itself, how should we build robust digital environments? In a survey of transfer practitioners conducted by Rosenberg and Griffin (2017), respondents were asked to list one "big idea" that they would like to see funded to improve transfer outcomes. After staff support and pathway development, the most wished-for item was technology improvements to the transfer support systems. Specific responses included broad-based upgrades in technology, such as a statewide or nationwide transfer information system, digital tools that would show course equivalencies, and a digital transcript processing system. While leveraging technology for these processes is crucial, using tools to facilitate launching students into the learning environments they will be expected to use in their academic career is also just as crucial in terms of retention and attainment.

To look at how digital environments are being created to help students "play college," the following two case studies offer viewpoints for leveraging the tools used in transfer orientation experiences. Both examples make the case for using online environments in the transfer process while demonstrating possibilities for campus-based and online institutions. Looking at the work of supporting transfer students in the blended and fully online realms provides a window into how institutions use tools available to support the students' journey from before they arrive at campus to graduation.

Case Study #1: Florida International University

Janie Valdes, assistant vice president for enrollment management and services at Florida International University (FIU) in the Office of Transfer and Transition Success, described the virtual orientation (VO) for transfers before they attend an in-person advising and registration day on campus. Several tools are used in the transfer process, specifically tools embedded in their existing virtual learning environment on campus and the use of short videos to give students verbal explanations of what to expect in the transfer process as well as what is expected of students in their academics.

The VO includes a tutorial created in the virtual learning environment (Canvas). The tutorials are organized under headings that indicate to students how to use the content. Headings include, "Get the most out of these tutorials that will help you learn how to access course content, take tests, turn in assignments and other course-related activities" and "This video series will help you learn how to use course tools to manage and communicate course work." These are both examples of clear signposting and transparency about not only the tutorial content but also how the content is intended to help students learn as well. In addition to these tutorials, there are additional videos related to registration procedures.

The Office for Transfer and Transition Success worked in partnership with the Center for the Advancement of Teaching to produce "Tutorials to Go" to outline successful student habits that lead to learning and retention (McGuire, 2015). These tutorials include brief videos on notetaking, effective communication, critical reading strategies, and study techniques.

Another approach describes the classroom environments listed among the online Transfer and Transition Services resources. To further orient students to the instructional culture of FIU, based on questions received by transfer advisors, Valdes added web pages defining different types of classrooms such as *active classrooms, flipped classrooms,* or *blended classrooms* since "our transfer students are not necessarily used to hybrid courses or active learning" (J. Valdes, personal communication, August 8, 2018) as learning experiences.

These online experiences are available before students arrive on campus for Advising and Registration Day to meet with advisors and discuss what it takes to succeed in college, a school, or a program. This day also includes an opportunity to meet with peer advisors who discuss their academic experiences and respond to general questions.

For students in STEM-related programs, there is a separate face-to-face orientation led by joint presentations by faculty members and staff of the Center for Academic Success. Faculty members discuss their expectations of the work required in STEM classrooms as well as the type of active-learning experiences to expect. Students have the opportunity to hear from faculty members as well as a transfer student panel where Valdes noted that "students are very honest about their experiences transitioning to FIU, the adjustments they've had to make in terms of study habits and time management" (J. Valdes, personal communication, August 8, 2018).

In terms of helping students make a successful transition into academic classes and thereby improve their retention, FIU made significant gains in redesigning mathematics gateway courses. Students in these courses experienced carefully designed course structures embedding inclusive pedagogies and assessment that contributed to retention and significant decrease in DFWI rates. In college algebra gateway courses, the 2010 passing rate was 30% in the baseline year. After redesign in 2015, the college algebra passing rate increased to 69% (McGowan et al., 2017).

There are other specific tools provided for transfer students to smooth their transition to FIU. When students transfer from three area colleges—Miami Dade College, Broward College, or Palm Beach State College—they are assigned an FIU bridge advisor who uses a proprietary online tool to help advisors and students keep track of meetings as well as what was discussed in those meetings thus creating a digital footprint of students' experiences prior to their time at FIU. Once these students transfer to FIU, they are assigned an academic advisor in their major and are given an introduction to other supportive platform tools such as the Panther Success Network, which supports a student's continuous contact with key support staff like advisors, tutors, and success coaches. Another online tool, the Panther Degree Audit, provides visible documentation of academic progression toward graduation. Taken together, FIU leverages digital learning environments to form an initial, supportive network before students reach campus with many of these well-crafted early exposure experiences reflective of the digital tools used during their on-campus academic experiences.

Case Study #2: Southern New Hampshire University

The next case study looks at the transfer experience within a blended institution, Southern New Hampshire University (SNHU). Seventy-one percent of students at this institution are transfer students. Jasmeial Jackson (associate dean of first-year experience and retention programs) shared the SNHU approach to helping students transfer into the learning processes expected of them in their academic experiences.

Jackson shared that initial feedback on students' orientation experiences pointed out that students did not feel part of the institution and were not aware of people who were there to support them. Even though SNHU had a suite of welcoming videos from senior administrators, Jackson decided to expand their video offerings to demonstrate to students that the senior administrators were not the only ones invested in their success.

SNHU developed a space and environment to address the following areas identified for transfer students to know about the transfer process: (a) understanding academic expectations, (b) navigating college, (c) valuing the curriculum, and (d) developing insight into particular programs. Setting students' expectations for learning included knowing how to engage in online environments such as understanding what a syllabus is, understanding the assessment process and the use of rubrics, and knowing how to leverage discussion boards. According to Jackson, by focusing on these important aspects of the learning process SNHU wanted to concentrate on these "impactful" components of what students would be asked to do in their courses.

The second aspect of orienting students to a digital learning environment encompasses a support series to help them "know where they are" and where to find the services and resources they might need. This included an initial scavenger hunt. The university also produced videos for students on goal setting for short- and long-term goals to help them understand how to navigate college.

An important aspect of their program leveraged data from students who had already graduated. They were able to group aspects of success based on students who succeeded versus those who did not. These data turned into developing a resource that identified the five successful habits of students at SNHU. To increase consistency and messaging of content, Jackson partnered with the administrative and advising teams in order to share applicable content for transfer students. Jackson cited this information as vital to students for them to understand important traits to emulate in order to succeed.

The third aspect focused on helping students understand the "full picture" and reasons for entering a general education curriculum. The narrative around their curriculum outlines the skills students will build and how these skills are situated within specific majors. Jackson identified an engaging infographic for students to understand the foundational skills they will develop within their degree thus visualizing their attainment again as a form of focused concentration. The final aspect of this orientation program allows students to delve into specific programs supporting their knowledge of people involved, and those people provide short videos outlining what students need to know. Students view newsletters from the program to keep them informed of events and program-related content that will increase their success and engagement. Jackson found that students who completed this orientation program still wanted access to it even though they were meant to complete the orientation before their studies started. This indicated that further online support was needed. Therefore, he developed an additional orientation that includes personalized information for different student populations such as veterans or first-generation students. Using principles of accessibility and inclusion, these student groups are equipped with checklists to help them balance expectations during the program with the intention of keeping them on task for graduation and beyond. The digital learning environment at SNHU is the pathway itself from transition to graduation for the substantial number of transfer students the institution serves.

Taken together, these case studies illustrate the possibilities and directions for creating inclusive digital learning environments through meaningful campus partnerships, strategic use of resources already available, and most importantly, a primary focus on the needs of transfer students in development and delivery. The careful design of resources evident in these case studies reflects an understanding of student needs at both FIU and SNHU.

From a blended, institutional perspective, the SNHU case study demonstrates the need to make the support structure explicit—one that encompasses a clear map for students to understand the environment they are entering. The key point made by Jackson was the importance of generating a sense of support and encouragement within the orientation that students felt they needed following the orientation. Leveraging digital solutions to indicate to students what their trajectory will be and where they are headed visualizes a path for them that contains a record, a digital footprint within the ecosystem. This does not replace the advising system or faculty members in this process yet strengthens the support network in place for students.

The FIU case study demonstrates a more blended experience. The institution collates digital tools into a threshold where students will pass from the VO to the face-to-face supportive learning environment of bridge advisors and coaches to newly designed gateway courses where there is a renewed aim to capture and retain the capabilities of all students who enter the university.

Digital Learning as Ecosystem

These case studies point to what an effective "digital ecosystem" might look like in which digital technology, student learning, and educational values combine to support student learning. Bass and Eynon (2016) discuss a *digital ecosystem* as a "whole constellation of learning technologies—institutional and non-institutional—that characterizes our contemporary life" (p. v). This element of a digital ecosystem corresponds to the earlier definition on environments and the need for breadth and depth in how college and university stakeholders build an ecosystem of support for student learning. Furthermore, Bass and Eynon situate an effective digital ecosystem in a framework of liberal-education values where integration of key elements around engagement, community, and mentorship form additional fundamental themes to any tools used within a digital ecosystem. Some of the digital tools identified within their ecosystem as contributing to developing institutional values are ePortfolios (Eynon et al., 2014); electronic systems to support the advising process (as seen in the FIU case study); and adaptive tools in learning management systems that provide visual, documented progress indicators or "microcredentialing"—for students to use in reflecting on and seeing their own progress.

Based on our working definition and its themes, these case studies of effective practice, and the notion of a digital ecosystem to support transfer students, the following recommendations serve as initial guidelines to consider in creating (or reviewing) "transfer-affirming" (Handel, chapter 5, this volume) institutional digital environments:

1. Take the *digital learning* definition in this chapter as initial criteria for evaluating your own digital learning environments on campus. Consider how digital environments support learning, assessment and improvement, employability, and ensuring that the design of the environment is transparent and rational.
2. Use data to inform and justify why particular tools work well for transfer students in order to make the case for continued use and support.
3. Monitor transfer student experiences consistently. Ask the useful question, "What do you wish you had known?" to understand the surprises, frustrations, or puzzlement of transfer students, particularly in the realm of their digital learning experiences.
4. Involve students in both the development of digital resources as well as face-to-face events.
5. Conduct usability design testing with staff and students to understand the digital pathway for transfer students from start to finish. This will inform the design of environments.

Conclusion: Moving Toward Effective Digital Learning Ecosystems

Our working definition for *digital learning* encompassed the themes of authenticity, transparency, and learning as a process within a digital learning environment. Bass and Eynon (2016) also addressed the themes of authenticity and the development of key learning skills as crucial in the development of "digitally-enhanced strategies" where "students analyze and apply information to address authentic problems and build the skills of critical inquiry" (p. 22). In the context of supporting transfer students through the case studies presented here as reflections of the *digital learning* definition developed during this funded project, six themes emerged as crucial for transfer students when considering the type of digital learning environment they require to be successful: authenticity, engagement, transparency, learning, mentorship, and community. Both case studies situated their "digitally-enhanced strategies" within the institutional community and the needs they identified from transfer students, thus generating authentic, tailored solutions to engage transfer students into the campus community and learning environments. Both institutions in the case studies embedded transparency in their approaches to reflect potential successes and the reality of transferring into a new learning culture. Both case studies identified the use of transfer student panels at face-to-face orientations and videos of graduates discussing their learning journey as key to being transparent and honest in conveying the tools to succeed and overcome potential challenges.

The key to enacting our working definition of *digital learning* returns to the theme of the ecosystem in thinking there is no individual, unit, or app responsible for creating such an environment. Including students, faculty, administrators, and institutional researchers into these conversations is imperative to develop the digital learning environment each institution deserves. This stands in vital contrast to the persistent, at times pernicious, belief that "ed tech" is the answer to most of our institutional challenges. The answer lies in the humans responsible for making the decisions regarding what we want students to remember about their learning experience in 20 years' time (Lang, 2018). Our goals for developing digital learning ecosystems for transfer students should encompass the themes represented here, and they should emulate the good work happening already within many institutions represented within this chapter as well as this book.

Discussion Questions

In closing, we encourage all institutional stakeholders to discuss the following questions to continue the dialogue in developing transformative educational pathways for transfer students and the role of digital environments in those pathways:

1. What are the examples of effective uses of digital tools currently happening on campus? How do you know they are effective from the learning standpoint?
2. How are technologies selected on your campus? And who is involved in making those decisions? Do you have members of your centers for teaching and learning and/or learning technologists who contribute to those decisions?
3. What are some of the consistent or ubiquitous uses of digital tools on campus? Which ones are most recognizable or used often by students?
4. How are faculty and staff trained in not only using digital tools but also situating their use in larger, educational frameworks discussed in the *digital learning* definition? How is professional development maintained for institutional stakeholders to signpost effectively to students?

Acknowledgments

I wish to thank the following colleagues who graciously took their time to talk with me about their work in relation to students and digital learning environments: Michelle Alvarez, Isis Artze-Vega, Jasmeial Jackson, Drew Koch, and Janie Valdes. In addition, I benefited from the expert editorial attention from colleagues John Gardner and Michael Rosenberg. Any student is fortunate to be in the hands of these dedicated, caring, and engaged educators.

References

Ambrose, S. A., Bridges, M. W., DiPietro, M., Lovett, M. C., & Norman, M. K. (2010). *How learning works: Seven research-based principles for smart teaching*. Wiley.

Bass, R., & Eynon, B. (2016). *Open and integrative: Designing liberal education for the new digital ecosystem*. Association of American Colleges & Universities.

Bransford, J. D., Brown, A., & Cocking, R. (1999). *How people learn: Mind, brain, experience, and school*. National Research Council.

Cohen, B. R. (2017, April 24). Jill Lepore on the challenge of explaining things. *Public Thinker.* http://www.publicbooks.org/public-thinker-jill-lepore-on-the-challenge-of-explaining-things/

Eddy, S. L., & Hogan, K. A. (2014). Getting under the hood: How and for whom does increasing course structure work? *CBE—Life Sciences Education, 13*(3), 453–468.

Eynon, B., Gambino, L. M., & Török, J. (2014). What difference can ePortfolio make? A field report from the connect to learning project. *International Journal of ePortfolio, 4*(1), 95–114. https://doi.org/10.1187/cbe.14-03-0050

Freeman, S., Eddy, S. L., McDonough, M., Smith, M. K., Okoroafor, N., Jordt, H., & Wenderoth, M. P. (2014). Active learning increases student performance in science, engineering, and mathematics. *Proceedings of the National Academy of Sciences, 111*(23), 8410–8415. https://doi.org/10.1073/pnas.1319030111

Greenhow, C., Robelia, B., & Hughes, J. E. (2009). Learning, teaching, and scholarship in a digital age: Web 2.0 and classroom research: What path should we take now? *Educational Researcher, 38*(4), 246–259. https://doi.org/10.3102/0013189x09336671

Hills, J. R. (1965). Transfer shock: The academic performance of the junior college transfer. *The Journal of Experimental Education, 33*(3), 201–215. https://doi.org/10.1080/002209 73.1965.11010875

Lang, J. M. (2018, September 30). What will students remember from your class in 20 years? *The Chronicle of Higher Education.* https://www.chronicle.com/article/What-Will-Students-Remember/244633

Linder, K. E. (2016). *The blended course design workbook: A practical guide.* Stylus.

Lovett, M., Meyer, O., & Thille, C. (2008). The Open Learning Initiative: Measuring the effectiveness of the OLI statistics course in accelerating student learning. *Journal of Interactive Media in Education, 2008*(1), p. Art13. https://doi.org/10.5334/2008-14

Means, B., Peters, V. Zheng, Y. (2014). *Lessons from five years of funding digital courseware.* SRI Education. https://www.sri.com/publication/a-review-of-the-bill-melinda-gates-foundation-postsecondary-success-portfolio-lessons-from-five-years-of-funding-digital-courseware-full-report/_

McGowan, S., Felten, P., Caulkins, J., & Artze-Vega, I. (2017, Winter). Fostering evidence-informed teaching in crucial classes: Faculty development in gateway courses. In A. K. Koch (Ed.), *Improving teaching, learning, equity, and success in gateway courses* (New Directions for Higher Education, no. 180, pp. 53–62). Jossey-Bass. https://doi.org/10.1002/he.20261

McGowan, S., & Koch, A. K. (2017). "Definition of digital learning." In A. K. Koch (Comp.), *John N. Gardner Institute for Excellence in Undergraduate Education planning grant report for investment OPP1160998* (p. 3). John N. Gardner Institute.

McGuire, S. Y. (2015). *Teach students how to learn: Strategies you can incorporate into any course to improve student metacognition, study skills, and motivation.* Stylus.

Nilson, L. B., & Goodson, L. A. (2017). *Online teaching at its best: Merging instructional design with teaching and learning research.* Wiley.

Rosenberg, M. J., Griffin, B. (2017). *Views of transfer practitioners: Results of a national JNGI survey.* John N. Gardner Institute for Excellence in Undergraduate Education. http://www.jngi.org/surveytransferpractitioners/

Veletsianos, G. & Shepherdson, P. (2016). A systematic analysis and synthesis of the empirical MOOC literature published in 2013–2015. *The International Review of Research in Open and Distributed Learning, 17*(2), 198–221 https://doi.org/10.19173/irrodl.v17i2.2448

Walker, R., J. Voce, and J. Ahmed. (2012). *2012 survey of technology enhanced learning for higher education in the UK*. Universities and Colleges Information Systems Association. https://www.researchgate.net/publication/264309353_2012_Survey_of_Technology_Enhanced_Learning_for_higher_education_in_the_UK

Wang, X. (2017). Toward a holistic theoretical model of momentum for community college student success. In M. B. Paulsen (Ed.), *Higher education: Handbook of theory and research* (pp. 259–308). Springer.

PART FOUR

CASE STUDIES: TRANSFER IN ACTION

16

A DEEP COMMITMENT TO TRANSFER STUDENT ACCESS AND SUCCESS

The University of Central Florida Story

Maribeth Ehasz and J. Jeffrey Jones

The University of Central Florida (UCF) committed to transfer student access and success from its founding in 1963, and that dedication set the stage for current and future collaborations. This chapter describes how the university built an organizational structure dedicated to strengthening relationships with transfer-sending institutions and supporting transfer students prior to enrollment and during their transition. It introduces the establishment and development of the DirectConnect to UCF consortium and outlines the impact of assessment and continuous improvement with the John N. Gardner Institute for Excellence in Undergraduate Education's Foundations of Excellence Transfer Focus program. The contributors provide tips for replication, reinforcing that it is a process, not an event. They detail plans in development to create a stronger transfer support system that eliminates duplication of services and streamlines student support prior to and after enrollment. In addition, the contributors offer a preview of UCF's next adventure—a downtown campus where future transfer students and current students will learn, study, live, and engage together on one campus.

Transfer students have attended UCF since its beginning—they are an essential part of UCF's foundation and future. UCF was established in 1963 specifically to serve the residents of nine counties in east Central Florida (Sheinkopf, 1976). There was a sense of urgency associated with establishing the university because there were predictions of "phenomenal growth in college enrollment in the 1960s and '70s" (Sheinkopf, 1976, p. 4). In addition, with its proximity to the Florida Space Coast and with the rapid acceleration of the aerospace industry in the region, there was a demand for technical and scientific talent in areas like engineering and computer science.

261

UCF's first day of classes was Monday, October 7, 1968, when 1,891 new first-time freshmen alongside junior-level transfer students enrolled at the Orlando main campus and two regional sites. From UCF's founding, access and success of transfer students have been integral parts of our framework—unlike older American universities, which were created without a thought that such transfer students would ever exist.

Fifty years after the first classes began at UCF, transfer students represent more than half of the undergraduate student enrollment (UCF, 2018). As predicted from the start by UCF's inaugural president, Charles Millican, UCF was destined to be a large university (Sheinkopf, 1976), and in fall 2018, enrollment reached over 68,500 with over 59,000 of those students being undergraduates (UCF, 2018), making UCF one of the largest public universities in the United States (U.S. News and World Report, 2018). However, since its founding, Millican's educational philosophies of "accent on the individual" and "accent on excellence" continue to guide UCF's commitment to access and success for all students (Sheinkopf, 1976).

Providing for the higher educational needs of the citizens and industries in the Central Florida area, particularly in the metropolitan Orlando community, continues to be a priority for UCF. At the time of UCF's founding, there were limited higher education offerings in the Orlando area including a junior college (Valencia Community College) and a small private college (Rollins College) (Sheinkopf, 1976). Although the number of higher education institutions in the Orlando area and Central Florida region has expanded, the state's population has also grown rapidly. In 1960, 3 years before UCF was established, Florida's population was 4,951,560. Today, Florida's population is 21,640,000 (World Population Review, 2018) and Central Florida is one of the fastest growing regions in Florida. Current estimates show that about 1,086 residents move to Central Florida weekly (Millsap, 2018).

In 2015, UCF launched a strategic plan entitled "Collective Impact," a 20-year vision and a 5-year course of action to chart a path to become a leading 21st-century preeminent institution. UCF's plan is to achieve preeminence by "leveraging our scale and our constant pursuit of excellence to create greater cultural, economic, environmental, and social impact for our students, community, region, and beyond" (UCF, 2017, p. 12). Priority metrics, thematic team leaders and members, and an institutionalization plan were identified and are currently being followed. Our experiences—both challenges and achievements—to enhance transfer student access and keep student success a priority at UCF will be the focus of this story.

Phase One—Commitment to Transfer Student Access and Success

In the early 1990s, UCF estimated that approximately 22% of all associate of arts (AA) degree completers from the Florida Community College System enrolled at UCF. During this same period UCF welcomed its fourth president, John C. Hitt, the coauthor of this book's Foreword, who recognized the importance of improving access to higher education to meet the needs of our growing Central Florida region.

President Hitt's commitment to growth mirrored state funding models, which at that time supported enrollment growth.

Since UCF enrolled such a substantial number of AA transfers—in addition to transfers from all sorts of colleges and universities—the university needed to establish an office dedicated to the development of trusted relationships and positive interactions with transfer-sending institutions. An office of Community College Relations in the Department of Undergraduate Studies was established and staffed with one director. The focus of this office was to work with transfer-sending institutions to improve student access and success. The main work of the office was the preparation of articulation agreements that guaranteed the successful transfer of community college courses for specific bachelor's degree programs at UCF. In the Community College Relations office, more time was spent with community college representatives than with students.

In 1999, recognizing the importance of direct contact with students to enhance their access and success, UCF established the Office of Transfer Services in the new division of Student Development and Enrollment Services, which reported directly to the president (Dodge, 2017). This office expanded the mission of the former office of Community College Relations to also focus on pre-enrollment services for students attending community colleges and other higher education institutions. UCF recognized that some students plan to transfer and complete their bachelor's degrees and others need to transfer because options to complete degrees at their previous institution or institutions were not available. The office became a resource for all prospective transfer students, including what are known as "swirlers" (students attending multiple institutions), 4-year college and university transfers, and community college transfers. The common denominator among all transfers was interest in understanding more completely the best pathways to completion of their anticipated bachelor's degree programs. In addition to developing pathways to graduation, students also received assistance with the admission and financial aid processes. Professional development sessions and yearly transfer manuals were developed to inform staff from transfer-sending institutions about updates in bachelor's degree curricula so that the transfer-sending institutions could advise students accurately about UCF academic programs while students were still at their colleges (Collins et al., 2011).

An enhanced commitment to the access and success of transfer students at UCF expanded again when the office changed its mission and name to Transfer and Transition Services (TTS) in 2004 (Stinard, 2012). UCF realized that only a small portion of new transfer students reached out to UCF prior to their enrollment at UCF. Also, many transfer students did not decide to continue their education until they were enrolled in their final courses to complete their AA degrees. To address these issues, TTS added another priority—to support transfer students in their transition to UCF especially in their first term as UCF students. A priority was placed on engaging transfer students in the life of the university. This was to combat what Hills (1965) first referred to as "transfer shock" or the academic and social adjustment period many transfer students have after they transfer.

In the same way investments had been made by UCF and many other institutions across the nation to support the first year of new first-time-in-college (FTIC) students, this was UCF's attempt to intentionally support transfer students in their first semester at UCF. The principles guiding UCF's work revolved around a three-stage intervention model (Collins et al., 2011). The first stage involved a greater commitment to readiness for success at UCF, not only through early contact initiated by prospective transfer students but also, more importantly, through UCF staff reaching out and having a regular presence at regional state college campuses to meet directly with students. This endeavor was further enhanced by embedding services and staff at regional state college sites throughout Central Florida through a new DirectConnect to UCF inter-institutional initiative that will be discussed more completely in the next section.

The second stage of our efforts revolved around more intensive and intentional transition programs such as enhancements in mandatory orientation so transfer students experienced curricular, cocurricular, and social engagement opportunities in the same way as new FTIC students. Welcome week activities were also broadened to include experiences for new transfer students at UCF. These activities included more family-friendly entertainment for students with children. Opportunities for transfer students to live in UCF-owned, managed, and affiliated housing also became available. The most popular accommodations for transfer students are apartment-style plans and those at our Rosen College of Hospitality campus in the center of the region's hospitality district. Transfer students represent close to half of the students living in UCF housing at the Rosen campus and at our new shared downtown campus (Varner, 2019).

The third phase emphasized progression once new transfers moved past the transition stage of their enrollment. In other words, now that these students had enrolled at UCF, what did they need from the university to ensure their continued success? The progression stage involved the creation of intentional university-wide efforts to advocate and highlight the needs, concerns, and barriers that interfered with transfer student success at UCF. One example was the formation of a registered student organization (RSO) at UCF to allow transfer students to advocate for themselves, plan social events aimed at transfer students, and help transfer students find a network of peers.

This enhanced approach to transfer student access and success did not come without its challenges. Although embraced by our transfer-sending institutions because of long-term trusted relationship building, these enhancements were not readily accepted by all of UCF's internal partners, such as our academic colleges. Some of our faculty members maintained a perception that transfer students were inadequately prepared for the rigors of a university. Internal relationship building became necessary to expand an understanding that the needs of transfer students once they became UCF students were different than the support that could be provided by any one academic unit alone. In many ways the creation of a centrally identified "transfer center" (Collins et al., 2011) such as Transfer Services and its evolution to Transfer and Transition Services brought university-wide attention to the need for all of UCF faculty and staff to make transfer student access and success a priority.

This development of central support, coupled with the creation of the division of Student Development and Enrollment Services mentioned before, reflected the evolution at UCF that transfer student access and success involved more than an articulation agreement with an institution—and, more importantly, that transfer is a student-focused and student-centered enterprise. This effort also reflected the university-wide recognition that transfer student access and success involved the development of both institutional and student relationship building. The creation of transfer success initiatives while students were enrolled at the sending institution and during the start of and progression toward completion of a bachelor's degree at the receiving institution were critical components of UCF's efforts to support transfer students.

Phase Two—DirectConnect to University of Central Florida Partnership

In 2004, UCF and four regional community colleges—Brevard Community College, Lake-Sumter Community College, Seminole Community College, and Valencia Community College—formed the Central Florida Higher Education Consortium. In April 2005, the brand and the product of that consortium was born—DirectConnect to UCF—and its first students were enrolled. To manage and grow this new partnership, all UCF regional campus leaders who were operating independently were reorganized into a new division, UCF Regional Campus Administration, led by a new vice provost for regional campuses recruited from the community college system.

The intent of this formal partnership was to ensure that regional citizens would continue to have access to UCF, which, due to increased demand, had become more selective over time. The concern on the part of local higher education leaders—raised by Valencia College president Sanford Shugart, the other coauthor of this volume's foreword, to UCF's then-president John Hitt—was that increased selectivity at Central Florida's only state university would limit baccalaureate degree options for local residents.

To provide continuing access to UCF, DirectConnect to UCF guaranteed admission to UCF for any student earning an AA degree from any of the four community college partners. Although this guarantee still didn't provide direct admission to limited enrollment programs (e.g., engineering, nursing), students could attend the university without any additional conditions.

However, the mission of the community colleges legislatively changed on July 1, 2009. An update to Florida State Statute 1007.33(4)(C) enabled Florida's state community colleges to issue a limited number of baccalaureate degrees to address the need for more workforce-focused college graduates. With this change to their college portfolios, the names of the institutions also changed—becoming Eastern Florida State College, Lake-Sumter State College, Seminole State College, and Valencia College.

With the implementation of DirectConnect to UCF, one traditional pattern of student enrollment changed. The guaranteed admission for AA graduates incentivized community college students to stay at their state college and complete their AA degree. Previously, some community college students left their college before graduation to attend a 4-year university. Before DirectConnect to UCF, some expressed worries UCF was poaching students from the community colleges before they could graduate, potentially affecting community college graduation rates and ultimately state funding. DirectConnect to UCF addressed these concerns.

When students completed their associate degrees before enrollment at UCF, their general education requirements at UCF were also considered complete. As a result, students saved a considerable amount of money and time. Tuition and fees at the state colleges are a little less than 50% of the amount charged at the state universities. Students matriculating had only upper-division coursework for majors, minors, and electives remaining to complete the bachelor's degree at UCF. This is the equivalent to students completing their first 2 years of a baccalaureate degree program for a 50% discount.

Through DirectConnect to UCF, transfer students had at least three options: stay at one of the UCF regional campus sites to complete the UCF baccalaureate degree, complete their degree through one of UCF's online degree programs, or attend another UCF campus in Orlando. Faculty employed by UCF taught courses at the regional campuses, allowing many students to complete degrees without the need to travel to the Orlando main campus of UCF. At each site, enrollment specialists, student affairs coordinators, and DirectConnect to UCF advisors tended to the needs of students planning to attend UCF both before and after matriculation.

Faculty members from each of the Central Florida Consortium institutions began to meet to discuss curriculum alignment—how the respective faculties can work together to align courses to ensure students are prepared for next level courses. Originally beginning with STEM courses such as calculus and biology, these activities have now expanded to include writing and rhetoric and speech communications.

Phase Three—Collaboration—Continuous Improvement

As UCF contemplates the next 20 years, the institution's commitment to access and success for all students will continue to be core values. UCF will not be able to reach its goals and aspirations alone and will need the continued support of regional state college educational partners to sustain and enhance its student success mission. Collaboration will continue to be the "secret sauce" that will solidify UCF's collective commitment to provide access, ensure quality, and achieve success as more students begin their journey through higher education at a state college and transfer to complete their undergraduate degrees at UCF.

UCF's state college partners agree that all member institutions have a responsibility to own student success, both before and after attendance at one or more of the consortium partner institutions. Data sharing has become a priority, so each institution can use outcome data for all other partners through a shared dashboard hosted by UCF. Recently, Valencia College and UCF, along with Orange County Public Schools and the School District of Osceola County, embarked on a data-sharing project called the Central Florida Education Ecosystem Database (CFEED), designed to formalize and operationalize data sharing across the pre-K–20 spectrum to support student success.

DirectConnect continues to grow. In November 2015, with the unanimous support of the existing DirectConnect to UCF presidents, two additional partners were added—College of Central Florida and Daytona State College.

Despite the success of DirectConnect to UCF, continuous improvement in access and success for all students continues to drive the partnerships. In 2014, UCF engaged with the Gardner Institute for Excellence in Undergraduate Education and its Foundations of Excellence (FoE) Transfer Focus program. This effort focused on transfer students and their needs. It involved a self-study of transfer policies, practices, and procedures. This study involved over 200 administrators, faculty, staff, students, and external stakeholders, including colleagues from DirectConnect to UCF partners, and resulted in 118 recommended action items, including an emphasis on reverse transfer. During the 2017–2018 school year, almost 400 Valencia College AA degrees were awarded because of the reverse transfer initiative. UCF sent back to Valencia College records of coursework completed by students who had transferred to UCF without the AA degree, thereby completing the requirements to obtain the Valencia College AA.

Future Plans

As we move into the next phase of our partnership—one of true and deep collaboration—the conversation has shifted to a discussion of DirectConnect to UCF 2.0. What does the next generation of the partnership look like? Currently, more students transfer to UCF than any other university in the United States (Ross, 2018). Of all Florida transfer students, 28%, including 30.7% of all Florida state college AA graduates who go on to attend a Florida university, transfer to UCF (Pumariega, 2018).

The Foundations of Excellence action plan was rebranded as the UCF Transfer Alliance. The implementation of the recommendations is in various stages of execution, and institutional momentum for improved transfer student success continues. A sustainability plan has enabled ownership of various initiatives among university offices and units.

With the continued decrease of face-to-face courses offered on the UCF Regional Campuses, the division's name of UCF Regional Campus Administration was changed to UCF Connect in order to reflect the new needs of our DirectConnect to UCF students. The regional campuses were once the only option for students who were geographically constrained, but the growth of online courses at UCF opened the door for students to complete baccalaureate degrees from anywhere.

UCF Online now offers 80 undergraduate and graduate degrees fully online. In order to capitalize on the unique strengths that UCF has demonstrated in transfer student success, the decision was made to limit UCF Online undergraduate degree programs to transfer students. To meet the needs of these online learners, UCF established a success coaching model. The duties of staff located in the regions evolved from enrollment and financial aid specialists, student services specialists, and DirectConnect to UCF advisors to the more comprehensive role of success coaches. In this new role, staff work to develop relationships with students to ensure that those students are empowered to be successful. Fewer transactions are necessary due to increased student access to technology, and the regional campuses are now making the transition to become regional Success Centers. Students can connect with success coaches at those centers, either in person or virtually, and seek coaching to assist in their eventual transfer to UCF. These coaches are trained to help empower a student to address academic, social, and personal challenges that might be standing in the way of achieving the student's life goals.

Replication

UCF and the consortium partners are honored frequently by inquiries and guests from institutions interested in modeling or replicating a transfer program using components of the DirectConnect to UCF programs. Replication by other institutions is possible and certainly has the potential to positively affect other institutions or consortia, regardless of scale, location, number of partners, or other regional factors.

To enable a similar program, or perhaps to improve an existing partnership, our experience shows a few things that should be in place to ensure success and continued growth. Many institutions examining DirectConnect to UCF can be deterred from the comparison to our infrastructure, including human assets devoted to it, because of the sheer size of this enterprise. We advise institutions to resist looking at the description of this current collaboration as their starting point. DirectConnect to UCF scaled up over time and is now in its 14th year, recently awarding the 50,000th degree through the program (Kruckemyer, 2019). We advise institutions to be willing to start with limited resources, just as UCF did initially, but to make mutual commitments, redeploy existing resources, and stay centered on what is best for the students that they serve—not the institutions. By building effectively on the existing resource base, institutions can begin to positively affect student opportunities, access, and success.

Campus leaders should be ready to share power and control through a robust, transparent governance structure. Unilaterally establishing a program is much easier, since the ability to control resources is so attractive. However, to create a program that truly holds to the overarching desire to do what is best for students, shared governance among all partners is fundamentally important. DirectConnect to UCF succeeds in part because of such a unique governance structure.

This structure begins with the top-down support of the Presidents' Council. Consisting of UCF's president, provost, and the presidents of each state college partner, this council meets annually to review the consortium's operation and efficacy, to consider any potential policy changes, and to set the vision for the continued growth and vitality of the collaboration. A steering committee consists of chief academic and student affairs officers from UCF and each consortium partner, along with key stakeholders from each of their staffs. This group functions to lay operational groundwork and to smooth out "pinch points" for students, faculty, and staff where feedback suggests the need for further attention and adjustments.

The Consortium Academic Collaboration Council (CACC) consists of the chief academic officers from each state college partner along with two vice provosts from UCF. Among other things, this group vets proposed baccalaureate degree programs from the state college partners. This collaboration, which many would see as a loss of autonomy by the state colleges, was imposed by the Presidents' Council to ensure that degree programs had an existing workforce need (not duplicative) and make efficient use of state and regional resources. Another six consortium committees monitor workforce needs, consortium data and reporting, and joint philanthropy, among other responsibilities.

Meanwhile, UCF continues to examine its internal structures to maximize resources devoted to transfer student success. Currently, planning is underway to more carefully design a system in which TTS and DirectConnect to UCF define more explicitly respective roles in serving transfer students both prior to and after transferring. The intent of this planning will be to ensure that there is a "smooth handoff" of students during the transfer process, while preventing an inefficient duplication of effort.

UCF's partnership with Valencia College reached new levels when we together committed to building and operationalizing a new downtown campus that opened in fall 2019. We are creating a new model for higher education delivery where students working toward the AA at Valencia College and planning to pursue the bachelor's degree will be enrolled in the same lower division courses as UCF FTIC students. The goal of the downtown campus is to create a seamless and unified education experience. Students, whether from Valencia College or UCF apply for and utilize university housing, recreation, community service, leadership, involvement, and learning in a uniform fashion. The downtown campus will be fueled by workforce data, providing specific industry- and community-based majors that benefit and are benefited by the community because of their location in downtown Orlando. The potential for enhanced learning, greater success outcomes, and critical community impact is significant as UCF and Valencia College strengthen their partnership with the creation of the downtown campus.

Like any other meaningful relationship, the downtown campus collaboration requires constant nurturing. Communication must be open, resource discussions need to be transparent and meaningful, and occasional disagreements must be resolved with equity and efficiency. Initially, start slow and begin to build seamless on-ramps for transfer students while constantly assessing results in both student access and success. The moment that students decide that they are interested in pursuing their degree at another institution is the moment that they become the shared responsibility of the state college and the university. Waiting until they arrive for their first day of class is too late! Once they are on campus, the institution's responsibility continues to provide the best experience possible while always keeping student needs at the center of the work.

Conclusion

The following are key points to consider for future action as you build your transfer network:

1. Don't be afraid to begin with limited resources—get started!
2. Shared governance among consortium members is critical; take time to develop, advance, and continuously improve.
3. Commitment by partners' executive leadership is key to continued success.
4. Operational matters will be best handled by chief academic officers, student affairs officers, and student success officers.
5. Formal agreements should be executed by governing boards and chief executive officers.
6. Finally, a shared commitment to access and success is the underlying principle that drives the commitment to the program—share stories of impact!

Discussion Questions

1. Since transfer students come from many different institutions and pathways, what are the similarly significant differences in students' needs, expectations, and success outcomes?
2. What are the differences in success outcomes for students making early contact either through personal interaction or inquiry and students who never connect with the transfer receiving institution until orientation?
3. What characteristics and experiences are associated with strong transfer student affiliation to the university as alumni, athletic boosters, and philanthropists?

References

Collins, J., Navarro, C. P., & Stinard, C. (2011). *Transfer students in higher education: Building foundations for policies, programs, and services that foster student success.* National Resource Center for the First-Year Experience and Students in Transition First-Year Experience Monograph Series, 54, 55–68.

Dodge, J. (2017). *Abbreviated history of TTS.* (Unpublished internal UCF report).

Florida State Statutes. (2009). *1007.33 Site-determined baccalaureate degree access.* http://www.leg.state.fl.us/statutes/index.cfm?App_mode=Display_Statute&Search_String=&URL=1000-1099/1007/Sections/1007.33.html

Hills, J. R. (1965). Transfer shock: The academic performance of the junior college transfer. *Journal of Experimental Education, 33*(3), 210–215. https://doi.org/10.1080/0022097 3.1965.11010875

Kruckemyer, G. (2019, April 24). DirectConnect to UCF to award 50,000th degree. *UCF News and Information.* https://today.ucf.edu/directconnect-ucf-award-50000th-degree/

Millsap, A. (2018, March 23). Big metro areas in Florida keep getting bigger. *Forbes*. https://www.forbes.com/sites/adammillsap/2018/03/23/big-metro-areas-in-florida-keep-getting-bigger/#6825ea6a671d

Pumariega, M. (2018, June 28). *Florida Department of Education–Florida 2+2 presentation*. Florida Board of Governors meeting, University of Central Florida, FAIRWINDS Alumni Center.

Ross, K. (2018). 10 colleges that attract transfer students. *U.S. News & World Report*. https://www.usnews.com/education/best-colleges/the-short-list-college/articles/2018-02-13/10-colleges-that-attract-the-most-transfer-students

Sheinkopf, K. G. (1976). *Accent on the individual: The first twelve years of Florida Technological University*. Florida Technological University Foundation.

Stinard, C. (2012). *Transfer and Transfer Services document*. (Unpublished internal UCF report.) University of Central Florida. (2016, May 26). *Collective impact*. https://www.ucf.edu/wp-content/uploads/2012/08/UCF-Strategic-Plan-BOT-FINAL-052616-Web.pdf

University of Central Florida. (2016). *Creating our collective impact: An overview of our promises and strategies*. https://www.ucf.edu/strategic-plan/files/2017/07/Creating-Our-Collective-Impact-rev072017.pdf

University of Central Florida. (2018). *UCF facts 2017-2018*. https://www.ucf.edu/files/2018/03/UCF-FactsFlyer-2017-18-v2.pdf

U.S. News and World Report. (2018). *Most transfer students*. https://www.usnews.com/best-colleges/rankings/most-transfers

Varner, M. (2019). *Transfer students in housing*. (Unpublished internal UCF report.)

World Population Review. (2018). *Florida population 2019*. http://worldpopulationreview.com/states/florida-population/

17

CREATING A CULTURE OF TRANSFER AT ARIZONA STATE UNIVERSITY

The Story of the Arizona State University Transfer Transformation

Maria Hesse

Arizona State University (ASU), one of the largest universities in the United States, has a strong commitment to serving its sizable transfer population. In summer 2009, we began undertaking a broad-reaching and comprehensive plan for reform and improvement by visiting every community college president in Arizona, on-site at their college, asking for their thoughts and ideas about improving transfer student success. We subsequently signed agreements with the stated purpose to "create a culture of transfer" between each college and ASU. Open, honest, and consistent dialogue helped us build strong relationships and increased interaction between the university and the community colleges at all levels.

Every year in her role as ASU's vice provost for academic partnerships, the contributor of this chapter visited each of the 21 community and tribal college presidents in the state to share progress, provide data, answer questions, and listen to concerns. Furthermore, she invited community college administrators to visit the university to meet colleagues and learn more about transfer student resources and initiatives.

In spring 2018, one such visit by a group of more than 20 educators from Arizona Western College included their president and vice presidents, along with faculty leaders, the transfer center staff, advisors, and other student affairs professionals. ASU tailored the agenda so they were able to meet with specific academic and service units of their choosing. Some of these community college guests were making either their first visit to the university or their first in many years.

ASU's director for community college relations, who reports to the vice provost for academic partnerships, meets with transfer center and advisement center directors

272

and staff at each community or tribal college every semester to provide updates and answer questions.

Seven ASU transfer specialists who work for ASU's admissions department visit with students individually on site at community colleges, as well as through phone and video appointments. Transfer specialists answer thousands of questions through emails, text messaging, and phone calls. They provide students with tours and visits, webinars, and special events.

A faculty conversation series provides community college and university counterparts in a given discipline with an opportunity to get on a first-name basis with one another, while promoting better alignment of curriculum, allowing them to learn about one another's programs and encouraging ongoing professional dialogue. These sessions are held face to face at either the university or the community college. It is a constant back and forth for the purpose of jointly improving transfer student success.

Improving the Student Experience

Although we instituted many changes over the course of the past 10 years (since 2009), the foundation of our work was the creation of curricular pathways that made the transfer process clear and seamless. We used the very successful ASU eAdvisor concept as the basis for our transfer pathways program. ASU's eAdvisor is designed to assist students with personalized, on-demand tools to guide and support them toward success in their college journey. ASU uses the terminology *major map* to describe the sequenced curricular pathway to degree completion. Playing off that theme, we developed the Maricopa to ASU Pathways Program (MAPP) with the Maricopa Community Colleges, the Transfer Admission Guarantee (TAG) program at other community colleges throughout the state, and the Guaranteed Program for Admission (GPA) for out-of-state transfer partners. In aggregate, we describe these as our Guided Pathways to Success (GPS).

There are slight differences between the MAPP, TAG, and GPA programs; so, for the purposes of this section, we'll focus on our collaboration with the Maricopa Community College District, our primary transfer partner. Located in the metropolitan Phoenix area, the Maricopa Community Colleges enroll approximately 200,000 students per year, and approximately 40% of those students indicate a desire to eventually transfer and earn a bachelor's degree. Annually, more than 5,100 new transfer students from the Maricopa Community Colleges enroll at ASU, which accounts for approximately 30% of ASU's new transfer enrollment. About half of these students are part of the MAPP, which was initially implemented in fall of 2009. There are several elements that made the MAPP distinct from other transfer partnership programs that ASU and other Arizona universities had undertaken in the past.

1. These pathways build in the appropriate Arizona General Education Curriculum (AGEC) and a full-transfer associate degree. Thus, when students enter the university, they come as "true juniors" with a maximum of 60 credits remaining for graduation.

2. Credits on a pathway transfer and apply to the student's designated major. This is both cost-effective and time efficient, as there is no loss of credit if community college students follow their MAPP.

3. The ASU critical tracking course requirements are built into pathways, so community college students are taking the same courses as their university peers, which helps students determine if they are an appropriate fit for given majors.

4. Courses on a pathway are identified in the "language" of a community college, that is, the community college course numbers and titles are used so students and advisors do not have to reference other tools or compare college catalogs.

5. Our pledge to students is "no surprises." Any special requirements for a specific major are clearly identified. If a given major requires a higher grade-point average for admission or anything about which the student or advisor should be aware, it is easily seen on the document.

6. These pathways have benefits for all parties involved. They help the community colleges with their degree completion initiatives because the pathways build in a completed associate degree. They help the university because they incentivize students to come academically prepared, and thus, they are more likely to persist to bachelor's degree completion. Most of all, they help students because the programs are designed around student success data and provide incentives for completing major milestones along the route to success.

Transfer pathways are available on the university website. Initially, interested students signed up for a pathway with their community college advisor. In recent years, we have moved to an electronic sign-up process that allows students to sign up online, at any time of day or night. The electronic sign-up process also allows community college and university faculty and staff to work with individual students or groups of students who can pull out their phones and sign up during a class discussion or while meeting at an event or activity.

Students agree to complete the prescribed course sequence that includes the general studies curriculum, associate degree, and the outlined lower-division coursework specific to their major. The names and additional information about those students who sign up are transmitted to ASU, which starts a flow of communication from the university to the student. For those readers who are wondering how our institutions can share sensitive student data, students provide their FERPA compliance when they sign up for the MAPP. We explain to them that in order to facilitate their success across our institutions, we need to be able to share their demographic and academic data.

To encourage student participation in the pathways, benefits for students are tied into the program. Students still need to apply to the university when they are ready to do so, but if they have completed the pathway requirements, they are guaranteed admission to their major and have a maximum of 60 semester credits remaining to be completed at the university. And during their time at the community college, they have access to ASU transfer advising and other pre-enrollment services. Students from the Maricopa Community Colleges have 4 years at their community college to complete the pathway before transferring to ASU, which allows students who may be attending part time or need to take developmental coursework at the community college, for example, to be involved in the program.

Additionally, ASU annually provides more than $8 million in transfer grants and scholarships to students from the Maricopa Community Colleges. These grant and scholarship dollars are not Pell funds or Veterans Administration benefits, and there are no loans included in this figure. In Arizona, there is no state-based student aid. These transfer scholarships are internal university funds made available specifically for these transfer students.

> The MAPP was beyond helpful in making the transfer process smooth and easy. It set a goal for me, there were benefits involved, and I wasted no time at the community college, because all 60 of my credits transferred. (Martine Garcia, B.S. in Communication, personal communication, May 29, 2019)

As part of the MAPP, students obtain an ASU account, which allows them to access critical information and services, even while enrolled at the community college. For example, students in the program have access to ASU's Career and Professional Development Services for the purpose of engaging in career interest inventories and skills assessments. ASU can assist with identifying potential internships and finding on-campus and off-campus jobs.

Students in the MAPP program are encouraged to visit ASU while still enrolled at their community college; they are invited to attend university events; and they receive communications with university news in order to prepare them for what lies ahead. They are further encouraged to participate in transfer orientation and welcome week activities.

Following the development of the MAPP program, we developed more specific pathways for career and technical education programs (AAS to BAS pathways). In 2009–2010 we developed the Transfer Admission Guarantee (TAG) program for other community colleges and tribal colleges in Arizona, and by 2012–2013 we began the Guaranteed Program for Admission (GPA) for out-of-state transfer students.

There has been a considerable investment of university resources over 10 years to get our pathway programs up and running. These Guided Pathways to Success are one of several programs and projects overseen by the Office of Academic Partnerships, which is a unit of ASU's Office of the University Provost. The program also requires support from many other ASU units such as Undergraduate Education, Enrollment Services, Educational Outreach and Student Services, the University Technology Office, the Office of Institutional Analysis, and academic units.

Implementation of transfer pathways has also required a significant investment of time from the state's community colleges, as they also had to rework their systems, amend FERPA agreements with ASU, establish data sharing systems, review curriculum, undertake many other tasks to get these pathways in place, and help students learn about these programs. A generous gift of $1 million from the Kresge Foundation allowed the early development of several of the transfer technology tools that provided support to students in pathways programs. ASU has continued to enhance and expand the tools and resources available to transfer students. While these tools were developed internally by ASU, primarily because there were no tools available in the market when this initiative started, there are now pathway software packages available from technology vendors.

Using Technology to Provide a Personalized Experience at Scale

A major challenge was figuring out how to serve the increasing numbers of transfer students coming to the university and provide personalized information relevant to their specific majors and unique needs and circumstances. The ASU pathway programs were integrated into the University's eAdvisor system. Over a period of years, we built several online, self-service tools to help students, as well as community college and university advisors, with the transfer process. In some cases, we were able to refine existing tools to include a transfer component.

- The Degree Search tool helps students learn more about various majors and related careers. It serves as an online catalog for students, and it now includes several components that are of interest to transfer students, such as information on transfer admissions to a given major, and links to transfer pathway programs. The Degree Search tool is linked from ASU's main webpage or can be accessed directly at https://webapp4.asu.edu/programs/t5

- The Transfer Guide allows students to see how courses taken at their current community college or elsewhere will "count" at ASU. A student or an advisor can search for course equivalencies from in-state and out-of-state, public and private, associate and bachelor's degree–granting institutions to confirm if a course equivalency exists at ASU. Many transfer students will have earned credits at multiple colleges and universities, and one key to helping community college advisors and students develop a comprehensive educational plan is to know how the university will count previous coursework. If a course equivalency does not exist, there is an easy online process for the student to submit course materials for evaluation. This tool is available at http://tcg.asu.edu

- MyASU is an online student portal for community college students who have signed up for a transfer pathway program identifying transfer resources and tools. Information is personalized for each student based on their community college, intended ASU major, academic record, and their sign-up form. This personal portal provides links to the student's transfer specialist, their academic advisor, a calendar of important dates for transfer students, financial resources, and more. This tool is available at my.asu.edu, but students must have a username and password to enter their account.

The Pathway Progress Tracker tool allows a student from one of the Maricopa Community Colleges to view a pathway audit to see how courses taken fulfill pathway requirements. A student can see which courses have been completed, are currently in progress, or remain to be completed pertinent to the specific university major the student aspires to achieve. This is accomplished via the electronic exchange of transcripts. The Pathway Progress Tracker tool is available within the student's MyASU account. Maricopa Community College advisors and other staff also have access to these ASU tools for their transfer students.

The Degree Search tool and the Transfer Guide are available and useful for in-state and out-of-state students. A new feature of the Transfer Guide will take an ASU major map (a sequenced curricular plan for degree completion) and display equivalent coursework from a community college or another institution using the current equivalencies we have available in the Transfer Guide database. Students can see easily which coursework from their institution has relevance to the ASU degree they aspire to complete.

These are just a few of the tools available for students. Other tools help students determine career interests, and analytic tools for ASU administrators and academic units build pathways, track student progress, and evaluate program effectiveness. Technology tools have allowed us to serve many more students in a personalized and effective manner. Further, because we can automate certain transfer processes, such as course equivalencies, we can ensure that all students are treated in a fair and equitable way.

Providing More Options for Students

Many of our transfer students are adults (average age is 26 years old) working full time or part time, often with children or other family obligations. To help more students succeed in completing their degrees and moving on to their career ambitions, we needed to begin offering more options to serve our increasingly diverse student population.

The growth of our online options has been a significant element in serving our transfer student population. As of spring 2019, ASU has 90 undergraduate degree options available fully online, with six start dates per year. So, students don't need to wait until the following fall, or even a semester, to start. The flexibility of online coursework with robust online student support services has provided many transfer students with the ability to pursue their degree while managing their work schedule and other responsibilities. Our transfer pathway students can identify their interest in online programs when they sign up during their community college years, so that we can assist them in exploring their online options.

Some students are place-bound, meaning that their job or other commitments don't allow them to move to Phoenix to complete their degree, but they are also not fully comfortable in online programs. In 2012, the university began expanding the availability of bachelor's degrees in face-to-face and hybrid formats in various locations around the state of Arizona. In partnership with Arizona community colleges, ASU now offers bachelor's degrees on-site in Thatcher, Yuma, Prescott, Sierra Vista, and Casa Grande, and we are expanding options in Tucson.

In each of these communities, we started by researching local career opportunities that require a bachelor's degree. Then, we looked for degrees that met employer needs, those in which the community college had an adequate number of students enrolled, and university degree programs with upper-division courses that could be completed on-site. Student enrollment at these sites tends to be small, with cohort sizes from 15 to 25 students pursuing one of the handful of degree options offered. For example, with Eastern Arizona College in Thatcher, ASU currently offers bachelor's degrees in nursing, elementary and secondary education, and organizational leadership, while at Arizona Western College in Yuma, we currently offer criminal justice and secondary education.

Students in these programs follow a prescribed sequence of classes, along with a peer group, which limits choices for electives and requires scheduling of classes when most people can attend. The university has been able to hire faculty associates from the local community, sometimes even individuals who also teach for the community college. Faculty hiring and general oversight of the program is provided by the ASU academic unit that offers the degree. Academic Partnerships, a unit of the Office of the University Provost, provides coordination for the university's academic and service units that support these programs and manages the relationship with the community college.

By way of our partnership agreements, community college alumni who enroll in these university bachelor's degree programs can use the community college libraries, computer labs, parking and fitness facilities, and feel part of an educational community while they are taking their ASU classes. These students sometimes pile into vans and come to the Phoenix area to attend ASU football games and special events, and nearly all these students come to ASU commencement and convocation ceremonies. While it is a challenge to maintain these off-site programs, community leaders are often grateful for the university's partnership with their local community college to develop the workforce needed for businesses in their area.

Raising Awareness Within the University

During the first several years of our more concerted effort interacting with community colleges, we focused on how to help transfer students while they were at the community college. As we surveyed students about their transfer experience, we learned that we also needed to look internally at the university.

ASU has already made significant progress in developing transfer pathways, providing support services for community college students, offering more course formats and options, and building stronger relationships with community colleges. There is an internal culture of innovation and a relentless focus on constant improvement that led us to undertake a significant initiative in 2015 and 2016 related to our transfer student population.

That year, we contracted with the John N. Gardner Institute for Excellence in Undergraduate Education and used their Foundations of Excellence Transfer Focus process to undertake an initiative designed to study all aspects of the transfer student experience and to produce a plan for institutional improvement leading to higher levels of transfer student learning, satisfaction, and graduation. After outlining the process, some of the specific changes taken by the university will be described.

We called this project "Transfer Matters," meaning that it pertained to all matters related to the transfer process and our transfer students. However, we also wanted to make the point internally that our success as a university was dependent on the success of our transfer students, and that should *matter* to all of us.

Following on the heels of the successful ASU "First Year Forward" self-study initiative in the College of Liberal Arts and Sciences, which was also facilitated by the Gardner Institute using its Foundations of Excellence First Year process, a group met with the university provost to garner support for undertaking a similar process of data analysis and self-reflection related to transfer student success. The provost was supportive and formed an executive committee to lead the effort that included two vice provosts, one college dean, and two associate deans who were also faculty leaders at the university.

We sent a team of 13 ASU representatives and two colleagues from the Maricopa Community Colleges to the Gardner Institute for training in summer 2015. The Gardner Institute has nine aspirational principles, termed *Foundational Dimensions of Excellence*. By early fall, we identified co-chairs for nine committees, each of which would focus on a specific aspect of transfer, aligned with the nine Dimensions. We also recruited people who would assist with data collection, survey implementation, and logistics.

A kickoff event followed by committee meetings helped us orient several hundred employees, students, and community college staff to the task at hand, to become a more efficient and effective institution for our transfer students. A group of faculty and staff completed the Foundations of Excellence Current Practices Inventory; distributed, collected, and compiled the student and faculty and staff surveys; and dug into the task of data collection. The results were available to all those involved with the project through the Foundations of Excellence technology system (FoEtec).

As we built momentum, committees planned their approach to the analysis of their Dimension reports and began meeting and corresponding regularly. Many faculty and staff members participated in webinars offered by the Gardner Institute, which helped them gain clarity and learn how other institutions were tackling similar tasks.

In early January, we held a "midyear recharge" for all who were contributing to the project. Each committee reported on progress to date and plans for the spring semester. Our consultant, John Gardner, keynoted the event, speaking passionately about this often overlooked and underserved population of students. Gardner then made himself available to meet individually with committees.

Committees collected additional evidence by calling peer institutions, convening student focus groups, examining current practices and policies, learning about existing programs and services at ASU, and more. Each committee was charged with producing a report summarizing their processes and data analysis, and presenting recommendations for change or improvement. Draft reports were submitted to our advisor for feedback and then revised, sometimes multiple times.

At the end of the spring 2016 semester, we held a wrap-up and recognition event for everyone involved in the initiative. In addition to recognizing those who had assumed leadership roles and thanking everyone who contributed, including students, faculty, staff, and community college colleagues, we had everyone engage in an activity to prioritize the recommendations.

During the summer of 2016, the project executive committee reviewed all the Dimension reports and recommendations, as well as the sizable amount of group feedback on one another's results, to produce an institutional action plan and blueprint for improvement. After meeting with the university provost, decisions were made about which items to prioritize for implementation over a series of years.

It is beyond the scope of this chapter to describe results in detail, or the rationale and data behind each of these actions, but what follows are some concrete examples of the changes that have occurred at ASU. Hopefully some of these examples may provide ideas for other institutions too.

The most pervasive problem that arose during the Transfer Matters project was that information about transfer was desultory at the university. Even for faculty and staff who were attuned to transfer students and their issues, it was difficult to figure out which academic or service units had responsibility for certain functions, much less how to create a coherent plan for improving transfer student success. We pursued a number of things to help us improve internal communication and coordination related to transfer.

- We formed a *Transfer Operations Team* composed of representatives from community college relations, admissions, and curriculum articulation, which meets every semester with each college within the university to review transfer student data; share information about services, tools, and best practices across the university; strategize about communication and collaboration with community college partners; and discuss ideas and develop plans for improving transfer student success. The vice provost for academic partnerships appoints this body and provides oversight, but the operations of the group are coordinated by the director for community college relations.

- We created *transfer data reports* for each academic unit within the university, as well as special populations of students. These reports provide information such as academic level at entry, race/ethnicity, gender, age, Pell grant status, first-generation status, veteran or military status, full-time and part-time status, average enrolled hours, average transfer hours, last institution attended prior to ASU, associate degree completion, leading transfer institutions for the unit, leading degree majors for new transfers, courses with the highest new transfer enrollment, courses with the highest D and E (failing) rates for new transfers, courses with the highest withdrawal rates for new transfers, retention rates for new transfers in the majors offered by a unit, and more. These reports are used during the Transfer Operations Team meetings to help focus discussions but are also provided to the administrators charged with oversight of academic and service units.

- *Transfer Town Halls* address broader themes in the transfer student experience that pertain to many academic and service units at the university. For example, the fall 2017 Transfer Town Hall included information on transfer student housing; transfer scholarships and financial aid; enhancements to the MAPP, TAG, and GPA programs; a recap of Welcome Week activities and participation rates; and more. The Office of Academic Partnership convenes these town halls, inviting representatives from all academic units and service units to attend. Presenters come from across the university.

- A *Transfer Forum*, an internal conference for ASU transfer-serving faculty and staff to share best practices related to transfer, took place in July 2018 for the first time. This is an annual opportunity for sharing what is working, drawing on the expertise of faculty and staff who have become interested in the transfer student experience. The Office of Academic Partnerships coordinates this conference, but proposals for presentation were submitted by many different units within the university.

- *New faculty* receive a one-page digest about our transfer student population in their orientation packets. The digest includes our philosophy statement on transfer, demographics of our transfer student population, key contacts related to community college relations, curriculum articulation, and recruitment and admissions for transfer students. The Office of Academic Partnerships coordinated the production of the document, but the document is distributed by the vice provost for academic personnel.

- We created *distribution lists* to communicate regularly to all university units about transfer student issues, programs and services. One list is for administrators with responsibility for academic programs or support services related to transfer students; another has messaging geared for operational staff who need to understand processes in more detail and who appreciate reminders at particular times of the year. The lists themselves as well as the content of the messages are coordinated by the Office of Academic Partnerships.

Another group of recommendations from the Transfer Matters work related to creating a smoother transition for students who are moving from the community college to the university follows.

- With a more visible and enthusiastic welcome for new transfer students to ASU, the Transfer Family Reception kicks off a series of *Welcome Week* events. Throughout Welcome Week, workshops and programs are held for transfer students on topics ranging from success in ASU classrooms, career and professional development, use of campus technology, campus tours, and more. Programming is available at all ASU campus locations and offered at a variety of times to meet the needs of the transfer student population. Welcome Week is coordinated by the Office of New Student and Family Programs, but all others at the university are expected to participate and provide support. Because there are so many activities available, the associated website now has a drop-down menu on the calendar of events that allows transfer students to pull forward those events that are specifically designed for them.

- A *Transfer Online Orientation* was originally created in 2015 as an avenue for reaching a larger majority of the incoming transfer students. An enhanced online transfer orientation was launched in 2017. The new digital orientation platform contains modules, interactive quizzes, and dozens of videos featuring current students to help new transfer students make a successful transition to ASU. Participation is not mandatory and varies by month. Five months (March to July) have the highest participation numbers with between 400 to 700 students per month.

- *Transfer Student Ambassadors* (TSAs) provide a peer perspective on the transfer process and what it's like to be a student at ASU. They connect with students in a variety of ways, including in person through classroom and club presentations, and via phone and email. In addition to sharing their transfer story and helping to connect prospective students to the tools, resources, and contacts at ASU, the TSAs play an important role in explaining pathway programs, passing out print materials, and providing a welcome call and email to all new path way students. This peer support program was begun in 2015 and is managed by a program coordinator in the Office of Academic Partnerships. The program has grown as a result of the Transfer Matters recommendations. For example, the TSAs now handle several call campaigns, they initiate cases in Salesforce that require follow-up by professional staff, and they support many more events and activities at the university and at community colleges.

The TSA program is important, because it allows students to obtain information from a student's perspective, it's not a view that is coming from an advisor or a recruiter; communicating peer to peer provides a level of trust that makes what the ambassador says believable. (Carletta Miller, B.S. in the Science of Healthcare Delivery)

One of the recommendations from the Transfer Matters report was to have a mandated one-credit course for new transfer students, similar to ASU's first-year orientation course. After discussions with deans, it was determined that most general resource information was available through the digital orientation for transfers and the Welcome Week events. They felt that rather than adding another credit to the student's academic plan, focusing on adjustment to the specific academic unit or discipline was more valuable. Some academic units have implemented transfer student orientation courses, while others have focused on embedding activities that would be helpful to new students (e.g., information on engagement in undergraduate research or support services) into existing courses with considerable new transfer enrollment. Several units already have robust transfer student support systems in place. For example, the Ira A. Fulton Schools of Engineering at ASU runs a Motivated Engineering Transfer Students (METS) Center that provides staff support, along with short courses and workshops on success strategies specific to engineering. In addition, because many of their transfer students are commuter students, the METS Center includes individual and group study spaces; access to computers, printers and other equipment; and a lounge that includes amenities such as a refrigerator and microwave.

The Transfer Matters project defined *student success* as completion of a bachelor's degree. So, several changes have been made at ASU related to early identification of issues that might impede success.

- ASU implemented a *Transfer Connections survey*, distributed to all new transfer students each fall and spring semester. This non-anonymous survey allows us to quickly identify and provide direct support for transfer students who need additional assistance in their transition and engagement at ASU, while also identifying larger trends that might require systemic solutions for the future. This process includes a system for tracking individual and aggregate responses and a system for outreach and follow-up on those students who request support. The University Office for Institutional Evaluation and Effectiveness manages the survey.

- Success coaching, offered through the First-Year Success Center, is now available for transfer students, with the goal of helping students on everything from transition (adjusting to university life) to transformation (realizing potential and dreams). While we have marketed the program primarily to transfer students with a 2.5 GPA or below, this service is available to any transfer student.

- GetSet, an ed tech tool, aims to reduce college dropout rates by matching students instantly with someone at the university who has already overcome similar challenges. Tips from classmates help new students get comfortable and overcome obstacles. ASU began using GetSet with first-year students in 2016, and in fall 2018, ASU implemented GetSet for transfer students. The vice provost for student success and his staff within the Office of the University Provost are taking the lead in coordinating this effort.

Currently, we are working on the implementation of additional elements of our Transfer Matters action plan, as well as other related plans. Our enrollment services team is exploring the use of microscholarships to incentivize transfer students toward the behaviors that we know help them be successful. A team is investigating how we might identify students who are "new to ASU" on class rosters. Imagine how helpful it would be, for example, for faculty members to know that half the students in their

300-level class are new to the university. They might describe an assignment in more detail or direct people to university resources with more clarity than if they assume that all the students have already been attending for years. A team that works on ASU's online interactive career quiz and helps students chart an academic pathway to find a major that leads to a career the student desires, is working on a community college version of the tool. ASU faculty and their community college counterparts will continue meeting to collaborate on applying for grants that will assist community college students in their pursuit of certain careers, with financial support, with undergraduate research experiences, and with professional development opportunities. The work will never be "done"—this is a reiterative process of assessment and improvement.

Making a Difference

Our goal was and continues to be the improvement of transfer enrollment and, more importantly, student success toward completion of associate and bachelor's degrees. Development of curricular pathways was an important element in making the avenues to the bachelor's degree more visible and clear. Although they are foundational, in and of themselves they are insufficient for transfer student success. With hopes of better addressing student needs, we're continually adjusting in the following ways:

- A reverse transfer of credit program allows Arizona community college students who transfer prior to completing their entire pathway to receive an associate degree on their way to the bachelor's degree.
- We routinely provide advisor training for both community college and university advisors.
- We publish electronic newsletters to keep advisors, faculty, staff, and administrators informed and engaged.
- Student success stories are included in every newsletter to keep staff inspired and motivated about the important work they are undertaking.
- We'll continue making the rounds of community colleges, asking for their input and advice and reflecting on how things are working and what needs improvement.

What progress has been made toward our goals? Since we began our concerted effort to improve transfer student success in 2009, we have seen steady increases in new transfer student enrollment at ASU from community colleges. Even though community college enrollment nationally has declined, and some Arizona community college districts have lost from 10% to 25% of their enrollment in this time frame, ASU has more than doubled its transfer enrollment in less than 10 years, as can be seen in Figure 17.1.

Additional factors contributed to this substantial enrollment growth including the expansion of online undergraduate degree programs and offering more responsive

Figure 17.1. ASU new transfer student enrollment.

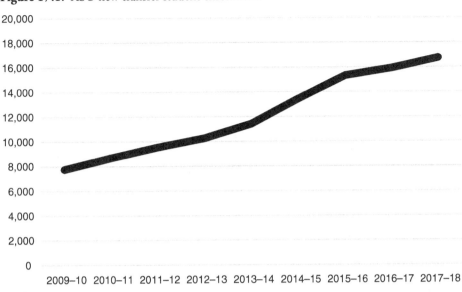

Note. ASU Office of Institutional Analysis (2011, 2018)

Figure 17.2. Transfers with an associate degree.

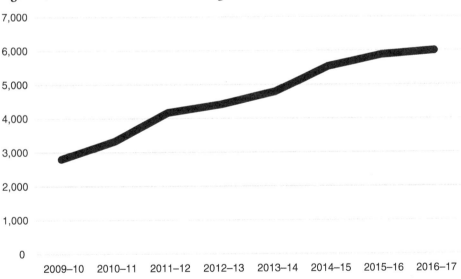

Note. ASU Office of Institutional Analysis (2011, 2018)

options for this population of students, which were described earlier in this chapter. Figure 17.2 shows that the number of students who are transferring as upper-division students, prepared for success in their majors, has increased as we have encouraged completion of associate degrees prior to entry at the university.

Our transfer students are diverse with 39% being minority, 42% receiving Pell grants, 34% reporting themselves as the first in their family to attend college, 10% veterans, 46% attending part time, and an average age of 26.4 years.

Assessing the effectiveness of some of these newer programs in terms of impact on *student success*, defined as completion of the bachelor's degree, is premature. We implemented some of the first Transfer Matters recommendations in the 2016–2017 academic year, and even if a student transferred to ASU that fall, that student may not have graduated at the time of this writing.

The Maricopa-to-ASU Pathways Program has been in place for 10 years, as of this writing, so we have an initial sense of the effectiveness. In terms of persistence to baccalaureate, students who come to ASU with a completed transfer pathway and begin as an upper-division transfer student tend to persist to bachelor's completion at significantly higher rates than students who do not follow their transfer pathway. In some cohorts, the differences in success between those who come as lower-division transfers and those who come as upper-division transfers exceeds 15%. Approximately 85% of all transfer students, including those in online programs, are retained from their first fall to the next fall semester, and approximately 75% graduate within 4 years of their transfer to ASU. Those are rates which the university is striving to improve through the variety of programs that have been described here.

There are no easy fixes to the challenges of supporting transfer students before, during, and after their transition from the community college to the university, but at ASU, in collaboration with our community college partners, there has been significant progress in our ongoing effort to support transfer student success.

Recommendations

1. Focus on first-generation and financially challenged students. Data still show that socioeconomic background factors are significantly correlated with academic success and bachelor's degree completion.
2. Disaggregate your data to look at specific majors, special populations of students, full-time/part-time status, and other factors.
3. Consider whether your institution would benefit from a comprehensive self-study on transfer to examine your institutional data, and create a plan for improvement of transfer student success.

Discussion Questions

1. Many higher education catalogs are confusing to students, particularly community college students, who have to negotiate their way through not just one, but two or more institutions. For students who are beginning at other institutions, what is the mechanism at your community college or baccalaureate college/university for figuring out what will "count" at your school or move a student closer to associate and bachelor's degree completion?

2. Many students who start their postsecondary education in a community college have vague notions about their talents or interests, career possibilities, and recommended educational paths for specific careers. How do we "front load" meaningful discussions about career options, educational pathways to those options, and additional experiences needed in order to succeed in the career?

3. How often do key people from your community college have discussions with your largest transfer partners? How often do key people from your college or university have discussions with your community college partners? What is the content of those discussions and how do you hold one another accountable for addressing or resolving the issues raised?

References

Arizona State University Office of Institutional Analysis. (2011). *2005-2006 through 2010-2011 new transfer students—Applied, admitted and enrolled* [UOIA Census Tables #6586]. UOIA Website. https://uoia.asu.edu/

Arizona State University Office of Institutional Analysis. (2018). *2012-2013 through 2017-2018 total university new transfer students—Applied, admitted and enrolled* [UOIA Census Tables #9506]. UOIA Website. https://uoia.asu.edu/

CONCLUSION

Where Do We Go From Here? Synthesis and Recommendations

John N. Gardner, Michael J. Rosenberg, and Andrew K. Koch

In our handbook's conclusion, we want to offer some of our own ideas, as the editors and compilers of this work, for what we think can and must be done to improve transfer student success. We have been greatly influenced by what the thinkers assembled in this volume have presented to you. In addition, the three of us have been influenced by our collective experience working directly with transfer students and/or those educators responsible for their learning and success.

This conclusion will present our specific recommendations. Most of them are relevant to both 2- and 4-year institutions, although some are more relevant to a particular sector. We do not believe all institutions must undertake all of them at once, but we encourage institutional representatives to thoughtfully consider them and determine where to start. We also believe there may be elements not on our list that should be on yours. In higher education, as in politics, all policies and practices are local!

While we are mindful that your own conclusions and recommendations matter most, we hope you followed the suggestion from our introduction that you form or be part of some kind of institutional task force, study group, book club, online gathering, or some other group that can consider the ideas in this book to extract the most relevant explanations, insights, and recommendations for your institution. (If you haven't done this yet, it's certainly not too late!) This intentional follow-up can be done on campus or in a retreat setting convened for a wide variety of stakeholders, internal and external.

There can be no significant movement on increasing transfer student success without more evidence-based discussion and action. At a minimum, this book invites you to talk about transfer students and what you are doing/not doing with and for them. It's never too late to begin this conversation. Ideally, your conversations will lead to a comprehensive plan that you will then implement. That is our greatest hope for you and your institution.

Our recommendations are found in the following sections.

Institutions Must Make Transfer Student Success a High Priority! There Will Be No Progress or Justice by Maintaining the Status Quo

Everything we do as higher education professionals is a function of our priorities, both as individuals and institutions. Priorities determine attention, resources, status, imprimatur, power, and outcomes. Our current transfer outcomes flow from our current priorities. In our experience, very few institutions imbue transfer with a high priority.

Let's start with the archetypal sending institutions, community colleges. One could and should make an assumption that transfer is a high-priority mission for all community colleges, given the demand for baccalaureate degrees and the role these colleges have assumed as the primary entry point for the majority of America's beginning students. Our experience has taught us that for many community colleges, transfer is not a high priority at all. Why not?

To begin with, getting beyond certain founding principles, policies, practices, and traditions can be difficult. Community colleges were founded, initially and primarily, to provide "terminal" degrees and other credentials and/or to separate "less serious students" from others who would go on to study for an "upper-level" degree. There was not a perceived need for lifelong learning and continual updating of credentials. Additionally, there was no assumption that community (or junior) colleges would function as the largest intake institutions for first-time-in-college students in a democratized postsecondary education system. The transfer function was not assumed to be a major function on any widespread basis. Moving beyond a culture where the education provided in this sector was "terminal" and an exception to the norm has not happened. Sadly, for large numbers of students in community colleges, their education is still "terminal," ending with no credential at all, even though that is obviously not the intention of these institutions.

Given the historic underfunding of community colleges in comparison to other sectors, their leadership's attention understandably would be captured by more immediate sources of revenue than the tuition and fees generated by transfer-bound students. Instead, major grants and contracts for workforce training provide powerful financial incentives from both governmental sources and private businesses for retraining. Further, community college attention has also been focused on performing the extremely challenging "developmental" (formerly "remedial") education function. This very resource-intensive and inefficient undertaking has not yielded impressive outcomes. On the much more attractive side, community colleges have received great attention for their success at creating selective admissions academic programs to meet high demand societal needs such as the education and training of health-care professionals.

Fast forward to the present. With the recovery from the Great Recession and the historically inverse relationship of community college enrollments with the overall health of the economy, we have seen significant declines in community college enrollments in recent years. With the COVID-19 pandemic upon us at the time of this work's publication, the jury is out as to whether that economic dislocation will encourage or discourage community college enrollments. Why would rational thinking, resource-driven, community college leaders prioritize sending their best students on to any other institutions any sooner than they have to? The incentives rest with keeping those students enrolled at the community college level, ultimately awarding associate degrees.

In our experience, competing priorities place real pressures on community colleges to have institutional priorities elsewhere than increasing transfer student attainment rates. This is why we have included a chapter in this book on the need for reverse transfer to recognize community colleges for their significant accomplishments in creating successful transfer students who earn additional credentials.

The baccalaureate transfer-receiving sector has other priorities than transfer, as well. One of those priorities has always been attempting to ensure that those students who start at a 4-year campus get "the whole thing"—even though an ever-increasing percentage of baccalaureate completers earns credits from multiple institutions. This sector has developed most of its history and institutional traditions based on "non-transfer" students.

Until recently, 4-year institutions have had to pay the most attention to the subset of student demographic information that they have been required to report by federal statute in the Integrated Postsecondary Education Data System (IPEDS): data on first-time, full-time undergraduates. Those students have been the institutional focus for the all-important retention and graduation-rate metrics on which funding, rankings, and prestige have been based. Until very recently, transfer students have not been included in this public accountability focus.

Four-year institutions have other competing priorities that matter more than service to transfers: number and quality of majors, faculty matters, pursuit of research grants and contracts, and so on. All these priorities, especially those related to the traditional-aged, full-time, first-time-entering degree-seeking students, have had powerful advocates with titles, offices, budgets, and so on. Transfer students have not been so fortunate. One need look no further to see the enormously disproportionate attention now paid to first-year students. Nothing remotely resembling the attention to this first-year population has been paid to transfer students, even though transfer students may be a larger proportion of the undergraduate student body at many institutions than those who came to the institution as traditional first-year students.

To make transfer a high priority, we encourage institutions to undertake the following actions:

1. Give service to transfer students a high priority in the institutional mission statement, which comprises the basis for reaffirmation of regional accreditation.
2. Make sure that this same level of commitment is evident in the institutional strategic plan.
3. Make sure that transfer is understood, acted upon, and supported as a social justice imperative.
4. Make sure that this priority is reflected in the regular talking points that institutional leaders make in their many public appearances. Words matter.
5. Deeds matter, too. In these public statements about the importance of transfer students, share some recent action(s) taken to shore up support for this population.
6. Include transfer outcomes among the most important metrics that institutional leaders focus on, talk about, and are held accountable for by a wide variety of external stakeholders.

7. Work with governing boards to ensure their actions also reflect this priority and assure that it carries over from the administration of one CEO to the succeeding one.

8. Vest responsibility for transfer student success in particular offices and individuals. Make sure the rest of the campus knows where these responsibility centers are. Given that, ultimately, the transfer outcome that matters most is the attainment of an academic credential, the "buck should stop" with a senior academic leader. Enrollment management leaders play a hugely important role for transferring students in or out, depending on institutional type. However, once admitted, articulated, advised, registered, and in class, the fate of transfers is fundamentally an academic one.

Start With the End in Mind: Provide Experiences and Support for Beginning Students That Increase the Likelihood They Will Thrive

Assuming you accept our expanded definition of the *transfer experience* as the entirety of the academic experience at both transfer-sending and -receiving institutions, then the beginning of the academic experience at the sending institution must be a major focus. Institutions must help students be academically successful in the beginning of and throughout their college careers, typically at the 2-year institution. Where specifically should the 2-year sector focus?

We encourage 2-year colleges to undertake the following actions:

1. Provide orientation that is targeted to the realities of transfer-bound students' lives and those of their families and made mandatory.

2. Offer career services that are delivered early to clarify purpose and educational decision-making with respect to courses and programs of study.

3. Maintain a focus on academic advising. Transfer student advisors need special expertise in transfer options and requirements of degree programs at receiving institutions, as well as in helping students access necessary resources on and off campus.

4. Include an emphasis on "guided academic pathways." Since transfer students need to make good choices from a vast array of academic offerings, potentially at multiple institutions, specific academic "pathways" need to be created for transfer students that will yield the maximum number of transferable credits.

5. Redesign gateway courses as needed to increase student success. If all institutions do is to create new pathways containing the same courses which have failed these students before, nothing changes.

6. Shift attention to faculty because of the huge impact they can have on transfer students. Pay more attention to faculty development relating to the special needs of transfer-bound students.

7. Don't forget the impact of adjuncts. These instructors have to be paid their proper due for the impact they have on transfer-bound students. This means

increasing their compensation, integration into departmental affairs, access to faculty development support (with compensation), and assuring them respect, for instance, in some kind of honorific title.

8. Require a college success courses for all potential and actual transfer-bound students. These course have a long-established positive impact on student success, and actual transfer should be included as a metric of success.

9. Create a transfer center on each campus. Transfer-bound students should have a centralized "one stop shop" that can interface with advising, career services, 4-year admissions efforts, and so on. Make sure everyone on your campus knows where it is, too!

The 4-year sector also has a "beginning" upon which to focus. Just because they get in, they don't always get out! Hence, in like fashion, we encourage 4-year institutions to undertake the following actions:

1. Pay more attention to the orientation of transfer students, especially by making it required. Orientation needs to be at both the institutional level and within the department the transfer student will enter. Transfers should begin immediately to meet department-level faculty, staff, and administrators.

2. Find viable alternatives for transfer students who have a sufficient grade point average for collegiate admission but lack qualifications for certain high-demand majors. These not-yet-fully engaged students can easily flounder without proper attention.

3. Pay more attention to who provides academic advising to incoming transfer students and ensure these advisors have appropriate expertise, knowledge, and availability. Ideally, each transfer student should be provided a faculty advisor in their intended major in addition to a professional staff advisor.

4. Design and offer specific versions of college success courses adapted to the unique needs of transfer students. Preferably, make these required and credit-bearing courses, even if they carry only one academic credit. A course with any credit impacts students more than a course with no credit.

5. Ensure that there are some consistent standards of attention to the particular needs of transfer students—such as academic advising and support, career planning, social integration—across the units that become the students' administrative and degree homes. In reality, there are as many cultures for transfer students as there are majors, departments, and other units that house them—and the amount of attention and support for these students varies accordingly. Take steps to address the cottage-industry nature of these subcultural unit variabilities so all students can assume they will be accorded certain consistent standards of treatment, attention, and respect.

6. Pay attention to "gateway courses" in the major. Courses with high percentages of enrolled transfer students that have correspondingly high rates of DFWI grades need to be targeted for redesign.

7. Consider more centralized academic responsibility and coordination for the welfare of transfer students. More specifically, more authority and ownership over transfer should be exercised by the institution's chief academic officer (CAO). Only the CAO has the authority and power to effect these changes in concert with academic deans, department chairs, and, ultimately, mainline faculty. As we reported in the introduction, the most common administrative home for transfer students is enrollment management. While the advocacy role of chief enrollment officers is critical, they cannot address many of the inequities and challenges transfer students face at the receiving institution. In both this spirit and substance, we refer you back to chapter 12 and our contributing CAO Mark Canada on the transfer-supportive role of chief academic officers.

8. Take advantage of your regional accreditor's options for undertaking a "quality" initiative for purposes of reaffirming your institution's reaccreditation and focusing that initiative on the improvement of educational outcomes for transfer students. Whatever any institution chooses as a focus for reaffirmation of accreditation is a true reflection of priority because, for most places, there is no higher priority than getting reaccredited. This then is a suggestion of how to use the priority that the accreditation spotlight on a campus can provide for the benefit of an often lower-status population.

Use Data to Understand Your Students and for Decision-Making to Improve Student Learning and Success

As multiple chapter contributors for this book have indicated, there are many misunderstandings and even myths about transfer students, especially the often-held assumption that they are less academically capable, less likely to graduate, and more likely to have an educational experience where "life gets in the way" than are nontransfer students. We regard such blanket categorizations as evidence-free prejudice that often leads to discriminatory actions and other unfair practices—and certainly inequitable outcomes.

In reality, we need to understand *all* our students better so that we can make more data-informed decisions about educational improvements. Institutions must analyze more data—both quantitative and qualitative—on transfers, but these data must be widely shared and applied to ensure continuous improvement of the educational experience. This requires various institutional communities of practice to gather and discuss the implications of these data.

The federal government has given advocates of transfer students a boost by requiring 4-year institutions to report, as part of IPEDS data accountability requirements, transfer progression and graduation rates. But those statistics alone certainly don't tell the whole story. What else do we need to know? We encourage institutions to utilize data by undertaking the following actions:

1. Disseminate disaggregated data on the transfer student cohort by race, ethnicity, gender, first-generation status, full-time/part-time status, veteran's status, and, if applicable, residency status (on/off campus).
2. Also, make available data to respond to the following questions:
   a. From which institutions do the students transfer?
   b. How many credit hours do the students bring with them?
   c. What are the outcomes for these students with respect to degree attainment?
   d. How do they perform in our courses in terms of grades received, again, disaggregated and compared to non-transfers?
   e. How do degree attainment rates vary across different sending institutions?
   f. Overall, what can be determined about predicted versus attained levels of academic success and degree attainment of transfer versus non-transfer students?

Conduct a Voluntary Self-Study of the Transfer Experience to Produce and Execute a Comprehensive Plan to Improve Transfer Student Success

At the risk of offering a suggestion that could elicit a groan from many academics, one of the most productive actions we have discovered and developed to actually do something with data is to incorporate it into a "self-study" of how the institution is actually performing with respect to its transfer students. One example of this process is called Foundations of Excellence-Transfer Focus developed by the Gardner Institute in 2007–2008, piloted with the University of Texas at El Paso, and revised in 2010 with the American Association of State Colleges and Universities and a national cohort of community colleges.

This self-study approach offers a set of aspirational standards for excellence in transfer in terms of institutional practices, policies, and outcomes. These standards (Foundational Dimensions) are in the public domain and can be accessed, used, adapted, and modified at no charge by any institution. From 2007–2019, Foundations of Excellence Transfer Focus has been undertaken by approximately 75 2- and 4-year institutions including some of the universities featured in case studies in this publication. The major outcome of this self-study process is the institution having for the first time in its history a comprehensive plan for improving transfer student outcomes—and hence higher attention and priority for transfers.

Intentionally Involve Faculty in the Discussions Around Transfer Student Success

We emphasize the inclusion of faculty in institutional planning related to transfers not to exclude or diminish the role of nonfaculty, but to make sure that faculty themselves *are included*. In our experience, since transfer is typically considered an administrative function, faculty are often left out of the conversation. Doing so removes the heart of the academic experience—what goes on in the classroom—from the discussion about transfer student success.

The voices of faculty who teach courses frequently taken by transfers at both sending and receiving institutions must be part of the discussion. That discussion should include the evidence collected as part of the previous recommendation arguing for the merits of conducting an institutional, voluntary, self-study. Offer instructors of all kinds—tenured, tenure-track, adjunct, research—an opportunity to build greater awareness of what is actually going on with and for transfer students at their respective institutions. Faculty, in concert with administrators and staff from various areas, can use that knowledge to make and act on evidence-based recommendations.

In addition, institutions should not forget to build and maintain faculty relationships between those who teach in the same disciplines at primary sending and receiving institutions. The classroom experience—whether online, face-to-face, or some blended hybrid version thereof—is the one experience all transfers have in common. Faculty-to-faculty affinity-based relationships, interactions, groups, and projects—whether intra- or interdisciplinary—influence how faculty understand, interact with, support, evaluate, and make judgments about transfer students. Efforts to enhance those connections must be included in transfer reform efforts.

Ideally, we encourage faculty involved in transfer-redesign efforts to

- teach transfer students without prejudice or bias, and gain appropriate perceptions of them from other faculty who know them best;
- engage with transfer students out of class;
- understand and shape the institutional or departmental process associated with the awarding of transfer credit;
- make consistent and evidence-based judgments about what are/are not corresponding equivalent courses between sending and receiving campuses; and
- study transfer student outcomes in gateway courses, and use that information to help refine both preparation of students at the sending institution as well as placement and awarding of credit at the receiving institution.

Identify Institutional Barriers to Transfer Student Success

We invite you to refer to chapter 2 of this volume and its insightful focus on institutional barriers. Specifically, we encourage you to explore the barriers identified in Fink and Jenkins's research that may apply to your own institutions. Then ask these questions:

1. Which of these barriers can you see in evidence on your campus?
2. How would you rate these barriers in terms of their relative significance as barriers to student progress at your institution?

3. How well recognized, understood, and accepted do you believe these barriers are?
4. Do you see currently the institutional will to address these barriers?
5. Do you see the knowledge needed to provide corrective action?
6. What are the policies in place that may constitute these barriers?
7. What are some of the organizational structures in place that may function as barriers?
8. Are there certain offices that have come to represent barriers?
9. Are there certain individuals who constitute individual barriers?

Undertake an Institutional Audit to Determine the Extent of Prejudice Against Transfer Students

Another way to combine the use of data/information is to conduct a "policy audit." No one on any campus will know all the relevant rules and policies, and as there will be no single written compendium of such, you should produce one!

We have found that the best way to do this is through group brainstorming. Put together a group of administrators, staff, faculty, and students to compile all the different rules that are directed at or apply to transfer students. With this lens in mind, proceed to compare the treatment of transfer versus non-transfer students at your institution in terms of policies for the following:

- Admissions (deadlines for application, costs for application, deadlines for notice of acceptance, award for financial aid, recognition of prior credit and learning experiences)
- Financial aid (deadlines for application and notification, criteria for eligibility, amounts and types of aid, designations specifically for transfer versus non-transfer students, criteria for renewal and maintaining eligibility)
- Eligibility for on-campus housing
- Priority for course registration
- Availability of required versus elective programs, opportunities, courses to support student success (e.g., orientation, academic advising, college success courses, etc.)
- Provision of academic advising—is it optional or mandatory and for which populations?
- Eligibility for internships, co-ops
- Eligibility for study abroad or the National Student Exchange
- Eligibility for on-campus employment—supported by Federal Work-Study or regular institution funds
- Eligibility for academic awards, prizes
- Existence of specific offices/programs dedicated to support transfers

Conduct an Audit of the Student Success Artifacts That May Suggest Transfer Students Are or Are Not Valued

Just as our observation in the previous section on how the institutional policy structure can reveal how your institution may be throwing barriers ahead of transfer student success, an audit of institutional practices and supports can also provide very useful information.

This additional audit would reveal how much the institution values a focus on transfer student success. The audit will undoubtedly uncover considerable evidence suggesting the extent to which we value, are conscious of, and are intentionally supporting our transfer students. In this vein, consider these questions:

1. How obvious and easy to find are transfer student opportunities, requirements, and activities on your website? What would you conclude from your website to be the relative priority given to transfer at your institution? And more specifically, how many "clicks" does it take for a transfer student or transfer advisor to find needed information?
2. Do you confer any awards to faculty, staff, or students for the exemplary support they provide transfer students? And at what kind of ceremonial venue/occasion do you present such awards, assuming that the highest status relevant events are commencements and honors and awards days?
3. Do your internal and external public relations' communications report on accomplishments and distinctions of transfer students? If so, how frequently and in what communications media does this happen?
4. Do you have any displays in your public spaces to call attention to the accomplishments of transfer students?

Do your official publications have specific sections that are clearly and conspicuously devoted to transfer students and how they are supported and recognized in the following functional areas:

- Admissions
- Financial aid
- Registration
- Academic advising
- Orientation
- On-campus employment
- Equity, diversity, and inclusion
- Career services
- Counseling
- Residence life
- Athletics
- Student activities

- Parking/transportation
- Childcare
- Health services and insurance
- Opportunities for family involvement

Showcase the History of Transfer Students at Your Institution and Those Who Have Supported and Championed Them

One way to encourage greater advocacy for transfer students is to identify those who have come before and who took a stand to support transfers. As Stephen J. Handel illustrates at the start of this volume, transfer has a long history in U.S. higher education. To understand how your institution is functioning now with respect to transfer students, you should know your own history in this regard. Consider these questions:

1. How long has your institution been admitting transfer or transfer-bound students?
2. How have your policies regarding them evolved?
3. What is your history with respect to their numbers and types?
4. How has your institutional culture toward this subpopulation evolved?
5. If your institution has an official historian and a published institutional history, how can you use these resources to help you research the treatment of this population?
6. If you have a campus museum, do you have any exhibits that reflect aspects of serving transfers?
7. Do you have campus displays or websites that call attention to this cohort and its contributions?
8. Do you have noteworthy alumni who came to you as transfers or began as transfer-bound students?
9. As you look at your institutional history and consider the extent to which your transfer policies have evolved, to what kind of forces do you attribute these changes?
   a. Was it external policy from the state?
   b. Were there actions taken by specific leaders to be more receptive to these students? Who were these leaders and what moved them to encourage your institution to become more accommodating, welcoming, supportive, or celebratory of student transfer?

If this line of thinking about your past and how it influences your future has appeal, how could you present this important history to your larger institutional community? One suggestion is to involve some of your best campus thinkers from the fields of history, education, public relations, and the arts.

Take Steps to Be Inspired by What Is Possible: Visit Other Institutions to Learn About Their Success With Transfer Students

We can't suggest strongly enough the advisability of putting some teams together and hitting the road to visit institutional transfer exemplars. A number of them are featured in case studies presented in both this book and in the Online Compendium. Also, there will likely be institutions in your geographic region that have a reputation for excellent service to transfer students. Look beyond factors like size and resources and consider instead what replicable action steps were taken by other institutions to help this population. Always remember, what you see when you arrive on another campus may have taken years, even decades, to evolve to a present state of committed excellence. You have to start somewhere, just as they did.

Establish a Stakeholder Institution-Spanning Advocacy Group

Some of the best clues to the value system of any postsecondary institution is the specific areas of focus enshrined in officially constituted committees, councils, and task forces. A priority for the success of transfer students needs to be in this constellation. We can all truly say, "Show me a list of institutional committees, and I will know what this place values!"

Unlike traditional first-year students and other non-transfer students, transfer students generally lack advocates—and they sorely need them. In addition to having a special unit/office/center that advocates for transfer students, another excellent mechanism is an institutional advocacy stakeholder group.

Ideally, this group should consist of representatives of key units including academic programs, academic administration, faculty, student affairs/student success professionals, enrollment management, key staff-driven functional areas, and, most importantly, transfer students themselves. The group should be vested with both formal and informal power to identify issues, problems, and needs affecting transfers.

Such a group should be an institutionalized, standing entity, not an ad hoc body, with regular open meetings and with issues and actions communicated publicly across the institution. This group should have reporting lines to institutional cabinet-level officers and be empowered to make official recommendations to forward through official policy review and approval channels.

Proactively Develop Peer-to-Peer Relationships Between Sending and Receiving Institutions

Much of what seems to make positive differences in transfer student success comes down to the informal relationships between peers. The challenge is how to institutionalize, formalize, and sustain these relationships. The foreword of this volume was written by John Hitt and Sanford Shugart, two visionary college/university CEOs who leveraged their individual relationships to create one of the most successful, institutionalized partnerships in enhancing transfer student success in U.S. higher education.

In that mold, one of the most important peer-to-peer structures is that of relationships between CEOs for geographically contiguous institutions. Hopefully, your CEO is already cognizant of this and practicing it. If not, consider how to encourage this connection and develop an awareness of how it can advance both institutions. One way to encourage this type of partnership is by developing peer-to-peer relationships across these critical roles:

- CAOs
- Chief student services/student success officers
- Chief enrollment management officers
- Chief financial aid officers
- Chief business officers
- Chief library officers
- Chief athletic officers
- Chief facility officers
- Chief officers for distinct academic disciplines
- Chief academic support officers
- Chief developmental education officers

Ask Your Students, "How Transfer Friendly Are We?"

We highly recommend you ask your transfer students how "transfer friendly" they think your institution is based on their experiences. You could do this by using focus groups and surveying current and former transfer students. We recommend a combination of both quantitative and qualitative data. One commercially available survey is the "Foundations of Excellence Transfer Focus Student Survey" owned and serviced by SkyFactor, a unit of Macmillan Higher Education. This instrument provides transfer student perception data on how students perceive the institution is functioning according to nine "dimensions" of excellence that are components of the Foundations of Excellence Transfer Focus process (previously described in this chapter).

An excellent way to learn more about the current state of the practice and art of enhancing transfer student success is to either attend yourself or at least have your campus participate in the annual conference of the National Institute for the Study of Transfer Students (www.nists.org). Drawing hundreds of faculty academic/student affairs/student success/transfer experts and proponents each year, it is the only national, annual event focused exclusively on the success of transfer students. The University of South Carolina's National Resource Center for The First-Year Experience and Students in Transition (www.sc.edu/about/offices_and_divisions/national_resource_center/) also provides an excellent annual professional development conference known as "Students in Transition" with an included, but not exclusive, focus on transfer students.

Additionally, many state and regional professional organizations that focus on advising, admissions, and orientation also offer workshops and conferences on transfer student success. Some regions and states are also founding their own transfer-related groups, such as NETA, the New England Transfer Association and NYSTAA, the New York State Transfer and Articulation Association.

Review the Recommendations in the Concluding Sections of Each Chapter in This Book

As we prepared this volume, we asked each of our content experts to prepare a set of recommendations and discussion questions for your consideration. Hopefully, you and your institution have—or will—create a task force/reading group for consideration of our book's information and recommendations. Ideally, you would consider each of the recommendations and see how they might apply to your particular institutional setting. We believe it would be interesting, revealing, and instructive to inventory and enumerate just how in accordance with our experts' recommendations your institution is or is not.

Final Thoughts

We return here to the place where we began, namely, with a reminder of the lens that we have suggested you use in seeking to improve transfer outcomes. This lens focuses broadly on the entire educational experience of transfer students—everything that happens to them from the time they begin at a sending institution to everything they experience at the receiving institution. A more limited focus, such as the mechanics of transfer credit articulation, while necessary, is insufficient. Essentially, we have to create successful, mobile learners who can thrive throughout their multi-institutional experience. If they aren't successful learners, they ultimately won't accumulate enough credits to earn the credentials they seek.

Our contributors and colleagues joined us in this effort because of our shared belief that improving the success of transfer students is not just possible, but necessary to expand the opportunity and quality of life in our country. Without improving transfer student educational outcomes, we cannot fulfill the possibility of American higher education truly becoming a means to the social justice we seek for all our students.

We wish to thank you for your consideration of what we have laid out in this volume. We wish you our best in our shared effort to bolster transfer student success through whatever means of transfer advocacy your position in our society permits. If there is anything we have learned in our work on this book, it is that these students do not have nearly enough advocates on both sending and receiving campuses. You can help offset that by becoming a transfer advocate. We welcome hearing from you about your own efforts and having you contribute to our knowledge of important efforts being made to enhance transfer student success.

EDITORS AND CONTRIBUTORS

Editors

John N. Gardner is an undergraduate student success thought leader and a social justice advocate. He is chief executive officer and chair of the nonprofit John N. Gardner Institute for Excellence in Undergraduate Education, co-founded by him and his wife, Betsy O. Barefoot, in 1999. Gardner is also distinguished professor emeritus and senior fellow at the University of South Carolina at Columbia. He was also the founding executive director of both the National Resource Center for the First-Year Experience and Students in Transition, and the University 101 Programs. He served from 1983–1996 as vice chancellor for Academic Affairs for the University's five regional campuses. He is the founder of the international reform movement to improve what he coined in 1982 as "the first-year experience." Over his career he has worked with hundreds of institutions in the United States and abroad to increase student success in the transitions of the first-year, sophomore year, transfer, and senior year experience. He is coauthor of seven books on undergraduate education and, with his wife, of a series of textbooks for "college success" courses. He is also the recipient of a dozen honorary degrees. He is the recipient of the University of South Carolina's highest awards for teaching, committing to partnering with student affairs professionals, and advancing affirmative action. He is also a proud veteran of the United States Air Force.

Michael J. Rosenberg is a nationally recognized expert on transfer student policy. He is director of planning for Penn State University's Office of Planning, Assessment, and Institutional Research. A higher education practitioner by trade and training, his extensive background includes experience in student affairs, academic advising, judicial affairs, residence life, and enrollment management. For the past decade, he has championed policy solutions for transfer students by examining the student experience through a social justice lens. As the inaugural director of transfer at Gateway Community and Technical College and as chair of the Kentucky Community & Technical College System's statewide transfer task force, he helped drive the conversation in his home state around improving outcomes for this important population. His doctoral work at the University of Kentucky in Educational Policy and Evaluation and scholarship thereafter focuses on adult transfer students and transfer student capital. He holds a master's in higher education from the University of Arizona and a bachelor of arts in English with a certificate in women's studies from Duke University. He is a college basketball aficionado, a decent cook, and author of *The Naked Vine: Wine Advice for the Rest of Us*—an online wine education column.

Andrew K. Koch is the president and chief operating officer for the nonprofit John N. Gardner Institute for Excellence in Undergraduate Education, which he joined in 2010. In his role, he provides strategic leadership and operations oversight for the Institute in its efforts to help colleges improve teaching, learning, student success and, in the process of doing so, mitigate inequitable outcomes and advance social justice. Prior to coming to Gardner Institute, Koch spent nearly 20 years working in both independent and public postsecondary institutions on student enrollment, access, success, accreditation, learning, and completion efforts with an emphasis on first-generation, low-income, and historically underrepresented students. He holds a BA in history and German from the University of Richmond, an MA in history from the University of Richmond, an MA in higher education administration from the University of South Carolina, and a PhD in American studies from Purdue University. He has served as the principal investigator or coprincipal investigator on more than two dozen grant-funded research projects with support coming from sources such as the Bill & Melinda Gates Foundation, ECMC Foundation, GEAR UP, Kresge Foundation, Lilly Endowment, Lumina Foundation, and the National Science Foundation. His scholarship focuses on critical university studies and the role of colleges and universities in shaping culture, equity, and democracy in the United States. He has published widely on student access and success topics, with an emphasis on historically underrepresented and underserved populations, the first-year experience, gateway courses, and redesign of unjust education systems.

Contributors

Heather Adams currently oversees the UCLA Transfer Student Center. With 20 years of experience in public speaking, multimedia marketing, public relations, and career coaching in the entertainment industry, her work focuses on developing and implementing student success strategies and formulating collaborative campus efforts to better support transfer and post-traditional students.

Michelle Alvarez is currently a Digital Credentials Lab team member at Southern New Hampshire University (SNHU). She has 19 years of experience in curriculum design, including recent design work with competency-based degree programs. She is currently working with a team to recommend the microcredential strategy for SNHU.

Angela Bell is vice chancellor of research and policy analysis for the University System of Georgia. Her division meets information needs including data collection, fulfilling data requests, reporting, and analysis for decision-making and policy. She earned her doctorate in higher education administration at the University of Georgia.

Wallace E. Boston is president of the American Public University System (APUS), including American Military University and American Public University. His research work includes online postsecondary student, and he and is a frequent speaker regarding the impact of technology on higher education.

Boyd Bradshaw serves as the associate vice chancellor for enrollment management and chief enrollment officer at IUPUI. He is a strong advocate of serving transfers as a key part of enrollment strategy. He holds an EdD with a concentration in higher education administration from Saint Louis University.

Debra D. Bragg is director of Community College Research Initiatives at the University of Washington–Seattle and emeritus endowed professor of higher education and founding director of the Office of Community College Research and Leadership at the University of Illinois at Urbana–Champaign.

Catherine Buyarski is executive associate dean of University College at IUPUI. She leads efforts to assist students in the development of purposeful pathways to college and career success. Buyarski served as cochair of the Foundations of Excellence–Transfer process at IUPUI. She earned a PhD in educational policy and administration from the University of Minnesota.

Mark Canada is executive vice chancellor for academic affairs and professor of English at Indiana University Kokomo. His publications include five books and numerous articles on student success, pedagogy, American literature, and information literacy.

Jason Chambers has been an international transfer student advocate for his 7 years working in the admissions department of the University of Cincinnati. He graduated with a bachelor's degree in psychology from Miami University in Oxford, Ohio, and a master's degree in higher education administrative services from McKendree University in St. Louis, Missouri.

Erin Cogswell is the content manager at Phi Theta Kappa Honor Society. She attended a community college in Mississippi, was a Phi Theta Kappa member, and joined the staff in 2012. Previously, Cogswell was a reporter, writer, and magazine editor for *The Clarion-Ledger* in Jackson, Mississippi, having studied journalism at the University of Southern Mississippi.

Lee Colquitt is a professor and chair of the Department of Finance at Auburn University and the executive director of Tau Sigma National Honor Society. Colquitt has a BS in economics from Auburn and an MBA and a PhD from the University of Georgia. He is married and has three daughters.

José Del Real Viramontes is a visiting post-doctoral research associate in the department of Education Policy, Organization, and Leadership at the University of Illinois at Urbana–Champaign. His research highlights how Chicanx/Latinx community college transfer students engage in the cultural production of a transfer receptive culture at 4-year institutions.

Tess Diver serves as the assistant director of account management and learner experience at SNHU. She supports the development of new learning models to meet the evolving needs of learners and organizations at SNHU. She helped launch College for America, SNHU's competency-based degree program, in 2013.

Brent M. Drake currently serves as the vice provost of decision support at the University of Nevada, Las Vegas, where he focuses on data related to student attainment and learning, overall institutional effectiveness, institutional reporting, faculty activity, and data analytics. Drake earned all three of his degrees from Purdue, including his PhD in educational psychology in 2009, with an emphasis in both motivation theory and psychometrics.

Maribeth Ehasz is vice president for student development and enrollment services at the University of Central Florida (UCF). During her tenure, UCF has achieved significant gains in student enrollment, retention, progression, and graduation. She received UCF's first VIP Diversity Award for making diversity and inclusion a priority for her division.

John Fink is a senior research associate at the Community College Research Center at Teachers College, Columbia University. Fink's research seeks to uncover structural barriers within higher education that result in inequitable access to educational and economic opportunity for racially minoritized, low-income, and first-generation students.

Pamela K. Fly currently serves as associate vice president for academic affairs at Northeastern State University where she provides oversight for accreditation, curriculum, state and federal reporting requirements, remediation and general education, external projects, and policy. Her scholarly interests center on curriculum development, teacher education, and secondary literacy.

Stephanie M. Foote is the associate vice president for teaching, learning, and evidence-based practices at the John N. Gardner Institute for Excellence in Undergraduate Education. Formerly a professor of education, Foote's research spans aspects of student development and transition, engagement in online learning, and metacognitive teaching and learning.

Charles Fox is the associate dean of English and the Decatur Campus for Perimeter College at Georgia State University. He holds an MFA in creative writing from George Mason University, and he is the author of *Creative Control: Creative Writing Prompts for the Composition Class* (Kendall Hunt, 2010).

James Gladden leads the IUPUI Division of Undergraduate Education as associate vice chancellor for undergraduate education, dean of University College, and acting dean of the Honors College. He provides leadership for campus-wide student success programs and curriculum from orientation through graduation.

Betsy Q. Griffin is vice president and resident scholar at the Gardner Institute where she advises institutions working to improve student success. She is a professor emeritus of psychology at Missouri Southern State University where she served as assistant vice president for academic affairs.

Stephen J. Handel is the executive director of higher education strategic assessment use and opportunity for the college board. Prior to this position, he served as the chief admissions officer for the University of California (UC) System, working to strengthen the transfer pathway between UC campuses and California's community colleges.

Maria Hesse served as vice provost for academic partnerships at Arizona State University from 2009–2019, helping to create and sustain productive relationships with community colleges and other institutions. Prior to that, Hesse served for 25 years in the Maricopa Community Colleges, including as president for Chandler-Gilbert Community College.

John C. Hitt served as the fourth president of the University of Central Florida between March 1992 and June 2018. With Valencia College's Sandy Shugart, Hitt was a principal architect of DirectConnect to UCF, one of the most effective transfer pathways in the United States.

Jamie Holcomb is associate dean of first-year experience and education at SNHU. Holcomb supports faculty and students, develops curriculum, and works with institutional partners to enhance the learner experience. She also creates content to enhance the onboarding experience for new learners at SNHU.

Jennifer L. Ivie currently serves as an assistant professor of psychology at Tulsa Community College (TCC). During the Tulsa Transfer Project, she served as the director of institutional research at TCC. Her scholarly interests focus on effectiveness of programs, services, learning experiences, and assessment in higher education.

G. Edward Hughes was the second president of Hazard Community and Technical College (KY, 1985–2001) during the development of the University Center of the Mountains. He was the founding president of Gateway Community and Technical College (KY, 2001–2015). Currently, he is president of The Hughes Group and partner with STAR Educational Programming.

Danielle Insalaco-Egan, assistant provost for student success at Montclair State University in New Jersey, has focused on advising structures, technology-mediated advising, and high-impact practices for 25 years. Prior to that, she was assistant dean for student support at Stella and Charles Guttman Community College of the City University of New York. She holds a doctorate from New York University in English and American literature.

Dimpal Jain is an associate professor in educational leadership and policy studies at California State University, Northridge. Her research centers on the relationship between community colleges and universities, specifically how universities can implement a transfer receptive culture for students of color. Her scholarship utilizes critical race theory and womanist frameworks.

Davis Jenkins is a senior research scholar at the Community College Research Center at Columbia University's Teachers College. He works with institutions and states across the country to find ways to improve educational and employment outcomes for students, particularly students of color and those from low-income families.

Kathy E. Johnson serves as executive vice chancellor and chief academic officer at IUPUI. She was instrumental in the founding of the Office of Transfer Student Services and was an active leader in the Foundations of Excellence-Transfer project. Johnson holds a PhD in psychology from Emory University.

J. Jeffrey Jones serves as vice provost for UCF Connect and UCF Global at the UCF. UCF Connect is well known for its innovative transfer program, DirectConnect to UCF. UCF Global is charged with international partnerships, international student recruitment and support, and university international credentialing.

Chet Jordan is an assistant professor of interdisciplinary studies at Stella and Charles Guttman Community College of the City University of New York. His research focuses on the study of urban higher education, particularly community college and transfer students.

Julie Landaw is director of the Ivy Tech and IUPUI Coordinated Programs (Passport) Office and an adjunct instructor of anatomy at IUPUI. Landaw has an extensive background in transfer student initiatives at multiple institutions. Landaw received her MEd from the University of Nevada, Las Vegas.

Melissa Layne, assistant vice president of research and innovation at American Public University System, serves as editor-in-chief for the *International Journal of Open Education Resources* and contributes to several journal editorial boards. Her research on retention, emerging technologies, and open educational resources has been recognized by distance learning organizations including the OLC, NUTN, and DLA.

Sarah Mackey has an extensive background in international student services and international admissions. She currently serves as the assistant director for international recruitment and outreach at the University of Cincinnati, where she manages the university's overseas offices and agent network.

Janet Marling is executive director of the National Institute for the Study of Transfer Students. She holds a PhD in higher education administration from the University of North Texas, an MS in counseling psychology from the University of Southern Mississippi, and a BS in psychology from Texas Christian University.

Heather N. McCambly is a PhD candidate in human development and social policy at Northwestern University and is a research affiliate at the Office of Community College Research and Leadership. Previously, McCambly worked for nearly a decade on issues of racial equity in higher education in various governmental and national nonprofit contexts.

Susannah McGowan is the associate director for curriculum design at the Center for New Designs in Learning and Scholarship and the Designing the Future(s) of Higher Education at Georgetown University. She is also a Gardner Institute fellow working on supporting faculty members in course design through the Teaching and Learning Academy.

Jonathan Mercantini is acting dean of the College of Liberal Arts at Kean University where he has taught since 2007. He earned his PhD in American history from Emory University in 2000.

Mary A. Millikin serves Rogers State University as the associate vice president for academic affairs where she is responsible for coordinating university-wide efforts toward institutional effectiveness, institutional data analysis and reporting, strategic planning, assessment of student learning, and accreditation processes. Research interests include organizational effectiveness, teaching effectiveness, and learner advocacy.

Deronda Collier Mobelini is the executive director of the University Center of the Mountains (UCM) and an academic dean for heritage and humanities at Hazard Community and Technical College (HCTC). She has conducted research and coauthored two publications focusing on transfer and the rural community college student.

Karen Ramos is from Ohio and has a passion for travel and learning languages. During her undergraduate studies, Ramos studied abroad in Mexico. She later earned her doctorate in educational leadership from Northern Kentucky University in 2019. She is the international program director at the University of Cincinnati's medical campus and teaches Spanish.

Rose Rojas, director of curriculum and transfer articulation at the Maricopa Community Colleges, oversees the district's curriculum development, university transfer, academic support, policy development, and prior learning assessment. Rojas is a community college graduate and holds an MA in education leadership from Northern Arizona University.

Patricia A. Shea is the former director of academic leadership initiatives for the Western Interstate Commission for Higher Education (WICHE) where she was employed for 23 years before retiring in 2019. During her tenure, she led two membership organizations of chief academic leaders and their related projects, including Interstate Passport.

Sanford Shugart has served as the fourth president of Valencia College since January 2000 and, with John Hitt, was a principal architect of DirectConnect to UCF, one of the most effective transfer pathways in the United States.

Kathy Silberman focuses her work in curriculum and transfer articulation at the Maricopa Community Colleges (AZ) on supporting transfer partnerships, developing advising resources and promoting student transfer. She presents on transfer trends, successful transfer partnerships, articulation models, and prior learning assessment. She holds an MEd from Arizona State University.

Deborah Skibitsky is acting assistant dean for the College of Liberal Arts at Kean University in Union, New Jersey. She earned her master's of public administration from Kean University and her bachelor of arts in marketing from Trenton State College (now The College of New Jersey).

Vernon Smith, provost of the American Public University System, is a pioneer in the development and delivery of online higher education including quality, assessment, and retention strategies. He is an early adopter of big data for predictive modeling and teaching excellence to promote student success in online settings. He serves as chair of the WICHE Cooperative for Educational Technologies Executive Council.

Jason Taylor is an assistant professor of higher education in the Department of Educational Leadership and Policy at the University of Utah. His broad research interests are at the intersection of community college and higher education policy, and educational and social inequality.

Emily Tichenor serves as the director of university transfer at Tulsa Community College, where she is responsible for the development and coordination of transfer pathways, resources, and relationships. Tichenor is a lifelong Tulsan and has served for 13 years in library and higher education leadership roles. She is a certified project management professional (PMP).

A. Hope Williams is in her 29th year as president of North Carolina Independent Colleges and Universities (NCICU), the statewide office of the 36 private, nonprofit colleges and universities. She earned her undergraduate degree from Duke University, master's from North Carolina State University, and PhD from the University of North Carolina at Chapel Hill.

Niesha Ziehmke is associate dean for academic programs and planning at Guttman Community College. She is leading efforts to integrate transfer and career success into the academic curriculum, all through an equity lens. Throughout her career, she has focused on finding systematic ways of improving equity and inclusion in education.

Faculty Development books from Stylus Publishing

Advancing the Culture of Teaching on Campus
ow a Teaching Center Can Make a Difference
Edited by Constance Cook and Matthew Kaplan
Foreword by Lester P. Monts

Faculty Mentoring
A Practical Manual for Mentors, Mentees, Administrators, and Faculty Developers
Susan L. Phillips and Susan T. Dennison
Foreword by Milton D. Cox

Faculty Retirement
Best Practices for Navigating the Transition
Edited by Claire Van Ummersen, Jean McLaughlin and Lauren Duranleau
Foreword by Lotte Bailyn

The Prudent Professor
Planning and Saving for a Worry-Free Retirement from Academe
Edwin M. Bridges and Brian D. Bridges

Teaching Across Cultural Strengths
A Guide to Balancing Integrated and Individuated Cultural Frameworks in College Teaching
Alicia Fedelina Chávez and Susan Diana Longerbeam
Foreword by Joseph L. White

Why Students Resist Learning
A Practical Model for Understanding and Helping Students
Edited by Anton O. Tolman and Janine Kremling
Foreword by John Tagg

Graduate and Doctoral Education books from Stylus Publishing

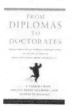

From Diplomas to Doctorates
The Success of Black Women in Higher Education and its Implications for Equal Educational Opportunities for All
Edited by V. Barbara Bush, Crystal Renee Chambers, and Mary Beth Walpole

The Latina/o Pathway to the Ph.D.
Abriendo Caminos
Edited by Jeanett Castellanos, Alberta M. Gloria, and Mark Kamimura
Foreword by Melba Vasquez and Hector Garza

On Becoming a Scholar
Socialization and Development in Doctoral Education
Jay Caulfield
Edited by Susan K. Gardner and Pilar Mendoza
Foreword by Ann E. Austin and Kevin Kruger

Developing Quality Dissertations in the Humanities
A Graduate Student's Guide to Achieving Excellence
Barbara E. Lovitts and Ellen L. Wert

Developing Quality Dissertations in the Sciences
A Graduate Student's Guide to Achieving Excellence
Barbara E. Lovitts and Ellen L. Wert

Developing Quality Dissertations in the Social Sciences
A Graduate Student's Guide to Achieving Excellence
Barbara E. Lovitts and Ellen L. Wert

General Interest books from Stylus Publishing

Are You Smart Enough?
How Colleges' Obsession with Smartness Shortchanges Students
Alexander W. Astin

The New Science of Learning
How to Learn in Harmony With Your Brain
Terry Doyle and Todd D. Zakrajsek
Foreword by Kathleen F. Gabriel

Of Education, Fishbowls, and Rabbit Holes
Rethinking Teaching and Liberal Education for an Interconnected World
Jane Fried with Peter Troiano
Foreword by Dawn R. Person

Managing Your Professional Identity Online
A Guide for Faculty, Staff, and Administrators
Kathryn E. Linder
Foreword by Laura Pasquini

Teach Yourself How to Learn
Strategies You Can Use to Ace Any Course at Any Level
Saundra Yancy McGuire with Stephanie McGuire
Foreword by Mark McDaniel

Pitch Perfect
Communicating with Traditional and Social Media for Scholars, Researchers, and Academic Leaders
William Tyson
Foreword by Robert Zemsky

Job Search/Staff Recruitment & Retention books from Stylus Publishing

The Complete Academic Search Manual
A Systematic Approach to Successful and Inclusive Hiring
Lauren A. Vicker and Harriette J. Royer

Debunking the Myth of Job Fit in Higher Education and Student Affairs
Edited by Brian J. Reece, Vu T. Tran, Elliott N. DeVore and Gabby Porcaro
Foreword by Stephen John Quaye

Establishing the Family-Friendly Campus
Models for Effective Practice
Edited by Jaime Lester and Margaret Sallee

Job Search In Academe
How to Get the Position You Deserve
Dawn M. Formo and Cheryl Reed

The New Talent Acquisition Frontier
Integrating HR and Diversity Strategy in the Private and Public Sectors and Higher Education
Edna Chun and Alvin Evans
Foreword by Andy Brantley and Benjamin D. Reese, Jr

Search Committees
A Comprehensive Guide to Successful Faculty, Staff, and Administrative Searches
Christopher D. Lee
Foreword by Edna Chun

Professional Development books from Stylus Publishing

Adjunct Faculty Voices
Cultivating Professional Development and Community at the Front Lines of Higher Education
Edited by Roy Fuller, Marie Kendall Brown and Kimberly Smith
Foreword by Adrianna Kezar

Authoring Your Life
Developing an INTERNAL VOICE to Navigate Life's Challenges
Marcia B. Baxter Magolda
Foreword by Sharon Daloz Parks
Illustrated by Matthew Henry Hall

The Coach's Guide for Women Professors
Who Want a Successful Career and a Well-Balanced Life
Rena Seltzer
Foreword by Frances Rosenbluth

Contingent Academic Labor
Evaluating Conditions to Improve Student Outcomes
Daniel B. Davis
Foreword by Adrianna Kezar

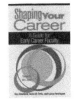

Shaping Your Career
A Guide for Early Career Faculty
Don Haviland, Anna M. Ortiz and Laura Henriques
Foreword by Ann E. Austin

What They Didn't Teach You in Graduate School
299 Helpful Hints for Success in Your Academic Career
Paul Gray and David E. Drew
Illustrated by Matthew Henry Hall
Foreword by Laurie Richlin and Steadman Upham

Race & Diversity books from Stylus Publishing

Building on Resilience
Models and Frameworks of Black Male Success Across the P-20 Pipeline
Edited by Fred A. Bonner II
Foreword by Tim King

Diverse Millennial Students in College
Implications for Faculty and Student Affairs
Edited by Fred A. Bonner II, Aretha F. Marbley, and Mary F. Howard-Hamilton

Answering the Call
African American Women in Higher Education Leadership
Beverly L. Bower and Mimi Wolverton

The Department Chair as Transformative Diversity Leader
Building Inclusive Learning Environments in Higher Education
Edna Chun and Alvin Evans
Foreword by Walter H. Gmelch

Multiculturalism on Campus
Theory, Models, and Practices for Understanding Diversity and Creating Inclusion
Edited by Michael J. Cuyjet, Chris Linder, Mary F. Howard-Hamilton, and Diane L. Cooper

Creating the Path to Success in the Classroom
Teaching to Close the Graduation Gap for Minority, First-Generation, and Academically Unprepared Students
Kathleen F. Gabriel
Foreword by Stephen Carroll

Race & Diversity books from Stylus Publishing

Advancing Black Male Student Success From Preschool Through Ph.D.
Edited by Shaun R. Harper and J. Luke Wood

Contested Issues in Troubled Times
Student Affairs Dialogues on Equity, Civility, and Safety
Edited by Peter M. Magolda, Marcia B. Baxter Magolda and Rozana Carducci
Foreword by Lori Patton Davis

Critical Race Spatial Analysis
Mapping to Understand and Address Educational Inequity
Edited by Deb Morrison, Subini Ancy Annamma, and Darrell D. Jackson

Closing the Opportunity Gap
Identity-Conscious Strategies for Retention and Student Success
Edited by Vijay Pendakur
Foreword by Shaun R. Harper

Beyond Access
Indigenizing Programs for Native American Student Success
Edited by Stephanie J. Waterman, Shelly C. Lowe, and Heather J. Shotton
Foreword by George S. McClellan

Critical Mentoring
A Practical Guide
Torie Weiston-Serdan
Foreword by Bernadette Sánchez

Student Affairs & Campus Issues books from Stylus Publishing

The Curricular Approach to Student Affairs
A Revolutionary Shift for Learning Beyond the Classroom
Kathleen G. Kerr, Keith E. Edwards, James F. Tweedy, Hilary
Lichterman and Amanda R. Knerr
Foreword by Stephen John Quaye

Esports in Higher Education
Fostering Successful Student-Athletes and Successful Programs
George S. McClellan, Ryan S. Arnett and Charles M. Hueber

Islamophobia in Higher Education
Combating Discrimination and Creating Understanding
Edited by Shafiqa Ahmadi and Darnell Cole
Foreword by Shaun R. Harper

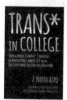

Trans* in College
*Transgender Students' Strategies for Navigating Campus Life and the
Institutional Politics of Inclusion*
Z Nicolazzo
Foreword by Kristen A. Renn

**Rethinking College Student Development Theory Using
Critical Frameworks**
Edited by Elisa S. Abes, Susan R. Jones and D-L Stewart

Straddling Class in the Academy
*26 Stories of Students, Administrators, and Faculty From Poor and
Working-Class Backgrounds and Their Compelling Lessons for Higher
Education Policy and Practice*
Sonja Ardoin and becky martinez
Foreword by Rev. Jamie Washington, PhD

Teaching and Learning books from Stylus Publishing

Of Education, Fishbowls, and Rabbit Holes
Rethinking Teaching and Liberal Education for an Interconnected World
Jane Fried With Peter Troiano
Foreword by Dawn R. Person

Creating Wicked Students
Designing Courses for a Complex World
Paul Hanstedt

Dynamic Lecturing
Research-Based Strategies to Enhance Lecture Effectiveness
Christine Harrington and Todd Zakrajsek
Foreword by José Antonio Bowen

Designing a Motivational Syllabus
Creating a Learning Path for Student Engagement
Christine Harrington and Melissa Thomas
Foreword by Kathleen F. Gabriel

Course-Based Undergraduate Research
Educational Equity and High-Impact Practice
Edited by Nancy H. Hensel
Foreword by Cathy N. Davidson

Creating Engaging Discussions
Strategies for "Avoiding Crickets" in Any Size Classroom and Online
Jennifer H. Herman and Linda B. Nilson
Foreword by Stephen D. Brookfield

Gardner Institute

Since its founding in 1999, the not-for-profit John N. Gardner Institute for Excellence in Undergraduate Education (Gardner Institute) has worked with colleges, universities, philanthropic organizations, individual postsecondary educators, and higher education member organizations to improve teaching, learning, retention, and completion. Through doing so, the Gardner Institute strives to advance higher education's larger equity, social mobility, and social justice goals.

The Gardner Institute's work includes redesign of the first college year, gateway courses, teaching and learning, academic advising, the curriculum, and, of special importance of this book, transfer. Through all that it does, the Gardner Institute strives to create a day when race/ethnicity, family income, gender and other demographics are no longer the best predictors of who succeeds in college and gains the broader societal benefits associated with doing so.

Visit www.jngi.org/transfer-experience for more information.